# FAMILY MEDIATION: THEORY AND PRACTICE

# FAMILY MEDIATION: THEORY AND PRACTICE

## Second Edition

**Jane C. Murphy**
*Laurence M. Katz Professor of Law*
*University of Baltimore School of Law*

**Robert Rubinson**
*Professor of Law*
*Director of Clinical Education*
*University of Baltimore School of Law*

ISBN: 9781632809490
Ebook ISBN: 9780327177210

| Library of Congress Cataloging-in-Publication Data |
| --- |
| Murphy, Jane C., author. |
| Family mediation : theory and practice / Jane C. Murphy, Laurence M. Katz Professor of Law, University of Baltimore School of Law; Robert Rubinson, Professor of Law, Director of Clinical Education, University of Baltimore School of Law. — Second Edition. |
| pages cm |
| Includes index. |
| ISBN 978-1-63280-949-0 (softbound) |
| 1. Family mediation—United States. 2. Domestic relations courts--United States. 3. Dispute resolution (Law)—United States. 4. Domestic relations—United States. I. Rubinson, Robert, author. II. Title. |
| KF505.5.M87 2015 |
| 346.7301'5—dc23 |
| 2015005800 |

NOTE TO USERS
To ensure that you are using the latest materials available in this area, please be sure to periodically check the LexisNexis Law School web site for downloadable updates and supplements at www.lexisnexis.com/lawschool.

Editorial Offices
630 Central Ave., New Providence, NJ 07974 (908) 464-6800
201 Mission St., San Francisco, CA 94105-1831 (415) 908-3200
www.lexisnexis.com

MATTHEW◊BENDER

# Dedications

To Chris, Brendan, Katie, Margaret, Cat, and Gracie, with thanks for your love and patience — JCM

To my wife Randi Schwartz and to my children Stella and Leo, with love and gratitude — RR

# Acknowledgements

This book is a collaboration in the full sense of the word. We have benefited enormously from the help of others. Wendy Seiden made substantial contributions to Chapter 5, Child Welfare Mediation. She along with Lydia Nussbaum and Eve Hanan contributed to the teaching simulations included in the Teacher's Manual. Don Paris provided a practitioner's perspective to the complex task of mediating financial disputes in Chapter 6. Andrew Schepard was a supporter of this project from its earliest stages and his critique of an early draft of the text was of incalculable importance. We are also grateful to the many family mediators who have contributed to our classes and our understanding of mediation, including Theresa Furnari, Mark Scurti, Amaza Scott Reid, Jay Knight, and Eileen Coen. We have also received wonderful research assistance on the second edition from University of Baltimore law students Lauren Vint, Brittaney Fabiano, and Victoria Narducci. We also thank Library Director Adeen Postar and her talented colleagues in the University of Baltimore law library for all their help in the preparation of this book.

There are many others, too numerous to name, who have been de facto co-authors. Our work has been enriched by the many mediators we have spoken to, mediated with, and observed. Our students in our Family Mediation Seminar and Clinic have taught us a great deal about teaching, learning, and mediation and have provided helpful feedback on earlier versions of the text.

We also thank the University of Baltimore Foundation for its financial support and the many faculty and administrators at the School of Law who have provided encouragement and various kinds of expertise while we were writing the book, especially Shavaun O'Brien and Dean Ronald Weich.

Finally, our deepest thanks to the many participants in mediation we have represented and with whom we have mediated. They have been the greatest teachers of all.

# Preface to the Second Edition

The second edition of this book updates and expands upon the material in the first edition. We have made substantial changes, both in response to the rapidly changing world of family dispute resolution and in response to feedback from the many students and faculty who have used our first edition.

While mediation has spread as a means to resolve virtually all types of disputes, in no area has this been more apparent — or more controversial — than in family law. Mediation is part of a paradigm shift in family dispute resolution that is now firmly entrenched. Legislatures and courts in numerous jurisdictions have adopted rules and statutes that encourage and sometimes mandate that family law cases be mediated and set forth procedures under which such mediations are to take place. Many thousands of family mediations happen every day. More and more private family mediators are starting to practice. As a result, mediation and family law are increasingly intertwined in a web of procedures and practices that has generated a new, distinct subject: "family mediation." Knowledge of mediation or knowledge of family law no longer suffices for a modern family lawyer. Family mediation melds the unique characteristics and challenges of family law with the unique characteristics and challenges of mediation. The many issues of practice and policy this implicates are the subject of this book.

In addition to expanding and updating the prior material in the first edition, this new edition explores a range of recent developments that have arisen since the publication of the first edition. One is how family lawyers are increasingly participating in "collaborative" or "cooperative" law — processes which, without a mediator, are designed to approach resolving family disputes in a constructive, non-adversarial way. Another development is the expanding use of different types of dispute resolution besides mediation, such as arbitration, or of "hybrid" processes that include some combination of ADR processes. We have also added a chapter on pro se parties who now represent the majority of family law litigants in 21st century courts. The chapter explores the profound implications of this influx of large numbers of unrepresented parties on the role of mediators and the mediation process. One impact of this development is a broader endorsement of the educating role of the mediator. In response to this and to feedback from users of the book, we have also included sections that provide an overview of the legal norms that might be helpful in some mediation contexts. Finally, we address how the many changes in family composition over the last several years, including the impact of the remarkable spread of the legal recognition of same-sex marriage, has or will change family mediation.

As we noted in the first edition, we continue to be guided by a number of core principles in writing this text. First, while mediation can be extraordinarily effective, family mediation — like any activity — can be done well or poorly, can be appropriate or inappropriate, can be effective or ineffective. We do not shy away from asking these difficult questions. Second, new family lawyers might or might not find themselves mediating, but all new family lawyers will represent clients in mediation. We thus include materials on representing clients in mediation. Third, we do not assume a perfect world, where parties have resources to hire attorneys and a mediator with abundant time to facilitate a resolution. Family mediation is contextual not only in terms of "facts" but also in terms of where and how it is practiced. We do our best to reflect this in the text. Fourth, we recognize that mediation can sometimes pose serious risks for participants, and we offer different views of when this might be the case and how it can be dealt with. Finally, family mediation is interdisciplinary, and thus experts in family dynamics and child development have important things to teach all of us. We include a sampling of their conclusions in the text.

We welcome readers to an exciting and challenging subject that is at the forefront of how we, as lawyers and as a society, approach resolving the most intimate and, in many respects, consequential of disputes.

# Table of Contents

# Table of Contents

## Table of Contents

# Table of Contents

# Table of Contents

# Table of Contents

# Table of Contents

# Chapter 1

# AN OVERVIEW OF FAMILY MEDIATION

## A.  INTRODUCTION

Family mediation is an amalgam of distinct disciplines: family law, mediation (itself a multidisciplinary undertaking), and the psychology of family relations. Each of these disciplines has an individual history and role to play in understanding and, ultimately, mastering the intricacies of family mediation. Although we will assume a working knowledge of family law, we make no such assumption about knowledge of mediation generally or family mediation in particular.

This Chapter will begin the process of understanding and, even more importantly, internalizing ways of thinking that are alien in a culture — both legal and non-legal — that is dominated by the norms of adjudication. What follows traces briefly the history of mediation and of family mediation.

## B.  AN INTELLECTUAL HISTORY OF MEDIATION

The history of family mediation is necessarily bound up with the history of mediation more generally.

Mediation has a long intellectual history. The following excerpt introduces intellectual forebears of mediation. Some, but not all, of this excerpt addresses family mediation. In reviewing this material, filter these ideas through the lens of family disputes. Are the ideas expressed particularly relevant to family mediation?

### *MOTHERS AND FATHERS OF INVENTION: THE INTELLECTUAL FOUNDERS OF ADR*[1]
16 Ohio St. J. On Disp. Resol. 1, 1–37 (2000)
By Carrie Menkel-Meadow

[The ADR Movement] has been an eclectic field intellectually, and we have used, borrowed, and elaborated on ideas that have come to us from many different fields, not only from law and legal theory, but from anthropology, sociology, international relations, social and cognitive psychology, game theory and economics, and most recently, political theory . . .

[In the 1920s] Mary Parker Follett, one of the leading "mothers" of invention in

---

[1] This article was first published in the Ohio State Journal on Dispute Resolution. Copyright ©2000. Reprinted with permission.

ADR, talked about "constructive conflict" in the context of organizational and labor disputes . . . It is her story we often tell when we describe integrative solutions, when she was one of two readers in a library, arguing about an open window. She wanted the window closed because of a draft; the other patron wanted fresh air; the solution was to open a window in another room for indirect air to circulate. In her view, the likelihood of integrative solutions, in which parties do not necessarily have to give anything up, are increased by bringing differences out into the open, facing the conflicts and underlying desires, evaluating and re-valuing desires and preferences when the other parties' desires are made known, and looking for solutions in which the "interests may fit into each other." . . .

[The anthropologist Laura] Nader reminds us that disputing processes are intimately tied to the culture in which they are situated . . . Nader reminds us that methods of dispute resolution, in all of its forms, are not neutral — they are designed and implemented by parties, court administrators or governments with substantive agendas. Thus, we must always interrogate the purposes for which a process of dispute resolution is being invoked. How did this particular institution come to be? What values does it serve? Who is achieving what with the particular structure of the system in place? . . .

Nader's attention to the social and cultural situatedness of dispute resolution has resonated with a number of critics of ADR, both about mediation and arbitration, usually in their compulsory or mandatory forms. Thus, where mediation is thought to be designed to provide flexible, future-oriented solutions, critics point out that in cases of divorce, wronged and financially less secure women may be manipulated to compromise and give up too much. Similarly, others have argued that without the protection of the "rule of law" and the formality of the courtroom, racial and ethnic minorities as well as the economically disadvantaged will be taken advantage of by the more contextually powerful within the informal settings of ADR. Though she is not the only one, Nader's political and anthropological critique has provided an important standard against which to measure whether justice is being compromised in the quest for other values, like peace, harmony, or simple caseload reduction. . . .

In his efforts to elaborate the different structures, functions, and moralities of different legal processes, [Lon] Fuller wrote the first description of, and most sustained argument for, mediation. He said that this conciliatory process, which did not require a decision of state-made law, would "reorient the parties to each other" and "brin[g] about a more harmonious relationship between the parties, whether this be achieved through explicit agreement, through a reciprocal acceptance of 'social norms' relevant to their relationship or simply because the parties have been helped to a new and more perceptive understanding of one another's problems." For Fuller, as for other theorists of mediation, its principal functional strength lay in its release of the parties "from the encumbrances of rules and of accepting, instead, a relationship of mutual respect, trust and understanding that will enable them to meet shared contingencies without the aid of formal prescriptions laid down in advance" . . .

Soia Mentschikoff, one of the first women to leave a deep imprint on legal institutions, also argued for the particular strengths of non-adjudicative forms of dispute resolution . . . Like a wise and modern student of ADR, Mentschikoff refused to pronounce on which processes were "better" than others . . . [I]t could not be said that any one process was perfect or appropriate for all kinds of matters . . .

Though few have made the argument explicit, much of the current penchant for "menus," "multi-door courthouses," and "fitting the forum to the fuss" can find its historical roots in the work of the Legal Process scholars, Henry Hart and Albert Sacks . . . Hart and Sacks make among the first references to the lawyer's role as negotiator and dispute resolver by suggesting that the lawyer's function as a "representative in the private settlement of disputes without litigation" was every bit as important as the more well-known role of the lawyer in court . . .

Much of the underlying and often implicit assumptions of negotiation and bargaining processes in modern ADR theory draw from the work of George Caspar Homans [who noted that what] might be good for trial (narrowing issues) is actually dysfunctional for settlement — the more issues, the merrier, for more possible trades . . .

Some legal scholars of dispute processing and conflict resolution have also drawn on the work of fathers in cognitive science to help us understand why resolving conflict is sometimes so difficult. In Kenneth Arrow's edited volume on Barriers to Conflict Resolution, psychologists describe the various reasoning errors and biased heuristics we use when reasoning alone or with others in the negotiation process . . .

So, what principles or teachings do we take away from the mothers and fathers of invention who founded our field, whether wittingly or not? From these intellectual founders, I take the following major precepts:

1. Conflict can be good and a potential source of creativity. It is not always to be resolved or squelched. Conflict handled appropriately can put the parties (and the rest of us) in a better position than we were before or than we might be in if left to our own devices (or litigation).

2. Good resolutions of conflicts and problems in the law can occur when people realize that valuing different things differently is good. Money need not be a proxy for everything, an assumption that can lead to bitter zero-sum games and distributive or unnecessary compromise outcomes. More issues and more trades enhance the likelihood of both the number and quality of possible resolutions.

3. Different dispute resolution processes produce different kinds of outcomes. Where there is a need for a decision, with a reasoned and reported basis, adversarial argumentation may be more important to framing the resolution. Where there is more than one party or more than one issue ("polycentric" disputes), however, single decision outcomes may not be wise, and mediation, or a negotiated consensus, rather than a single issue, externally imposed decision may be better.

4. Settlements or mediated solutions do not have to be compromises or "split the difference" outcomes. By exploring different values and underlying interests, creative solutions and integrative outcomes may be possible.

5. . . . Different dispute institutions will have their own special competencies, expertise, and morality for handling particular kinds of matters, which may change over time, developing a kind of "process integrity."

6. Processes produce different kinds of outcomes — there are no universal processes that will always be better, fairer, or more efficient than others . . .

7. Variations and choices in processes used to resolve particular matters or to plan future arrangements or transactions in a society are likely to increase participation in and legitimacy of the outcomes reached.

8. The human conditions under which peaceful collaboration and cooperation versus conflict and aggression exist are variable, and we continue to need more theory and more practice to elaborate when we mortal actors can influence each other's behavior.

## NOTES AND QUESTIONS

1.   Many of Menkel-Meadow's "mothers and fathers" focused on dispute resolution in ways other than traditional adjudication. When and under what circumstances is traditional adjudication most appropriate? When and under what circumstances is it least appropriate?

2.   Are the ideas described particularly appropriate given the nature of family conflicts?

3.   Menkel-Meadow describes how a range of disciplines influenced the development of mediation. What particular expertise does a lawyer bring to mediation that you believe would be helpful? Would any be unhelpful? How about mental health professionals, such as social workers and psychologists? Clergy?

4.   Whether family mediation subordinates women has been a controversial issue and one to which we will turn in Chapter 9. However, Menkel-Meadow's article — embodied even in the title of the article — notes how many of the intellectual founders of mediation are women. If a female perspective differs from a male perspective culturally or innately (a contested issue in and of itself), does a female perspective somehow resonate with the development and practice of mediation generally and with family mediation in particular?

5.   Consider in particular the ideas of Laura Nader. What sorts of "motivations" could institutional actors have in promoting mediation? Are these motivations fully or partially inconsistent with what mediation is designed to achieve?

## C.   THE DEVELOPMENT OF FAMILY MEDIATION

### 1.   History

Reliance on mediation rather than litigation is a central feature of a broader shift in dispute resolution that occurred in family courts during the late 20th century. Most early work in family mediation involved divorcing couples — first in mediation designed to facilitate reconciliation between husbands and wives and, later, to resolve issues related to divorce and other family conflicts. Family Mediation has now become what one scholar has called "the workhorse of family dispute resolution.[2] This "paradigm shift" in family dispute resolution had a number of important historical antecedents.[3]

The elimination of fault as a prerequisite to divorce made the traditional adversary system much less useful for resolving divorce-related matters. No longer was it necessary for a court to determine whether a spouse had engaged in behavior defined as "fault" under state divorce law — backward-looking tasks for which the adversary process was arguably well suited. Instead, the primary role of the court — in cases where the parties had not already reached agreement — was to determine the financial and parenting consequences of the marital dissolution. For these more forward-looking tasks of family reorganization, adversary procedures were, at best, unwarranted. With the shift from fault to no-fault divorce, the court system largely abandoned its role as the moral arbiter of marital behavior and ceded to divorcing couples themselves the authority to determine whether and how to end their union. Unlike formal adjudication, mediation offered divorcing couples a way to exercise this authority privately and to order their own post-divorce affairs.

Perhaps even more important than the shift from fault-based to no-fault divorce was the displacement of the prevailing sole custody regime as the exclusive remedy in a contested custody case. Virtually all states now authorize courts to award joint custody — both legal and physical — to both parents following divorce or parental separation. Under the sole custody regime, the job of the court in resolving contested custody cases had been to identify a single, preferred custodian and assign that parent primary legal rights to the child. The shift from sole custody to joint parenting required a rethinking of the procedural role of the custody court. Under a post-divorce co-parenting regime, the court's job is no longer to make a one-time custody allocation, but rather to supervise the ongoing reorganization of a family. The mediation process is much better suited than adjudication and adversary procedures to accomplish these forward-looking, managerial tasks.

In addition to these changes in family law doctrine, family mediation grew in response to a consensus among many law and mental health practitioners and researchers that the adversary system is ill-suited to resolving most disputes involving children. Traditional child access proceedings embody adversarial norms intended to minimize direct communication between parties and maximize the court's role in decision making. Divorce or custody actions are initiated by a lawsuit naming a plaintiff and a defendant, and settlement negotiations are conducted in the "shadow of the law."[4] Parties, if represented and advised by lawyers, reach agreements by making difficult predictions about who will "win" at trial. Under prevailing legal standards, the party who prevails is the parent who most successfully depicts the other parent as unfit, or who can most effectively assign blame for the parties' failed

---

[2] Nancy Ver Steegh, *Family Court Reform and ADR: Shifting Values and Expectations Transform the Divorce Process*, 42 FAMILY LAW QUARTERLY 659, 660 (2008).

[3] *See generally*, Jane C. Murphy and Jana Singer, *Divorced from Reality: Rethinking Family Dispute Resolution* (NYU Press 2015).

[4] Robert Mnookin and Lewis Kornhauser, *"Bargaining in the Shadow of the Law: The Case of Divorce,"* YALE LAW JOURNAL 88 (1979): 968.

relationship. The research tells us that the acrimony between parents engendered by this system harms children.

All of these developments contributed to the creation of family courts with a significantly expanded vision of the role of the court in resolving disputes. According to this expanded vision, resolving disputed legal issues is too narrow an objective for an effective family court. Rather, to achieve its mission, an effective family court must address not only the parties' immediate legal needs, but also the underlying family dynamics and future well-being of the children and families who appear before it. Moreover, because divorce or parental separation no longer signals the end of a relationship, but rather the restructuring of a continuing parenting partnership, both the range of relevant issues and the potential duration of court involvement in family life have expanded dramatically. Mediation is central to this expanded vision.

One commentator recently offered another reason for the spread of mediation — the enthusiasm and "zealous" belief in the process by its practitioners:

> [M]ediation appears to be more of an ideologically driven movement than most dispute resolution processes, resulting in a zealous commitment to the process and the field by its proponents. Because the ideals of self-determination, empowerment and collaboration are firmly embedded in the roots of the mediation process, it is viewed by some not merely as another mechanism through which to resolve disputes, but something entirely different. . . .

> The idealism and enthusiasm surrounding the mediation movement has helped to spur an entire industry, including myriad international, national, state and local professional mediation associations; a vibrant continuing education and training community; academic programs including degree programs, certificates, mediation clinics and a related body of scholarly work; and numerous books, journals and other publications. In more than twenty years of participating in and observing family dispute resolution (and having been a mediation idealist and enthusiast), I have witnessed passionate responses to many new ideas and processes; however, in my opinion, none have generated near the level of sustained and widespread activity and enthusiasm as mediation. (citations omitted)

Peter Salem, *"The Emergence of Triage in Family Court Services: The Beginning of the End of Mandatory Mediation?"*47 FAMILY COURT REVIEW 371, 374 (2009)

As family mediation grew, a number of organizations stepped in to begin to regulate the practice and offer guidelines for best practices. The Association of Family and Conciliation Courts (AFCC) and the American Bar Association have been leaders in developing standards for family mediation. In 1984, the AFCC drafted Model Standards of Practice for Family and Divorce Mediation, and the ABA's Family Law Section drafted Standards of Practice for Lawyer Mediators in Family Law Disputes. In 2000, the ABA, the AFCC, the Association for Conflict Resolution, and other organizations substantially revised the Model Standards of Practice for Family and Divorce Mediation.

As family mediation has grown and families have become more diverse, the range of family conflicts in mediation has also changed. Conflicts following divorce are no longer the central focus of mediation. Court-sponsored programs address primarily child access issues — custody and visitation involving both married and unmarried parents as well as disputes between parents and third parties who have acted as parents — grandparents, stepparents, and same sex partners without legal parent status. These child access disputes may also raise issues of paternity and, in some programs, child support. While child access related disputes remain the focus of most family court mediation programs, private mediation has expanded to address a wide range of other issues, including financial issues related to family break up.

## NOTES AND QUESTIONS

1.   As discussed in the excerpts above, a number of circumstances contributed to the growth of both private and court based family mediation. Much of it related to the view of many lawyers and mental health practitioners that the adversary system harmed children. What was the basis for this belief?

2.   How did the changes from fault to no-fault divorce also help fuel the growth of mediation to resolve family disputes? How did the law's endorsement of joint parenting increase reliance on mediation?

## 2.   Emerging Critiques of Family Mediation

Most mental health professionals, lawyers, and participants have viewed the pervasive use of mediation in family courts as a positive development that offers parties a more economical, efficient and less harmful process for resolving disputes. For courts, it offers a cost-savings approach to clearing increasingly crowded family dockets. For lawyers, it offers an alternative role in representing a client in family conflict. But some critics of family mediation have emerged, particularly as it is practiced in many family courts. In survey conducted from 1998–2004, the Association of Family and Conciliation Courts' survey found that 92 percent of family court service agencies offered mediation. As a result, mediation has become the "default" option for most parties involved in contested child access claims in court. The two excerpts below describe the most common objections to such programs.

## *BURDENING ACCESS TO JUSTICE: THE COST OF DIVORCE MEDIATION ON THE CHEAP*[5]
73 St. John's L. Rev. 375, 390–93, 397, 473–74 (1999)
By Carol J. King

Programs mandating or encouraging divorcing parties to mediate and pay for the service raise significant legal and policy questions concerning access to justice. Mandatory referral schemes, in which divorcing parties are ordered to attend mediation and pay the costs, are certainly effective in increasing the use of mediation while holding down court expenditures. If mediation is not voluntary, and parties are required to attend and are obligated to pay the mediator, constitutional due process

---

[5] Copyright ©1999. Reprinted with permission.

and equal protection issues may be implicated. Further, as a practical matter, parties may be denied access to adjudication of their cases because they lack the funds to pay for the prerequisite mediation. Particularly in divorce cases, when partners are setting up two households on the same income that formerly supported only one, money is tight. Divorcing parties who are mandated to use and pay for mediation services may be unduly pressured to settle on unacceptable terms because they cannot afford to pay lawyers' fees for trial or further negotiation, in addition to the fees they have been forced to spend for mediation.

Originally, most divorce mediation practitioners were privately retained and paid by the parties, while a few community mediation centers provided free services. This was in line with one of the primary rationales for advancing the mediation movement — avoiding the court system. Mediation was intended to provide a dispute resolution process that differed greatly from the adjudicatory model, by emphasizing consensual, voluntary participation in both the process and outcome of mediation. People were not ordered to attend mediation. Instead, they were given the opportunity to negotiate freely. Mediators were philosophically opposed to forcing a settlement on an unwilling party. One of the goals of mediation was to address the root causes of the conflict by generating understanding and consensus. Rather than focusing on fault-finding or seeking to impose a decision on the parties in conflict, mediation sought to promote lasting resolutions.

Recently, mediation has begun to diverge greatly from many of the precepts originally guiding the movement and mandatory mediation is no longer viewed as being antithetical to the goals of mediation. Early experience in community mediation pilot programs showed that voluntary usage rates were low. In many cases, one party was interested in trying mediation, but one or more of the other parties would decline to participate. Policy makers grew more interested in mandating participation, particularly in light of studies indicating that satisfaction rates were high even under mandated conditions. Interest in expanded use of mediation through mandatory participation was not limited to the types of cases typically seen in neighborhood or community mediation centers. Family courts began to explore mediation when possible systemic benefits, such as docket reduction and cost savings, became known. In the past few years, there has been a significant increase in the number of states authorizing mandatory divorce mediation — there was a vast leap in a single year, from reports of four to six states in 1993, to thirty-three states in 1994. Courts have taken several different approaches to funding mandatory divorce mediation programs. On one end of the continuum, courts fully fund mediators for the disputants. On the other end, judges are permitted to refer cases to private providers at party cost, manifesting little official concern for the financial constraints on the parties.

. . . Sometimes, free services are made available at least to some of the very poor. Unfortunately, many low-income divorcing parties, who are unable to pay mediation fees on their own, do not qualify for free services. A few programs attempt to mitigate the financial strain on lower-income mediation participants through sliding fee scales. The actual affordability of mediation services offered under sliding fee scales remains unexamined. Statutory provisions allowing parties to request fee waivers may be ineffective because the parties are often unaware of them. Some courts do not address the affordability problem at all, and leave the allocation of fees to the court's discretion if the parties cannot agree. If the fees are substantial, which is often the case, the allocation of such fees is a deciding factor when parties are determining whether to pursue mediation . . .

Courts have encouraged greater use of mediation with hopes of controlling dockets and reducing the delays and costs of modern litigation. Domestic relations courts also aspired to reduce the negative impact of bitterly fought divorce and custody disputes on children by diverting cases to a forum seen as more capable of resolving the underlying conflicts between parents than traditional adjudication or attorney negotiation.

Totally voluntary mediation programs did not handle a sufficient volume of cases to have any significant impact on the court system's goals. Mandatory mediation became more appealing, especially as research showed continued participant satisfaction even when mediation was involuntary.

Unfortunately, as courts have demonstrated increased interest in adding mediation to the range of available dispute resolution services, money for funding new programs has become less readily available. Funding problems have led to the passage of statutes and rules allowing courts to require parties to use and pay for mediation as a prerequisite to having their cases heard in court. An increasing number of litigants, both in general civil and family law cases, have been compelled to pay for mediation in addition to the other costs of litigation.

. . . In the domestic relations case context, it raises serious concerns about functional denial of the due process guarantee of access to the courts where parties cannot afford both mediation and litigation. In addition, the practical reality of the significant financial constraints facing most divorcing parties makes a party payment approach punitive. It clearly places the interests of the court in case diversion ahead of the litigants' needs and interest in free choice of dispute resolution options. The weight of argument and preliminary research favor publicly funded divorce mediation as the best way to guarantee equal access to both alternative dispute resolution and the courts . . .

---

## *THE EMERGENCE OF TRIAGE IN FAMILY COURT SERVICES: THE BEGINNING OF THE END OF MANDATORY MEDIATION?*
47 FAM. CT. REV. 371, 377–78 (2009)
By Peter Salem

. . . [T]he times and conditions have changed in family court service agencies since many studies of court-connected mediation were conducted in the 1980s and 1990s. Today, many court-connected mediation programs struggle with growing caseloads, static or reduced staffing levels, and increasingly complex cases; they simply lack the resources to provide the five to six hours of mediation that yielded such positive long-term outcomes as those found in Emery's study of mediations conducted in the late 1980s. With triage, on the other hand, there is potential to reallocate resources, avoid duplication of services, and create a more efficient service delivery system. The contrast in the public agency environment is illustrated by my conversation with a family court services supervisor in the early 1990s. The supervisor's agency had identified a need for three additional court mediators/evaluators in order to keep pace with the growing number of referrals. In anticipation of having its staffing request reduced, the agency submitted a budget for seven new positions. Surprisingly, all seven positions were approved and the agency was *overstaffed*. Today, such an occurrence seems beyond the wildest dreams of court agencies.

Lacking sufficient resources, it is not at all clear that the mediation process in family courts today can embody, "the vision of self-determination that dominated the original mediation movement and inspired its broadly facilitative approach." Hedeen, writing generally about court-connected mediation in the civil, criminal and family contexts, writes, "While it is commonly held that mediators are expected to "honor, protect, and nurture parties' self-determination . . . [and] 'empower' the parties, 'enable' them to be 'ultimate decision makers' and 'satisfy' them", these expectations are not always realized in practice." (citations omitted)

If mediators lack sufficient time to conduct mediation, it is simply not possible to honor, protect and nurture parties' self-determination; to conduct a mediation process in which parties can fully express their views and develop their own agreements; to help parents work together; and to help them understand the impact of conflict on their children. And there is little disagreement about the lack of resources. In the previously noted AFCC survey, forty-eight percent of family court service programs surveyed reported increased workload for staff between 1998 and 2004; 39 percent experienced a reduction in direct service staff; 31 percent reduced administrative staff; and 24 percent reduced supervisory staff.

Adding to the challenges of inadequate resources is that cases referred to mediation have become increasingly complex over the last quarter century. According to Saposnek (2004), "Compared to disputed divorce cases in the 1980s, contemporary disputed divorce cases- . . . involve families with more serious and multiple problems, who use a plethora of public agencies . . . and disproportionately use the court's resources . . . Mediation approaches and techniques that worked quite well in the past often are inappropriate today" The complexity of cases, combined with lack of adequate time for mediation and the involvement of additional public agencies, make it that much more difficult for court-connected mediation programs to deliver on the promise of self-determination and empowerment . . . .

When constrained by time and challenged by families with multiple issues, mediators are faced with difficult decisions about the manner in which to conduct the process. One option is to become increasingly directive, making recommendations, predicting court outcomes and pressuring parties into agreement. It is not difficult to find anecdotes about such behaviors, including instances when the mediator virtually dictates the agreement terms or spells out dire consequences for the parties if they fail to settle. It is possible that this behavior is the exception and in and of itself it is not necessarily an indictment of the mediation process or the court-connected mediators. It may be that some mediators feel compelled to do whatever it takes to help parties reach settlements due to institutional pressures. Or an experienced mediator, recognizing that a facilitative mediation process is unlikely to succeed with a particular family, may shift to a highly directive process, taking the pragmatic view that it is more important to help the family resolve their issues than adhere to a particular mediation practice orientation.

It is difficult to identify research that chronicles these patterns of behavior. But behind closed doors, many court-connected mediators acknowledge that they cannot conduct a facilitative mediation process if they are to meet the expectations of their workplace. They express enormous frustration at being caught between a rock and a hard place as they are asked to deliver high quality mediation services in what they know to be a fraction of the time required to effectively do so, often with cases that are not appropriate for mediation. According to one veteran court mediator who requested anonymity, "In recent years, encouraging families toward self-determination and private ordering have taken a back seat. Mediation services, which are mandated, are adversely affected because administrators move their workforce toward evaluation services." Another mediator and court services supervisor referring to the common practice of recommending settlements said, "The process is called mediation and we settle cases, but it certainly isn't real mediation." (citations omitted)

---

# NOTES AND QUESTIONS

1. By statute or court rule, most courts hearing family disputes, make mediation an option for parties in family disputes. In some states or jurisdictions, it is voluntary. In many, mediation is mandatory for child access cases, with some exceptions (most commonly for families experiencing domestic violence). These statutes and court rules require parties seeking child access remedies to try mediation before they are permitted access to an adversarial proceeding to resolve the dispute. *See e.g.*, ME. REV. STAT. ANN. TIT.19-A § 251; W. VA. CODE § 48-9-202; MI Rules MCR 3.216. *But see*, COLO. REV. STAT. ANN. § 13-22-311(1) (2000) (party can be excused for a compelling reason including costs of mediation and lack of success in previous mediation).

What concerns do mandatory mediation programs in family courts raise for the participants? What about concerns for mediators mediating these cases?

# Chapter 2

# MODELS OF FAMILY MEDIATION

## A. INTRODUCTION

You might assume that when the word "mediation" is used everyone is referring to the same thing. This is not the case. Indeed, in recent years, there has been an intense debate about what mediation *is*. This debate is often framed in terms of what "model" or "style" of mediation is most appropriate, or even if certain "models" constitute real mediation at all. Another interesting, albeit less common, way to conceptualize different conceptions of mediation is through whether mediators can or should advocate or educate participants about what "norms" should be at play in mediation. This Chapter addresses all of these issues.

## B. AN OVERVIEW: THREE MODELS OF FAMILY MEDIATION

Most commentators identify three models of mediation: evaluative, facilitative, and transformative.[1] What follows briefly sketches the basics of each model in order to set the stage for a more in depth discussion in the material that follows:

### Evaluative Mediation

Evaluative mediators take an active role in conducting mediation. They will offer a range of assessments about a conflict. These assessments might be about, among other things:

- Predictions about how a court will decide a particular issue.

- Identifying what issues are in dispute and warrant resolution.

- Opinions about what agreements are "fair," such as particular child access schedules or division of property.

---

[1] The first articulation of the distinction between "facilitative" and "evaluative" was set forth by Leonard Riskin. Leonard Riskin, *Understanding Mediator Orientations, Strategies and Techniques*, 12 ALTERNATIVES TO HIGH COST LIT. 111 (1994); Leonard Riskin, *Understanding Mediators' Orientations, Strategies, and Techniques: A Grid for the Perplexed*, 1 HARV. NEGOT. L. REV. 7 (1996). Professor Riskin himself has more recently expressed reservations about how the distinction has come to be used. Leonard Riskin, *Decisionmaking in Mediation: The New Old Grid and the New New Grid System*, 79 NOTRE DAME L. REV. 1 (2003).

**Facilitative Mediation**

Facilitative mediators hold that participants, not mediators, should define and assess the nature of conflicts and how best to resolve them. Such mediators facilitate the process and do not make assessments.[2] They generally believe that evaluation of legal positions or assessing fairness of proposed resolution is inconsistent with the role of a mediator.

**Transformative Mediation**

Transformative mediators assume a less active role than a facilitative mediator. They reject that resolution of a dispute is the goal of mediation. They instead aim to create an environment through which participants may experience positive "shifts" in how they interact with each other. One shift would "empower" participants to better enable them to be heard by other participants. The other shift promotes the ability of one participant to "recognize" the perspective of another participant. Transformative mediators argue that these shifts reinforce each other because "empowerment" contributes to "recognition," and vice versa.

## C.  "EVALUATIVE" MEDIATION

Mediators who adhere to an evaluative model take an active role in the process and substance of mediation. Although this model of mediation is widely practiced among mediators, particularly those who are lawyers or current or former judges, it is relatively rare to find extended arguments in favor of it in the mediation literature. What follows is an example of such an argument.

### *EVALUATIVE MEDIATION*
in Divorce and Family Mediation 72, 73, 77–85 (Jay Folberg, Ann L. Milne & Peter Salem, eds., 2004)
By L. Randolph Lowry

. . . The evaluative approach to the mediation process either allows or, in many cases, establishes an expectation that the mediator will make assessments about the conflict as well as its resolution and communicate those assessments to the parties . . . . Evaluation involves at least three activities: (1) first assessing the strengths and weaknesses of the parties' case; (2) then developing and proposing options to resolve the case; and (3) predicting the outcome at trial if a dispute, not settled in mediation, were to be fully litigated. Notice the activity included in this definition — assessing, proposing, and predicting. Evaluation in mediation assumes the mediator's involvement in the substance as well as the process. It is active, decisive, and involved.

The primary arguments in favor of using evaluation in the mediation process follow:

1. Those who favor evaluative mediation cite its value in achieving the most important objective of mediation: getting an agreement. They point to the many cases

---

[2] This would not extend to reporting of child abuse or other circumstances where disclosure is mandated or permitted by applicable rules of ethics. See Chapter 12 for more details on these issues.

in which the moment in the mediation that was most influential and persuasive occurred when the mediator formulated and expressed an opinion about how the parties should view the case. It was at that moment that hard news was delivered to one, or both, of the parties that reconsideration of positions took place and that parties were motivated to move toward each other in the negotiation . . . .

2. [E]valuation represents the integration into the mediation process of expertise not available among the parties or perhaps even their advocates . . . . The need for additional expertise is evident . . . in the family law arena. Most parties in a divorce context are experiencing the trauma of that event for the first time. By definition, they have only limited experience with it. They cannot be expected to know all of the issues that will need to be resolved, the range of possible options, or the preferences of the court in resolving the conflict. Their emotion is certainly very real, but their knowledge of the law may be nonexistent. Those represented by lawyers may be more informed; still, additional expertise is often necessary for the resolution of the issues at hand. The mediator could be that resource . . . .

3. Evaluation benefits the mediation process by making it more efficient . . . . At some point, someone has to encourage a transition from unrelenting advocacy to problem solving. Often the expression of an opinion encourages such movement . . . .

4. Parties who have little or no influence on the opposing party benefit from the evaluative approach . . . When it comes to convincing the opposing party, the neutral third party has the platform from which to express a perspective and have it taken more seriously than if the same perspective were expressed by the other party . . . .

5. Evaluation by the mediator is a benefit because it gives the parties an excuse to agree. In highly entrenched family disputes, neither party may see the possibility of agreement on a particular issue . . . . For a variety of personal and professional considerations, the lawyer-advocate might find it difficult to suggest to the client that a case be settled. The lawyer cannot look "soft." Yet that same lawyer might recommend that the client carefully consider "what the mediator has said" and be thrilled that an outsider has said it. In that moment, the evaluation benefits the parties by allowing a socially acceptable way to move toward one another . . . .

6. The quality of the analysis and advice given by the mediator may be greater than most other information received. Who is to say that the parties know more about the application of law or the probable outcome of a matter in litigation than someone who might have mediated hundreds of cases with the same issues? Is it not a benefit to the party to receive the evaluation? Whereas the traditional view would be to defer to the party's expertise in mediation, those supportive of an evaluative model point to the value of correct information as an asset to the parties involved . . . .

## THE FOCUS OF EVALUATION

Experience suggests that there is a variety of directions an evaluative mediator might take . . . .

1. The mediator can evaluate the dynamics between the parties, their movement or lack of movement toward a negotiated resolution, and identify barriers that might

impede success. The evaluating mediator can also categorize the work of the parties in the negotiation in terms of their contribution, or lack of contribution, to progress as the communication process unfolds . . . .

2. Evaluation in mediation might focus on the behavior of parties . . . . The mediator is in a unique position to point out those actions or behaviors that may lead to an agreement or may keep an agreement from occurring.. . . .

3. The mediator's evaluation might focus on the priorities of the parties . . . . I am not advocating substitution of the mediator's priorities for the priorities of the parties; rather I am calling for the mediator's understanding of the parties' priorities so that they can be evaluated in light of what is actually achievable in a legal forum . . . .

4. The evaluation of a mediator might focus on particular plans proposed as solutions to the conflict . . . The evaluative mediator may have handled hundreds of similar cases, seen how lasting particular plans might or might not be, and understand the court's view or particular issues. The willingness to share an evaluation of a plan being proposed may be critically important to the success of that plan and to the best interests of the parties being served . . . .

5. . . . A mediator experienced in divorce and family law, or in the specific subject of dispute, can evaluate proposed solutions in the context of real-world alternatives. The evaluation directs the mediator either to encourage the acceptance of the proposed agreement or to consider the dangers in accepting the terms proposed. The mediator's experience or expertise is most helpful in that evaluative moment, whether that experience is in child development, financial planning, real estate, or another subject in dispute . . .

In looking closely at the work of a mediator, most observers would conclude that, on some level, all mediators evaluate. Mediators make informed decisions based upon the information presented. They mentally process information, formulate judgments, and respond according to their theoretical framework. They even decide what they think of the parties involved and what the outcome should be. If mediators did not evaluate (at least internally), it would be difficult to move the parties toward a settlement.

Perhaps the question is not whether to evaluate but, rather, should the evaluation by the mediator be expressed and, if so, how? If one considers the reality of at least the mediator's internal evaluation, then the focus becomes on what and how any of it might be shared. Does the mediator react to evidence, reveal a feeling about the case, or share an idea about what a settlement might look like? Does the mediator understand the reality of the circumstance and test the parties' understanding as well? Does the mediator ask questions with the intention of affecting the parties' perspectives? Many mediators, even those who would consider themselves more facilitative in approach, carry out those tasks without violating their commitment to the process and to the parties. It is not a question that something will be communicated but, rather, the degree of directness in that communication . . . .

## NOTES AND QUESTIONS

1. Assessing evaluative mediation is most valuable after more closely examining its primary alternative, facilitative mediation, which will be addressed next. Even at this preliminary stage, though, consider how evaluative mediation differs from, say, a settlement conference in which a judge encourages settlement.

2. Lowery argues that lawyers representing participants in mediation might welcome evaluative mediation. In fact, evaluative mediation seems to be on the rise in light of lawyers' increasing involving as mediators. Why do you think this is the case?

3. Do you agree with Lowery that all mediators evaluate whether they admit it or not? We will explore this issue more later in this Chapter.

## D. "FACILITATIVE" MEDIATION

Some have argued that evaluative mediation reflects a view of mediation that is not mediation. Rather, it is litigation, and operates in a way comparable to how a judge might conduct a settlement conference. Judges in settlement conferences do tend to take an active role in encouraging parties to settle a dispute, and in so doing a judge might offer an assessment of what a fair resolution might be.

Before stepping into this debate, however, the following excerpt sets forth how facilitative mediation differs from litigation.

### *CLIENT COUNSELING, MEDIATION, AND ALTERNATIVE NARRATIVES OF DISPUTE RESOLUTION*[3]
10 Clin. L. Rev. 833, 846–53 (2004)
By Robert Rubinson

The story of litigation has been so thoroughly internalized by litigants, judges, and lawyers alike that it operates below the level of consciousness. [E]verybody — lawyers and non-lawyers alike — knows what it is. In contrast, for a culture steeped in litigation, the risk in approaching [facilitative] mediation is in underestimating its strangeness. In its more sophisticated forms, mediation is bizarre indeed: it proceeds from fundamentally different premises as to what resolving disputes is about and, even more fundamentally, as to what a dispute is . . . .

Perspectives

[L]itigation is consumed with determining "what happened" in order to determine liability. Judges and juries decide "what happened" and sort liability (or penalties) accordingly. In contrast, mediation rejects the idea that "what happened" is a unitary or stable "truth" to be found "out there." Instead, a primary — if not the primary — thrust of [facilitative] mediation is that conflict resolution entails some recognition on the part of disputants that "what happened" is informed by perspective. Literature on

---

[3] Copyright ©2004. Reprinted with permission.

mediation is rife with this idea: a critical component of mediation is that parties "begin to acknowledge another view of the situation," or "[t]he challenge for mediation is to somehow lead people to a situation where they can, at the very least, allow two contending perceptions to coexist," or to "enable each person to see the other as the victim, and in the process, build a new moral framework" . . . .

### Rights and Wrongs in Mediation

Given the importance of "perspective" in mediation, the very notion of "judgment" is alien to mediation, as are notions of "fault" and even "responsibility." Issuing "judgments" (both in its legal and non-legal sense) and finding "fault" or "responsibility" impede mediation because mediators want parties to be the authors of their own mediation. A morality tale which identifies one party as "moral" necessarily brands the other party as not, and the "immoral" party is not likely to "own" a process that produces such a result.

### "Time" in Mediation

Litigation looks backward in time: it seeks to resolve disputes through historical reconstruction of past events. In contrast, mediation focuses on what needs to be done to resolve disputes in light of present and future interests. This is not to say that history — or at least perspectives on history — does not have its place in mediation: indeed, history in mediation might offer clues about how to resolve controversy in the here and now, or parties might require validation of their perspective on history — and the catharsis that describing that history might bring — as necessary before meaningful progress can be made towards resolving a controversy. Nevertheless, the past in mediation is typically not the foundation for resolving conflict . . .

### Narrowing and Expanding

[R]ather than narrowing issues, the mediation process tends to embrace openness in dialogue. Such openness encourages parties to discuss and disclose anything that would facilitate the resolution of controversy. The idea is that the more circumstances and possibilities are shared by the parties to mediation, the greater the chances that the parties, with the assistance of the mediator, can find creative ways to resolve disputes . . . .

## E.  THE "FACILITATIVE" VERSUS "EVALUATIVE" DEBATE

The debate between evaluative mediators and facilitative mediators can be vigorous. The following excerpt is one example. As you read it, reflect on the prior article on evaluative mediation. Do you agree with Love's arguments?

# THE TOP TEN REASONS WHY MEDIATORS SHOULD NOT EVALUATE[4]

24 FLA. ST. U. L. REV. 937, 937–38 (1997)

By Lela P. Love

## I. THE ROLES AND RELATED TASKS OF EVALUATORS AND FACILITATORS ARE AT ODDS

. . . [T]he evaluative tasks of determining facts, applying law or custom, and delivering an opinion . . . can compromise the mediator's neutrality — both in actuality and in the eyes of the parties — because the mediator will be favoring one side in his or her judgments . . .

## II. EVALUATION PROMOTES POSITIONING AND POLARIZATION, WHICH ARE ANTITHETICAL TO THE GOALS OF MEDIATION

When disputing parties are in the presence of an evaluator — a judge, an arbitrator, or a neutral expert — they act (or should act) differently than they would in the presence of a mediator. With an evaluator, disputants make themselves look as good as possible and their opponent as bad as possible. They do not make offers of compromise or reveal their hand for fear that it weakens the evaluator's perception of the strength of their case. They are in a competitive mind-set seeking to capture the evaluator's favor and win the case.

While adversarial confrontations between parties are helpful to a neutral who must judge credibility and clarify the choices he or she must make, such confrontations are not helpful to collaboration. Adversarial behaviors run counter to the mediator's efforts to move parties towards a different perception of their own situation and of each other. While parties typically enter the mediation process in a hostile and adversarial stance, the mediator seeks to shift them towards a collaborative posture in which they jointly construct a win-win solution. An atmosphere of respectful collaboration is a necessary foundation for creative problem-solving.

## III. ETHICAL CODES CAUTION MEDIATORS — AND OTHER NEUTRALS — AGAINST ASSUMING ADDITIONAL ROLES

The ethical codes explicitly include a preference to keep processes "pure." Consequently, a mediator undertaking to give an opinion on the likely court outcome of a particular claim or a fair resolution of a particular matter should give an accurate label of the new role he or she is assuming and obtain the disputants' informed consent for undertaking the new role . . . .

---

[4] Copyright ©1997. Reprinted with permission.

## IV. IF MEDIATORS EVALUATE LEGAL CLAIMS AND DEFENSES, THEY MUST BE LAWYERS; ELIMINATING NONLAWYERS WILL WEAKEN THE FIELD

If it is acceptable or customary for mediators to give opinions on likely court outcomes or the merits of particular legal claims or defenses, then only lawyers and substantive experts will be competent to mediate . . . While this result may be good news for lawyers, the mediator pool would be substantially weakened by the loss of the talents and perspectives of nonlawyers. Furthermore, if the field is theirs, lawyer-mediators will likely pull mediation into an adversarial paradigm. One noted authority in the mediation field, reacting to a Florida rule requiring mediators of certain cases to be either experienced lawyers or retired judges, proclaimed this requirement to be "the end of good mediation."

## V. THERE ARE INSUFFICIENT PROTECTIONS AGAINST INCORRECT MEDIATOR EVALUATIONS

Even assuming that mediators could be governed by and held to appropriate standards when they evaluate, growing concerns about the quality of justice that disputants receive when they are diverted from courts into private alternative dispute resolution (ADR) processes argue for leaving evaluation to adversarial processes where due process protections are in place. In the courts, disputants can appeal decisions they feel are wrong . . . . In mediation, little protection exists from a mediator's inadequately informed opinion. Confidentiality statutes, rules, and agreements keep sessions private. Quasi-judicial immunity in some cases can shield mediators from liability for careless opinions.

## VI. EVALUATION ABOUNDS: THE DISPUTING WORLD NEEDS ALTERNATIVE PARADIGMS

Mediation has the potential of being shifted towards an adversarial framework in which mediators "trash and bash" to get parties to settle. They "trash" the parties' cases, predicting loss and risk if litigation is pursued. They "bash" settlement proposals that the other side will not accept. We lose a great deal if mediation becomes a mere adjunct of the adversarial norm . . . .

## VII. MEDIATOR EVALUATION DETRACTS FROM THE FOCUS ON PARTY RESPONSIBILITY FOR CRITICAL EVALUATION, RE-EVALUATION AND CREATIVE PROBLEM-SOLVING

. . . The mediator's task of elevating the dialogue from recriminations and blame to the generation of possibilities and breakthrough ideas is a task we are just beginning to understand. If we allow mediation and mediators to slip into the comfortable (because it is the norm) adversarial mind-set of evaluation, we kill the turbo-thrust of the jet engine of idea generation. So-called "evaluative mediation" pulls mediation away from creativity and into the adversarial frame.

## VIII. EVALUATION CAN STOP NEGOTIATION

When mediators provide opinions, the opinions have consequences. An unfavorable opinion can seriously disadvantage one of the parties. When a party disagrees with the unfavorable opinion, the party is likely to withdraw from the mediation, believing that the mediator has "sided" with the other party. On the other hand, a party advantaged by a favorable opinion may get locked into an unacceptable claim or position and negotiations may stop altogether. Because mediators are charged with furthering negotiation, this result is undesirable.

## IX. A UNIFORM UNDERSTANDING OF MEDIATION IS CRITICAL TO THE DEVELOPMENT OF THE FIELD

When attorneys advise clients about the advantages and disadvantages of mediation, when courts and institutions create mediation programs and panels of mediators, when consumers go to the Yellow Pages to find a mediator, they should know what they are getting. They should have a clear understanding of the goals of the process and the tasks the neutral will perform.

## X. MIXED PROCESSES CAN BE USEFUL, BUT CALL THEM WHAT THEY ARE!

Parties sometimes request that neutrals assume a variety of roles. "Mixed processes" abound: med-arb, arb-med, mini-trials, summary jury trials, and mediation and neutral evaluation. These mixed processes can address particular needs of a situation and can be very helpful.

Mediators are not foreclosed from engaging in some other process or helping parties design a mixed process. Whatever the service being provided, however, it should be requested by the parties and accurately labeled. When a process is "mixed" and the neutral has multiple roles, he or she is bound by more than one code of ethics and is charged with separate goals and tasks. A properly labeled process — or, conversely, a label that has a clear meaning — promotes integrity, disputant satisfaction, and uniform practice . . . .

# NOTES AND QUESTIONS

1.   Are you convinced by Love's reasons why "mediators should not evaluate"? Why or why not? In thinking through your answer, consider how Lowry, the author of the prior excerpt on evaluative mediation, would respond to each of Love's "top ten reasons."

2.   While sometimes writers charge "evaluation" is never appropriate in mediation, such as in the excerpt above, others claim that the debate presupposes a kind of stylistic "purity" that is not to be found in practice. In other words, many — if not most — family mediators will sometimes be "facilitative" and sometimes "evaluative" along a continuum, with mediators deploying a particular "style" when the situation so demands. What do you think?

3.   A somewhat different argument made by some evaluative mediators, including Lowry, is that a mediator cannot help but evaluative: it is just that facilitative mediators will not admit it. This is as much a comment about human nature as it is about mediation. *See, e.g.*, Jacqueline M. Nolan-Haley, *Lawyers, Non-Lawyers and Mediation: Rethinking the Professional Monopoly from a Problem-Solving Perspective*, 7 HARV. NEG. L. REV. 235, 276–280 (2002) (arguing that all mediations contain explicit or implicit "evaluation" by mediators). What do you think of this argument? If it is true, do you believe the evaluative/facilitative debate is not as meaningful as the debate presupposes?

4.   Are some forms of evaluation more legitimate than others in family mediation? For example, should mediators "evaluate" — or at least share views — on what is best for children of divorcing couples? How about issues relating to finances? Does it matter that children are not formal "participants" in mediation?

5.   It appears that many of Love's arguments against evaluation are animated by a fear that evaluative mediation is simply an adversarial process under another name. Do you agree?

6.   Love argues that lawyer-mediators are likely to adopt an "evaluative" model because it embodies the norm of adversarial adjudication.[5] Some evidence suggests that this is indeed the case. Richard Baitar et al., *Styles and Goals: Clarifying the Professional Identity of Divorce Mediation*, 31 CONFLICT RESOL. Q. 57 (2013). Others express similar fears about judge-mediators. Noel Semple, *Judicial Settlement Seeking in Parenting Disputes: Consensus and Controversy*, 29 CONFLICT RESOL. Q. 309 (2012). Love ultimately suggests that limiting mediators to lawyers signals "the end of good mediation." Do you agree?

## F.   "TRANSFORMATIVE MEDIATION" IN FAMILY DISPUTES

In the 1990s, Robert A. Baruch Bush and Joseph P. Folger elucidated what they call "transformative mediation" — a model of mediation that, they argue, has different goals, practices, and premises than evaluative and facilitative mediation.[6] Transformative mediation has proven to be highly influential and, despite its relatively recent origins, has taken its place as one of the three widely recognized models of mediation. The following excerpt describes the goals of and practices of transformative mediation in the context of family mediation.

---

[5] Debra Berman & James Alfini, *Lawyer Colonization of Family Mediation: Consequences and Implications*, 95 MARQUETTE L. REV. 907 (2012).

[6] The latest edition of their seminal book is ROBERT A. BARUCH BUSH & JOSEPH P. FOLGER, THE PROMISE OF MEDIATION: RESPONDING TO CONFLICT THROUGH EMPOWERMENT AND RECOGNITION (Revised Ed. 2005).

# TRANSFORMATIVE MEDIATION: CHANGING THE QUALITY OF FAMILY CONFLICT INTERACTION[7]

*from* DIVORCE AND FAMILY MEDIATION 54: 556–60 (JAY FOLBERG, ANN L. MILNE & PETER SALEM eds., 2004)

By Robert A. Baruch Bush & Sally Ganong Pope

. . . [T]here are problems to be solved at the end of a marriage — the assets to be divided, the parenting plan to be created — and parties do want to solve those problems. The reality is, however, that they want to do so in a way that enhances their sense of their own competence and autonomy without taking advantage of the other. They want to feel proud of themselves for how they handled this life crisis, and this means making changes in the difficult conflict interaction that is going on between them, rather than simply coming up with the "right" answers to the specific problems. The corollary, explored below, is that in order to be useful to parties, conflict intervention must directly address the interactional crisis itself; it cannot be limited to problem solving and satisfaction of interests . . . . Therefore, what they most want from an intervener-even more than help in resolving specific issues-is help in reversing the downward spiral and restoring a more humane quality to their interaction . . . .

In the transformative model, reversing the downward spiral is the primary value that mediation offers to parties in family conflict. That value goes beyond the dimension of helping parties reach agreement on disputed issues. With or without the achievement of agreement, the help many parties want most in family conflict (and probably in all conflict) involves helping them end the vicious circle of disempowerment, disrespect, and demonization — alienation from both self and other. Because without ending or changing that cycle, the parties cannot move beyond the negative interaction that has entrapped them and cannot escape its crippling effects . . . .

[W]ithout a change in the conflict interaction between them, parties are left disabled, even if an agreement on concrete issues has been reached. Their confidence in their own competence to handle life's challenges remains weakened, and their ability to trust others in relationships remains compromised. The result can be lasting damage to the parties' ability to function, not only in family relationships but in general. "Moving on," therefore, necessarily means moving out of their negative conflict interaction itself, and parties intuitively know this and want help in doing it.

Conflict is . . . an emergent, dynamic phenomenon in which parties can and do move and shift in remarkable ways. They move from weakness to strength, becoming (in more specific terms) calmer, clearer, more confident, more articulate, and more decisive. They shift from self-absorption to responsiveness, becoming more attentive, open, trusting, responsive toward the other party. [T]hese shifts that parties make — from weakness to strength, and from self-absorption to responsiveness to one another — . . . are called "empowerment" and "recognition" . . . [T]here is a reinforcing feedback effect . . . . The stronger I become, the more open I am to you. The more open I am to you, the stronger you feel, the more open you become to me, and the stronger I feel . . . . What many divorcing parties want most from mediators, and what

---

mediators can, in fact, provide . . . is help and support in making these critical shifts from weakness to strength and from self-absorption to responsiveness . . . .

The transformative model . . . can thus help divorcing parties to "move on with their lives," with the capacities for living those lives restored-including both the sense of their own competence, and the confidence in their ability to connect with others . . . . Transformative mediators allow and trust the parties to find their own way through the conflict, and even more important, find themselves and each other, discovering and revealing the strength and compassion within themselves . . . .

## NOTES AND QUESTIONS

1. In another article, Bush and Pope claim that transformative mediation "differs markedly from the normal definitions found in training materials and literature on mediation." Robert A. Baruch Bush & Sally Ganong Pope, *Changing the Quality of Conflict Interaction: The Principles and Practice of Transformative Mediation*, 3 PEPP. DISP. RESOL. L.J. 67 (2002). Do you agree?

2. The authors argue that "transformative mediation" seeks to encourage "positive interactional shifts" with the parties rather than resolve specific controversies. Does facilitative mediation — at least in terms of its promise — seek to do the same thing, albeit as a means to resolve a specific conflict? Is the difference then one of emphasis rather than of kind?

3. Transformative mediation has been the subject of vigorous critiques. One of these critiques is directed at the idea that mediators must "follow" participants without influencing the path they wish to pursue. Consider this argument against this idea:

> [I]ntervenors must be aware of their own biases and understand their role in the dynamic. It is not enough to limit mediator behavior for fear of mediator bias, which is what Bush and Folger are increasingly doing. We all bring bias to the table; the question is, are we are aware of our bias, and how does awareness inform our work?[8]

Note that a similar critique was leveled at facilitative mediation by Lowry in his article on transformative mediation. Can a transformative mediator be free of bias? If not, can this bias be minimized?

4. Building upon the earlier article by Lela P. Love, formulate 10 reasons why a "mediator should not transform" and ten reasons why a "mediator should transform."

5. The goals of transformative mediation are ambitious. Do you believe that these goals have particular resonance for family mediation? Are there particular obstacles in meeting these goals in family disputes? Are there particular opportunities for meeting these goals in family disputes?

---

[8] Lisa P. Gaynier, *Transformative Mediation: In Search of a Theory of Practice*, 22 CONFLICT RESOL. Q. 397, 406 (2005). Bush and Folger have responded to some of these critiques. Joseph Folger and Robert A. Baruch Bush, *A Response to Gaynier's "Transformative Mediation: In Search of a Theory of Practice*, 23 CONFLICT RESOL. Q. 123 (2005).

6.    Is transformative mediation only plausible for parties who have adequate time and resources to secure private mediators? Do you believe that the principles of transformative mediation can or should inform mediation even where time and resources are limited?

7.    Do you believe courts would be inclined to support transformative mediation? In answering this question, consider not only potential time demands of transformative mediation, but also its promise of enacting positive change in how parties interact with each other.

8.    Bush and Pope argue that conflict "is an emergent, dynamic phenomenon." Are there particular ways that child access mediation might be "dynamic"? Does or should mediation draw upon this fluidity in conflict? Are financial issues in family mediation more or less dynamic than child access issues? Why?

## G.   CAN MODELS BE COMBINED?

For the most part, the materials in this Chapter have presented models of mediation as discrete or "pure." Others, however, argue that using elements from different models is the best way to practice mediation.[9] This, then, leads to a basic question: can mediators integrate different "models" when mediating? Mediators differ in their answers. Consider the following range of views:

- The distinction between "evaluative" and "facilitative" approaches is illusory. L. Randolph Lowry in the above excerpt argues in favor of this position. This view holds that even a "facilitative" approach necessarily involves evaluating positions. Can asking any question not embody an element of "evaluation"?

- Lela P. Love, as exemplified by the excerpt above, would strongly disagree. To her there is a profound difference between facilitating and evaluating disputes. Indeed, she argues that evaluation mediation is not mediation at all.

- Bush and Folger, the founders of transformative mediation, argue strenuously that transformative mediation entails a closed system of goals and techniques. In their view, it cannot be combined with any other model.

- Others disagree with Bush and Folger, and find their position regarding the exclusivity of their approach to be overly rigid. These commentators argue that such a position subverts the flexibility of approach that is the hallmark of good mediation.[10]

As you immerse yourself in the theory and practice of mediation, consider which of these positions you find most convincing.

---

[9] *See, e.g.*, Jeffrey W. Stempel, *The Inevitability of the Eclectic: Liberating ADR from Ideology*, 2000 J. Disp. Resol. 247.

[10] Lisa P. Gaynier, *Transformative Mediation: In Search of a Theory of Practice*, 22 Conflict Resol. Q. 397, 401 (2005).

## H.  ALTERNATIVE MODELS

Some have proposed other forms of non-litigation alternative dispute resolution processes that are not the standard choices of three models outlined above. Some examples are "parenting coordination," which is used when parties continue to experience conflict after a parenting plan has been negotiated and approved,[11] "mediation-arbitration," and "mediative evaluations."[12]

One interesting example is "Settlement-Focused Parenting Plan Consultation." Daniel B. Pickar & Jeffrey J. Kahn, *Settlement-Focused Parenting Plan Consultations: An Evaluative Mediation Alternative to Child Custody Evaluations*, 49 FAM. CT. REV. 59, 62–63 (2011). Pickar and Kahn describe a process through which a "parenting plan consultant" acts in a number of roles:

- A facilitative mediator who seeks to enhance communication and facilitate parents in developing integrative solutions.

- A "child custody evaluator," who undertakes an "information-gathering process . . . that follows the scientifically-informed approach to custody evaluations."

- A "child specialist in collaborative law,"[13] who "helps the parents focus on the children's needs and allows children to have a voice in the process of devising parenting plan arrangements that may affect them for the rest of their lives."

## NOTES AND QUESTIONS

1.  Both Daniel B. Pickar and Jeffrey J. Kahn are psychologists and the model they propose seems to assume some expertise in psychological testing. Would a lawyer be qualified to undertake this role?

2.  How would adherents to evaluative, facilitative, and transformative mediation assess models such as Pickar and Kahn's? How would you?

## I.  AN ALTERNATIVE CONCEPTION: "NORMS" IN FAMILY MEDIATION

Professor Ellen Waldman has offered an alternative framework for analyzing and discussing approaches to family mediation. As you read the following except, consider how much it aligns with the "models" we have been discussing. Are there ways in which it is more or less useful?

---

[11] Christine A. Coates, "*A Brief Overview of Parenting Coordination*," COLORADO LAW REVIEW 38, 61 (2009).

[12] Arnold Shienvold, *Hybrid Processes*, in DIVORCE AND FAMILY MEDIATION 112–126 (Jay Folberg, Ann L. Milne & Peter Salem, eds., 2004).

[13] We discuss collaborative law in detail in Chapter 14.

## IDENTIFYING THE ROLE OF SOCIAL NORMS IN MEDIATION: A MULTIPLE MODEL APPROACH[14]

48 HASTINGS L.J. 703, 704, 707–709, 723–32, 738–45, 753, 755–64, 768–69 (1997)

By Ellen A. Waldman

. . . This Article proposes a refinement of mediation theory in an effort to clarify discussion and comprehension of the field. It seeks to separate out the variety of processes grouped together as mediation and distinguish them based on their divergent treatment of social norms. It suggests that what passes as mediation today constitutes not one, but three separate models. It terms these models "norm-generating," "norm-educating," and "norm-advocating" respectively . . . .

Description of the Norm-Generating Model

[The] traditional "norm-generating" model of mediation . . . typically consists of several stages: introduction, storytelling, exchange of views, option-generating, option-selection, and agreement writing . . . [The] mediator introduces the parties to the process, secures agreement to particular ground rules, facilitates an exchange of viewpoints, structures an agenda, encourages brainstorming of possible options, assists in the selection of viable options, and records the understandings reached, if any, in a written agreement . . . .

In using these techniques, the mediator exercises considerable control over the parties' interaction. Like a symphony conductor, he directs the order, pace, tone, and pitch of dialogue. At no time, however, does the mediator serve as a constraint on the parties' power of decision-making. He may question whether one party's demands are realistic, given the needs articulated by the other. However, he does not restrain deliberations by referencing concerns extrinsic to the parties. That is to say, in the mediation model I have characterized as "norm-generating," the mediator does not remove identified options from consideration simply because those options conflict with existing social norms . . . .

The leitmotif of the norm-generating model, then, is its inattention to social norms. In an effort to spur innovative problem-solving, the model situates party discussion in a normative tabula rasa. The only relevant norms are those the parties identify and agree upon. As Lon Fuller has explained, traditional or norm-generating mediation "is commonly directed, not toward achieving conformity to norms, but toward the creation of the relevant norms themselves" . . . .

A Description of the Norm-Educating Model Using Mediative Techniques

What follows is an example of the norm-educating model applied in a divorce dispute. While the model is now used in a variety of settings, it is perhaps most closely identified with divorce mediation practice.

Dan and Linda had been married 15 years when they decided to divorce. Dan earns

---

$65,000 a year; Linda earns $300 a month as a part-time secretary at the local church. She is resistant to the divorce, but knows she cannot prevent it. They have two daughters, Denise, age three, and Marie, age nine. They have been separated for five months. In that time, Dan has had very little contact with Denise and Marie. To avoid acrimony and expense, Dan and Linda have decided to mediate their divorce.

At the first mediation session, the mediator, Ms. K., provided Dan and Linda detailed information about the goals and assumptions of the mediation process. She showed them a copy of her Rules and Guidelines (Rules) which discuss confidentiality, courtesy, the nonrepresentational, neutral role of the mediator, and the necessity of obtaining outside counsel to review whatever mediated settlement is reached. In addition, the Rules require the parties to refrain from selling marital property or incurring large debts without first obtaining the other's approval. She then inquired briefly about their most pressing issues. She learned that, for Linda, finances presented the most urgent problem, while, for Dan, his scant contact with his children was his greatest concern. After securing from both a commitment to the mediation process, Ms. K. then asked them to independently fill out a six-page questionnaire providing property, income, expenses, and other financial information before meeting for a second session.

Having assessed Dan's concern about not seeing his children as the most urgent, Ms. K. began the next session by suggesting that they begin talking about the children and custody issues. Ms. K. redefined the custody issue by explaining that the discussion was not about who would control the children, but rather an exploration of how both Dan and Linda could continue to be the kind of parents they wished to be. Ms. K. asked Dan and Linda to speak briefly about their hopes and fears about post-divorce parenting and to describe the parenting arrangements throughout the separation. After learning about the ad hoc arrangements that had developed, Ms. K. explained that current psychological data reveals that most couples and children benefit from having a definite exchange schedule. In this way, each family member can plan and be certain about his or her schedule. Ms. K. then drew a twenty-eight box grid on a flipchart, with each box standing for a day of the month, and began to work with Dan and Linda on developing a custody and visitation plan that would accommodate their own, and the children's schedules. The presence in Dan's apartment of Dan's new girlfriend was a sticking point for Linda. However, when Ms. K. reflected back to Linda her resentment toward the woman and probed the lack of connection between the girlfriend's presence and the children's ability to spend quality time with their father, Linda dropped the objection. By the end of the session, they had worked out a temporary schedule for the next month.

At the next session, Ms. K. complimented the couple on reaching agreement concerning the children and suggested moving to the financial issues. Both Dan and Linda listed their income and expenses and constructed a budget of what they needed to survive. Ms. K. pointed out that given their combined income and expenses, the couple as a whole were 786 dollars short each month. Ms. K. suggested that couples generally chose one of four options when facing a shortfall: 1) cutting expenses; 2) increasing income; 3) borrowing from assets; or 4) using tax-planning principles to reduce taxes, thereby yielding more income to meet their needs.

After Dan and Linda explained to each other the basis for some of the expenses listed, they agreed to divide the shortfall equally. Dan did state, however, that the finances would be easier if Linda would get a real job instead of "volunteering" her time at church. Linda expressed interest in developing a more lucrative career, and Ms. K. suggested she give some thought to a plan to increase her earning potential. Dan was asked to obtain detailed information about his pension plan.

At the next session, when Linda began to talk about her financial future, it became clear that schooling was essential. Linda's nursing studies had been interrupted by the marriage, and she now wished to continue those studies. Dan, however, did not want to pay the $4,000 per year tuition. Dan stated that Linda could pay for the tuition and books from her 1/2 share of the $18,000 money market account they planned to divide equally. Linda felt Dan should pay for tuition since she had dropped out of nurse's training in the first year of their marriage to help Dan obtain his M.B.A. degree. When Linda queried Ms. K. if she had a right to a share in Dan's M.B.A. degree, the mediator replied that several courts, particularly New York State Courts, had ruled that a wife had an ownership interest in her husband's medical degree.

As the conversation degenerated into bickering over who had worked harder at the marriage, the mediator interrupted, shifting the focus from the past to the future, from casting blame to solving problems. Ms. K. advised:

> I'm quite sure that if I sat here for the next three hours and listened to both of you, I would never be able to figure out all the facts exactly the way they happened. In fact, you didn't hire me to listen to the two of you present evidence about why Linda is now dependent on the marriage for support. I'm sure that each of you would have made very different choices during the last fifteen years had you known you would be sitting in my office today.

Ms. K. then pointed out that Linda and Dan shared a mutual desire to facilitate Linda's economic independence from Dan and suggested they work at brainstorming ways to accomplish that goal. They ultimately agreed that Linda would receive $14,000 from the money market account, and Dan would receive $4,000. Ms. K then wrote up the custody and financial agreements in a memorandum, and sent a copy to Dan and Linda, with copies to their attorneys to file with the court.

Clearly, the model which Ms. K. employed is similar in many ways to the [norm generating] model. Ms. K. proceeded through the standard mediation stages, beginning with an introduction to and explanation of the process, and moving on to storytelling, agenda-setting, option-generating, option-selection, and, finally, the concluding agreement writing stage.

In addition, Ms. K. availed herself of the full panoply of mediative techniques displayed in norm generating mediation. She engaged in active listening, reframed issues so as to avoid a win-lose perspective, encouraged empathic understanding of opposing views, separated needs from positions, helped the parties generate and evaluate options according to explicitly articulated criteria, and refocused the parties on the future instead of the past.

Ms. K.'s approach differed from the traditional norm generating approach in her reference to relevant social and legal norms, which she used to provide a baseline framework for discussion of disputed issues. She adverted to these norms twice: first when Dan and Linda were beginning to consider what sort of custody and visitation arrangement to adopt, and, second, when questions arose as to whether Dan should be required to pay Linda some share of her tuition. In the first instance, the mediator educated the parties about existing norms in the child psychology field. In the second, the mediator informed the parties about prevailing legal norms.

Ms. K. did not insist that the parties' agreement implement these norms. It is likely that if Dan and Linda both strongly desired to retain a visitation schedule that was ad hoc and changeable from day-to-day, the mediator would have assisted them in codifying that agreement. Similarly, if Dan and Linda both agreed that Dan's M.B.A. could fairly be excluded from all consideration, the mediator would likely have supported that conclusion, so long as she felt that the parties understood the implications of their decision.

This model, then, is a norm-educating model which utilizes mediative techniques. Contrary to the norm-generating model, where discussion of societal standards is thought to impede autonomy and distract parties from their true needs, this model's consideration of social norms is thought to enhance autonomy by enabling parties to make the most informed decisions possible . . . .

This model is most visible in the divorce arena. The mid-eighties divorce mediation literature reveals skirmishes between those who thought that divorce mediation should mirror the generic norm-generating model and those who believed that disputants should be educated about the norms encoded in family law. Today the battle has largely subsided. Most commentators agree that a divorce mediator should have some familiarity with family law issues. Descriptions of ongoing programs reveal that the mediator is active in ensuring that disputant negotiations are informed by relevant legal and social norms, either by educating the parties himself or by ensuring that they are educated by retained counsel . . . .

Identifying Paradigm Case(s) for Use of the Norm-Educating Model

Like the norm-generating model, the norm-educating model is appropriately used in disputes where party autonomy and relational concerns are the preeminent values for consideration. Yet, in these conflicts, unlike in disputes that call for the norm-generating model, application of social or legal norms is possible, conclusive, and relatively compelling. These disputes invoke norms that embody certain societal conclusions about what is just and unjust and confer entitlements on those who might otherwise remain disadvantaged and marginalized in private bargaining. Elsewhere, I have called these norms "protective norms" because they serve to protect one (or both) of the parties from exploitation or abuse. Norms that require payment of permanent spousal support to a nonworking spouse after breakup of a long marriage, or prohibit the firing of an elderly worker solely because of his age could be characterized as protective norms. These standards grant rights to the displaced homemaker or terminated employee and safeguard both from impoverishment and rank injustice. Because these norms are protective in design and effect, it is important that parties be informed of their existence before making decisions which unknowingly dispense with the conferred entitlements.

The fact that a dispute implicates norms of which the parties should be informed does not, however, imply that the parties must adopt or implement them. In disputes calling for the norm-educating model, the parties' interests in reaching settlement, even a settlement that disregards social and legal norms, outweigh whatever societal interest exists in the application of those norms. Disputes in which party interests in settlement subordinate societal interests in norm-enforcement often share certain qualities.

First, the parties approach the mediation with sufficient resources such that their waiver of a legal entitlement does not appear coerced by circumstance. Although the parties may not enjoy equal power, they each possess sufficient competency that a decision to settle for less than the law might award represents a conscious, capable expression of will rather than a capitulation to oppressive conditions. Second, the resolution of these disputes will primarily affect only the parties or entities at the table. The parties' resolution will not adversely affect third parties absent from the mediation. Equally important, while the dispute calls into play protective norms, they are not implicated so profoundly that their bypass will weaken social bonds and do violence to important public values. In certain contexts, the disregard of a protective norm, such as the antidiscrimination norms embodied in civil rights or gender equality legislation, creates a ripple effect. Far from affecting only the disputants, it places significant strains on the social fabric and casts doubt on the power and influence of the norm and its centrality in American life and institutions . . . . The norm-educating model is only appropriate in conflicts in which the relevant norms may be disregarded without weakening the ideals upon which our government and legal structure are based.

To further concretize this discussion, consider the custody dispute discussed in Part One. Imagine that both parents are relatively stable, resourceful, and powerful people. Imagine too that the father is threatening to withhold child support from the mother if she does not allow him to take the children five months of the year. In this situation, it is important that both parties be alerted to the legal norms which require noncustodial parents to pay child support, even when they object to existing custody arrangements. This norm protects both the child as well as the custodial parent, usually the mother. Now, with this information, the mother may agree to the proposed seven-five month split, even though a court might have awarded her primary custody over the children for eleven and a half months of the year, and the same amount of child support being offered by the father. If so, the mother's desire to avoid a judicial proceeding and to settle for "less" than she might have obtained in court should be respected, so long as her decision is not forced or coerced.

Another important consideration involves whether the arrangement is beneficial or harmful to the child, a third party whose interests are unrepresented at the mediation. If norms in the field of child development indicate that such an arrangement would be detrimental to the child, as it would likely be if the child were school age, then arguably the parents should not be allowed to waive the standards established by those norms.

Waiver of legal norms should also be discouraged if the resulting agreement would seriously undermine the norms of gender equality, as it would if the child support payments were so low as to represent an effective abandonment of the mother and child. Arguably, the "divorce revolution" of the last twenty years represents a societal commitment (though not entirely successful) to avoid the impoverishment of women and children following divorce. Private agreements which do injury to this commitment should be discouraged.

If, however, the parties' proposed custody and child support arrangement imperils neither the child nor the mother, and avoids seriously compromising the norms of gender equality, the parties should be permitted and encouraged to adopt and abide by it. Agreements which deviate from the legally determined outcome are permissible and encouraged, so long as the benefit to the parties outweighs any harms created.

The norm-educating model of mediation strikes a compromise between those who would bar discussions of law entirely from mediation practice and those who would outlaw mediation because it strays too far from the normative moorings of our adversary system. It stands for the proposition that the parties should be educated about their legal rights. However, if one or both of the parties decides to waive those rights, the mediator does not object. The norm-educating mediator views the parties, not society, as rightful possessor of the dispute. Consequently, the parties may, if they choose, reach a resolution that does not correspond entirely with societal norms.

This model, then, may be sensibly applied in disputes where the social or legal norms implicated are sufficiently important that the disputants should be made aware of them — but, the position of the parties and the context of the dispute does not demand their enforcement. In other words, the disputant benefited by these norms may waive them, and such waiver is unproblematic, both from the disputant's and society's vantage point.

Although parties under this model may waive their rights and entitlements, such waivers, in the face of complete knowledge, seem less likely to occur and will likely be less dramatic than in the norm-generating mediation model. Moreover, such rights-waivers, if made knowingly, may represent a party's conscious trade-off to obtain an alternate form of satisfaction. In such a situation, the legal right has served as an important bargaining chip, and, to the degree that the legal entitlement has empowered one party to advance claims that she would otherwise be poorly situated to assert, the right has served its purpose; the norm has been effectuated . . . In some contexts, however, the norm-educating model is insufficiently protective of party and societal interests. This is true when the power imbalance between the parties is so extreme that one party cannot provide a trustworthy waiver, when the institutions administering mediation have a mandate to enforce statutory law, and/or when the dispute involves public resources or implicates public values in such a profound way that their enforcement outweighs the disputants' interests in achieving settlement. In these instances, a norm-advocating model better suits the task at hand.

A Description of the Norm-Advocating Model

The following mediation case illustrates the model I term norm-advocating. It involves an ethical conflict which has arisen in the course of patient care. [Author describes a mediation involving a patient and her physician, both of whom want treatment withheld under circumstances that would violate the hospital's ethical standards and, possibly, constitute a crime. The mediation involves the patient and her doctor on one side and various representatives of the hospital on the other and is conducted by a "bioethics mediator."]

[In the norm-advocating model], the mediator proceeded through the familiar stages common to the norm-generating and norm-educating models, using a repertoire of standard mediative techniques . . . In this process, however, the mediator not only educated the parties about the relevant legal and ethical norms, but also insisted on their incorporation into the agreement. In this sense, her role extended beyond that of an educator; she became, to some degree, a safe guarder of social norms and values. She apprised the parties of relevant social norms, not simply to facilitate the parties' informed decision making and provide a beginning framework for discussion; she provided information about legal and ethical norms to secure their implementation . . . .

To some, norm-advocating mediation is a contradiction in terms. Yet, its growing use is undeniable. One explanation for this growth is that some disputes will be best resolved through a process which combines the informality of mediation with the reliance on legal and social norms characteristic of adjudication. These disputes often involve interconnected issues, ongoing relationships, and highly-charged disputant emotions. For these reasons, mediation's informal, communication-oriented approach offers clear benefits. However, these conflicts are ill-suited to a norm-generating or even norm-educating approach for one of two reasons. First, the conflict implicates important societal concerns, extending far beyond the parties' individual interests. Second, the conflict only involves the interests of the parties, but one party is so structurally disenfranchised that allowing her to negotiate away legal rights and entitlements would make the mediator complicit in her continued oppression . . . .

Where the norm to be applied is sufficiently open-textured that it permits several equally acceptable outcomes, then the mediation shifts to a norm-generating mode. Within the open boundaries that the norm establishes, the parties are free to bring their own interests, concerns, and creative thinking to bear on the problem. Thus, the differences between norm-advocating and norm-generating mediation are not as dramatic as might be originally imagined. The differences may be framed in high relief where the norms to be applied are precise and dictate the parties follow a particular action plan. The differences fade, however, in disputes where the norms to be applied are indeterminate, leaving the parties free to decide precisely how and in what manner those norms will be given content and effect . . . .

Why Recognition of the Three Models — and the Divergent Role Social Norms Play in Each — Matters

As the preceding sections demonstrate, many individual practitioners and institutions utilize either the norm-educating, or norm-advocating models, or some combination. Indeed, in delineating these three models, I do not mean to suggest that they are always, or even usually, used singly. Rather, many mediators will combine these various models, depending on the nature of the dispute. A divorce mediator, for example, may employ a norm-educating model when discussing spousal support and property division. She may shift to a norm-advocating model if the parents contemplate a visitation plan that would place the child at risk. And, she may adhere to a norm-generating model when assisting the parties in how property of only sentimental value should be divided.

Despite the prevalence of the norm-educating and advocating models, academic commentators and practitioners alike tend to conceive of the norm-generating model as the authentic article and recognize the more norm-based procedures, if at all, as aberrant step-children. Both Professor James Alfini, in describing "evaluative" mediation, and Professors Craig McEwen, Nancy Rogers, and Richard Maiman, in depicting Maine's lawyer-dominated divorce mediation program, question whether these procedures represent "real mediation." Scholars and mediators Robert A. Baruch Bush and Joseph P. Folger recognize two distinct mediator orientations which they label transformative and problem-solving. Both of these approaches, however, are based on the norm-generating model . . . .

In When Talk Works, researchers identified a persistent mediation mythology in which all mediation follows the norm-generating model. According to this mythology, mediators are passive actors, completely neutral with regard to the proposed outcome of the dispute, and unwilling to use social norms to constrain the disputants' settlement autonomy. Although the actual practice of the profiled mediators departed sharply from this theoretical ideal, the mediators nonetheless continued to adhere to the myths as formal virtues. Although the mediators were aware that many of their behaviors undercut and exposed the cleavage between myth and reality, this disjunction did not prompt them to question the myth's validity. This may be, as the researchers suggest, because the "mythic frame . . . gives direction and inspiration amidst uncertainty, isolation, and complexity." A concomitant explanation is simply that the norm-generating model, inspired by a communitarian vision of autonomous, self-actualizing individuals realizing mutual gains while rediscovering community norms, presents an attractive vision. While the vision may not bear a close resemblance to much that transpires in real life, it continues to command strong ideological allegiance. But, clinging to obsolete phantasms that no longer capture a dynamic reality poses numerous dangers for a burgeoning profession . . . .

## NOTES AND QUESTIONS

1. Professor Waldman offers an alternative framework for classifying approaches to mediation. Do her classifications relate, in any way, to the transformative, facilitative, and evaluative approaches discussed earlier? Do you find Professor Waldman's framework more or less useful?

2. What factors would Professor Waldman use to determine whether norm-educating or norm-advocating is the most appropriate model in a given mediation? How would these factors play out in some of the issues often present in family mediation, such as child access, child support, and property distribution? Why?

3. The excerpt concludes by arguing that "norm-generating" mediation is a myth, albeit a compelling myth. Do you agree? How does Professor Waldman's objection relate to arguments that all mediation should or must be evaluative?

4. Professor Waldman argues that there is now a consensus that the norm-educating model is most appropriate for divorce mediation because there is agreement that mediators should have knowledge of "family law issues." Is a mediator's knowledge of "family law issues" crucial in family mediation? Given that not all mediators are lawyers, is there a risk that "education" about legal norms by non-lawyers could constitute the unauthorized practice of law?

5. Professor Waldman's norms are not only legal. They might instead be psychological (such as the most appropriate custody arrangements for children) or based on a mediator's personal or professional experience (such as how parents have addressed situations where one parent lives a substantial distance away from a child). Is educating about non-legal norms more, less, or similarly appropriate than education about legal norms?

# Chapter 3

# AN OVERVIEW OF THE FAMILY MEDIATION PROCESS

## A. INTRODUCTION

Many mediators have found that it is helpful to conceptualize mediation as proceeding through a series of "stages." There are different views on what these stages might be. In the materials that follow we suggest six, but we do not claim that this is the only "right" number of stages or even the right way to characterize them. Rather, the purpose of this conception — or most conceptions — is as a practical tool to orient mediators as they are engaged in a fluid, shifting, and sometimes volatile process. Thinking in terms of stages is a tool for being situated in a process that resists linearity or structure.

Not all mediators, however, agree that conceptions of "stages" have value, or even that they are consistent with mediation. Transformative mediators in particular argue that stages presuppose a degree of mediator control that is anathema to the value of mediation — enhancing the quality of participants' interactions. They further argue that stages are directed towards a goal — agreement — which is not what mediation is about. We will return to these issues at the end of this Chapter. We will nevertheless present a process that reflects prevailing views about facilitative mediation.

## B. THE "STAGES" OF FAMILY MEDIATION

Few, if any, mediators would characterize mediation as linear. Rather, it is an open process driven by the participants. This lack of an imposed order and chronology reflects a fundamental difference with litigation, where order and chronology are imposed by rules of civil and criminal procedure as well as evidence. Moreover, family mediation often has the additional variable of an emotionally charged atmosphere. Emotions may surge or recede, or go back and forth, often in the blink of an eye — not a recipe for order.

A lack of linearity is not a shortcoming of mediation. It rather reflects a bedrock premise of effective mediation: participant control. Nevertheless, a free for all is not necessarily a positive given the limited time available for most mediations, which is especially true in the context of court-connected programs. There is value in identifying where a mediation is and appropriate strategies that might be deployed in order to facilitate a resolution of conflict. With that in mind, one approach sets forth six stages in mediation:

- Setting the stage

- Gathering information
- Identifying issues and interests
- Generating options
- Negotiation
- Formalizing decisions

We will briefly consider each of these in turn.

## 1.   Setting the Stage

### a.   Preliminaries

Certain preliminaries should be attended to in family mediation. What these are, however, varies based upon a number of variables.

One crucial factor is how much time is available for the mediation. Especially with court-connected programs or mediations available for low-income participants, a mediator may have limited time available — sometimes just a few hours. Participants might have personal obligations that limit how much time they can stay, such as a job with minimal or no time flexibility, child care responsibilities, or transportation challenges. Time also must be expended in filling out forms. Some programs have attempted to address these constraints by showing an introductory video. Nevertheless, almost always mediators will deliver an "Opening Introduction" — the substance of which will be discussed shortly — in the mediation itself.

In contrast, assuming adequate time and resources, a mediator might send prospective mediation participants packages containing "setting the stage" information. They then conduct a separately designated "orientation session" for participants to learn about mediation, ask the mediator questions about the process, and fill out paperwork relating to, for example, confidentiality, payment of fees, and detailed statements about financial matters. Depending on the mediator, this orientation may include an "Opening Introduction" (detailed below) or the mediator may defer the Introduction to the first actual mediation session.

Another factor to consider is whether family mediation can take place prior to or after the commencement of formal proceedings. Some participants still might hope to reconcile. Given that most family mediators do not conceive of their role as couples counseling, some mediators ask participants early in the mediation process whether they have decided to divorce, thus clarifying the mediator's role.

Yet another variable is the nature of the mediation itself. Are one or both of the participants represented? If so, will attorneys attend the mediation? Is the mediation what some mediators call "high conflict," perhaps involving protective orders or other indicia of intense conflict?

Finally, and most broadly, how and when mediators attend to preliminaries is a function of personal style and experience.

What follows is a range of options for preliminaries in mediation. As you review them, consider how these variables might have an impact on choices available to you.

### b.   Seating Arrangements and Space

A set of basic decisions await mediators even before the mediation starts.

First, what should seating arrangements be? This is a non-issue in formal adjudication where physical layout — bench, witness stand, and jury box — are embedded in the process itself. In contrast, many options are available in mediation.

Assume the mediator has a rectangular table. Which of the following arrangements would you choose and why?

**Arrangement 1:**

Mediator

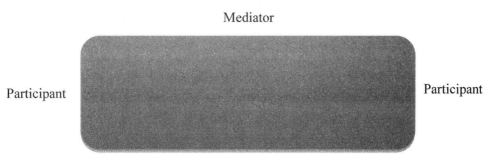

Participant                                            Participant

**Arrangement 2:**

Mediator

Participant                Participant

**Are there advantages to a round table, such as the following:**

How about the following:

- A square table.
- A coffee table.
- No table.

How about when attorneys are representing clients in mediation? Where would you, as mediator, suggest that attorneys sit in all of the above settings? Why?

There are other basic issues to be attended to. Whiteboards can be crucial as a means to capture information for all the participants to see, such as listing issues for resolution, potential solutions, financial arrangements, and child access schedules. Access to a computer can be important for calculating child support and drafting potential agreements. Assuming available technology, perhaps the best of all worlds would be a computer with a projector, which would enable participants to see all of the above. Some mediators also provide pads with pens or pencils to enable participants to write down issues that occur to them.

Some mediators also provide basic amenities, such as water, snacks, and tissues. These items are not mere conveniences. Physical discomfort impairs the ability and willingness of participants to think clearly about conflict, particularly given the intensity that often accompanies family mediation.

In addition, mediators should think through how they plan to conduct a private caucus. This would usually entail having some means for the participant who is not in caucus to wait in a comfortable setting where what is being said in the mediation room is inaudible.

### c.  The "Opening Introduction"

Almost all mediators deliver some sort of Opening Introduction. As noted above, many variables might influence the nature of the Opening Introduction. It is also important to consider what tone to employ and atmosphere to cultivate at this initial stage of the mediation.

Your initial challenge in preparing and delivering an Opening Introduction is to consider what the goals are of an Opening Introduction. Many mediators would view one goal as educating participants about relatively specific matters, such as explaining what mediation is, confidentiality, and, if relevant, legal procedures that will ensue should an agreement be reached.

An Opening Introduction, however, can be more than the communication of specific information. Mediators might wish to "model" in intonation and body language a calm and collaborative spirit that participants might emulate or absorb. Many mediators start on a note of optimism, perhaps congratulating participants on their willingness to participate in mediation. Another possibility is to offer participants an opportunity to make decisions about the mediation process such as, for example, eliciting a verbal agreement to mediate and suggesting to participants that they might call for breaks if they wish. More than explaining merely process, such communications convey that a mediator is not an authority figure like a judge. Indeed, these indirect actions are far more valuable than simply saying "this is your process" or that "I am not a judge." Participants are *experiencing* empowerment rather than merely hearing about it.

The following list offers a menu of options to consider as you develop your own Opening Introduction:

- Communicate optimism about a productive and successful mediation.

- Support, compliment, and confirm participants' decision to proceed with mediation.

- Make participants comfortable by discussing the location of rest rooms, the possibility of taking a break if needed, the availability of refreshments, and so forth.

- Inquire whether participants wish to be addressed by first or last names.

- Present and complete forms, such as agreements to mediate and to maintain confidentiality. If the mediation is court-annexed, certain forms are likely required by the court, but virtually all mediators have paperwork for participants to sign. Insure you have readily available copies of the relevant forms in order to convey competence to make efficient use of time.

- Introduce yourself, including your background.

- Describe the goals and process of mediation, including how mediation differs from litigation, the differences between the role of mediator and judge, and the voluntary nature of whether to participate or reach an agreement.

- Discuss private caucuses, including how you might ask to meet with each participant separately and how confidentiality will be handled. This process should be "normalized," that is, described as a natural part of mediation and not some sign that the mediation is "going badly."

- Discuss the nature and limits of confidentiality — a matter we will explore in detail in Chapter 12.

- Communicate "ground rules," such as, for example, discouraging interruptions or shouting.

- Discuss whether you plan on taking notes and, if appropriate, assuring participants that notes will be destroyed after the mediation.

## NOTES AND QUESTIONS

1. Decisions in an Opening Introduction are not only about *what* to raise, but *when* to raise them. Consider one example: the completion of paperwork. Assuming that you do not have time to send participants paperwork prior to the start of the mediation, when do you present the paperwork? Would you do it as the first thing to "get it out of the way" or do you wait to the end of the Introduction or somewhere in between? To what extent do you describe what the paperwork is?

2. In terms of introducing yourself, what should you say, if anything, about your experience? This is a particular challenge if you are a new mediator.

3. When do you inquire about children assuming this is child access mediation? Is this something to do immediately to emphasize the "real" concern of the mediation or should you wait until participants are more comfortable with you and the process?

Consider other strategies mediators employ when discussing children. Some mediators ask for pictures of children, and then place them in the middle of the mediation table. Some may explicitly emphasize that the wellbeing of children is a core issue in the mediation. Some ask participants to describe their children: their personalities, interests, and so forth. Some do nothing and wait for the participants to discuss their children as the mediation unfolds. Without knowing any details about a particular mediation, do you see pros and cons to these choices? What are they?

## 2. Gathering Information

### a. Beginnings

The "gathering information" stage usually begins with a joint session with all participants present. Most family mediators will first request that each participant present without interruption his or her perspective on issues. A mediator should not predefine what those issues might be. That is best left to the participants.

### b. What Is "Information"?

The term "gathering information" is perhaps misleading. "Information" in litigation is usually associated with "facts" yet it is important for mediators to avoid replicating patterns of litigation. It is all too easy for a mediator — as participants often do — to view this exchange as akin to an "Opening Statement" at trial. To counter this tendency, mediators may ask parties for their "perspective" or to "describe the situation" or to inquire about "what brings you to mediation." In light of research that shows that participants who speak second often "respond" to the first participant point by point and thereby cede power to the first speaker for setting the agenda for the mediation,[1] some mediators explicitly tell both participants that they need not engage in such a "response" and explicitly note that this exchange is about sharing information and perspectives. The litigation norm looms large at all points in mediation so mediators should be on the alert to educate the participants explicitly or implicitly about the distinctive norms of mediation.

Mediators often encourage participants to share as much background as possible in order to facilitate an opportunity to identify issues and generate options. Information in this sense might include emotions — things that might be not "relevant" in a legal sense — or anything else a participant deems relevant.

### c.   Who Goes First?

An initial question that often arises prior to this initial exchange is which participant should speak first in the mediation. Options abound. If there is some neutral basis upon which to make this decision — for example, the party who filed for divorce if there is pending litigation or the party who requested mediation — the mediator may ask this party to speak first, explaining the neutral reason why. Other mediators employ by design entirely arbitrary criteria — "I usually start with folks on my right" — which has the virtue of enhancing the message of neutrality. Some mediators ask participants who should speak first, thus signaling that this is the participants' process.

After this initial exchange, mediators often prompt participants to share information by asking open questions. Given that a hallmark of effective mediation is flexibility and openness as to conceptions of conflict, it is crucial to allow the participants to determine what *they* see as significant, even if these matters appear to the mediator or the other participant as irrelevant or counterproductive.

In addition, mediators need not always intervene at this or other stages of mediation. It may even be counterproductive to do so. The stereotype of high conflict divorce is common, but "amicable divorces" are common as well. Effective family mediators should cultivate no particular expectations as to which category (or middle category) a particular mediation might fall into, or the shifting nature of a conflict as it unfolds in mediation. If participants are collaborating in sharing information productively, the mediator should consider holding back and listen to what is being said. The mediator *facilitates*, but "facilitation" might simply be bringing participants together in a collaborative atmosphere. Saying nothing is a legitimate and sometimes advisable mediation technique, and one that can be difficult to put into practice.

Most family mediators, however, do gather basic information for the benefit of the mediator and the participants themselves. The mediator typically should know and, if necessary, elicit information about the following:[2]

- **Children**. It is important to know something about children, assuming of course there are children, in family mediation. This is true even where custody

---

[1] Sara Cobb & Janet Rifkin, *Practice & Paradox: Deconstructing Neutrality in Mediation*, 1991 LAW & SOC. INQUIRY 35, 54–59.

[2] Each of the following categories of information is addressed in more detail in Chapter 4 ("Child Access Mediation") and Chapter 6 ("Mediating Financial Issues").

is not being disputed. Apart from the obvious questions regarding names and ages, the mediator might wish to explore where each party believes the children should live, go to school, how the parents have made decisions about the children, and the nature of the relationship each hopes to maintain with the children. This does not mean that there is necessarily conflict about any or all of these issues, but having a grasp about such issues may enable a mediator to understand the participants' situation and thereby facilitate solutions.

- **Finances**. Even if the issue to be mediated is solely child access, it is rare that issues about finances, particularly child support, are not at least in the background. The degree to which it is necessary to delve into details, of course, is contingent on the nature of the mediation and the resources of the participants. When resources are at issue, however, detailed information about assets, liabilities, and cash flow are virtually always necessary. Even when participants have no or minimal resources, issues about child support may arise. These calculations are contingent upon the law of a particular jurisdiction and may not be within a participants' discretion, although even then mediators may assist in calculating awards or in exploring issues related to child support.

- **The participants' future plans**. How do the participants see themselves in the future? This may entail information about professional or personal goals or redressing personal problems, such as alcoholism or substance abuse, that may be inhibiting their ability to parent or work.

## 3. Identifying Issues and Interests

"Gathering information" often transitions into identifying issues in the mediation and the interests underlying those issues. A common mistake among mediators is to rush into issue identification without allowing "gathering information" to run its course. This is especially true for mediators who are also attorneys: law school, after all, focuses on "issue spotting" and the impulse to move there prematurely is hard to resist. Resisting, however, almost always enhances the quality of the mediation whether or not conflicts are ultimately resolved.

### a. Organizing Issues

Issue identification can be complicated. It can entail digging deeper into issues that warrant attention. Assume, for example, the following two issues that commonly arise in family mediation:

- Children
- Finances

Under each broad category, however, it is almost certain that there are sub-issues to be addressed. Consider additional issues regarding the broad issue of "children":

- Children
  - Where to spend the holidays

    o  Choices of school

    o  Transportation to and from each parent's house

Perhaps all or some of these are issues to be resolved. To dig down deeper, perhaps issues might break down as follows:

- Children
  - o Where to spend the holidays
    - Birthdays
    - Major family holidays (Christmas and Thanksgiving)
    - Days when school is not in session

These can be subdivided further. Consider the issue of what happens when school is not in session. These can be scheduled days when school is closed such as "professional development days," unanticipated absences due to illness, and extended breaks such as in the spring and especially the summer. This level of detail might not occur to participants.[3]

## b.  Techniques When Articulating Issues

The art of how to identify and articulate issues is not easy. Consider the following techniques.[4] Note that not all mediators would agree with all of these techniques. Which might you choose?

- **Get a Buy-In**

A mediator should not assume that participants agree that an issue a mediator has identified actually is an issue or that the way a mediator has articulated an issue is the correct way to articulate it. A mediator, then, often chooses to check in with participants about whether both the identification and articulation are correct. This technique — common in mediation and alluded to above when discussing the Opening Introduction — also serves a positive function in reassuring participants that they remain in charge of the process.

- **Neutrality**

It is all too easy to frame an issue in terms that are negative towards one participant. Consider the following: "Insuring Parent A does not impede Parent B's access to the children." Asking for buy-in can capture articulations that favor one participant, but it is best to not favor one participant to begin with.

- **Look Ahead**

As noted in the discussion of facilitative mediation in Chapter 3, a virtue of mediation is that it seeks to avoid reconstructing the past in order to define the future. Thus, framing an issue as a way to resolve a past conflict — "who called whom and

---

[3] A mediator might inquire as to whether these are issues. Another common means for reaching this level of detail are parenting plans, examples of which are included in Appendix B.

[4] This list is adapted from CARL SCHNEIDER, GUIDELINES FOR FRAMING ISSUES IN MEDIATION (MEDIATION MATTERS MANUAL 2005).

when" — is not likely to be productive. Note that participants usually have internalized the litigation mindset and thus might well view resolution of these issues as crucial. A mediator, however, might have a role in facilitating a forward looking perspective. Mediators should not be too doctrinaire on this point, however. For example, some exploration of caretaking patterns in the past may be necessary to understand how these issues might be resolved in the future.

- **Not About Finding the "Truth"**

Given the role of integrative solutions in mediation and promoting the recognition of alternative perspectives, it is often prudent to avoid framing issues as determining what is true or not. An example of what is best avoided would be "is it best to raise the child in mom's religion"?

- **Normalize**

Some mediators choose to assure participants that a given issue is not unique to them. For example, how to arrange child care in light of unpredictable work schedules is an issue with which many parents grapple. It is important not to minimize the challenge of the issue, but suggesting that a seemingly unsolvable issue has been solved before might give participants some optimism that they can do the same. Some mediators may feel free to offer a suggestion that other mediation participants have used to resolve a comparable issue — an example of normalizing combined with Ellen Waldman's idea of "norm educating" discussed in the Chapter 2.

- **Capable of Being Resolved in Mediation**

Some issues might not be capable of resolution in mediation. Some of these issues might be characterized as "value conflicts." Consider, for example, conflicts about the virtues of different religions or no religion or whether a certain type of discipline is more effective than another. Note that these issues are framed in terms of there being one right answer. It is, however, entirely legitimate, if not prudent, to note issues that do not presuppose a right or wrong answer, such as how best to accommodate different views on religion when raising a child.

- **Not Character**

It is common in family conflicts for each participant to claim that the other is wrong, or bad, or selfish. Such issues might be difficult, if not impossible, to be resolved in mediation and they also likely focus on the past instead of how to move ahead.

- **No Advice/Solutions**

It is a significant challenge for mediators to withhold generating options before facilitating issue identification. As noted above, this is especially a challenge for lawyers and law students, who are trained to "issue spot" and then immediately "analyze." Note also that by immediately turning to option generation, the mediator risks controlling the mediation and shortchanging participants from defining their own conflict.

## c.  Interests Versus Positions

A foundational tenet of mediation is that it should help participants identify "interests" rather than "positions."[5] A classic description of the difference between "positions" and "interests" is a couple planning a vacation. The husband wants to go to a beach; this is his "position." The wife wants to go to the mountains; this is her "position." If one considers, however, *why* the husband wants to go to a beach, it is because he enjoys swimming and sunbathing. These are his "interests." If one considers *why* the wife wants to go to the mountains, it is because she enjoys hiking. This is her interest. While "beach" and "mountains" seem incompatible "positions" with no room for compromise, understanding what motivates these "positions" helps to generate possible compromises. One possibility, for example, would be a trip to a mountain lake.

Participants to family mediation, drawing from litigation norms, often take "positions" akin to the beach/mountains. Here a few examples:

- "I want sole custody."
- "I need to get the house."
- "We have to sell the house."
- "There's no way your mother will have anything to do with our daughter."
- "Our son cannot be at your house when your girlfriend is there."

How may a mediator facilitate participants' recognition and articulation of interests in the often emotionally charged environment of family conflict? One technique is to ask "why" or "what for" questions. Responses to these tend to elicit interests rather than positions.

Another technique is more subtle. "Positions" are usually embedded with some expression of an underlying interest. A parent might, for example, state that he wants "joint custody," which is a "position" that might be incompatible with the other parent's position that she wants "sole custody." Nevertheless, a position that a parent wants joint custody may embody a desire to maintain a close and continuing relationship with a child. In such cases, a mediator listening to a party closely can glean underlying interests, state them, and thereby enable each party to better understand what the other party wants. It is usually advisable in such instances for the mediator to confirm with a party that a mediator's statements about interests are accurate — the "buy-in" alluded to earlier.

## 4.  Generating Options

### a.  The Option Generating Process

Once some progress has been made in identifying issues and underlying interests, the participants and mediator can collaborate in generating options.

---

[5] This groundbreaking distinction is from ROGER FISHER & HAROLD L. URY, GETTING TO YES: NEGOTIATING AGREEMENT WITHOUT GIVING IN (2d ed. 1991).

Literature on problem solving suggests that it is most productive to generate as many potential solutions to problems as possible before eliminating them as not feasible or inappropriate. While this is easy to state, it is exceptionally difficult in practice, especially in family mediation which so often embodies intensely felt views of what is "right" or "wrong." Thus, it is the norm and not the exception for participants to immediately reject many potential options suggested by another participant. On occasion, however, a new idea might arise that the other party — or even the party stating the new idea — might not have thought of before.

It is usually advisable for the mediator to defer supplying options prior to insuring that the participants suggest their ideas. This can take a prodigious amount of self-control on the part of the mediator: the mediator will defer expressing what seems to be a transparently obvious solution. Nevertheless, what is transparent to the mediator might be opaque or wrong to the participants, and, conversely, the participants themselves are experts on their own situations and are likely to offer potentially creative, constructive, ideas that would never occur to the mediator. Moreover, the notion of participants as controlling the subject of mediation and the mediator as facilitator suggests that premature option generation by the mediator might be counterproductive.

If the problem-solving phase is not productive or no other options are forthcoming from the participants, it might be advisable for the mediator to suggest a possibility to the participants — a "trial balloon." This might be accepted with enthusiasm or rejected immediately or met with a reaction that is something in between. As always, it should be the participants who are the ultimate decision-makers in how they choose to accept or reject or reformulate options.

## b.  Framing Options

As with identifying issues, options can be framed in multiple ways suggested by the participants or by the mediator. Note that in facilitative mediation, mediators may choose, when appropriate, to subtly shift how an option is articulated either in joint session or private caucus, again with the ever-present buy-in advisable.

Consider the following example. The distribution of an art collection is at issue. While the following excerpt addresses negotiation, not mediation, it starkly demonstrates the fluidity of potential options and how these options may be framed. As you read this discussion, consider how a mediator may facilitate the different potential dispositions of the collection and determining whether different dispositions might accord with the participants "interests" relating to the collection.

## AN INTRODUCTION TO THE PLANNING AND CONDUCT OF NEGOTIATIONS
### (1989)[6]
### By Anthony G. Amsterdam

. . . If personal property is being divided upon the divorce of a wife (a lawyer) and a husband (an architect), the art collection can be handled by giving a portion of it to each party, or by giving the entire collection to one party and "balancing" it by giving some property of equal value to the other. The party urging the latter disposition can argue that it is appropriate (or "natural") to "keep the collection together" for aesthetic reasons, or for economic reasons. Notice that the very description of the subject matter as an "art collection," rather than as "the pieces of artwork in the house" works subtly in favor of keeping it together. If the collection is divided, it may nevertheless be "natural" to keep some subparts of it together. Again, differing divisions can be urged. It can be said to be "natural" to keep the Daumier prints together (for the same aesthetic or economic reasons, or others), or "natural" to keep all of the prints from the living room (which include some but not all of the Daumiers) together. The latter disposition will be more "natural" if the furniture has been divided earlier in the negotiation, on a room-by room basis. If the Daumiers are kept together, it may be "natural" to give them to the wife because they deal with legal subjects, or "natural" to give them to the husband because he was the one who originally selected them. Or it may be "natural" to sell the art collection and split the proceeds equally. The party who urges this course will point out that the art collection was "held for investment" — indeed, that the couple has previously claimed tax deductions for framing which were allowable only because the art collection was "held for investment."

## NOTES AND QUESTIONS

1.  Consider the impact of the different formulations described by Professor Amsterdam. To what extent are they merely descriptive? To what extent do they characterize what the art collection *is*?

2.  Art collections, of course, are not the only options that might be subject to the verbal reformulations detailed in the above excerpt. Consider how to recharacterize the following:

- A house purchased by a divorcing couple with children in which the mother currently resides with the couple's children.

- A girlfriend who currently resides with the husband of a divorcing couple.

- A 10-year-old child from a prior marriage of the wife of a divorcing couple who has resided with that couple.

---

[6] Copyright © 1989. Reprinted with permission.

## 5.  Negotiation

This stage in mediation involves choosing options generated as a result of working through the prior stages.

One question is the order in which to tackle issues. Some mediators may suggest beginning with something "easy" or likely to generate agreement as a means to establish positive momentum. Alternatively, some mediators may tackle a difficult problem first, in the hopes that a successful resolution will generate momentum that will carry everything else along to a positive conclusion.

Another concern in choosing order is to avoid appearing partial to one participant. One issue may be of greater importance to one participant, or may involve the giving up of something that a participant currently has. In such situations, mediators should try to "alternate" issues to ensure that participants feel that the mediation is proceeding fairly.

As always, mediators should seek to elicit participants' "buy-in" as to the order or consideration of a particular issue. Mediators should also always keep in mind the option of a private caucus. It is often at this negotiation stage that individual meetings with participants can generate positive movement towards agreement.

## 6.  Formalizing Agreements

How agreements reached in family mediation are formalized depends on the posture of the matter and the jurisdiction in which the mediation takes place. In mediation generally, it is often typical for a mediator to draft a "Memorandum of Understanding" to memorialize the participants' agreement and to guide the participants' future conduct. This "Memorandum" may then serve as a contract, the breach of which may entitle the aggrieved party to seek damages in a lawsuit. While such a document may be the result in some forms of family mediation, more typically the ultimate goal of the mediation — the granting or modification of a child access order, for example — may only be ordered by a court, even if the mediation is "private" and not court-annexed. A court also may be required by law to undertake an independent review of custody arrangements agreed to in mediation or ensure that an agreement does not violate some other law relating to, for example, child support. It is thus often the case that an agreement reached in family mediation must be put into a form appropriate for judicial review.

The extent to which a mediator may draft such a document is a matter of some dispute, but as a practical matter it is important to note that the mediator is not acting as a lawyer even if the mediator is a lawyer. The mediator should view her role more as scrivener, albeit one whose expertise in law might help ensure that an agreement conforms to the format courts look for or expect. We will defer for now the difficult ethical issues that may arise when a mediator who is a lawyer recognizes that an agreement will differ from the result likely be obtained in court.

A final point about the Formalizing Agreements stage is to keep in mind that the idea of "stages" imposes a linearity on the mediation process that rarely occurs in real life. Conflicts can arise at any point and one stage might go "backwards" or meld into one another. It is rare indeed for a mediation to proceed logically in line with discrete stages. To the dismay of many a new mediator, this can happen even after participants seem to have reached an agreement as to all matters and the mediation has reached the point of writing down the agreement. If conflict should flare at the formalizing agreement stage, this is not necessarily a "failure" or "setback." Rather, it might suggest more work needs to be done by the participants and mediator, and this work might enhance the chances of a durable and comprehensive arrangement and understanding. Viewed in this way, it can demonstrate the power and effectiveness of mediation.

## C.  JOINT SESSIONS AND PRIVATE CAUCUSES

There are two primary procedural mechanisms family mediators use in mediation: the "joint session" and the "private caucus."

### 1.  The Joint Session

*Joint sessions* are sessions in which all participants are present, including attorneys if the participants have them and the attorneys have chosen to attend. Almost all facilitative mediators view joint sessions as the norm. After all, having all participants present offers the best chance that the many virtues of mediation — recognizing perspectives, developing integrative solutions, enhancing communication — can be achieved.

One interesting aspect of a joint caucus is how anything that is said has multiple audiences. When a mediator speaks, the mediator is being heard by all participants. This is true even when the mediator directs a question to one participant. Similarly, when one participant speaks, the mediator and other participant(s) are hearing what is said, even if the comment is being directed to the mediator. When one participant is speaking to another participant, the mediator should pay attention to both the speaker and the listener. To take a simple example, if a mediator asks one spouse a question, the other spouse hears both the question and the response. Mediators should be aware of reactions on the part of non-speaking party at all times. These reactions can be non-verbal, such as through facial expressions or body language. Thus, a mediator should be attentive to everything said or done in a joint session.

### 2.  The Private Caucus

A *private caucus* is when a mediator meets separately with a party and, if the party is represented, the party's attorney. Mediators vary widely in how often or even whether they use private caucuses. Among the situations where a private caucus might be warranted are:

- When participants are too emotional or volatile to be productive in a joint session. Sometimes this situation is referred to in shorthand as "high conflict mediations," although there might be disagreement as to what fits that description. Some mediators will even begin a mediation with a private caucus should there be indicia that a joint session would be counterproductive. This might be the case, for example, should there be a potential for violence or particularly intense volatility. Some mediators, however, would argue that such a conflict is not suitable for mediation at all.

- When the mediator believes that a participant may share information confidentially with the mediator that is too intimate or sensitive to share with the other participant.

- To help one participant consider or make a proposal or suggest ways of framing issues or proposals in light of the other participant's perspective.

- When impasse looms or the mediation seems "stuck."

- When a mediator believes there might be child abuse, domestic violence, or other issues that would render mediation inappropriate or might even trigger an obligation for the mediator to report such circumstances to an appropriate agency. To take one example, a participant experiencing domestic violence might feel inhibited sharing information while the abuser is sitting across the table. A private caucus might enable the victim to feel freer to share information.

There are some basic rules to follow in conducting private caucuses. These tend to be more definitive than many of the other choices available to mediators.

- Never conduct a private caucus with only one participant without then conducting a private caucus with the other participant.

- If you are co-mediating, both co-mediators should meet with each participant at the same time.

- Ensure that all participants understand confidentiality "ground rules" prior to the private caucus and that you, as mediator, strictly adhere to these ground rules. Two choices are available in this regard, and mediators are divided on which is the best. Some mediators advise participants that unless a party requests otherwise, all information shared in the private caucus may be shared with the other participant either in a private caucus with the other participant or in a joint session. Alternatively, some mediators advise participants that everything said in the private caucus will be kept confidential unless a party explicitly authorizes the mediator to make a disclosure.

- Ensure that the participants understand that they can request a private caucus if they wish.

## D.   "STAGES" AND TRANSFORMATIVE MEDIATION

The stages described in this chapter describe a process that, even if non-linear, succeeds when an agreement is "formalized." This might seem a self-evident goal, and it is indeed assumed as such by most mediators except for transformative mediators. Transformative mediators take issue with the idea of "stages." Consider the following:

> Transformative practice moves away from a linear, stage model of the process that typically instructs mediators to help the participants progress through a

series of sequential stages. Instead, in transformative practice, the mediator conceives of the process as emergent — resulting from the ongoing interactions of all the participants (including the mediator) during the mediation session.[7]

In this conception, then, mediation should follow a path "emerging" from interactions among the participants in mediation. Where, when, and how that path emerges is something a transformative mediator should not control or influence. This is because transforming the interactions of the participants, not settlement, is the goal of transformative mediation. Settlement of a dispute, should it be reached, is a byproduct, not a goal, of the mediation process.

This debate represents a fundamental disagreement about what mediation is. As you continue to learn about family mediation and mediation more generally, you will develop your own conception about these crucial issues.

---

[7] ROBERT A. BARUCH BUSH AND JOSEPH P. FOLGER, THE PROMISE OF MEDIATION: THE TRANSFORMATIVE APPROACH TO CONFLICT 109–110 (new and rev. ed. 2005).

# Chapter 4

# CHILD ACCESS MEDIATION

## A. INTRODUCTION

Mediation has traditionally been viewed as especially appropriate for disputes involving child access, traditionally referred to as custody and visitation disputes. As discussed in Chapter 1, almost all states have enacted statutes or court rules that encourage or mandate participation in court-sponsored mediation for child access disputes between parents or between a parent and a third party.

The potential virtues of mediation and the problems with the adversary system seem to make mediation particularly appropriate in the child access context. The adversary system, with its emphasis on the past and parental fitness, may encourage parents to focus on weaknesses of the other parent and thus escalate conflict and destroy relationships between individuals who will have to co-parent after the dispute is resolved. Social science research over the last two decades has made a strong case that children's well-being following parental breakup depends upon their parents' behavior during and after the separation process. Much of the research concludes that the higher the levels of parental conflict to which children are exposed, the more negative the effects of family dissolution.

Crowded court dockets for contested custody trials also result in delayed decisions which are particularly problematic for children who need certainty and predictability to reduce the harm from parental break-up. Applying the legal standard governing most child access disputes, the "best interests of the child," calls for an understanding of the particular child(ren) involved in the dispute and expertise about child development that are not ordinarily part of judges' range of talents or knowledge. Finally, the decision or order in a litigated custody case is usually limited to the allocation of "custody" and "visitation" that do not permit nuanced and detailed plans for children, often resulting in post-judgment proceedings in court.

Mediation, on the other hand, is said to look to the future rather than the past and encourages parents to rethink their roles as parents for the common goal of helping their children. Mediation generally leads to quicker resolution of child access disputes in a setting that permits more privacy than litigation to discuss intimate details of family life. Mediation's flexibility also permits the involvement of more interested parties and informal consultation with experts. Mediation facilitates detailed planning for children resulting in agreements that often contemplate greater involvement of both parents than existed while they were together. To the extent the agreements reflect genuine agreement and realistic expectations, mediated agreements may require less judicial intervention for clarification or enforcement than court-imposed solutions.

Mediation may be particularly helpful in cases where existing legal standards do not adequately address the interests of particular family members. These include non-biological "de facto" parents or cases where there may be multiple potential parents as a result of artificial reproductive technology or other circumstances. Finally, unlike litigation, mediation can occur online and thus presents logistical benefits for parents who live in different states or countries.

This Chapter will explore mediation in "private' family disputes — those involving disputes between parents or between a parent and a third party. The following chapter will look at mediation in the context of cases where the state has intervened as a party to protect children, sometimes referred to as "public" family law. The sections below examine legal and social science norms related to child access, the role of the child in mediation and the use of parenting plans.

## B. NORMS THAT GUIDE DECISIONMAKING IN CHILD ACCESS MEDITATION

While party self-determination is a central feature of mediation, mediators and participants often draw on external norms to develop options and guide choices. Depending upon the setting and the choices made by mediator and participants, mediation of child access disputes may consider both legal norms — what the law says about child access choices — and mental health norms — what child development experts say about what is best for children. The relevance of norms drawn from the mental health field is generally well understood and accepted in mediation. While the importance of legal norms is more contested, there is a growing consensus that legal norms have a role in child access mediation. Because courts have continuing jurisdiction over issues like child custody, visitation and support until a child is 18, many agreements on child access issues will end up before a court to be evaluated against legal norms. Legal norms may also be relevant in understanding the impact of child access decisions on other issues including the amount of child support to be paid and eligibility for public benefits. The following sections provide an overview of both legal and social science norms relevant to child access disputes.

### 1. Legal Norms

#### a. Child Access Disputes Between Parents

Typically courts apply the best interests of the child standard when resolving disputes about child access between parents — what most courts still call child custody and visitation. This standard permits judges to exercise broad discretion when reaching decisions. The following model statute lists factors courts typically consider when applying this standard:

Uniform Marriage and Divorce Act: Best Interests of the Child

The court shall determine custody in accordance with the best interest of the child. The court shall consider all relevant factors including:

1.  the wishes of the child's parent or parents as to his custody;

2.  the wishes of the child as to his custodian;

3.  the interaction and interrelationship of the child with his parent or parents, siblings, and any other person who may significantly affect the child's best interest;

4.  the child's adjustment to his home, school, and community; and

5.  the mental and physical health of all individuals involved.

The court shall not consider conduct of a proposed custodian that does not affect his relationship the child.

In most jurisdictions, a court uses the best interests standard to determine both physical (residence) and legal (decision making) custody. The court can award either type of custody to one (sole) or both parents (joint custody). Agreements between parents about child access issues — parenting plans — often use terms like residential time and decision making. But when such plans are incorporated into orders courts will most often revert to the legal terms of custody and visitation. A parent seeking modification of custody or visitation decisions must prove that a substantial change in circumstances occurred since the initial child access decision that warrants a fresh look. Continuing jurisdiction over child custody lasts in most jurisdictions until the child turns 18.

While joint custody or shared parenting, particularly joint legal custody, are frequently agreed to in mediation, the term covers a wide variety of parenting arrangements under the law. The following excerpts discuss the evolution of joint custody under the law and complexity of crafting and implementing agreements or orders for both joint physical and legal custody.

## *FROM THE RULE OF ONE TO SHARED PARENTING: CUSTODY PRESUMPTIONS IN LAW AND POLICY*
52 Fam. Ct. Rev. 213, 217–220 (2014)
By Herbie DiFonzo

. . . A number of scenarios have been swept under the joint custody umbrella: that both parents have legal custody (decision-making) but only one parent has physical custody (residence); that the parents share both legal and physical custody in approximately equal proportions; and that the parents share legal custody but one parent predominates in the residential placement of their child. This last scenario resembles the traditional sole custody award to one parent with visitation rights to the other. Even decreeing that physical custody will be equally shared opens the door to other questions: will the child spend alternate days (or weeks or fortnights or longer set periods) with each parent; will the child live with one parent on weekends and holidays while residing during school days with the other; or — a rare option — will the child live in the family home while each parent takes turns residing in it?

In light of these permutations, the joint custody-sole custody distinction is best viewed along a continuum, not as a sharp divide. Most states distinguish between joint legal and joint physical custody, allocating to the former the authority of both parents to participate equally in making significant long-term decisions regarding their child's health, education, and welfare. Joint physical custody implies that the child is in the physical care of both parents. But there is no accepted formula for how many hours per week, month, or year the child must reside with each parent for the arrangement to qualify as joint physical custody.

. . . Forty-seven states and the District of Columbia have statutory provisions authorizing courts to award joint custody in one form or another (legal or physical). The remaining three states permit these orders through case law. A number of states have joint custody presumptions or preferences, while others have avoided either term and have instead directed that the courts order as much parenting time with each parent as is reasonably possible. The terminological vagaries make it strikingly difficult to fairly categorize these statutes, and any effort to assess their impact on family life based upon the statutory language alone would be foolhardy. All states continue to frame the custody resolution norm in terms of the best interests of the child, and therefore presumptions, preferences, and the other legal terms are subservient to that hallmark custody standard.

. . . A generation ago, New York's highest court announced its perspective on joint physical custody in what has come to be known as the "Braiman rule." The court asserted that "alternating physical custody" would generally "further the insecurity and resultant pain frequently experienced by the young victims of shattered families." Thus, the court viewed joint custody as "a voluntary alternative for relatively stable, amicable parents behaving in mature civilized fashion." But the court warned that as "a court-ordered arrangement imposed upon already embattled and embittered parents, accusing one another of serious vices and wrongs, [joint custody] can only enhance familial chaos."

Although this assessment dates from 1978, New York and other courts still consider those same "relatively stable, amicable parents behaving in mature civilized fashion" to be the gold standard for participants in joint custody. The other half of the Braiman rule has also continued in force as the well-established principle "that joint custody is not appropriate where the parties are antagonistic toward each other and have demonstrated an inability to cooperate in matters concerning the child, even if the parties have agreed to the joint custody arrangement."

In contrast to the major decision-making components at the heart of legal custody, physical custody generally means "the right and obligation to provide a home for the child and to make the day-to-day decisions required during the time the child is actually with the parent having such custody." When physical custody is entrusted to the parents jointly, it is generally "divided" custody, as each parent normally has a separate residence to which the child travels. Divided physical custody will rarely be *equally* divided, and "most commonly will involve custody by one parent during the school year and by the other during summer vacation months, or division between weekdays and weekends, or between days and nights."

Nor should an award of joint legal custody be seen as the prologue to joint physical custody. In the words of the recently-enacted Arizona statute, "[s]hared legal decision-making does not necessarily mean equal parenting time." Logistical and other practical reasons generally lead to the far greater frequency of joint legal than joint physical custody awards, especially if the latter involves a 50/50 split of the children's time between the parents.

## *JOINT LEGAL CUSTODY PRESUMPTIONS: A TROUBLING LEGAL SHORTCUT*
52 Fam. Ct. Rev. 263, 264 (2014)
By Nancy Ver Steegh

## II. THE NATURE OF JOINT DECISION-MAKING

\* \* \* \*

When physical custody is at issue, a great deal of time and energy is often focused on creating detailed parenting arrangements that regulate contact between parents, anticipate problem areas, and divide the child's time with specificity. These plans provide predictability for cooperative parents and a protective structure for others.

For many families, considerably less effort is spent planning for legal custody. This difference stems, in part, from the fact that future decisions about a child's medical care, religion, and education can't be calendared and charted in the same way as physical care.

For example, it is difficult to predict whether an infant will later need special education, whether a parent will undergo a change in religious beliefs, or whether a teenage daughter will seek parental permission for an abortion. More typically parents may disagree about what school a kindergartner should attend, whether orthodontics are really needed, or whether a child should attend counseling:

Legal custody primarily involves major decision making about the child's life, including choices about religion, residence, choice of school, course of study, extent of travel away from home, choice of camp, major medical treatment, lessons, psycho-therapy, psychoanalysis or like treatment, part or full-time employment, purchase or operation of a motor vehicle, especially hazardous sports or activities, contraception and sex education, and decisions relating to actual or potential litigation involving the children . . . .

Precisely because of the nature of the decisions associated with legal custody, frequent parental contact and conferral may be required. This is in contrast to physical custody arrangements, which may be more easily structured to avoid contact between the parents.

———————

### b.  Child Access Disputes Between Parents and Third Parties

The increase in families in which grandparents, stepparents and other adults play a central role in parenting children has contributed to the rise of child access disputes between parents and third parties. Although parents have equal footing before the court, when a third party seeks custody or visitation, courts generally defer to a fit parent's decision about where the child will live and whom the child will see. This parental preference is grounded in constitutional principles of parental autonomy and can only be overcome where the parent is unfit or other extraordinary circumstances in which the loss of contact with the third party would risk harm to the child. *Troxel v. Granville*, 530 U.S. 57 (2000). "Extraordinary circumstances" have been found where grandparents or other third parties have acted as parents for the child for a substantial period of time and the legal parent attempts to cut off or limit contact with the "de facto parent." While some jurisdictions treat de facto parents as legal parents, many do not but will award visitation over the objection of the parent based on extraordinary circumstances. *See e.g., McAllister v. McAllister*, 779 N.W.2d 652, 662 (granting stepfather reasonable visitation because of his strong relationship with the child).

## 2.  Social Science Norms: Studies on Child Development and the Impact of Conflict on Children

Although psychology or social work experts are occasionally called to testify in custody trials, reliance on psychological and child development research is rarely apparent in judges' custody and visitation decisions. Because mediators often come from the mental health professions, they will frequently rely on such research or their own clinical experience in facilitating agreements. Social science research can help parents to develop age appropriate parenting plans or understand how their conflict impacts their children. The importance of family mediators (and family lawyers) understanding the impact of parental conflict on children and basic child development principles is increasingly recognized in mediation training and law school curricula. *See e.g.*, Mary E. O'Connell and J. Herbie DiFonzo, *The Family Law Education Reform Project Final Report*, 44 FAM. CT. REV. 524, 525 (2006) (arguing that law school family law courses should include knowledge of the current research on such issues as effects of conflict and loss of parental contact on children); MD Rule 9-205(C)(2)(b) and (c) (including among qualifications of family mediators "the emotional aspects of separation and divorce on adults and children" and "an introduction to family systems and child development theory").

The following excerpt summarizes findings of social science research on children and parental separation, which is crucial information for family lawyers and mediators to understand.

# Children's Psychological Responses to Divorce and Parental Conflict

## Jennifer McIntosh, Ph.D.[1]

- By age 15, 40 percent of children in the USA experience the dissolution of their parents' partnership.

- Acrimonious divorces with ongoing levels of poorly resolved or uncontained conflict between parents constitute about one third of these separations.

- The re-structuring of family life necessitated by divorce involves multiple and complex adjustments for children, including transitions of home and school, change in parent and extended family contact, economic strain, periods of diminished parenting, parent conflict, sadness and grief.

- These factors combine to elevate risks of poor outcomes for children of divorce, across psychological, social, health and academic domains, reaching through to adulthood, with increased risk of diminished emotional, economic and educational attainment.

- Ongoing parenting conflict after divorce further increases the nature and magnitude of developmental risk for children.

- Through its prevalence and the nature of risk it carries, parental separation may fairly be regarded as a public health issue for children.

- The way in which family law practitioners intervene in parenting disputes can make a difference to family adjustment and children's outcomes.

## Current Relevant Issues

### 1.  Children's responses to parents' separation

- Children rarely wish for their parents to separate and divorce for many represents the collapse of a vital, archetypal structure in their world and in their experience of who they are.

- Most children experience considerable sadness in the first stages, with anxiety, anger, resentment, confusion, guilt, loyalty tensions and somatic symptoms being common responses in the first six months post separation.

- Over time, adjustment and robustness generally improve within a stable, supportive care-giving environment.

- However, the independent impacts that separation brings to bear on children's development remain notable . . . .

---

[1] Jennifer McIntosh is a clinical child and family psychologist. She directs a clinical practice devoted to the treatment of family trauma, and specializing in divorce trauma. Her research interest is in family law interventions and their impacts on children's developmental outcomes This excerpt is from materials collected on the website maintained by The Family Law Education Reform Project, which is co-sponsored by the Association of Family and Conciliation Courts, Hofstra University School of Law Center for Children, Families and the Law and William Mitchell College of Law. *See* http://www.flerproject.org/pdf/000053-Children_Psychological_Responses_to_Divorce.pdf.

## 2. Infants' responses to parents' separation

- Separation brings substantial complexity for infants and pre-school children. It is their 'developmental response' as much as their emotional response that concerns current researchers.

- Like older children, infants (even from a few weeks of age) recognize and react to parent's distress and to overt conflict between their parents.

- Unlike older children, infants are further behind in their formative journey. Disruptions to primary attachment and patterns of care brought about by separation can de-stabilize important segments of an infant's developmental pathway. Ongoing, inflammatory and poorly contained conflict between parents, while emotionally overwhelming for parents, can be developmentally overwhelming for the infant.

- Parents need to be supported to manage these risks, to continue to provide a nurturing, steady presence, within developmentally appropriate care arrangements that evolve at the infant's developmental pace.

## 3. The developmental risks of divorce

Contemporary social scientists recognize parental separation as a coat of many colors, experienced by and affecting children differentially, over time. There are controversies and complexities, but there are also some established "truths":

- Marital conflict and divorce create risks for all children, and higher risk for those already vulnerable through other factors

- Unresolved parental conflict and diminished emotional availability impact children's psychological growth

- Children and adolescents of divorced families (compared to never divorced families) are significantly more likely to experience greater economic, social and health difficulties through childhood and early adulthood (for example, more likely to use alcohol, cigarettes and drugs, to give birth as a teenager, to drop out of school early, to receive psychological treatment, and to have earlier marriages, with increased propensity to divorce)

- Co-parenting conflict is a significant predictor of ongoing distress for adolescents and adolescent antisocial behavior.

## 4. The type of conflict that damages

- High conflict is a generic term, which can look like many things, but typically includes significant levels of anger and distrust, verbal conflict, poor communication and cooperation over parenting, ongoing negative attitude to the ex-spouse, lack of support for children's relationship with their other parent, covert and overt hostility, allegations about the ex-partner's behavior and parenting practices, ligation and re-litigation.

- Frequent, intense, threatening or poorly resolved conflict between parents pose the greatest risks to children.

## 5. How does conflict impact children?

- Children's development is profoundly influenced by the quality of their care-giving relationships, the "soil" in which they grow. Nothing grows well in toxic soil, and children are no different.

- Children soak up their parents' conflict in two ways: by directly witnessing it and by bearing the brunt of how the conflict impacts their parents' emotional availability.

- The developmental tasks most vulnerable to "stressed" parenting are the establishment of core trust, the development of attachment, regulating emotions, beliefs about oneself, understanding the social world, and learning.

- Children who witness intense/frequent marital discord exhibit higher levels of emotional and physiological reactivity, associated with poor outcomes. For example, children of conflicted divorce are more susceptible to stress-related health problems.

- It is important to note that in the case of domestic violence, a single exposure to parental violence can result in trauma of diagnostic proportions.

## Children interpret conflict through a developmental lens.

- Three to six year olds are unlikely to understand that conflict is about divergent goals and are more likely to be self-blaming. Conflict and its resolution is understood in behavioral terms; the fight is over when the shouting stops. Young children are likely to take sides in parents' arguments with the goal of cognitive simplification, rather than true alignment with one parent over the other.

- Older children, ages seven through ten years, readily recognize more subtle types of conflict and are sensitive to whether an argument has been resolved or not. These children's dominant emotional response to arguments in which they are the topic is of guilt.

- Older adolescents are most likely to try to avoid the conflict, and will "vote with their feet," often by leaving home much younger than their peers from never separated families.

- There are notable gender effects in how children make sense of marital conflict. Boys tend to experience a higher level of threat and girls a higher level of self-blame. Both of these appraisal styles influence their patterns of adjustment.

- All children are sensitive to parental anger, but children with histories of spousal violence respond with greater intensity. The fact that some children from high conflict marriages have been shown to prosper following parental divorce suggests that divorce may be helpful when it removes stress from children's lives.

6.  **Managing the risks**

    - Children's distress is diminished as a direct function of whether divorce conflicts are resolved, and the degree of resolution.

    - Parental warmth, supportive and responsive care taking and overall emotional "scaffolding" of the child play vital roles in buffering the impact of conflict, as does an environment that reduces daily stress for the child, through consistency of rules, routines and expectations within the household, and quality of parental monitoring.

    - When parent conflict post-divorce is low, increased father involvement appears to be closely associated with better child outcomes.

    - Quality of sibling support ameliorates the negative impact of parental conflict on self-esteem, competence, social skill and global self-worth.

7.  **Children's adjustment and the relationship to parent contact**

    - Parenting arrangements play an important role in the child's adjustment to divorce. The field awaits definitive longitudinal research in this critical area.

    - A commonly held and uncontentious view would hold that children's responses to divorce are facilitated by the active, warm and responsive involvement of both parents in their lives. Conflict as ever poses a problem in this equation.

    - An important current issue facing practitioners, courts and policymakers is whether shared physical parenting can be beneficial to children when there is high parent conflict. Transitions between warring parents unable to conceal their feelings require the child to use considerable energy to ensure their emotional safety, actively and constantly monitoring their allegiances, loyalties and the general 'emotional weather' they encounter in each parent's home. The potential developmental difficulties for infants and young children who do this on an ongoing basis are far reaching. The presence of active and unresolved conflict requires a cautious approach to shared arrangements.

8.  **Implication for family law practitioners**

    The findings summarized here about children's responses to divorce are sobering and the challenge they throw down to the practice front is real. Mindfulness of the needs of children and the merits of child centered dispute resolution are at the core of current practice developments in family law, with a growing body of research showing clearly that the way in which practitioners assist parents to resolve their disputes can significantly impact children's outcomes.

---

Despite the acknowledged importance of social science research, there is still much debate about how to apply such research to individual family situations and how to reconcile conflicting findings. For example, while studies generally find that continuing contact with both parents is most helpful to children of separated parents, they also point to the ongoing parental conflict that may result from shared parenting as a predictor for problems for their children. Researchers themselves caution about the limits of using such research to construct "rules" about the value of particular parenting arrangements:

> Some areas of research are established with sufficient quantity and quality of information to offer bright-line recommendations (e.g., the effect and conditions under which conflict undermines children's positive development), but these must be distinguished from studies that offer preliminary information, yet do not create an adequate body of research to suggest a policy direction for a broad subsection of family populations. For example, areas of research with strong supporting bodies elucidate both the harm to children due to continued exposure to parental conflict, and the important protective factor of positive quality parenting by both parents. In contrast, under what conditions and how best parents in moderate conflict can continue to share decision making and parenting time exemplifies an area about which we do not have a sufficient body of knowledge to recommend policy. Similar concerns underlie the question of when having children alternate between two homes on a regular basis becomes more anxiety producing than beneficial.

Marsha Kline Pruett and J. Herbie DiFonzo, *Closing the Gap: Research, Policy, Practice, and Shared Parenting*, 52 Fam. Ct. Rev. 152, 161 (2014)

## NOTES AND QUESTIONS

1.   When mediating child access cases, are the legal norms likely to be helpful in facilitating an agreement? Does your answer depend upon the type of conflict and circumstances of the case? How are they relevant if you are an attorney representing a parent or third party in a child access dispute that is being mediated?

2.   What are the two or three findings in the social science research that you believe are most relevant to child access decisions and post-separation parenting? Is any of the research in conflict — i.e., leading in different directions when developing a parenting plan?

3.   Mediators working with parents domiciled or planning to live in different countries should alert parties to issues surrounding international custody conflicts. In addition, families where one or both parents are non-U.S. citizens who seek mediation of child access disputes may be subject to the jurisdiction of a foreign court or to a foreign custody order. One particular situation involves a child access dispute in which a parent residing in one country has custody of a child and a parent in another country seeks the "return" of the child. Such disputes are subject to the Hague Convention on the Civil Aspects of International Child Abduction, which has been signed by 74 countries since its promulgation in 1980. Under the Convention, the country in which the child currently resides is not permitted to "decide on the merits of rights of custody" until it is determined that the child should not be returned to another country. The Convention's language has been interpreted to permit mediated resolutions of these disputes, and a substantial number of signatories to the Convention have opted to do so. For those interested in learning more, see Nuria Gonalez Martin,

*International Child Abduction and Mediation: An Overview*, 48 Fam. L.Q. 319 (2014).

4. Online Dispute Resolution (ODR) has proven to be helpful in child access mediation. As the name suggests, it involves two or more parties and a neutral, usually a mediator, communicating by electronic means in an attempt to reach an agreement. Communication can be either synchronous (e.g., via Skype) or asynchronous (e.g., via email). The increasing mobility of families has created a substantial need for low-cost and cross-jurisdictional dispute resolution methods. This is particularly true where the conflict involves parents who live in two different countries that might be thousands of miles apart. The main advantage of ODR is its efficiency, as it saves both time and money. People who resolve their disputes online do not have to travel or attend meetings, instead negotiating from their computers at home. In addition, settling a conflict online may force disputants to narrow their focus to the issues that need to be settled instead of being distracted by the emotional aspects of the conflict. Do you see any downsides to this process? Does it undermine the mediation process? If so, how?

## C. PARENTING PLANS

### 1. Introduction

Parenting plans are agreements providing for co-parenting by parents who do not reside together. They have become widely used in both private and court based mediation. The use of parenting plans evolved in part from the desire of mediators to approach co-parenting between separated parents in a holistic manner:

> The approach outlined in [the parenting plan used by the authors] follows the understandings first discovered by a small group of mediators in the early 1980s who noticed that it was much easier to reach resolution of the custody issues when the entire content of the parenting arrangements were first agreed upon prior to engaging in discussions about custody labels. This approach attempted to neutralize the framework of the adversarial system of divorce by eliminating the connection between winning custody as the key to so many other "prizes" that are attached to the custody label. Although at the time we did not think of it in terms of building a Parenting Plan, the approach essentially called for the mediator to refuse to mediate *custody* and to instead mediate schedules, housing, even how the clothes would be exchanged or handled.

Marilyn S. McKnight and Stephen K. Erickson, *Plan to Separately Parent Children After Divorce*, Divorce and Family Mediation, 129–133 (Jay Folberg, Ann L. Milne & Peter Salem, Eds.) (2004).

A number of states now require parties to submit parenting plans in any divorce in which minor children are present.[2] These plans may be individually crafted or adapted

---

[2] Katherine T. Bartlett, *U.S. Custody Law and Trends in the Context of the ALI Principles of Family Dissolution*, 10 Va. J. Soc. Pol'y. Law 5, 6, 7 (2002) (finding that about half of states have statutes requiring parenting plans and/or parenting coordinators). *See, e.g.*, Fla. Stat. § 61.125. Wash. Rev. Code Ann. § 26.09.181(1)); N.H. Rev. Stat. Ann. § 2.18 (a)(1) (2014); Tenn Code Ann. § 36-6-404(a).

from forms or a menu of acceptable plans promulgated by the state courts or private sources.[3] They generally include each parent's area of responsibility in providing for the child's physical care, emotional stability, and well-being, both at the present time and as the child ages. They also may incorporate agreements for methods of resolving future disputes. Examples of parenting plans, both a form used in court ordered mediation to more extended plan developed in multiple session private mediation, can be found in Appendix B. The following chart reflects the shift in language from the terms used in court orders and the terms commonly used in parenting plans:

---

## CHILD ACCESS MEDIATION REFRAMES

| Custody/Visitation Orders | → | Parenting Plans |
|---|---|---|
| "The Parties" | → | Participants/Parents |
| Physical Custody | → | Residential Plan |
| Visitation | → | Parenting Time |
| Legal Custody | → | Decision making |

---

## 2.  Developing Parenting Plans to Meet the Needs of Diverse Families

Given the social science research supporting continuing contact with both parents, enthusiasm for joint or shared parenting is a consistent theme in mediation literature. *See, e.g.,* Carol Bohmer & Marilyn Ray, *Effects of Different Dispute Resolution Methods on Women and Children After Divorce,* 28 FAM. L.Q. 223, 227, 233–234 (1994). Parenting plans have become an important tool in achieving that goal. As family composition becomes more diverse and complex, however, some have challenged the across the board promotion of shared parenting. Some families come to child access mediation with little or no experience co-parenting or a long history of co-parenting marked by conflict or even violence. The nature of these relationships may make shared parenting impossible or at least unlikely to succeed without support from the courts and others. As one commentator noted:

---

[3] *See* Appendix B in this book. *See also, Alaska Court System Model Parenting Agreement,* http://courts. alaska.gov/forms/dr-475.pdf (last visited Nov. 30, 2014); *Model Parenting Time Plans for Parent/Child Access,* http://www.azcourts.gov/portals/31/parentingTime/PPWguidelines.pdf (last visited Nov. 30, 2014); *American Academy for Matrimonial Lawyers Model for a Parenting Plan,* www.familylawfla.org/pdfs/ AAML_Parenting_Plan.pdf (last visited Jan. 5, 2015).

Some parents who are capable of sharing major decisions prefer for a variety of reasons not to make decisions jointly. In some cases joint decision-making is not practical, such as when a parent is on military deployment, travels extensively, lives far away, or is otherwise unavailable. One parent may have substantial expertise in an area, such as a medical doctor making health-related decisions or a teacher making educational decisions. Sometimes one parent has strong religious beliefs and the other does not. It is possible that one parent excels at decision-making while the other avoids it. Other parents may aspire to joint decision-making but recognize that they presently lack the skills or foundational relationship needed to avoid impasses that would harm their children. They may require a period of education and support to determine whether it is feasible. For example, some unmarried parents may not have had a substantial or lengthy prior relationship. Unfortunately, for some families joint legal custody will escalate conflict and lead to other detrimental effects. For those with a history of intimate partner violence, child abuse, substance abuse, mental illness, or deep-seated and unresolved dis-agreements on major parenting issues, joint legal custody will exacerbate problems and trap children in untenable situations.

Nancy Ver Steegh, *Joint Legal Custody Presumptions: A Troubling Legal Shortcut*, 52 FAM. CT. REV. 263, 265 (2014)

———

The following excerpt discusses some of the challenges of shared parenting facing nonmarital and low income parents. The author identifies barriers to joint parenting and suggests mediators and policy makers exercise caution in recommending joint parenting plans as a "one size fits all" child access approach and work to develop support for such families to realize the objectives of shared parenting.

———

## *SHARED PARENTING AND NEVER-MARRIED FAMILIES*
### 52 FAM. CT. REV. 632, 633–35 (2014)
### By Solangel Maldonado

Never Married Parents

. . . Almost forty-one percent of children born in the United States in 2012 were born to parents who were never married to each other, a figure that has remained relatively unchanged for the last five years. Approximately fifty percent of never-married parents have never lived together with the child and forty percent of the couples who were cohabiting when the child was born will separate before the child's fifth birthday. As compared to married parents, never-married parents are generally less educated, have significantly lower income, are more likely to have been incarcer-ated (which negatively impacts income earning ability), and are disproportionately African American or Latino. Studies have repeatedly found that children who grow up in single-parent homes are more likely to underachieve academically, become teen parents, abuse drugs, engage in delinquent behavior, and experience behavioral problems. While studies have found that a close relationship with both parents may reduce the risk of these poor outcomes, nonmarital fathers disengage from their children at alarmingly high rates. One study found that only sixty percent of nonmarital fathers see their one-year-old child at least once a month. By the time the child is five years old, only fifty-one percent of unmarried fathers visit at least once a month and one-third have no contact with their children at all. Never-married fathers are also significantly less likely than married fathers to share decision-making authority or parenting time.

Consequently, millions of nonmarital children are in need of parenting plans that will help their parents take care of them and that will maximize the likelihood that children will have a meaningful relationship with both parents . . . . Never-married parents face many barriers to shared parenting that divorced parents do not face. First, a never-married father must establish paternity before he can seek parenting time. In contrast, a married man is presumed to be the father of a child conceived during the marriage and thus is entitled to seek parenting time without first establishing paternity. Establishing paternity can be quite simple, requiring only that the parents execute a voluntary acknowledgment of paternity, which many parents do at the time of the child's birth. In some cases, however, establishing paternity can be quite burdensome. Sometimes the mother is unable to locate the father, or the father is unable to find the mother or even confirm the child's existence. In those cases, the parties may have to go to court to establish paternity.

Second, even after establishing paternity, in many states an unmarried father is not entitled to parenting time until he petitions for it, and in some states that petition must be filed in a separate proceeding. Until the court enters a custody order, the mother has sole decision-making authority and sole residential custody. As a result, mothers have the power to deny unmarried fathers access to their children. Some unmarried fathers do not know that they have a right to seek parenting time and many who are aware of their rights lack the resources (both financial and otherwise) to file a parenting time petition. Fathers who are denied access, or who believe they will be denied access, are unlikely to seek shared parenting. In contrast, married fathers have the same rights as mothers until the court decides otherwise. Third, the majority of unmarried parents never cohabited or did so for a short period of time only. As such, in contrast to the majority of divorcing parents who shared parenting responsibilities while they lived together, many unmarried parents have never shared parenting responsibilities. The unmarried father who never lived with the mother and child may not have had an opportunity to do much parenting. Not surprisingly, he may not feel confident that he can take care of a child for more than a few hours at a time and the mother may not trust that he can either. Interestingly, when never-married fathers lived with the mother and the child, they assumed fewer parenting responsibilities than married fathers. Parents who did not share parenting when they were romantically involved are unlikely to agree to share parenting when the relationship has ended.

Never-married parents lack the necessary tools to craft and implement effective parenting plans and the law does little to facilitate shared parenting of nonmarital children. As Professor Huntington has observed, our legal system has a mechanism to help divorcing parents transition into their new parenting roles but has no such mechanism for unmarried parents. Courts will generally not grant a divorce until custody and parenting time issues have been addressed. By the time a divorce decree is issued, parents have generally either agreed to a parenting plan or the court has imposed one on them. In addition, some states require divorcing parents to submit a parenting plan, which forces them to at least attempt to figure out how they will co-parent their children after divorce. Requiring divorcing parents to submit a parenting plan signals that both parents are expected to be involved in parenting their children. Many states also require divorcing parents to attend parenting education classes and attempt to mediate parenting time disputes. These services, although not perfect, reflect the state's determination that children should maintain close bonds with both parents after divorce and that each parent should have significant parenting time with the child. In contrast, the legal system does little to help unmarried parents share parenting.

Although unmarried parents have the option of creating a parenting plan and unmarried fathers who have established paternity have the right to file a petition for custody and parenting time, most will not. The majority of never-married fathers cannot afford to hire a lawyer to represent them and, although they could theoretically file a petition pro se, these fathers, many of whom have had prior dealings with the legal system, are hesitant to go to court. Without a court order, these fathers have no right to see their children and access is dependent on the relationship with the mother, which is not always amicable.

Low Income Families

Ideally, income would have no effect on how often a parent sees his/her child or the type of parenting arrangement that best serves a child's interest. However, income plays a significant role in whether parents have a parenting plan and the terms of the parenting plan (if any) that they agree to or the court imposes on them. Low-income parents (who also tend to be never-married parents) are significantly less likely than higher income parents to share parenting. Researchers in Wisconsin, a state that has strongly encouraged shared parenting for over a decade and which enjoys high rates of shared parenting, found that the percentage of families who shared parenting increased as family income increased. While eleven percent of divorcing parents with a combined family income of $25,000 per year shared parenting, sixty-four percent of families who earned $150,000 or more shared parenting. Other studies have similarly found that fathers with higher levels of educational attainment and greater financial resources had higher rates of shared parenting.

Low-income parents face many obstacles to shared parenting. Shared parenting requires that each parent maintain a home that is appropriate for the children to spend a significant amount of time in. Many low-income fathers live with extended family members or share a small apartment with friends. Others are homeless. Even fathers who have their own apartment cannot afford the larger space they would need to accommodate children or the costs of two households. Low-income fathers generally do not have an adequate home where their children can spend one night, much less thirty to thirty-five percent of their time as required for shared parenting.

Shared parenting is common when parents have legal representation and are informed of their options. Low-income fathers are unlikely to have access to legal representation and, as such, may not be aware that they have a right to seek substantial amounts of parenting time with their children over the mother's wishes. Mothers who lack legal representation may not be aware of the research demonstrating that shared parenting may be beneficial to both children and parents.

. . . Many low-income fathers are significantly behind on child support payments and are unlikely to file a petition for parenting time because they fear that they will be arrested for nonpayment of child support. Even when they have obtained a legal parenting time order or the mother is willing to grant them access to the child without a court order, some low-income fathers avoid contact with their children because they are ashamed of their children's economic circumstances and inability to contribute to their support.

## NOTES AND QUESTIONS

1.  Appendix B includes the Parenting Plan developed by the Erickson Institute and a Parenting Plan used in a court sponsored mediation program in Baltimore, Maryland. What are the primary differences between the plans? Evaluate the pros and cons of each plan and consider which you would prefer to use in your mediation practice and why.

2.  Do parenting plans encourage any particular type of child access (custody) arrangement? One of the stated benefits of such plans is that their detail provides for a wide range of post-separation situations not contemplated in the usual separation agreement or court- imposed custody and visitation order and therefore may result in fewer trips back to the court. Others claim that these plans actually encourage greater involvement by the courts. Which view do you find more persuasive?

3.  Many of the benefits attributed to child access mediation result from the power given to the parties, rather than the court, to make agreements about the care of their children. Indeed, in many jurisdictions trial courts are either not permitted to award joint custody over the objection of a parent or are required to make a series of factual findings before ordering it over the objection of either party. *See, e.g., Taylor v. Taylor*, 508 A.2d 964 (Md. 1986) (finding an award of joint custody reversible error unless evidence in the record that parents have a "capacity to communicate and to reach shared decisions affecting the child's welfare"). Is it ever appropriate for a court to overrule a mediated agreement when neither party is alleging unfairness or, for other reasons, seeks to set aside the agreement? *See, e.g., In re Marriage of Sutton*, 233 S.W.3d 786 (Mo. App. E.D., 2007) (trial judge did not abuse his discretion when changing the parenting plan to eliminate each parent's access to the children by telephone while the children were in the custody of the other parents because it was in the best interest of the children); *Sleater v. Sleater*, 42 S.W.3d 821 (Mo. App. E.D. 2001) (trial court judge was permitted to reject the parenting plan on custody and visitation but was required to make written findings detailing the specific relevant factors that resulted in the rejections of the parties' proposed agreement.)

4.  What are some of the barriers faced by non-marital parents who seek to share parenting after separation? Barriers for low income parents? Is there anything a

lawyer representing a client can suggest including in a mediation agreement to overcome such barriers? Is it appropriate for a mediator to take into account the parties' shared parenting experience or income circumstances when facilitating an agreement?

## 3.  "Child-Informed" Mediation

### a.  Introduction

Most discussion of children's participation in child access disputes has focused on litigated cases. Judges in most states have discretion to determine whether and how to consider a child's views in deciding custody and parenting matters. In some jurisdictions, judges exercise this discretion by routinely interviewing children in chambers or appointing attorneys or experts for the child. Scholars and practitioners are just beginning to pay attention to the participation of children in non-adversary family dispute resolution. Most court-connected mediation programs have been reluctant to involve children directly in the mediation process. For example, a 1996 study of California family courts found that less than 16 percent of court-connected mediators interviewed the children. More recent evidence confirms this reluctance. For example, the *Model Standards for Family and Divorce Mediation* provide that "Except in extraordinary circumstances, the children should not participate in the process without the consent of both parents and the children's court-appointed representative." The usage of the phrase "extraordinary circumstances" sets a deliberately high barrier, and in scenarios where one parent supports a child's inclusion and the other parent objects, the objecting parent can terminate the mediation rather than be required to involve the child.

Moreover, there is a divergence of views among mediators regarding the value of children's participation. *See e.g.* Cassandra w. Adams, *Children's Interest-Lost in Translation: Making the Case for Involving Children in Mediation of Child Custody Cases*, 36 U. DAYTON L. REV. 353 (2011) (describing the pros and cons of child inclusive mediation) While some mediators favor the inclusion of children at mediation sessions, others maintain that a child need not be physically present to have his or her voice heard. Still others oppose the involvement of children at any point in the mediation process, citing concerns about creating loyalty conflicts, as well as undermining parental autonomy or compromising mediator neutrality. Mediators who are trained as lawyers are less likely than those from a mental health background to favor the involvement of children in mediation.

In contrast to the prevailing wisdom in the United States, reformers in other countries have developed mediation models that emphasize the inclusion and perspective of children. *See e.g.*, PATRICK PARKINSON AND JUDY CASHMORE, THE VOICE OF A CHILD IN FAMILY LAW DISPUTES (Oxford University Press 2009). For example a model developed in Australia has two variants of child informed mediation, both intended to encourage parents to consider the perspective of their children during the mediation process. One is "child-focused mediation" in which the mediator responsible for mediating the dispute gave parents general information about the effects of divorce and parental conflict on children, and helped parents consider how the information applied to their particular children. The other is "child inclusive mediation" in which a separate mental health professional, designated as a child consultant, interviewed the parties' children and shared information from that interview with the parents prior to the first mediation session; the child consultant also provided general information about the effects of divorce and parental conflict. Evaluation of child informed mediation has yielded promising results. A study conducted one year after intervention found that parents who participated in both variants of child informed mediation experienced improvement in family functioning, including lower inter-parental conflict.

Some research in the United States has built on these studies. Researchers in Indiana conducted a randomized trial that compared the two "child-informed" mediation models with a more traditional mediation approach that did not focus explicitly on children's perspectives. Robin H. Ballard, Amy Holtzworth-Monroe, Amy G. Applegate, Brian M. D'Onofrio, & John E. Bates, *"A Randomized Controlled Trial of Child-Informed Mediation,"* 19 PSYCHOLOGY PUBLIC POLICY AND LAW 272 (2013). The results of this study suggest that child-informed mediation models may offer significant benefits to these families. Although parents in both traditional and child-informed mediation were highly likely to reach agreement, parents in the child-informed groups were more likely to report that they and the other parent had learned something in mediation. Mediators were also more satisfied with the child informed models than with the more traditional approach and thought that the child-informed approaches worked.

## NOTES AND QUESTIONS

1.   As a mediator, what do you think is the proper role, if any, for children in mediation? What are the relevant factors in making this decision?

# Chapter 5

# CHILD WELFARE MEDIATION: WHEN THE STATE IS A PARTY TO THE CONFLICT

## A. INTRODUCTION

This Chapter explores mediation and other dispute resolution processes in "public" family disputes — cases where the state has intervened and made claims of abuse or neglect against parents or other caretakers. Because of the presence of the state in these cases, commonly called "child welfare" cases, mediation and other informal processes raise different issues than the more established child access mediation where the state does not appear as a party.

### 1. What Is Meant by Child Welfare?

The child welfare system involves government agencies, usually called Departments of Social Services or Children's Services, and a combination of federal, state and local laws to protect children from physical abuse, emotional abuse, or neglect by the child's parent or parents. Child welfare cases usually come under the jurisdiction of a Juvenile Court, Family Court, or Unified Family Court. States may refer to the structure that governs child welfare cases as dependency, Child in Need of Assistance (CINA), or Persons in Need of Supervision (PINS) or other terms. While the nomenclature of the public entities may vary by state, the structure of the child welfare system is governed by federal mandate, and these cases differ vastly from private child custody disputes in purpose, process, and law.

Child welfare cases generally begin with a call or written report by a family member, school teacher, or other citizen to the county's Child Protection Services child abuse hotline. The hotline worker, usually a Department of Social Services child welfare worker, determines whether the report merits an investigation. If the case is investigated, another initial determination is made by the worker, often an intake worker, about whether the child or children should be removed from the home pending an initial court hearing. If the child is removed, the states generally have between 24 and 72 hours before they must present the case to a judge or hearing officer. Whether the child is removed or remains in the home of the accused parent, the court may hold a jurisdictional or adjudicative hearing to determine if the court will exercise control over the care of the child. If the court determines that the child is at risk, and therefore takes jurisdiction, the court will also hold a disposition hearing, during which it determines the appropriate placement type for the child. Another hearing is held by the court or an administrative agency every six months, until the child is returned to the home or the reunification period, usually consisting of six to 18 months of social services to the parent and child, has ended. If a child remains in the foster care system past the point of termination of services to the parent, another review hearing is held at least every 12 months.

Mediations take place throughout this process but most often, prior to a jurisdictional hearing, at disposition, after review hearings, and at times when the child's placement is in question. In almost every state, parents and children are routinely appointed attorneys or sometimes in the case of children, guardians *ad litem*, to represent their interests. The parents and children, their representatives, the assigned child welfare worker, county counsel, foster parents, community support people, and psychosocial experts may participate in mediations. Ultimately, by federal law, if the child is out of the home for 15 of 22 consecutive months, the case generally must move toward termination of services for the parents and may move toward termination of parental rights and later, adoption. Post-adoption contracts between biological and adoptive parents are often mediated toward the end of the child welfare process.

## B.   HOW SHOULD CHILD WELFARE CASES DIFFER FROM PRIVATE DISPUTE RESOLUTION?

Child welfare cases pose unique challenges to the family mediator, and some jurisdictions have or are contemplating special qualification requirements for individuals mediating child welfare cases. In contrast to child custody cases between private parties, which presume parents to be 'fit' to make decisions for their children, the child welfare system only comes into play when the fitness of the parent is in question by the state or the well-being of the child is at risk. For this reason, mediations that take place in child welfare cases begin with an imbalance of power, in that parents alleged to have brought harm to their children mediate with child welfare workers, the state agents assigned to protect and at times, remove, children from their homes. In addition, children often participate in these mediations, necessitating that the mediator have some grounding in child development or at least have the capacity to use age-appropriate language and child-friendly processes. Child welfare statutes, in contrast with child custody statutes, are rooted in federal law and tend to be more complex and involve more case law than custody matters. Child welfare cases often involve disparate but interrelated issues within a case, such as the need to apply for immigration status, the concurrent filing of criminal charges, delinquency court involvement, special education appeals, school discipline proceedings, public benefits barriers, adoption processes, substance abuse, poverty, domestic violence, and mental health issues.

Due to the complexity of interwoven law and the depth of emotions that often come to the surface during child welfare mediations, jurisdictions have experimented with having child welfare mediation facilitated by co-mediators with divergent expertise and experience. One formula would involve a mediator with a legal background co-mediating with a mediator schooled in social work or psychology. Similarly, at least one jurisdiction employs a co-mediator who herself traversed the child welfare system as a parent. The cross-pollination of insight from the complementary fields and first-hand experience assists the co-mediators in their effort to accurately reflect the feelings and values of the participants as well as to bring attention to the specific needs of the individual families.

The following excerpt discusses the results of a pilot child welfare mediation program in five California counties in the 1990s. The article speaks to the fears experienced by professionals — attorneys and child welfare workers — not accustomed to using mediation. She then discusses their experience, and that of the participating clients, once the pilot project was underway.

## *AN EVALUATION OF CHILD PROTECTION MEDIATION IN FIVE CALIFORNIA COURTS*[1]
### 35 Fam. Ct. Rev. 184, 184–85 (1997)
### By Nancy Thoennes

This article presents the results of an evaluation of five California counties utilizing court-based mediation services to process child maltreatment cases filed with the court. The programs employed a variety of different service delivery approaches and targeted cases at a variety of different stages of case processing. The results indicate that mediation is an effective method of resolving cases and may offer a number of benefits over adjudication, including more detailed treatment plans and fewer contested court hearings. At the Center for Policy Research we have been fortunate to have the opportunity to conduct research in a number of courts providing dependency mediation. Some of our earliest research gave us the chance to consider the programs operating in Los Angeles and Orange counties in California and throughout Connecticut. That research reached the following very general conclusions:

Settlement rates ranged from 60 percent to 80 percent of the cases seen by mediators; Mediated treatment plans were produced, on average, a month sooner than nonmediated plans; In some, but not all, sites there were significant differences between the degree of compliance with mediated and adjudicated plans. Where there were differences, compliance was better in mediated cases;

Children were more likely to be mentioned as the recipients of services in mediated versus adjudicated plans;

Professional participants reported that mediation makes the court experience a little faster, and less foreign and more understandable to parents.

The results of this study have been documented elsewhere. In the present article, I offer the results of a similar study conducted in five California counties. The California evaluations provide an opportunity to see whether similar results are found in dependency mediation programs initiated years later, and employing a variety of different formats . . .

---

[1] Copyright ©1997. Reprinted with permission.

## REFERRAL PROCESS

At most of the California pilot sites, judges had discretion about which cases would be referred to mediation. However, efforts were generally made to refer contested jurisdiction and disposition cases to mediation. Programs generally also encouraged the parties to request mediation at any time they felt it might help, and judges were inclined to order mediation when it was requested. The professionals interviewed in this study were able to cite examples of situations in which they did request mediation, For example, attorneys who represent children and parents reported that they sometimes requested mediation because discussions were at an impasse, because an issue needed immediate results, or because they needed to get direction in a case. One attorney who represents parents explained why he requests mediation:

> I'd ask for it if the social worker was being evasive and didn't talk to the parents. Or maybe there's a specific problem, like I had a caseworker who did a home visit to a client who doesn't speak English and there was no interpreter there. I request it if I have a parent who just needs to vent. And some attorneys use it . . . to find out what's really going on.

Attorneys who represent parents sometimes requested mediation because they felt they had nothing to lose and might get a better deal. Others wanted their client to get another "reality check," that is, to hear from people other than their attorneys that their demands or expectations were unreasonable. Finally, in fast-moving cases, mediation was an opportunity to get fresh information about events that had happened between the time the caseworker's report was written and a court hearing was scheduled. Attorneys who represented the child protection services agency reported that they tended to request mediation when there was a visitation issue, intrafamily conflicts, or when they felt their client, the social worker, needed to reevaluate her position.

## PARTICIPANT REACTIONS

. . . The surveys indicated that parents felt "heard" in mediation. More than 90 percent of the parents at each site reported they had a chance to talk about the issues important to them, felt others listened to and understood what they had to say, and felt mediation clarified what they needed to do in order to have the child protection services agency close their case. Somewhat fewer parents indicated that mediation helped to clarify what the caseworker would do to meet the goals of the treatment plan, which suggests an area in which mediation can improve.

Parents were also asked to compare their experience in mediation with prior experiences they may have had in court. Although a few of the parents said they were simply unsure of how mediation and court compare, parents who were able to provide an assessment clearly felt that mediation was "better than a court hearing before a judge."

Although the parents were usually receptive to mediation, initial resistance to the idea of mediation was common among caseworkers, attorneys, and even some judges and hearing officers. When they first heard about the pilot project, social workers at most sites admitted to having fundamental doubts about its utility. Speaking candidly, workers at most sites said they initially suspected that mediation would prove to be a waste of time. Workers tended to feel that they could reach settlements with reasonably cooperative and motivated parents on their own, and believed that it was impossible to achieve mediated settlements with less cooperative families. These caseworkers were concerned that mediation would be used by parents and their attorneys to challenge the workers' professionalism and honesty. There was concern that "mediators would be deciding things and the caseworker would be undermined."

Legal counsel for the caseworkers worried at the outset that public defenders would simply use the session "to get some free discovery" with no intention of settling in mediation. These attorneys said they did not want to participate in the process if that meant "negotiating about what the law said or coming up with agreements that were contrary to the law."

The prospect of mediating dependency cases also met with some initial resistance by the attorneys who represent parents in dependency court proceedings. Some public defenders doubted that the process would remain truly confidential, although experience has since convinced them that confidentiality is respected. With the exception of a new disclosure that puts someone at risk, nothing goes out of the mediation session. Participants at each site now agree that "judges never ask about mediation," and that the confidential nature of the process has been honored. Some public defenders also maintained that mediation would be like every other settlement effort: "just another way to get parents to submit." Thus they worried that the compromise in mediation would be done by parents, never by the department.

Resistance to mediation on the part of the professionals was typically short lived. Education about the process and exposure to it, along with the careful selection of a mediator, served to overcome initial resistance. Once they tried mediation, most case-workers and attorneys supported the process. Some caseworkers even credit mediation with opening up communication channels between the parents and the caseworker and helping them work together. One worker said:

> I had a client who wouldn't talk to me before mediation. She saw me as sort of like the police . . . . You don't talk to them unless they ask you a direct question. Once we got into mediation, she understood the role of the caseworker and was willing to work with me.

Caseworkers noted that in court the agency becomes the "enemy." Parents "hear all this incredibly negative stuff about themselves and feel awful." The presiding dependency court judge in one site recognized that mediation might help caseworkers bridge the conflicting demands of the social services and legal systems:

> Juvenile court has two contradictory missions going on at the same time. We are supposed to be obtaining proof of bad acts and simultaneously putting the family back together. Some social workers are busy putting together the legal case and don't really do a very good job of delivering services. Others focus on services without making the legal case.

Caseworkers now agree that mediation can help reconcile the helper and investigator roles. As a result, a strong sentiment among caseworkers is that there is "nothing to lose by mediating," and that unlike trial, "mediation has never made things worse." Parents' attorneys came to value mediation after discovering that it could be the place where all the parties are held accountable, and all the parties "test their reality." For parents who were insisting on unreasonable, hard-line positions against the advice of their attorneys, the input of the mediators was most helpful. One defense attorney noted:

> There's really no other place where someone can tell the caseworker "you need to talk to the parents" or tell the parents "you need to shape up." The mediators have a clear grasp of the dynamics among the parties and they are equally demanding on all sides.

Another attorney for parents noted that mediation was far more candid and revealing than other settlement efforts. In a system where attorneys admit they often appear in court before they know who their clients are, mediation also ensured that parents got some undivided attention. Parents' attorneys also acknowledged that parents got a lot of practical information in mediation, which was important because not all attorneys take the time to answer questions and ensure that clients fully understand the situation.

Finally, after trying it, the professionals generally came to view mediation as beneficial even when no agreement is reached. The process is believed to be effective in promoting communication and wrestling with the "real impasse issues." One defense attorney noted that "at a minimum, you will clarify the issues in mediation and maybe you will work out some interim arrangements on things like visitation that will hold you over to trial." Attorneys were even supportive in Contra Costa County, where they did not participate in the session. Initially, these attorneys expressed skepticism, but, as in other settings, their attitudes changed over time.

One key to the success of dependency mediation in each of the pilot sites was judicial support. The courts in the pilot sites fully recognized their leadership role. One presiding judge noted:

> If the judiciary doesn't support this, it won't work. Programs that are initiated more from the bottom up sometimes have trouble getting people to show up and participate. Others have to see value in mediation for themselves, but they won't go unless the judge is clear that it is required . . . .

## SUMMARY

The evaluation of the California pilot projects had several limitations, as have all dependency mediation evaluations. For example, the time line did not allow us to follow cases over a lengthy period of time to discover what ultimately transpired with respect to savings in court time, length of out-of-home placement, or compliance patterns. In addition, the programs were evolving even while the evaluation took place. However, despite these limitations, we can note the following:

*   Mediation can produce settlements at all stages in case processing: contested jurisdictional, dispositional, and post dispositional cases.

* All types of cases settle in mediation. There is no evidence that certain types of maltreatment should be screened out of the process.

* The decision to mediate jurisdiction and disposition generally met with some early resistance from all professional groups. However, today there is widespread support for the continuation of the service, although time constraints continue to pose problems.

* Parents reported that they understood the mediation process and felt it provided them with a place to be "heard" and to hear what was required of them. Most parents preferred mediation to a judicial hearing.

* The agreements produced in mediation are similar in many respects to those promulgated by judges. However, mediated agreements are more likely than other agreements to include detailed visitation plans for children in out-of-home placements. They are also more likely to address communication problems between family members or between the family and child protection services agency. They are also more likely to have the parent specifically acknowledge the need for services.

* Evidence suggests that mediation produces savings in time and money for the dependency court. Cases mediated, rather than adjudicated, at jurisdiction and disposition are less likely to result in subsequent contested review hearings.

* Mediated settlements enjoy greater compliance by parents, at least in the short run.

* A variety of mediation models are effective.

## NOTES AND QUESTIONS

1. What are some of the perceived dangers of child welfare court mediation programs, as outlined by the Thoennes article? Do you think public defenders were justified in their concern that mediation would be used as "just another way to get their clients to submit"? Do these types of dangers exist in child access cases as well? What is your impression of the attorneys who wanted to use mediation to afford their clients "another 'reality check' "as to their demands and expectations? Do you think the attorneys were justified in thinking that mediation would be used for "free discovery" by some attorneys?

2. Thoennes writes that "mediators have a clear grasp of the dynamics among the parties and they are equally demanding on all sides." Does this description suggest any particular style of mediating that may have been used in these California counties? What style do you think would work best?

3. Thoennes argues in her summary that "there is no evidence that certain types of maltreatment should be screened out of the process." Do you think any particular types of issues, such as domestic violence or child sexual abuse, should be screened out from child welfare mediation?

## C. CRITIQUE OF CHILD WELFARE MEDIATION

Not all reviewers of child welfare mediation have been as positive as Nancy Thoennes. In the following article excerpt, Amy Sinden critiques mediation and other informal methods for resolving disputes in the child welfare context.

### WHY WON'T MOM COOPERATE?: A CRITIQUE OF INFORMALITY IN CHILD WELFARE PROCEEDINGS[2]

11 Yale J.L. & Feminism 339, 339–40, 353–54, 355, 356–57, 379–81, 386–87, 391–92, 396 (1998)

By Amy Sinden

Reams of paper have been filled with the ruminations of countless judges and legal scholars on the subject of criminal procedure. It is the central concern of four of the ten constitutional amendments that make up the Bill of Rights. It is a major course offered at every law school. And it is the paradigmatic context in which we frame much of our debate about the relationship between the state and the individual in a democratic society.

But there is another system that exists in every county across the country, in which the state hauls private citizens into court against their will, accuses them of acts that trigger severe social reprobation, and threatens them with a deprivation of liberty that, for many people, strikes at the very core of their identity and threatens to remove the most profound source of purpose, fulfillment, and happiness from their lives. This is the child welfare system. . . .

[T]he predominance of social work norms and discourse creates significant pressure on parents to resolve these cases through non-adversarial, informal means. Social workers are trained to be effective by building non-adversarial relationships characterized by cooperation and trust. From a social worker's point of view, she fails professionally if her relationship with her client becomes adversarial. While lawyers' training steeps them in the discourse of individual rights and prepares them to operate in formal, procedure-bound environments, social workers are steeped in the discourse of relationships and cooperation and trained to value informality over formality as a means of gaining trust and building rapport.

A key word in the prevailing social work discourse is thus "cooperation." This word often forms the focal point of the meetings and conversations that take place in the hallways of the courthouse: "If mom would just cooperate . . . " Running as an undercurrent to this refrain are powerful cultural stereotypes and expectations attached to motherhood. Mothers are supposed to be nurturing, loving, and above all protective of their children. Conflict is viewed as harmful to the child, and therefore the mother accused of child abuse who creates conflict by failing to "cooperate" harms her child a second time. This language of "cooperation" cloaks the substantial power differential that exists between the child welfare agency and the accused mother. The word "cooperation" implies a collaboration between equals in which each party contributes and makes compromises. In the child welfare context, however, "coopera-

---

tion" is frequently just a code word for the parent doing whatever the social worker tells her to do. Where there is disagreement between the parties, it is the mother, not the social worker, who is labeled "uncooperative," and therefore blamed for creating conflict.

. . . .

In addition to these implicit pressures that operate on a day-to-day level to de-formalize the existing adversarial system, there is currently a movement to explicitly de-formalize the child welfare court system by introducing alternative dispute resolution ("ADR") mechanisms, primarily mediation. . . .

Proponents of mediation cite a number of benefits in addition to its ability to ease crowded dockets. Mediation is said to encourage participation by parents by giving them a sense of inclusion, validation, and empowerment. This decreases the likelihood that parents will withdraw from the process and leave their children feeling rejected. The parties' sense of inclusion and investment in the process is also said to give mediated agreements a greater chance of long-term success. But primarily, mediation is touted as an antidote to the adversarial process, which is viewed as inherently destructive to families and harmful to children. The adversarial process is said to break down communication, polarize disputants, create hostility, and "tear at the thin fabric that holds these families together." . . .

The formal adversarial process is designed to produce accurate decisions by bringing out all relevant facts and limiting bias and prejudice. Because adversaries each present their position in an attempt to persuade the judge to rule in their favor, each side is motivated to ferret out all the evidence that supports its position. Each side is also motivated to view its opponent's evidence critically and to undermine it through cross-examination and the introduction of contradictory evidence or evidence showing bias or lack of credibility. This motivation is critically important, particularly in a system in which professionals are juggling high caseloads. The parties' adoption of a conciliatory stance toward each other raises the danger that they will accept statements uncritically and fail to seek out contradictory evidence.

The formal rules that govern trial procedure also help to assure accuracy. Witnesses testify under oath under threat of penalty for perjury. The judge excludes unreliable evidence, like hearsay, as well as evidence likely to cause prejudice. The requirement that judges state the basis for their decisions helps to ensure that decisions are based on a rational view of the evidence and not on prejudice or bias. Numerous rules governing judges' conduct in adversarial proceedings encourage impartiality and the appearance of impartiality. Thus, judges sit higher than and at some distance from the parties, and usually address only the lawyers. When they do address the parties directly they do so formally and on the record. And they do not communicate with one party out of the presence of the other party.

Of course, these mechanisms are far from perfect, and it is beyond question that trials can and often do reach inaccurate results skewed by judges' prejudice and partiality. Where decision making occurs without these formal constraints, however, it is even more susceptible to being swayed by prejudices, stereotypes, and snap judgments based on innuendo and rumor. Mediators are trained to maintain impartiality and neutrality, but because their role is to facilitate communication between the parties rather than to judge, they do not maintain the same kind of physical and psychological distance from the parties that judges do. They sit closer to the parties, talk to them directly in an informal style, and may speak to one party without the presence of the other and without subsequently relating to the other what was said. This more intimate and informal setting may make mediation "an environment in which prejudices can flourish."

The danger that prejudice or incomplete or unreliable information will distort decisions is particularly acute in the emotionally-charged arena of dependency and termination cases. Where so much is at stake — the suffering of children — the players in the system are all the more likely to make snap judgments based on gut feelings and instinct and to cut corners in an attempt to manipulate decisions to conform to their own view of the right outcome. Imagine, for example, a social worker who is convinced in his gut that a mother is severely beating her child. Maybe it is because the look in her eyes is exactly the same one he saw in another mother who seriously injured her child after he failed to act quickly enough. In the face of such a feeling, imagine how tempted the social worker must be to remove the child immediately without bothering to confirm all the facts — to perhaps accept at face value the estranged father's hearsay statement that the doctor had said the broken bone could only have been the product of abuse. Because of these pressures, the evidentiary constraints and protections against bias and prejudice afforded by formality are particularly important in the child welfare context . . . .

Proponents of de-formalization, however, argue that informal proceedings lead to more just outcomes because when parties are not locked in an adversarial win/lose posture and are able to step back from the rhetoric of blame and rights that dominates formal proceedings, they are able to find a third way — creative solutions that meet all parties needs. Certainly it is possible to imagine such a dynamic producing positive results in a child welfare case. A mediation process may encourage the parties to think outside the box of the adversarial paradigm that insists on winning and defines winning narrowly: for the parent, a dismissal; for the agency, placement of the child in foster care. Instead, in the non-confrontational, needs-centered atmosphere of media-tion, the mother may be able to admit that she needs drug treatment while communicating to the agency the sincerity of her desire to improve and the strength of her bond with her child. The agency may be able to re-frame its position from insisting on foster care to simply needing assurance that the child will be safe. Out of this softening of positions the possibility for a third way — placement of the mother and child together in a mother-child drug treatment program — might arise.

But in the child welfare context, the vast disparity in power between the parties distorts this process. Too often informality results in the weaker party — the parent — simply capitulating to the agency rather than pushing the agency to find the creative third way. The "win-win" solution so frequently touted by the proponents of informality requires a creative tension between the parties that tends to arise only when the parties are roughly equally matched in power. Otherwise there is no leverage to dislodge the stronger party from its position. This is particularly true in the child welfare context where the agency's position can often be well entrenched. First, because the agency inevitably equates its own win with the best interests of the child, it may often approach a dispute resolution proceeding with the intransigence of those who believe they are "on the side of the angels." Secondly, in the child welfare context, the creative third way often involves the agency providing some innovative service to the family that allows the parent and child to stay together while addressing the problem that led to the agency's involvement — for example a mother-child drug treatment program, a supervised group home for teenage mothers, or financial assistance in obtaining housing. But these solutions are usually more costly than the standard package of services and require initiative on the part of the agency social worker. Unless the parent has sufficient power to exert some leverage on the agency, such solutions are frequently out of reach. Parents can sometimes exert leverage in a formal adversarial process by seeking a court order compelling the agency to provide innovative services in order to fulfill its legal mandate to make reasonable efforts to preserve the family. No such leverage is available in an informal proceeding, however.

Additionally, the "win-win" solution depends on the parties having a set of shared values so that there is some set of cultural norms in common that can form a basis for agreement. Otherwise informality will simply result either in a stand-off or in the weaker party capitulating to the cultural norms of the more powerful party.

Much of the rhetoric promoting the use of informal procedures in child welfare cases is borrowed from the domestic relations context, where mediation has been used extensively for many years in divorce and custody cases. But the domestic relations paradigm cannot simply be transplanted to the dependency context. The alignment of the parties is fundamentally different. Domestic relations cases involve disputes between private parties. There may be some disparity of power between them, and, indeed, many feminists have criticized the use of informal procedures in domestic relations cases for that reason, especially in instances where the power disparity is particularly acute, like those involving battering. Still, in domestic relations cases the vast power disparity between the individual and the state that exists in child welfare cases is absent. Moreover, in the domestic relations context, the parties have an existing intimate relationship which they entered into voluntarily and which they will often need to preserve — though in some altered form — in order to continue to share parenting responsibilities. Thus, often in a domestic relations case, determining accurately what occurred in some past event is less important than reaching a compromise that addresses both parties' needs and preserves a workable relationship for the future. Additionally the fact that there was at some point a voluntary intimate relationship between the parties indicates a set of shared values or at least a commitment to reconciling conflicting values.

The move to de-formalize child welfare cases attempts to squeeze these disputes into the domestic relations paradigm, locating them in the realm of family therapy rather than adjudication. Thus, one particular mediation program is touted as "cathartic" and as providing the parents a chance to "vent." The issue is viewed not as whether the parent committed some act of child abuse or neglect that warrants state intervention, but how to facilitate communication between the participants and how to reach a compromise that meets all of their needs. Principles of blame and rights are replaced with the rhetoric of compromise and relationship. The conflict is "styled as a personal quarrel, in which there is no right and wrong, but simply two different equally true or untrue views of the world."

By identifying communication as the problem, however, the proponents of mediation presume that the state is entitled to have a relationship with the parent. This involves two false assumptions: first, that all parents are guilty (i.e., intervention is warranted), and, second, that intervention is always helpful to a family (or at least not harmful.)

. . . .

Conclusion

. . . .

I have argued that, at least in termination of parental rights cases and at the initial adjudicatory phase of dependency cases, traditional formal adversarial process offers the best hope of protecting against the distortions of power imbalance and the dangers of prejudice and snap judgments. I do not mean to argue that formality offers the perfect solution. My analysis has proceeded largely based on what is, with little speculation about what might be. By endorsing formality as the best among existing alternatives, I do not mean to suggest that a better third way might not be imagined.

## D.  ALTERNATIVE PROCESSES

At least two additional forms of self-determinative multi-party forums have been established in the child welfare arena: the Family Team Decision Making Meeting (FTDM) and Family Group Conferencing.

### 1.  Family Team Decision-Making Meetings

In states where Family Team Decision-Making Meetings (FTDMs) have been established, the meetings occur any time a change in the placement of the child is contemplated, including, in some states, at the child's initial removal from the parent or parent's home. Participants at the FTDMs may include parents, the child at issue, the attorney for the child, foster parents, therapists, community members, service providers, a Court Appointed Special Advocate for the child, and anyone else that the family believes can help them determine the most appropriate living arrangement for the child. Unlike mediations, the FTDMs follow a specific format, beginning with introductions and a recitation of child and/or family strengths, and then move into the sharing of ideas among participants. But, like all child welfare mediations, the parties discuss the matter against the backdrop of knowledge that if they do not reach a consensus on the best plan for the child, the child welfare worker assigned to the case will determine the placement for the child. The participants, of course, can always challenge that placement in court.

### 2.  Family Group Conferencing

Family Group Conferencing (FGC) found its way to the United States child welfare community by way of New Zealand, where the government introduced FGC to child welfare cases. The goal of Family Group Conferencing was to strive for a formula that

stemmed from the way of life of the Maori Tribe and other native peoples of New
Zealand which emphasizes family strengths and relies on involvement of community in
family decision making. While Team Decision Making meetings are used by the child
welfare system to determine placement for a child, Family Group Conferencing is
perhaps best used to build a service and recovery plan for the family. As a family
strength-based practice, Family Group Conferencing becomes a tool to enhance the
chances that a child will be able to return *safely* to the biological family. One aspect
unique to Family Group Conferencing is the family time portion of the meeting, during
which all service providers depart from the conferencing room and leave the family
and extended family members to discuss and iron out the issues privately.

# *RIGHTS MYOPIA IN CHILD WELFARE*[3]
## 53 UCLA L. Rev. 637, 674–84, 687 (2006)
### By Clare Huntington

## I. Origins, the Process, and Theoretical Underpinnings

Family group conferencing is part of the broader restorative justice movement,
which seeks to reform the justice system to incorporate victims and to allow the
offender to "restore" the status quo. Although largely focused on criminal justice, the
restorative justice movement has also addressed other systems, including child
welfare. In that context, family group conferencing is the practice of convening family
members, community members, and other individuals or institutions involved with a
family to develop a plan to ensure the care and protection of a child who is at risk for
abuse or neglect.

Simplified descriptions of two cases, one receiving traditional child welfare services
and one receiving a family group conference, illustrate the marked differences
between the two approaches. In a child welfare case under the current system, after
the state agency receives a credible report of child abuse or neglect sufficient to
warrant removal, a caseworker goes to the home and assesses the danger to the child.
Assuming the caseworker finds sufficient evidence of such danger, the caseworker
removes the child and places her in foster care pending a more thorough investigation.
The state agency then files a petition in court seeking temporary custody of the child.
The child is assigned a guardian ad litem to represent her interests. The caseworker
then develops a case plan for the parents, requiring the parents to, for example, obtain
drug treatment and attend parenting classes. If the parents do not comply with this
case plan within the specified period, generally twelve to eighteen months, then the
state agency files for a petition for the termination of parental rights. If the court
agrees that parental rights should be terminated, the child is freed for adoption. The
majority of decisions in this model are made by professionals: caseworkers, therapists,
guardians ad litem, and judges.

In a family group conferencing case, the story and decision makers are decidedly
different. In a typical family group conferencing case, after receiving a report, a social

---

[3] Copyright ©2006. Reprinted with permission.

worker conducts an initial investigation to determine if there has been abuse or neglect. If the social worker concludes there is evidence of abuse or neglect, she refers the case to a coordinator, who has the authority to convene a family group conference. The coordinator contacts the parents, the child, extended family members, and significant community members who know the family. Before the conference, each potential conference participant meets separately with the coordinator to learn about the process. In these meetings, the coordinator screens for potentially complicating factors, such as a history of domestic violence, to determine whether the case is appropriate for family group conferencing and, if so, what additional supports may be needed for the participants.

There are three stages of the conference. In the first stage, the coordinator and any professionals involved with the family, such as therapists, teachers, and the investigating social worker, explain the case to the family. In the second stage, the coordinator and professionals leave the room while the family and community members engage in private deliberation. During the private deliberation, the participants acknowledge that the child was abused or neglected and develop a plan to protect the child and help the parents. After the participants reach an agreement, they present the plan to the social worker and coordinator, who likely have questions for the participants. Parents, custodians, social workers, and coordinators can veto the plan produced by the conference and refer the case to court. In practice, this rarely occurs: The participants come to a decision, and the social worker and coordinator accept the plan (perhaps with a few changes) if it meets predetermined criteria. The coordinator writes up the plan, sends it to all participants, and then sets a time for a subsequent conference to assess developments in the case.

The plan typically includes a decision about the safety of the child, including whether the child should be placed outside of the home for a certain period of time, and, if so, with whom. If the child is placed outside the home, she is almost invariably placed with a relative or other conference participant. The plan also identifies the services and supports needed by the parents. Finally, the plan determines which participants will both help the family and also check in on a regular basis to ensure the child is safe and the parents are complying with the plan. As is apparent from this description, five principles characterize the philosophy of family group conferencing. First, children are raised best in their own families. Second, families have the primary responsibility for caring for their children, and these families should be supported, protected, and respected. Third, families are able to make reliable, safe decisions for their children, and families have strengths and are capable of changing the problems in their lives. Fourth, families are their own experts, with knowledge and insight into which solutions will work best for them. Finally, to achieve family empowerment, families must have the freedom to make their own decisions and choices.

As one of its proponents has stated, "[f]amily group conferences amount to a partnership arrangement between the state, represented by child protection officials; the family; and members of the community, such as resource and support persons; with each party expected to play an important role in planning and providing services necessary for the well-being of children." Family group conferences are not a means for child protection officials to relinquish their responsibilities, but rather are a different method for exercising those responsibilities. The intent is to strike a balance between the interests of child protection and family support. Family group conferencing represents a radical reorientation of child protection: Many child protection approaches attempt to enforce community standards (accountability) but lack any way for the community to reach out and weave the family back into the community fabric with the development of shared, voluntary commitments to community standards. Consequently, those strategies often create short-term relief, but do not change behavior in the long term. Those strategies also rely heavily on outside enforcers, the professional system, to solve the problem.

Family group conferencing originated with the Maori and other First Nations around the world, and New Zealand was the first country to incorporate the process into its laws. To avoid the removal of Maori children to non-Maori families, and to incorporate Maori traditions of involving extended family members in decision-making, legislative changes were made to New Zealand's child welfare system in the Children, Young Persons, and Their Families Act of 1989. The changes were in response to several government reports documenting discrimination against Maori families in the child welfare system. The legislative changes were not limited to Maori families. Rather, the law required that all substantiated cases of child abuse and neglect be referred for family group conferencing. The premises of family group conferences resonated with the idea, long-espoused by social workers, "that lasting solutions to problems are ones that grow out of, or can fit with, the knowledge, experiences, and desires of the people most affected."

There are four hallmarks of the family group conferencing process (and these hallmarks reflect the principles set forth above). First, the process is intended to find and build on a family's strengths, rather than to place blame. One method for achieving this is to focus on the problem, rather than the person, and to concentrate on healing. Although the current system is supposed to preserve families, in practice social workers often do not look for the strengths in a family and instead focus on the dysfunctional elements. Thus, family group conferencing facilitates a strengths-based practice because it requires the family and community to look within to find solutions. Second, the process respects and values important cultural practices of the relevant community. Third, the process involves the extended family and community. Those individuals with information to share, individuals who love the child, and individuals with a stake in the outcome are all included in the conference. Finally, the process views the community as a resource for the family.

In addition to the four hallmarks of family group conferencing, there are several key features of the process that set it apart from other alternative dispute resolution methods and are essential for its success. These key elements include sufficient preparation of the participants by the coordinator (often a total of thirty-five hours of preparation per conference, private family time without professionals present, consensus on the plan, and monitoring and follow-up by the conference participants and the state.

Although no country other than New Zealand requires the use of family group conferencing, many countries have started to experiment with it. In the United States, child welfare agencies have been experimenting with family group conferencing since the early 1990s. Although its use is by no means widespread, states and localities are using some version of it with increasing frequency. Notably, in the United States, social workers, rather than lawyers and legislators, have pushed for its adoption.

## B. Early Empirical Research

Studies on programs implemented around the world and in the United States demonstrate that family group conferencing has had substantial success in improving child welfare systems. First, studies suggest, but are not uniform in concluding, that families who participate in family group conferences have lower levels of subsequent abuse and neglect than the typical child welfare case. This may be due in part to the way family group conferences enlist family members in monitoring the safety and welfare of children.

Second, research indicates that in the vast majority of cases families are able to devise a plan for the care and protection of their children. Family members, including fathers, participate in numbers far greater than in the traditional child welfare model. Caseworkers report that the plans devised by the participants often require more of the parent than the agency typically would. Conference participants play an active role in finding a solution for the troubles facing the family by providing, for example, child care, home furnishings, transportation, housing, and help with managing the household. Although participating family members have multiple problems, including substance abuse and histories of violence, these participants are able to create thoughtful and detailed plans to keep the children safe. These plans draw on familial and professional resources. . . .

Third, participants report satisfaction with the process and result. For example, one mother described her experience as follows:

There comes a time when you think "I can take control now" and that's when I think the normal way of running social services departments falls down. Yes people come initially because they do need a certain amount of support and a certain amount of help. But if you go on trying [to] nursemaid and suffocate that person then their growth isn't going to take place. The social services, the way it's run at the moment actually doesn't allow the person who has to . . . take control, they're very reluctant to give that person back the control of the family. So social services becomes the head of the family, and the mother and the father, or one of them, becomes more or less like a child themselves, and they regress into no responsibility, because they're instructed all the way, what their responsibilities are. But they are not actually helped to rebuild their confidence to enable them to take up the full responsibility.

Fourth, there is evidence that family group conferencing fosters development of a strong support network within the child's extended family and community. For example, when the plan does recommend placement outside of the immediate family, children are more often placed with extended family members. . . .

The process also fosters stronger ties between the family and the community. Research has demonstrated that ties to the community are particularly important to help an at-risk child overcome difficult family circumstances and that emotional support outside of the immediate family can be a crucial protective factor for children who grow up in high-risk environments.

Finally, to the extent the process prevents the placement of children in the foster care system, it could well generate significant savings for federal, state, and local governments. . . .

Family group conferencing holds great potential for the child welfare system. Although it may be no panacea for the very difficult issues facing the system, the relevant question is whether family group conferencing, and a problem-solving model more generally, is a marked improvement over the current legal framework, which clearly is not serving the interests of parents or children.

## NOTES AND QUESTIONS

1.   What do you see as the primary distinctions between Family Group Conferencing and other forms of alternative dispute resolution? What makes Family Group Conferencing particularly well-suited to child welfare cases? Can you think of other forums in which Family Group Conferencing would aid in the resolution of disputes?

2.   Would you suggest using Family Group Conferencing in child access cases? How would this practice change the nature of child access mediations? What would be the advantages and disadvantages of using such a practice? What is meant by "strength-based practice" and how could this apply to child access and other types of mediation?

3.   What do you think of the practice of the participants meeting in private session, without any of the professionals? Should it be necessary that they "acknowledge that the child was abused or neglected" during this private meeting? Why does this acknowledgement happen as part of the private session? What else do you imagine might happen during the private session?

4.   Why do you think Professor Huntington describes Family Group Conferencing as falling within the restorative justice movement? Who is restored? Would you describe other forms of mediation and alternative dispute resolution in this way?

5.   Do you think that these alternative methods of resolving child welfare matters can change the nature of this system from one of accusation and defense to one of gathering resources from and for the community?

6.   Dorothy Roberts and other legal scholars accurately point to a disproportionate percentage of children of color and poor families embroiled in the child welfare system in the United States. In 2000, African American/Black children represented 36 percent of the foster care population, even though they comprised only 15 percent of the general child population. *See, e.g.,* Dorothy Roberts, *Under-Intervention Versus Over-Intervention, in* Symposium: *Advocating for Change: The Status & Future of America's Child Welfare System 30 Years After CAPTA,* 3 Cardozo Pub. L. Pol'y & Ethics J. 371 (2005). What do you see as reasons for this disparity and how should alternative dispute resolution mechanisms be structured in light of this reality? Compare the manner in which New Zealand responded to the family system and needs of the Maori Tribe with the way in which the United States removed Native American children from their tribes and families en masse in the last two centuries. Do you think

that Family Group Conferencing might be particularly well-suited in cases involving Native American children in the United States?

# Chapter 6

# MEDIATING FINANCIAL ISSUES

## A. INTRODUCTION

Family mediators are often called upon to mediate issues concerning the finances of a divorcing couple. Mediation of financial issues is most common in private mediation but some states are beginning to include financial issues in court sponsored mediation programs. One commentator summarized the reasons why more states might mandate the mediation of financial issues:

> Courts and legislatures, buoyed by the success that mediation seems to have had on docket clearing, reductions in re-hearings, and party satisfaction, might expand jurisdiction to include other matters that are taking court time. Academic theorists corroborate that mediation is a better way to proceed in divorce, observing that money and custody issues are interrelated. A mediator's resolution of custody matters often directs the resolution of financial matters; therefore, the separation of issues is artificial. Parties who find that mediation helped them settle custody and visitation matters amicably, and who want to resolve everything that way, might be dismayed to discover that the mediator cannot address matters outside her jurisdiction. These parties may want to expand mediation's scope so that they can have one-stop shopping. . . . Mediators may see an expansion of the scope of their jurisdiction as a way to increase the number of hours for which they can charge the courts for their services. They also may feel that they are underserving their clients when they are prohibited from addressing financial matters in the divorce. (footnotes omitted)

*Mandating Mediation of Money: The Implications of Enlarging the Scope of Domestic Relations Mediation from Custody to Full Service*, 35 WILLAMETTE L. REV. 485, 495 (2000)

When courts resolve financial issues, they tend to view "finances" as a series of related but discrete issues — marital property, alimony, or child support. Mediation, however, enables families to take a more holistic approach to their finances. Where children are involved, mediation allows parents to focus on what the children's financial needs will be post-divorce rather than only the parents' legal rights to property. It also may promote collaboration among participants to craft budgets that permit adults to meet increased expenses post-separation rather than to maximize financial gain under existing legal norms. Despite these different approaches, mediation of financial issues is generally recognized to be an area where legal norms are relevant, and participants involve lawyers and financial specialists more often than is done in child access mediation.

The readings in this Chapter provide an overview of the law typically applied to resolve financial issues, a discussion of the skills and techniques of mediating financial issues and an excerpt from a mediation that included conflicts about the division of marital property and alimony, including the mediator's reflections on the interplay of legal and participant-generated norms when mediating such issues.

## B.  LEGAL NORMS

### 1.  Child Support

In the United States, parents are primarily responsible for bearing the cost of raising their children. Both parents, whether married or not, have a legal obligation to support their biological or adopted minor (usually through 18) or adult disabled children. Over the last century, states struggled to develop methods of calculating child support awards that are fair to both parents and provide sufficiently for the child. More recently, the legal landscape with respect to child support has changed dramatically. Primarily as result of federal intervention, states adopted mandatory child support guidelines. Consequently judges no longer exercised so much discretion and, in contrast to other areas of family law, uniformity and predictability are valued over in-depth consideration of individual needs.

If parents do not meet the basic needs of the children, the state provides support in the form of public assistance. As a result, the development of the law regarding child support has been driven largely by the requirements of public assistance programs. For example, one of the first federal interventions into the child support arena was to require public assistance recipients to cooperate in obtaining and enforcing child support orders and assign their rights to child support to a state. If a child support is paid for children receiving public assistance, it goes to the state not the custodial parent. Thus, although the child support system is administered pursuant to state law, those laws and their enforcement have been substantially shaped by federal public welfare policy.

State child support guidelines constitute a rebuttable presumption that the amount of support awarded under the guidelines is correct. Although one or both parents can seek a deviation from the guidelines amount, courts rigorously apply them. When deviations are approved, they are likely to involve either upper deviation because the parent paying child support (obligor) has agreed to pay more or downward deviations because the obligor is making other payments to benefit the child.

States have adopted child support guidelines based on different underlying models. The majority of states use some form of the Income Shares Model discussed below. Although state guidelines constitute a rebuttable presumption that the amount of support awarded is correct, courts may exercise some discretion in applying the guidelines. For example, parents may seek deviations from the guidelines, obligors may contest the definition of income and, under certain conditions, courts may impute income to one or both parents if they are "voluntarily impoverished" — i.e., able to work but under or unemployed.

## 2.  Spousal Support

Spousal support, alimony, and maintenance are terms used interchangeably to describe the obligation of one spouse to provide income to the other spouse during and after divorce. The obligation to pay such support is generally limited to an individual the obligor has married as opposed to parties who have cohabited without marriage.

The conceptual basis of spousal support has deep historical roots, and judicial decisions regarding spousal support often reflect different perspectives on marriage and divorce. For example, historically husbands and wives were considered to be one person, and the husband had a duty to support the wife throughout her life unless she committed adultery or left the marital home without provocation. Today spouses are viewed as equal partners and it is no longer assumed that the husband will provide for the wife upon divorce. As a consequence statutes and court decisions regarding spousal support and its duration have become more complicated and more difficult to predict. Unlike child support, formal statutory guidelines to determine the amount of support are not uniformly required in every state. While some courts may use formal or informal guidelines, judges are vested with broad discretion to determine whether to award alimony and how much should be paid. Statutes and courts tend to fashion spousal support awards toward a specific purpose or purposes. For example, rehabilitative support is designed to enable a former spouse to gain training and education in order to become financially independent. Reimbursement spousal support compensates a spouse for financial sacrifices made during the marriage. Courts may view divorce as analogous to a breach of a contract or dissolution of a partnership and may employ spousal support as a tool to apportion financial consequences more fairly. In some states spousal support may also serve to compensate a spouse who suffered from his or her partner's marital misconduct.

## 3.  Marital Property

When a marriage dissolves and the parties are unable to negotiate or mediate how property will be divided, the matter must be resolved by a judge. As discussed in earlier readings, the parties and judge have guidelines to resolve the child support issue. Its resolution is not dependent, except to the extent alimony might affect the amount of income each party has, on how alimony and property are decided. Alimony and property, however, are inter-related and the principle way marital assets are divided at divorce.

There are three primary property distribution systems that have been used at various times to divide the assets of a divorcing couple: 1) the separate title system; 2) the community property system, which is used today in about nine jurisdictions; and 3) the equitable distribution system, which is used today in over 40 jurisdictions.

At common law, a majority of states used the title system to divide property when a divorce occurred. This meant that each party was entitled to retain an asset that was titled in his or her name at the end of the marriage. In a pure title jurisdiction, a spouse obtained ownership interest in the property titled in the other spouse's name only upon the latter's death to the operation of dower, curtesy, or statutory forced share. Thus, one spouse can emerge from divorce owning all the property acquired during the marriage. The separate title system was criticized as unjust, especially in during a time when most of the property was titled in the husband's name. She (almost always the wife) was left with little but a claim for alimony, which often proved difficult to obtain or impossible if the wife was found to be at fault. The title system did not recognize non-monetary contributions to the marriage, such as child rearing. The obvious unfair treatment of a homemaker under the title-based system has been a driving force in bringing about major reform in divorce law over the past 50 years. This has resulted in title-based jurisdictions moving to some form of equitable or equal distribution of marital property throughout the country. The title-based system is no longer used by any states.

## Community Property

The community property theory, used in this country in its earlier form in several Western states, is an outgrowth of the civil law influence of France, Spain, and Mexico. Today, Arizona, California, Idaho, Louisiana, New Mexico, Nevada, Texas, Washington, and to a large extent, Wisconsin are recognized as community property states.

The community property partnership concept applies during a marriage, upon the dissolution of the marriage or upon the death of one of the partners. In general both spouses are vested in all the property acquired during the marriage, other than property that by statute is specifically excluded from the community, such as a gift to one partner but not the other, or an inheritance to one partner but not the other. In general, a community property state considers a marriage a partnership, in which each spouse possesses an undivided one half interest in property acquired by spousal labor during the relationship. It is presumed that property possessed by either spouse during or on dissolution of marriage is community property. Usually, community property is divided when a marriage is dissolved and each partner is entitled to immediate control over that partner's community property interest.

## Equitable Distribution

1. Underlying Theory: Recognition of economic and non-economic contributions to the marriage

The equitable distribution system also views marriage as a joint enterprise whose vitality, success, and endurance is dependent on the joint efforts, both financial and non-financial, of both parties. The non-remuneration efforts of raising children, making a home, and providing physical and emotional support, among other non-economic ingredients to the marital relationship are seen as essential to the maintenance of the marriage as are the economic factors. Equitable distribution recognizes that when a marriage ends, each of the spouses, based on the totality of the contributions made to the marriage, has a stake in and a right to a share of the marital assets accumulated because they represent the capital product of what was essentially a partnership entity.

2. Three step approach

When distributing property in a contested dissolution in an equitable distribution jurisdiction, a judge has three tasks. First the judge must identify and classify the property by creating a complete list of all assets involved in the action and then determine whether the property is marital or non-marital property. Second, once the list is prepared and has been classified as either marital or nonmarital, the next step is to place a reasonable value on the assets. Finally the court determines, based upon statutory factors, how the property should be "equitably" distributed.

## C.  IMPLEMENTING APPROACHES TO MEDIATION OF FINANCIAL ISSUES

The intended outcome of any mediation is an agreement that is durable — i.e., will withstand the test of time. In order to accomplish that, the mediator must 1) obtain competent and complete data and 2) understand the foundation behind the "positioning" that the parties bring to the mediation. The mediator also must understand and educate the parties as to the impact of the potential agreement, both short term as well as the long-term implications. What is thought as fair and equitable today may look very different when viewed though a long-term lens. Mediators who only view the settlement in today's lens may find that one or both parties have financial issues down the road, which could have been spared or solved had they been dealt with during the mediation.

Mediation of finances uses the law as a "reference point" rather than as a mandate. Instead of the parties relying on a judge to make decisions relating to their finances, they are making the decisions themselves. Except in community property states, the only legal requirements are that child support be included at or above the guidelines amount and that the property division be fair and equitable. Judges define what is fair and equitable differently depending on the facts and circumstances of the cases, allowing them much discretion in reaching a decision on alimony and marital property. This "moving line" allows the parties to decide what is fair and equitable within reason in mediation. The mediator's role is to help the parties in understanding what they can agree will be fair and equitable, as well as to guide them to this result. This collaborative approach toward achieving fairness strengthens the agreement, resulting in a more durable agreement.

So, what is competent data? In order for any mediation be successful, there must be cooperation and full disclosure of the parties. From the finance side, generalities as to assets, liabilities and budgets are both dangerous as well as elusive. Accordingly, though the mediator may wish to begin the mediation with a general understanding of the financial condition of both parties, the mediator must obtain a more specific understanding of all the finances by the end of the mediation. This would include obtaining copies of statements showing bank, retirement and investment accounts, tax returns, pay stubs and credit cards. Should the parties have children, it is always best to obtain copies of health insurance premium notices, child care expenses, and any other item relating to child support guideline calculations. Obtaining this level of competent data helps to ensure that the settlement is based on sound decisions, while reducing the possibility that one spouse may not be truthful about financial condition.

A household may include two adults who have relatively equal knowledge of financial matters or may have one party who takes care of the family finances, while the other spouse attends to other family matters. This often leads to certain ignorance as to the family finances by one spouse. As a result, the mediator must spend adequate time not only aiding the knowledgeable spouse to compile the data necessary to deal with the finance issues surrounding the mediation, but often must spend time with the "non-finance" spouse educating him or her as to the financial issues that exist today, as well as the financial outcome of the settlement discussed.

Most mediators try to get the participants to see their finances in a holistic way. The participants develop a budget based on their needs in creating two households and adjust it as they look at current and potential income. Despite this holistic approach, agreements for transfers of income and assets often get described in the written agreement as alimony, child support and marital property. This allows parties to submit the agreement to a court as part of the process of obtaining a divorce or other order. Each of these components of the agreement are discussed below

### Alimony/Spousal Support.

In most states, alimony is not required, but is allowed to be paid by one spouse to the other. There are a number of types of alimony, i.e., permanent, rehabilitative and reimbursing alimony. All alimony must be discussed as part of the budgeting phase of the mediation in order to ensure that the agreement on alimony is affordable. Without reviewing the impact of alimony on the budget, the agreement may be doomed before it is even ratified. Alimony is typically terminated upon certain events under law, i.e., death of either party, remarriage of the recipient party, and, in some cases, cohabitation by the recipient party with another consenting adult for a specific period of time. The legal norms in a particular jurisdiction should help guide the agreement on alimony but do not bind the participants in the same way as child support law binds the participants. The mediator must approach the discussion with care, allowing the parties to see this issue as part of a larger process of reallocating resources so that both participants can sustain a household after divorce. In addition to deciding how much alimony will be paid and when it will be terminated, the mediator must also help the parties to discuss whether the alimony is modifiable or non-modifiable, dealing with the possibility that financial conditions may change. Finally, a discussion must be included about the tax implications of alimony, i.e., the alimony will probably be deductible by the payor spouse and includable in income of the recipient, or non-deductible/non-includable.

### Child Support.

This is an issue where the "three legs of the stool meet", i.e., the law, child access decisions and finances. As discussed earlier, unlike other financial issues, there are legal requirements about both how child support will be calculated and how to enforce such obligations. Child support is based not only on income and certain expenses of the parents, but how the child's residential time is divided which should be worked out before turning to support. One would think that this would lead to a simple calculation of the child support obligation that may be due. However, this is not the case. Instead, once child support has been calculated, a decision must be made as to how to make this payment. Payment may be made from the obligated spouse to the recipient spouse, to child care or health providers, or even in some cases to the state where the child is receiving public assistance. Finally, using the budgets of the parties, there must be discussion of whether the child support is affordable. Given that the parties have little discretion about the amount of child support (at least about the minimum to be paid), there is often a discussion surrounding changes needed in other areas of the family budget in order to ensure that child support payments can be made in a complete and timely manner.

**Marital Property.**

**Marital Home**. A marital home, should the couple own one, is typically the largest financial investment that the couple will ever make. Division of the asset can have both emotional as well as financial repercussions. From the emotional side, this may be the home that one party grew up in, or the home that they both raised their children in. Unfortunately, logic may not always dictate the result when emotional considerations are overriding. Sometimes even pointing out that maintaining the marital home is unaffordable will make little difference to the outcome. Though this condition is unfortunate, all the mediator can do is point out the financial ramifications to the clients and let them make their own decisions. However, when the clients understand the finances, and do not weigh the emotional considerations to be more important than the financial, the mediator can aid them in understanding the options and decisions to be made. These may include: (a) whether to keep or sell the home, often considering the children's needs, (b) which party should reside in the property, (c) whether the property may be refinanced and how to re-title the home so that one spouse (not both) is liable on the mortgage, (d) how to understand and evaluate issues relating to disproportionate amounts each spouse may have contributed to the down payment or maintenance of the property, and (e) how to divide anticipated proceeds from a sale of the house. From a property transfer perspective, aside from pensions and retirement assets, the mediator may spend significant time dealing with issues related to the marital residence.

**Pension and retirement assets.** This is a complex area where the mediator or another neutral expert may often need to assume an educational role. First, the mediator will need to clarify the nature of the asset. Many people refer to a Defined Benefit retirement account as a "Pension" and a 401k or IRA account as a Retirement Asset. They are all governed by Section 401 of the Internal Revenue Code. The difference between these retirement assets really lies in how they are valued and the form of the benefit paid in retirement.

A Defined Benefit retirement account allows you to predict with some certainty the anticipated "benefit" that the participant will receive at a certain date or age, e.g., the monthly payment at a future date. Although the payment at a future date can be calculated with a Defined Benefit plan, it is complex to calculate the current value of the plan. To estimate the present value of a Defined Benefit account, the mediator (or more likely a pension valuation expert) must make actuarial calculations based upon: (a) the number of years until retirement, (b) the number of years the participant will live, and (c) the anticipated investment experience (discount rate) that the account will likely have. Once this calculation is made, most mediators will draw from legal norms to the let the parties know what portion of the pension would be considered marital property. In most jurisdictions, this is done by determining the number of years the owner of the pension was working while married. If he or she were married the whole time the pension was acquired, the asset is 100 percent marital property. If he or she was only married for half the time the pension was acquired, only half the pension is marital property. Again, in mediation these norms do not bind the parties but provide a guideline about what is considered fair and equitable under the law.

A 401(k) account, an Individual Retirement Account (IRA), or a Profit Sharing account are the most common examples of Defined Contribution accounts. Unlike a Defined Benefit plan, Defined Contribution accounts can easily be valued. You can simply obtain the most current statement for the account and see the value. While it is difficult to predict what the future monthly retirement payment will be for these plans, the current value of these accounts is easy to ascertain. As with the Defined Benefit plan, the mediator can also help the parties understand what portion of the Defined Contribution account is marital property by looking at the number of years the participant contributed to the plan while married.

As with the marital home, the mediator should be prepared that discussions about how to divide this asset may have both a financial and an emotional dimension, e.g., "I saved and you didn't," or "I worked all these years and you got to be with the children." Educating the participants about legal norms on what is considered fair in this complex area may be the mediator's best tool in helping the participants reach an agreement that both believe is fair and equitable.

**Miscellaneous Issues**.

**Life Insurance**. In order that the recipient spouse is guaranteed that agreed upon payments are made in the event of death of the payor spouse, the participants will often agree that the payor spouse will maintain a life insurance policy with the former spouse as beneficiary.

**Tax Issues**. The participants should discuss allocations of tax deductions as well as exemptions, e.g., who will take deductions for the marital residence and how will the exemptions available for the children of the marriage be divided. There are default rules for this by the IRS but the parties are free to deviate from them in a way that makes the most economic sense in their circumstances.

**Circling back**.

After the participants have reached an agreement on the financial issues, the mediator should circle back and discuss the most efficient method to implement the agreements. This is done by reviewing the assets and liabilities so that as few divisions/transfers as possible are made. As an example, it is generally preferable to have one Qualified Domestic Relations Order (QDRO) written, rather than multiple QRDOs, calling upon reallocation of the retirement plan division. Remembering that Individual Retirement Accounts (IRA's) do not require a QDRO, an attempt should be made to use these in lieu of retirement accounts where a QDRO or COAP may otherwise be required, saving the parties the attorney fees to prepare these documents. Where there are many cash or investment accounts calling for asset transfer, try and narrow it down to as few accounts as possible to distribute. This same principle may be used for unsecured debt, e.g., credit cards. Look for credit card or other unsecured debt accounts which may equal the sum of smaller accounts. This approach to finalizing the financial settlement will lead to a simpler result, without compromising the agreement.

## NOTES AND QUESTIONS

1.   Does the existence of state imposed child support formulae help or hinder the mediation process? What are the policy reasons for adhering to fixed formulae in the mediation context versus allowing parties to make their own agreements regarding the support of their children? Is there any room for deviation from the guidelines in a mediated agreement? *See, e.g., Pursley v. Pursely*, 144 S.W.3d 820, 825 (Ky. 2004); *See also*, LAURA W. MORGAN, CHILD SUPPORT GUIDELINES: INTERPRETATION AND APPLICATION (2nd Ed., 2014-updated annually).

2.   Mediators often emphasize the need to approach financial issues "holistically." What is your understanding of this term in this context? What benefits or risks do you see from this approach? A tool many mediators use to implement this approach is some version of budgeting software that builds in child support guidelines and tax consequences and helps the parties plan for a post-separation budget. Most software allows parties to test a variety of scenarios when generating options to understand the impact of changes on expenses and income. As one mediator described it, "This approach engages the parties' mutual goal of 'meeting everyone's needs' which can generate a much more productive discussion than a debate over entitlements to child support and alimony." For one example, see Family Law Software http://www. familylawsoftware.com/)

## D.  MEDIATION OF FINANCIAL ISSUES: ONE EXAMPLE

A mediator makes a variety of choices throughout a mediation session depending upon the nature of the dispute. In addition, the choices made in mediation may also be affected by other issues such as the sophistication of the parties and the presence or absence of legal representation. As you read the following excerpt from a divorce mediation involving financial issues, consider the choices made by family mediator and lawyer Gary Friedman.

### *A GUIDE TO DIVORCE MEDIATION*[1]
70–72, 78–101 (1993)
By Gary J. Friedman

I received a call from a man named Martin one afternoon. He said that he and his wife, Claire, were stuck with a disagreement they couldn't resolve and wondered if mediation could help. I told him that the intensity of their disagreement had no bearing on whether or not mediation would be workable, and that the real question

---

[1] Copyright ©1993. Reprinted with permission.

was were they willing to work together to find a good solution? Martin immediately wanted to describe their situation, but I cut him off, explaining that the process would have a better chance of working if I heard the facts for the first time when we all met together, since I make it a practice not to begin a relationship with one mediation client alone. Martin seemed put off by my response, but agreed to come in with Claire. My first impression of Claire was of an articulate, bright, sensitive woman in her late thirties. Though she looked healthy, when she walked across the room she seemed to shuffle. In the last several years, as she would tell me, she had developed headaches that had only been aggravated by medical treatment. She was now so disabled that she could no longer focus her attention for long or perform any strenuous physical activity. She had not worked for the past three years. Before that she had worked for a variety of nonprofit organizations in low-paying administrative positions. Claire still had dreams of becoming an artist but little confidence that she would be able to support herself in that effort. Martin, in his early forties, was a folk singer with enough of a following to keep him busy on weekends. He taught guitar and piano to aspiring musicians during the week.

When I begin a mediation, I usually start by attempting to I find out what brought the couple to mediation. The variety of responses to this simple question still surprises me. Some people want to tell the whole story of what happened in the marriage. Others want to reveal as little as possible. Martin and Claire were willing to give me a little background, but mainly they wanted to get right to "the heart of the problem." They were too anxious to listen carefully to an explanation of the mediation process. While it is essential in the first session to give the parties a sense of how the process works, the nonverbal creation of a warm, open atmosphere is equally important, so I was willing to postpone my explanation. The room is intended to be a place safe enough for people to say what is on their minds and in their feelings, a place where a certain level of trust can develop.

In his opening remarks, Martin got right to the point. He said that he had become increasingly disenchanted with the life he shared with Claire, and eight months before had suddenly left her to live with another woman. Martin was still living with this new woman and Claire had remained in their house. For Claire, just being in the same room with Martin was very stressful. Before we could begin to talk about what mediation was, she needed to say how hard it was for her to be there. Turning her chair toward me and away from Martin, Claire addressed me directly. It was clear that it was difficult for her to look at Martin. It was almost as if she were making an effort to shut him out of the room.

> *Claire*: Martin's leaving was a great shock. I have been working very hard not to be victimized by my situation. I still don't understand what happened. I know that I can play the role of the rejected woman and have everyone feel sorry for me — my friends do. But I don't enjoy being pitied . . .

In explaining the mediation process to Martin and Claire, I compared it to the litigation option, in which each of them would hire a lawyer. Many people automatically compare mediation to going to court, but since only a small percentage of cases are ever heard by a judge, the fairer comparison is to lawyers negotiating a resolution, There are two major differences between mediation and a negotiated settlement: the directness of the communications and the basis of the decisions reached. In negotiation the parties communicate through their lawyers; in mediation they communicate directly. In negotiation the law is the exclusive basis for their decisions; typically, lawyers negotiating with each other refer primarily to their predictions of what a court would do in trying to reach an agreement. In mediation, although the law is consulted, the primary reference points are usually the parties' personal priorities and their sense of fairness. . . .

Claire's physical problems compounded her difficulty, and I knew it would be important that in her desire to get on her own feet she not blind herself to the very real limits on her capabilities. She would have to find her own way without reacting to Martin's demands so much that she lost sight of her own needs.

Martin's motivations for beginning mediation had their own complexities. On one hand, he felt guilty that he had left Claire. On the other, he was anxious to get on with his life and was, with reason, concerned that their case could drag on indefinitely if they went the way of lawyers and courts. Yet he genuinely cared about Claire — that was unmistakable. He didn't like the situation she was in any better than she did. And Martin was vulnerable to losing sight of his own needs in this process, too. Out of his concern for Claire, he could end up in a caretaking position that would keep him from moving forward with his life.

## IDENTIFYING THE BASIC DISAGREEMENTS

Two weeks later, they returned for the second session, having gathered their financial information.

> *Claire*: We bought our house three years ago for $90,000 with a down payment of $30,000, most of which came from money I saved before we married. As a result of the increase in real estate values in our area, the house is now worth about $150,000.

> *Martin*: There was $10,000 that came from my earnings, and I've been making the mortgage payments since we bought it.

> *Mediator*: When was the money for the down payment earned?

> *Martin*: Since we've been married.

> *Claire*: It's actually hard to say exactly where that money came from. Martin's books are very sloppy. I made some of that money. And even though Martin's been paying the mortgage, I've been taking care of the house.

As we explored this information, it became clear that disagreements over two separate issues had to be resolved: the house and spousal support. The specific questions regarding the house were, when would it be sold, and how would the proceeds be divided? As to support, the question was, how much would Martin pay Claire and for how long? In the middle of the session, I pointed out that the two issues were interrelated and asked them which issue they would like to work on first.

*Martin*: Well, I'd say the amount of spousal support is pretty well established. I've been paying the monthly mortgage, insurance, property taxes, and loan payments. And I'm willing to do it for a little longer.

*Mediator*: How do *you* see this issue, Claire?

*Claire*: I don't want to receive support from Martin any longer than I need to, but everything in my life is up in the air right now, so I don't know how long I'm going to need it.

*Mediator*: Is the present level of support satisfactory to both of you?

*Martin*: I don't mind paying what I'm paying. The question is, how long do I have to pay it?

*Claire*: I agree. I can get along all right with what he is paying now.

*Mediator*: So for you, Claire, it's hard to answer the question of how long without knowing what will happen with your career, and this depends to some extent on your health, right?

*Claire*: Right. But I also want to sell the house, so it will depend on that, too-on how much I get and when it sells.

*Mediator*: What can you tell us about your work plans for the future?

In response to this question, Claire looked at me as if she had just been assaulted, her cheeks flushed, eyes widened, an expression of shock on her face. Martin shot me a knowing glance with a hint of a smile.

*Claire*: Look, I'm not prying into Martin's life. Why does he get to pry into mine?

*Mediator*: You're uncomfortable with how we're going about this. How would you like to do it?

*Claire*: I don't know. I'm just sick to *death* of Martin's persistent questions about my work plans.

*Mediator*: Since it's you who needs the support, I think you are the one who should be defining your need here. That's why the focus is on you. But this isn't the only way of going about it. It's only Martin's strong desire to get this issue settled now that pushes us to decide the future of support. A court, for example, wouldn't require you to figure out at this point when support should end. In fact, it's probable that a judge would only set a time for review. Then at that time the judge would look at what had happened in the interim to determine whether and when spousal support should end or at least be reduced.

*Claire*: Listen, I know this man, and if we don't get this settled now, he will make my life miserable. I don't want to go through that.

*Mediator*: So you feel compelled by Martin to get this all resolved now?

*Claire*: Yes, but postponing the decision would be easier for me. Maybe I won't need the support for very long. I just can't tell now.

*Mediator*: This does set up a tension here, because to protect yourself from coming up short in case your life doesn't go as well as you hope, you need to ask for a longer period than you might actually need.

*Claire*: Oh, this is awful. I just don't know how to do this. [Breaks into tears]

*Martin*: [Looking pained] I don't either, but I think we have to have more information from you, Claire, in order to figure it out. I have told you before, I think you should talk to a career consultant and I'm willing to pay for it. That would give us a more objective basis for looking at this.

*Claire*: [Angrily through her tears] I've told you before and I'm going to tell you again. I'm not about to have some jerk who knows nothing about me, my life, or my values tell me what he thinks I should be doing. I've never led my life that way before and I'm not about to start now.

*Martin*: [Sighing in frustration] You sit there like some kind of queen. You don't have a job. You won't talk about your plans. You won't even see someone who could help you because you have too goddamn much pride.

*Claire*: [Enraged now] Pride! I lost that when you humiliated me eight months ago.

*Mediator*: Is this what you want to be talking about?

*Martin*: Absolutely not. What do you suggest?

*Mediator*: We can pursue this further to identify your disagreement more sharply and then look at what's behind it. Or we can move to other issues, which could shed some light on this one, and then return to it.

*Claire*: I'd like to talk about the house.

*Martin*: Yes, okay. I think we need to agree as to what my share of the house is worth and how I'll get paid if Claire wants to buy me out.

*Claire*: [Struggling to regain control of herself.] I'd agree to give you about fifteen thousand dollars or about a third of our equity, but I can't give you the money until I sell the house.

*Mediator*: When do you plan to do that?

*Claire*: I don't know. I think I might be ready to put it up for sale in the next year, but it would take about a year to sell it.

*Martin*: [To me] I think you'd better tell her I could force a sale of the house right now *and* receive half of the proceeds.

## THE CORE OF THE MATTER

This was a very charged statement. In using the word "force," Martin was at least indirectly threatening Claire with going to court. Why would he do that? People threaten others only when they fear they will not get what they want. So they reach out for a way to exert pressure on the other person. What was it that Martin was seeing slip through his fingers? My guess was a quick resolution-Martin wanted to get on with his new life. But a quick fix that didn't account for the uncertainties in Claire's future ran completely counter to Claire's stated goal, which was to extricate herself from the role of victim. To be a victim, one must have a persecutor. If Claire reached an agreement without thinking through her financial future, she could end up feeling victimized by Martin after the divorce. But out of frustration or the fear that he wouldn't get what he wanted, he was trying to pressure her to conform to his desires. Both positions were understandable and each conflicted directly with the other.

*Claire's Options*: Claire was in a bind, but she had several options. We spent several minutes identifying and assessing each in turn. She could succumb to Martin's pressure and continue to play the victim, giving up her own needs. Only one benefit could come from this: She could feel free to blame Martin and anybody else who supported him-including me-for her failure to move on.

A second option would be for Claire to disregard Martin's desires entirely and flatly deny him what he wanted. This route had two possible outcomes: a stalemate, or Martin's concession to Claire out of guilt, fear, or frustration. With either possibility, Claire would be breaking out of her role as Martin's victim. But neither alternative was actually in Claire's best interest. A stalemate would be counterproductive. On the other hand, if Martin agreed to her demand, she could discover that the result was not what she wanted at all, but rather an expression of her desire to keep Martin from getting what he wanted. Blocking his progress might give her a sense of power and increase her self-esteem, which would be preferable to her remaining a victim. Still, it would leave both of them unsatisfied in the long run. And in effect it would prove to be completely without value, for in operating in reaction to Martin, Claire would still be controlled by him.

A third option was for Claire to figure out what she wanted and assert her desires. Then, not only would she be likely to emerge from the process with more strength and a clearer idea of her direction, but she would have less reason to oppose Martin in his efforts to achieve his own goals. This choice would give Claire the chance to exert her power, but in a different way than a fight would do. Most of us make significant life decisions in conformity with or reaction to what others expect us to do rather than going through the difficult, confusing, and lonely process of deciding what we *really* want for ourselves. To reach that point is to feel the strength of true self-knowledge arid self-determination.

*Martin's dilemma*: Though Martin's suffering did not approximate Claire's, he too was trapped by the victim-oppressor pattern. As long as he wanted to exert control over her, he was playing into the problem. And his life was also on hold until hers straightened out. But while Claire seemed to have a pretty clear picture of their pattern of relating-she was seeing a therapist at the time, which undoubtedly helped her gain some clarity-Martin seemed much less aware of or interested in it. Claire seemed to see that the pain of aloneness could be a chamber through which she could pass to a new sense of herself. But without feeling distress analogous to Claire's that would motivate him to observe his pattern carefully and commit to the hard work of change, Martin was in danger of simply gliding into a new version of his old life.

## MEDIATION AND THE LAW

As mediator, I had a delicate task to perform. Martin's last remark "I think you'd better tell her I could force a sale of the house right now" opened two central issues that had been waiting to rear their heads: my own role in the mediation process, and the role of the law. The understanding between us from the beginning was that I would remain neutral regarding their final agreement unless what they decided seemed so unfair to me that I could not in good conscience draw up the contract. Under no circumstances would I serve as an advocate for either party. If either of them found they needed the protection of an advocate, then it would be better for them to leave mediation and hire a lawyer to carry on negotiations. Still, as a human being, I could not honestly call myself a detached witness. My main role in sorting through the options and proceeding toward an agreement was to monitor the process with respect to *fairness*.

I already knew I could not let Claire agree to her first option, acceding to all of Martin's demands. That such an agreement would be unfair was as obvious to Claire as to me. To be fair, the agreement these two finally reached would have to permit Claire to decide on and execute her plans for her life.

The agreement would also have to be measured against the law. Part of my job was to predict what the law would decide in their case so they could use that as a reference point in making their own decisions. Not only do the parties need to understand the legal context of the decisions that they are making for practical reasons, but they can also use it to develop and articulate their own sense of justice.

But the law is more than just a reference point in the mediation process. By continuing to mediate, the parties are implicitly deciding, sometimes from moment to moment, not to turn the case over to their lawyers. And throughout mediation, their understanding of the law and their decision to depart from it can be an empowering experience. But the option to stop and turn to lawyers is always present.

The trick for the mediator is to find a way to bring the law into the process without intimidating the parties into giving up their personal sense of how to resolve their dispute. I do this by trying to educate them about not merely the court decision in their case, but also the principles that would inform that decision. In that way they can measure their own sense of what's fair against the principles of justice that inform the law and society's sense of what's at stake in their dispute. I act as a neutral friend who happens to understand how a court would view their situation.

One hitch makes this job difficult for me: The law often is much less clear-cut and much more subjective than most people recognize. Judges base their decisions on their *interpretations* of the law, and lawyers can never be sure what a judge will do in a particular situation. All I could hope to give Claire and Martin was a neutral but educated guess as to how a judge would decide their conflict over the sale of their house.

This would be very delicate. As I interpreted the law, I would have to watch myself for any tendency to favor Claire in an effort to help her feel more powerful. On the other hand, I didn't want her to feel coerced by the law into going along with Martin-and thus betraying her own sense of fairness. Then we would have a double whammy to fight: her tendency to feel as if she always had to give in, and her inevitable conclusion that her personal sense of justice was in conflict with the law, a bitter notion that could weaken her further. If this happened, I would probably terminate the mediation as it would clearly be leading to a destructive end. So it was imperative that I remain neutral in delivering the law to Claire and Martin when in fact I wasn't neutral at all. I was very much against a destructive outcome.

## THE FATE OF THE HOUSE

I stepped into the mine field opened by Martin's threatening invocation of the law this way.

*Mediator:* So you'd like to talk about how a court would look at your situation?

*Martin:* At least as far as the house is concerned, I think Claire should know that I'm being very generous.

*Mediator:* How about you, Claire? Do you want to talk about the law now or would you rather wait until later? It's important to me that we have that discussion at some point, but only when both of you are ready.

*Claire:* Frankly, I'm not much interested in hearing about — the law at all.

*Mediator:* How come?

*Claire:* You said that the two of us will decide things here. We're not in court, at least not yet. If we go to court, I'll hear plenty about the law.

*Mediator:* So you'd prefer not to know the law at all.

*Claire:* I suppose we need to hear it at some point. You did say that the agreement would not be legally solid unless we knew what the law was. Do you think we should hear it now?

*Mediator:* What's important to me in doing this at any time is that regardless of what the law says, neither of you gives up your sense of what's fair. And you also need to know that although I'll give you my best opinion, there is some uncertainty in the law, so I could be wrong. That's another reason why you shouldn't defer to my opinion if it differs from what seems right to you. So knowing that, do you want to hear it now?

*Claire:* Yes.

*Martin:* All I want Claire to know is that I could force a sale of the house now and get half of the proceeds.

*Mediator:* That's not my opinion of what the court would do. First, the question of *when* a court would order the sale would depend upon when your case came to trial, and in this county it would take at least nine months before a judge would likely hear it. It is true that at that point you could force a sale, but only if Claire couldn't make an offer to buy your share that the judge considered fair. As for the rest of it, it is not at all clear that a court would order the proceeds to be divided equally.

*Martin:* Yeah? Well, read this.

Martin pulled out of his papers a photocopy of a very recent California Supreme Court decision. I usually know the updates in the law before my clients do, but this time I was caught short. I read the published opinion carefully. The California Supreme Court had decided in a case similar to Martin and Claire's that the proceeds of the house should be equally divided when both parties had purchased the house as joint tenants even when some of the down payment came from one of the parties' alone. Martin and Claire had bought their house in this way, with $20,000 of the down payment coming from Claire's pre-marriage savings. On the surface, it seemed as if Martin was right. But as I read further and reflected, I saw substantial differences between the two cases.

*Mediator:* Let me try to explain. For the last several years the courts here have been trying to clarify the question of how to treat a family residence when people divorce and the house is in both names. A few years ago, the law was clear. Unless you had an understanding or agreement to the contrary, if the house was in both names, you each would get half regardless of where the money came from to purchase it.

But a couple of years ago, the legislature decided that that law was unfair and changed it to read that upon the sale of the house each of you should be reimbursed any separate money you put in for the down payment or into improvements before dividing the rest of the proceeds. Still, it's not altogether clear whether that law would be applied in your case, because at least one court has decided that this reimbursement law might violate the guarantee in the United States Constitution that no one's property can be taken from them without due process of law. Since that challenge, the courts have been distinguishing between houses bought before and after the reimbursement law was passed, using the purchase date to determine whether the new law will be applied. Since your house was bought after the reimbursement law was passed, Claire would probably be entitled to be reimbursed for her contribution. The published opinion you brought in, Martin, was based on a purchase date that preceded the reimbursement law. So reading this opinion doesn't change my mind that the reimbursement law would be applied to your situation. Before either of you reacts to what I have said, do you both understand?

*Claire:* More or less. I've never had a lot of respect for the law, and seeing it flip-flop like that tells me that nobody has a very clear sense of what's right. So it doesn't seem very relevant to me.

*Martin:* You've explained the law as *you* understand it, but I was given this opinion by a lawyer who told me that this was the law. So who am I supposed to believe?

*Mediator:* That question goes right to the heart of mediation. Trust yourself after listening to everyone. Does it seem to you that what I'm saying makes more sense or less sense than what the lawyer said in interpreting the case you brought in?

*Martin:* Frankly, neither of you make much sense to me.

*Mediator:* What part of what I said doesn't make sense?

*Martin:* Why would it make any difference when the property was bought?

*Mediator:* If you bought the property before the reimbursement law passed, you would be entitled to half of the property. But in passing the law, the legislature would, in effect, be taking away some of your property without giving you a chance to fight it. And the Constitution doesn't permit that. That's what the challenge to the reimbursement law says.

*Martin:* So if we bought the property in 1983 instead of 1985, then I'd be entitled to more, is that what you're saying? So the legislature took away money from me by passing the law.

*Mediator:* Yes, but they actually passed the law before you bought the property. So at least theoretically, if you had known the law at the time, to protect your half interest, you would have known that you had to enter into a different kind of arrangement.

*Martin:* But I didn't know we were going to get a divorce.

*Claire:* And if you had, you probably would have gotten me to sign a paper giving you half.

*Martin:* That's not the point.

*Claire:* What *is* the point here? Do you really think you're entitled to half the value of the property after I put in most of the down payment?

*Martin:* I never said I thought it was *right* that I get half. I only wanted you to know I was trying to be easier on you by not insisting on my legal rights.

*Claire:* Look, I don't need you to try to go easy on me. I just want what's fair.

*Martin:* Then don't put me in the position of having to support you endlessly. I want an end to this and I want it decided now.

We'd hit bedrock — support was the issue that lay under the matter of the house. However support was resolved, the house would fall into place.

## THE QUESTION OF SUPPORT

*Mediator:* Do you want me to explain how the court would decide support?

*Martin:* This is the most important part to me. I don't care what the law says.

*Claire:* But we have to find out sometime. I am interested in knowing how long support would go on.

*Mediator:* If push came to shove and you decided that you *couldn't* decide at this point how long support should go on, there's little or no chance a court would decide now when support would end. The very thing that concerns you, Claire — the uncertainty of your future, particularly your work life and your health — would also concern a court. So a judge would be sure to order temporary support now and would probably set a time for that decision to be reviewed.

*Martin:* [Agitated] Hey, Gary, I thought you were supposed to be neutral. It seems to me you're aligning yourself with Claire, and I don't like it.

*Mediator:* I'm sorry you feel that way. But what I am trying to do is what I think you both asked for — to give you as clear an indication as I can about how the law would apply to your situation. I don't want either of you agreeing to something without understanding the legal context of the decision. I'm also trying to ensure that neither of you feels pushed into a decision you could regret.

*Martin:* Good luck, because I'm going to regret any decision that doesn't settle everything *right now*.

*Mediator:* That's clear enough to me. And if Claire agrees to that, too, then there will be no problem. But if Claire doesn't want that, it's important that both of you realize that on the issue of support, she has the legal power to put off deciding the question. You could get a court to decide the question of the amount of temporary support almost immediately, but not the termination date.

*Martin:* I think that stinks.

*Mediator:* How come?

*Martin:* Because we don't have kids. There's no reason in the world we should have to continue to be bound together financially. I need to know when I can quit sending Claire money, and I need to know it *soon*.

Martin had nailed it. In the matter of support, I was once more in danger of becoming Claire's advocate. Martin already felt alienated. The only thing worse would be if Claire began to perceive me as her advocate and fell back into a passive role, leaving me to deal with Martin. For me to play Claire's advocate would be implicitly suggesting that she was too weak to protect herself and robbing her of the chance to stand up for herself against Martin, thus sabotaging the whole mediation process.

Yet there was also the opposite danger that Claire would continue to play the victim by capitulating to Martin's wishes. That could spell disaster not only for Claire but for Martin as well: If she caved in now, she could go to court later to have the mediated agreement overturned on the grounds that she had been unaware of her legal rights or pressured into the agreement at the time. I realized that although it was necessary for both to understand Claire's legal rights, by emphasizing what a court would do, I might be inadvertently encouraging them to view such a conclusion as the "right" one, even if neither saw it as the best.

To add one further twist, if my effort to ensure that Claire understood her legal rights resulted in her agreeing not to exercise those rights, then the conversation we were having now would probably jeopardize the possibility of her chances of having the agreement overturned at a later date. From that perspective, it could be said that what I was doing now was more in Martin's interests than Claire's.

This kind of step-by-step analysis is absolutely imperative to my remaining in the middle. With the momentum of the conflict constantly propelling the two disputants toward confrontation, an important part of my role is to define the disagreement precisely. The delicate part is remaining objective while still being empathetic enough that both parties feel I understand them and care about what happens.

Deciding whether a person whose position is favored by the law is personally strong enough to stand up for his or her position in the mediation process is one of the most difficult assessments I need to make. With Martin and Claire, I was concerned about Claire's victim history and the very real obstacles she would face in her effort to become self-supporting. Her way out of the victimization pattern would be to articulate her needs for support precisely. It was essential that if she agreed to a termination date for spousal support she do it because it felt right to her and not because she was intimidated by or wanted to conciliate Martin. It was equally important that the date, if she gave one, be realistic, and that she would be able to manage or have contingent plans for surviving financially after support ended. I certainly did not want to be an agent of Claire's self-destruction.

For Claire to independently agree on a realistic date for termination of support could be an extraordinarily liberating and powerful act, a way of declaring her own independence and autonomy. So it might well be in her own best interests to do the very thing that Martin wanted her to do. I hoped that by my injecting the law, Claire would feel enough power to decide how much money she could realistically expect to earn and when she could become self-supporting. Although it was not clear to Martin yet, the worst thing that could happen at this point would be for Claire to succumb to his pressure on a termination date and thus remain dependent not only in her own eyes but in the eyes of a judge. That would keep both of them locked into their old pattern. The key to Claire's liberation would be Claire herself, and that is why it was so important for me to avoid a position where I was perceived as her advocate. Turning the spotlight on Claire was what we all needed to create the hoped-for balance between us.

**Mediator:** [To Claire] What is your view of this?

**Claire:** Frankly, I have mixed feelings. I know that if I don't agree to a specific date I'll pay the price of Martin's resentment. I don't want that. I know that we'll probably not be friends, and I'm not sure I would want that even if Martin did. But I sure don't want him to get any angrier.

But I also think that it would be helpful to me to be able to cut the cord that connects me to him. I need to do that for my *own* good. I don't *want* Martin to take care of me-he was never particularly good at it anyhow, and it's not really worth it to me to have to count on him. He'd always be hassling me about getting a job or a better job. I know that whatever I decided to do wouldn't be good enough for him, and I don't want to have to answer to him any more in my life. I've had enough of that. Still, I have to be sure that I'm going to be able to make it financially. And I just don't know what's going to happen in that regard. Some days I think I can do it. Others I feel lucky to be able to get out of bed.

*Mediator:* So what you would like is to have enough support from Martin to get you through this transition. It would make sense, I think, to look at various possibilities of what might happen: What's the worst that could happen to you? What's the best?

*Claire:* I'm not sure I want to do that. What I know is that I'll probably sell the house within the next year and buy a smaller place. I'll have to pay some taxes if I do that, but it would still give me some cash. If I knew I could count on the money from the house sale and have help from Martin *until* it sold, well-I guess I'd probably be willing to give up support beyond that point.

*Martin:* [Bursting out] That would leave me with nothing!

*Claire:* No, you'd still have your health, your business, and your relationship with what's-her-name. And that's a hell of a lot more than I can say for myself.

*Martin:* I wouldn't even get back the money that I've put into the house. And I've been paying the mortgage since we bought it.

*Claire:* I know that, but look; you say you want me to be financially independent. If you really don't want me knocking on your door, you have to give me a head start.

*Martin:* I'd be totally screwing myself if I agreed to this.

*Mediator:* How so?

*Martin:* The house is the only asset I have in the world outside of my paycheck. I don't even have any money in savings. Besides, she'd never get anything like this in court.

*Mediator:* That's true. And you wouldn't get the termination date. I think from your point of view, Martin, the question is really how important it is to you to get a termination date. I imagine that neither prospect at the moment is appealing: giving up your whole nest egg or paying out support indefinitely.

*Martin:* You're damn right.

*Mediator:* But you might consider that there are some real advantages to you in Claire's proposal. I would suggest that you sit with it a bit before you decide.

We ended the session on that note. Martin's impatience and sense of urgency were signals to slow down the process. I was afraid that he might now make a decision that he would later regret, so I was glad that our time was up before he had an opportunity to decide. When the parties are moving quickly toward a solution, my function often is to slow things down. If people have an opportunity to deliberate, their feelings frequently shift. Time is an important test of the solidity of a decision. I was not surprised when Martin came into the next session with a variation on Claire's proposal.

*Martin:* Here is what I am willing to do. I'll give up all of my interest in the house if you give up support. And I'll lend you $750 a month between now and when the house sells, if you pay me back with interest out of the sale proceeds.Martin: Here is what I am willing to do. I'll give up all of my interest in the house if you give up support. And I'll lend you $750 a month between now and when the house sells, if you pay me back with interest out of the sale proceeds.

*Claire:* Hell, no! I'm not about to pay you a dime of interest. You're not a bank. And *no*, I don't like the idea of the support money being a loan.

*Mediator:* Why doesn't this seem fair to you?

*Claire:* Damn it, he's acting as if we were never married.

*Martin:* What do you mean? I don't go around giving away my property, everything I have, to my business associates, you know. Giving up my share of the house is a huge concession. It's $45,000. [This was based on the present value of $150,000, reduced by closing costs and the mortgage balance of $60,000, divided by two.]

*Claire:* [Slowly] It's actually more like $25,000, if we followed the law. And I assume I'll be paying the taxes on the gain. That could cost $15,000. I do appreciate your being willing to give up your interest in the house, but making the other money a loan with interest feels awful.

*Martin:* Then get the money someplace else. [Long silence] Okay, look. I'll give you the $750 a month without interest, if that will make you feel better, but I want that money back. I've already been paying you for the past eight months.

*Claire:* Okay. [Strongly] But we'll only make the loan retroactive to four months ago and I want you to get all of your stuff out of the house within the next week.

*Martin:* Consider it done.

*Claire:* And I don't want *her* coming over to help you, either!

*Martin:* Yeah, all right.

DOUBLE CHECK

Claire got up and walked over to the window with her back to both of us. Martin seemed to sink deeper into his seat and breathed a sigh of relief. They had an agreement, but I still wasn't sure if it was mutually fair or realistic. I needed to find out.

*Mediator:* We need to be sure that this agreement is going to work for both of you, not just now but in the long run. So I need to ask you some questions to check that out. My main concerns are with you, Claire. [Claire shot me a look as if I were intruding on her.] What happens to you if your life doesn't work out as you hope? What happens if you don't get better, or if you get worse?

*Claire:* I'm not worried about the medical bills. They're covered by my insurance.

*Mediator:* But how will you pay your expenses?

*Claire:* I don't know. I guess I'll be okay until the house sells with Martin lending me the money. And then when the house sells, I'll have that money to live on. That will be at least fifty or sixty thousand dollars after I pay Martin back and pay taxes, the mortgage balance, commissions, and closing costs. And after that, I don't know. I might rent a house for a while or buy a smaller place. I guess I don't think that should be Martin's problem. But I'd still feel better if the money he gives me until the house sells isn't a loan.

*Martin:* It has to be a loan to give you incentive to sell the House quickly.

*Claire:* [Snapping] You back off. It's hard enough dealing with Gary's questions.

*Mediator:* And what happens if you can't sell the house for a long time? Or if you run through the house sale proceeds before you get a job?

*Claire:* I don't think that'll happen, but if it does, I don't think Martin should have to help me just because he's obligated to.

*Mediator:* Do you think he would help you if he weren't obligated?

*Claire:* Maybe, but it's not healthy for me to think that way. I need to think positively. I know what you're getting at, but I think that what he proposes, but without the interest, is reasonable. I think it'll work.

*Mediator:* You sound only half-convinced.

*Claire:* Maybe sixty percent.

*Mediator:* Is that enough to make an agreement?

*Claire:* Yes, I think it is.

*Mediator:* That's going to feel better or worse in the few weeks between now and when you sign the agreement. I don't want you to sign it if it feels worse, or even if it doesn't feel better.

*Martin:* What about me? I'm giving up all my property.

*Mediator:* I think that when you have this agreement reviewed by your lawyer, that person will advise you that you've probably done better financially than if you were to go to court. Under a judge's decision, your obligation to pay support would be open-ended and Claire would also be entitled to half of the value of your business, whatever that amounted to. Since you don't have any savings to fall back on in case you get sick and can't work, this is a big consideration. It's also true that if Claire were to remarry quickly, then from an economic standpoint you'd have paid more than you are legally obligated because support would end upon her remarriage.

*Martin:* That's right. And I've been paying the mortgage since we separated. Except for the mortgage, we're now debt-free. And — I didn't mention this earlier because I didn't want to ruffle Claire's feathers — but if she gets into trouble, her mother would help her out.

*Claire:* I told you to *back off.* You know how hard she is to deal with. If that's what you need to say to yourself to assuage your guilt about what you've done to me, then say it, but it's not true. My mother doesn't have the money to support me, and she wouldn't do it even if she had it.

*Mediator:* [To Martin] As I implied, Claire's lawyer is probably going to discourage her more strongly from accepting these terms than yours will you.

*Martin:* That would ruin all the work we've done to get to this point.

*Claire:* I know it. Martin, I know I'll stick to this agreement if you agree that I don't have to repay you the money you are lending me.

*Martin:* I won't do that. It's too open-ended, and I need to get something out of the house sale.

*Claire:* All right. I guess I'll go along with it.

Was this the victim operating again? How did Claire really feel about the agreement? I wasn't sure. Sometimes she seemed to be solidly advocating her position, and other times, not. It was a borderline situation for me. Whether I would draw it up was my next decision — I had been clear from the beginning that I would not draw up an agreement that I felt was unconscionable.

On the one hand, it seemed that Martin had won. Claire had given up support-so in the one area they disagreed upon most strongly, she had given in. On the other hand, she would be getting at least $25,000 to $30,000 or more in exchange for the right to any support and whatever interest she would have had in Martin's business. She undoubtedly would have gotten more money if she had had a lawyer negotiate for her, or at least the security of knowing that she could look to Martin for support, but she would be free of any scrutiny of her life by a judge or Martin. It also appeared to me that during the process, she had moved away from her place of victimization and toward a position of strength. If her health held out and she landed on her feet, I concluded, this would work well. If not, she could end up regretting this agreement. I didn't know whether we were finished or not, but drew up the agreement feeling that this was not so unfair that I would inject my opinion. And it was clear to me that they both understood what they were doing. It had taken us four sessions to reach this point.

When I sent Claire and Martin each a draft of the agreement to review with their consulting lawyers, and they sent me back copies marked up with minor changes, Claire enclosed a note saying that she was relieved it was over and that the agreement felt right to her, even though she felt under pressure to sell the house quickly. Her lawyer did not support the agreement, but that hadn't changed her willingness to commit to it.

A few months later, I ran into Claire. She looked wonderful, happy, and healthy. When she saw me, she came right over. "It all worked out well," she said. "Selling the house felt like getting rid of a great burden, and I never would have done it if I hadn't had to. As it turned out, the week after we signed the agreement, I got an offer on the house for $15,000 more than we thought it was worth, so I didn't have to borrow any more money from Martin. And I found a job designing greeting cards. It gives me a chance to be creative, the hours are flexible, and the pay's not bad." Then, looking at me, she winked. "And you know, my headaches have almost gone away."

## NOTES AND QUESTIONS

1.   Which approach or mix of approaches did mediator Gary Friedman use in the "Claire and Martin" mediation? Are there examples of transformative, facilitative, or evaluative mediation? Recall the discussion in Chapter 2 about the categories of norm generating, norm educating, or norm advocating. Identify examples of each in this mediation. Was the mediator's approach(es) "appropriate" and "effective" given the circumstances of these parties?

2.   In this mediation example, it was clear to the mediator that Claire's emotions were driving much of her decision-making. How did he respond? What other ways could he have responded? How would you have responded?

# Chapter 7

# LEGAL REGULATION OF FAMILY MEDIATION

## A. INTRODUCTION

The flexibility of mediation is in stark contrast to the procedural, substantive, and evidentiary boundaries of litigation. This is not to say that legal regulation does not have an impact on the conduct and framework for mediation. To the contrary, the interaction between law and family mediation can be subtle and complex.

This Chapter will explore an aspect of this large issue: In what ways is family mediation regulated by legislatures, court rules, and judicial decision-making?

## B. COURT-CONNECTED MEDIATION

While thus far we have made some reference to the different contexts in which mediation is practiced, a core distinction is between "private" mediation, through which participants engage in mediation outside the context of the courts, and "court-connected" mediation, through which participants mediate under the aegis of a judicial process.

The logistics of court-connected mediation vary. In some jurisdictions, a judge will order or encourage litigants to participate in mediation immediately after appearing for a scheduled hearing. Such hearings are not necessarily pre-identified as an opportunity for mediation. Other jurisdictions have a separate mediation program or office through which litigants may or must attend mediation. Some jurisdictions have mediation programs or a roster of mediators outside the court to which litigants are referred.

Apart from such logistics, designers of court-connected mediation programs have many options. We will explore some of these in the materials that follow.

### 1. Goals of Court-Connected Mediation

Why has court-connected mediation proliferated? The excerpt that follows traces differing, if not contradictory, answers to this question.

## COURT-CONNECTED ADR — A TIME OF CRISES, A TIME OF CHANGE
95 MARQ. L. REV. 993, 1002–1008 (2012)
By Yishai Boyarin

. . . Mediation was originally intended as a voluntary and informal process designed to empower parties to explore the resolution of their disputes on their own terms rather than within the existing adversarial and legally rigid formal process. These goals are often encapsulated within the concept of self-determination, originally understood as the promise that the parties will have the power to determine the outcome of their dispute in a non-coercive, voluntary environment. The process characteristics incorporated into mediation in support of this understanding of self-determination are the voluntary participation and decision-making by the parties, as well as the neutrality of the third-party mediator. Confidentiality is also a significant characteristic meant to guarantee the open and non-coercive nature of mediation. . . . These characteristics of mediation have been and still are central to the practice of mediation, even if the precise manner of implementation may vary in practice. Indeed, mediation proponents generally believe that adherence to the core characteristics of mediation in the actual practice of mediation is necessary to ensure that mediation meets the goal of self-determination.

In the court-connected context, these characteristics of mediation, as a manifestation of self-determination, were also relied on in support of the argument that mediation can be fair in a manner that meets the courts' mandate to provide for justice. Indeed, self-determination, defined broadly, was one of the central justifications for diverging from the formal protections and the legal norms that would be applied to the parties had they gone through the traditional process offered by courts. The fact that parties have the ability to voluntarily and meaningfully participate in the process of deciding their outcome, along with having the sufficient knowledge needed to make such a decision, is meant to provide for a fair process, however fairness is defined.

While self-determination (and its varying definitions) certainly plays a role in shaping court-connected mediation, perhaps the most significant factor in determining how mediation is actually practiced is administrative efficiency. . . . [E]fficiency can be constructed narrowly to encompass short-term judicial economy considerations: Does the intervention dispose of cases, free the court's dockets, and preserve court resources? Or, more broadly, it can be understood to include effectiveness in meeting the court's role of providing access to justice, administering justice fairly, and providing for long-term sustainable resolution. . . .

While a number of court mediation programs are not only carefully and thoughtfully designed and implemented, it appears that a fair number of such programs incorporate mediation based on narrow administrative considerations, due to a focus on case management and due to limited resources. The primary goal for mediation for courts with such a narrow focus has become more and more the efficient — quick and cheap — settlement of cases, which is certainly an important goal for court ADR programs, but one that must not trump other important goals, such as self-determination, fairness, and justice. Mediation driven primarily by narrow administrative efficiency considerations may include the following relatively coercive features found in various jurisdictions: mediation would be settlement focused, mandatory, and relatively short; allow for or require the evaluation of the parties' claims; and allow for or require the mediator to report parties' good faith participation and provide a recommendation to the court based on the content of the mediation. Each one of these features may not on its own compromise the quality of mediation being offered. For example, a more directive form of mediation, such as evaluative mediation, may be appropriate in some cases and, in fact, may be precisely what the parties want. Such features, however, can undermine self-determination to various degrees by undercutting voluntariness, neutrality, and confidentiality, and by taking away the ability of the parties to make their own decisions in a non-coercive environment. This is particularly so where the mediation programs that include such directive and relatively coercive features do not incorporate informed consent by the parties as a component of the process. This reality raises the question whether the benefits of mediation as it seems to be practiced on a fairly wide scale — benefits defined differently based on the perspective of different stakeholders — outweigh, or should outweigh, the potential harm to the parties and even the damage done to how people perceive courts as public institutions.

To justify the practice of mediation as part of the court system, mediation must be practiced in a manner consistent with its stated goal of self-determination and with the intertwined characteristics of neutrality, confidentiality, and voluntariness. As a starting point, this will require a clearer definition of self-determination in relation to these characteristics and the establishment of mechanisms that will relieve the pressure that is put on parties to settle as well as mechanisms that might also encourage mediators to not over-aggressively push for settlement where settlement is either not appropriate or not desired by the parties. What is needed most is the clear articulation of court mediation programs' goals and practices that are consistent with self-determination and the related characteristics of neutrality, confidentiality, and voluntariness not only within the operation of the actual mediation process itself but also within the manner that mediation is set up as part of the larger court process. Courts and mediation programs would have to ensure that mediators adhere to such goals.

[T]he level and type of institutional support will determine how the mediator will actually behave as much as, if not more than, the actual intentions of the mediator. While there are many others, some of the significant areas to be improved [are] providing for sufficient time in the mediation, allowing opportunities for additional sessions, and not pressuring the mediators to exclusively focus on achieving settlement at all costs . . . .

## NOTES AND QUESTIONS

1.	What goals of court-connected mediation does Boyarin identify? Can you think of others? Which do you think were the primary impetus for the development of court-connected mediation programs?

2.   Boyarin refers to how evaluative mediation might be particularly prominent in court-connected programs. Why? Do you think this is a good thing or a bad thing?[1]

3.   As we will see, court-connected programs are particularly prevalent in family cases, and sometimes family cases are the only or one of few designated types of cases for which mediation is available. Why? Is family mediation particularly appropriate or inappropriate in the context of court-connected programs?

## 2.   Should Court-Connected Mediation Be Mandatory?

The core value of self-determination and voluntariness in mediation reflects how participants should control the process and substance of mediation, and, ultimately, whether to engage in mediation or not. How then can mandatory mediation be mediation?

That question, however, has not stopped some — but far from all — jurisdictions from making mediation mandatory. Such "mandatory" jurisdictions *require* litigants to participate in mediation prior to having a judicial hearing or trial. In contrast, courts in "discretionary" jurisdictions may recommend mediation but litigants may "opt out" if they so choose. There are more "discretionary" than "mandatory" jurisdictions, although a substantial number do adhere to a mandatory process.[2]

One issue that "mandatory" jurisdictions have had to grapple with is what a litigant must do in order to fulfill the mediation requirement. Consider, for example, a litigant and/or a litigant's attorney who have no intention of participating meaningfully in mediation. They might, for example, enter a mediation room, sit down, listen to an Opening Introduction, and then leave. Others might not be so obvious. Some courts and legislatures have tried to address this issue by requiring that litigants participate in mediation in "good faith." How "good faith" is defined and what must be gleaned in order to make this determination is not an easy task.[3]

In any event, a number of arguments have been set forth for and against mandatory mediation. Arguments in favor of mandatory mediation include the following:

- Litigants might not be conversant in the benefits of mediation. Giving litigants a choice, then, is illusory: How can litigants make an informed choice about whether to engage in mediation if they have never experienced it?

- The inherent difficulty of a judge assessing the best interests of a child should mean, at least in the first instance, that parents or caregivers be given an opportunity to craft custody and visitation arrangements.

---

[1] For a more extensive discussion of the prevalence of evaluative mediation in the court-connected context, see Nancy A. Welsh, *Making Deals in Court-Connected Mediation: What's Justice Got to Do with It?*, 79 WASH. U. L. Q. 787, 846–851 (2001).

[2] As discussed in Chapter 10, mandatory jurisdictions may not require or prohibit mediation under certain conditions — typically domestic violence. *See* http://www.americanbar.org/content/dam/aba/administrative/domestic_violence1/Charts/2014%20Mediation%20Statutory%20Chart.authcheckdam.pdf

[3] For an overview of these issues, see Megan G. Thompson, *Mandatory Mediation and Domestic Violence: Reformulating the "Good Faith" Standard*, 86 OREGON L. REV. 600 (2007).

- While participating in mediation might be mandatory, reaching a settlement in mediation is not. Voluntariness in mediation thus remains intact.

- Family court dockets are overwhelmed. Being told to mediate means that litigants have an opportunity to focus on their situation in a way that a court does not have the time or resources to do.

Arguments against mandatory mediation include the following:

- Transforming a "voluntary process" into a mandatory one is inconsistent with self-determination in mediation.

- Even if a court advises litigants that there need not be a settlement in mediation, the mandatory nature of mediation communicates to litigants that courts expect a settlement. A failure would thus place a participant in a negative light.

- Litigants with resources can afford private mediation, or at least have an option to "opt out" of a court-annexed process. These litigants also often have the resources to retain an attorney. Forcing pro se litigants into a process with minimal oversight endangers the rights and remedies of those litigants under the law.

This last argument against mandatory mediation relates to the resource issues. Parties who can afford private mediation — often an expensive proposition — typically use these mediators prior to appearing in court. Assuming an agreement is reached in a private mediation, litigants present the agreement in court and there is nothing left to mediate. In contrast, litigants who do not have the resources to hire private mediators have no choice but to participate in court-mandated mediation programs. If court-annexed programs are strapped for resources, is it fair to force only lower-resourced litigants into a process that only has the trappings of actual mediation? This might be particularly troubling given that court-annexed programs must accommodate such litigants when mediation is mandated, even if the resources allocated to the programs are not inadequate.

In thinking through this issue, consider one report of how mediators describe their experience with mandatory court-connected mediation programs:

> [M]any court-connected mediators acknowledge that they cannot conduct a facilitative mediation process if they are to meet the expectations of their workplace. They express enormous frustration at being caught between a rock and a hard place as they are asked to deliver high quality mediation services in what they know to be a fraction of the time required to effectively do so, often with cases that are not appropriate for mediation. According to one veteran court mediator who requested anonymity, "In recent years, encouraging families toward self-determination and private ordering have taken a back seat. Mediation services, which are mandated, are adversely affected because administrators move their workforce toward evaluation services." Another mediator and court services supervisor referring to the common

practice of recommending settlements said, "The process is called mediation and we settle cases, but it certainly isn't real mediation."[4]

The argument could be made, then, that "mandatory mediation" only mandates that lower-resourced litigants participate in inadequately funded mediation programs that are designed to resolve a high volume of cases as quickly as possible. Assuming this is the case, would a "discretionary" model solve or diminish the problem?

A critique of court-mediated mediation, however, might assume that the litigation alternative is somehow superior. An assessment of the litigation process for low income, often pro se litigants[5] is not encouraging. Courts are overwhelmed with cases with limited resources for individualized adjudication. This is especially true in family cases.[6] With little or no expertise in many family law issues, especially related to child access, and little time to conduct trials or hear evidence, is litigation a better alternative to mediation?

### 3.  "Confidential" Versus "Recommending" Models

Another issue that has arisen in court-connected mediation involves the legitimacy of what is usually called the "recommending" model of mediation." Although few jurisdictions have adopted this model, one of them is California,[7] and perhaps because of the prominence of that state it continues to stir controversy. Unlike the mandatory mediation debate, which focuses on voluntariness, this debate raises primarily raises questions of confidentiality and the nature of the role of a mediator.

A "recommending" model of mediation operates as follows:

> [A] mediator may carry out a dual role of mediator and evaluator. Mediation participants are to be told about this dual role in written materials, again in the orientation sessions, and again by the mediator at the beginning of the session. If the negotiations reach an impasse, the mediator informs the parties of his or her shift in role. If issues still remain after further discussion, the mediator may elect to terminate the mediation and begin the recommendation process or refer the case back to the court for further deliberations or evaluation. . . . If the case warrants further investigation due to allegations of substance abuse, child abuse, psychological problems, or neglect of the child's educational needs, the mediator may also obtain signed releases from the parents to collect information from other sources such as day-care providers, teachers, doctors, therapists, agencies such as Child Protective Services, or services connected to social welfare or mental health . . . [A] recommendation [must] include "data collection and analysis that allow the evaluator to

---

[4] Peter Salem, *The Emergence of Triage in Family Court Services: The Beginning of the End Mandatory Mediation?*, 47 FAM. CT. REV. 378, 381 (2009).

[5] Chapter 11 discusses special issues facing pro se litigants in mediation.

[6] For an overview of "mass adjudication," including in the context of family cases, see Robert Rubinson, *A Theory of Access to Justice*, 29 J. LEG. PROF. 89 (2004–2005).

[7] Cal. Fam. § 3183 (2011). The California statute does not mandate a "recommending" model, but gives counties discretion to adopt it.

observe and consider each party in comparable ways and to substantiate interpretations and conclusions regarding each child's developmental needs, the quality of attachment to each parent and that parent's social environment; and the child's reactions to the separation, divorce or parental conflict."[8]

Such a model typically includes other procedures that make it vastly different from norms of mediation. Mediators may be called to testify about their recommendations. Litigants have an opportunity to review the recommendation and may contest its conclusions in court proceedings. While a recommendation does not bind a court, a court typically gives it great weight.

## NOTES AND QUESTIONS

1.   Do you see advantages or disadvantages of a recommending model?

2.   Are there certain issues in family mediation that should be subject to a mediator's "recommendation" or, conversely, that should be kept confidential? Can or should a statute distinguish situations that should trigger a mediator acting as an "evaluator"?

3.   Do any of the models of mediation described in Chapter 2 resonate with a recommending procedure? Why or why not?

## C.   FAMILY MEDIATOR QUALIFICATIONS

Whether and how to regulate the qualifications of family mediators is yet another issue with which jurisdictions have grappled. Consider some of the qualifications requirements states have adopted or considered:[9]

- **General knowledge requirements.** Such "knowledge" might include understanding of judicial procedures governing family law matters, community resources that might be appropriate for mediation participants, psychological issues relating to families and children, or family law.

- **Degree Requirements.** These requirements may be that all mediators have a bachelor's degree or a graduate degree in behavioral science or law.

- **Experience.** This may include requirements that a mediator have practice experience for a defined number of years in certain fields, such as family law or counseling.

- **Hours of Mediation Training.** This common qualification typically requires a certain number of hours attending training. These hours can range from 20 to 60. Statutes may describe in some detail the topics that the training must

---

[8]  Isolina Ricci, *Historical Context for Court-Connected Mandatory Family Mediation in* Divorce and Family Mediation 399, 408–09 (Jay Folberg, Ann L. Milne & Peter Salem eds., 2004).

[9]  This list is based on *Note: A Survey of Domestic Mediator Qualifications and Suggestions for a Uniform Paradigm*, 16 Ohio St. J. on Disp. Resol. 1 (2000). The specific categories of qualifications listed above are quoted from this article.

include, including designating a certain number of hours of training to family issues.

- **Observation or Participation with an Experienced Mediator.** States may require a certain number of hours engaged in such observation or participation.

Note that states vary regarding which, if any, qualifications are needed for family mediators. Appendix A-2 includes representative examples of such statutes.

## NOTES AND QUESTIONS

1. Some jurisdictions only impose requirements on mediators involved in court-annexed programs. They do not extend to private mediators. Why do you think jurisdictions draw this distinction? Do you think it is a good idea?

2. Do more rigorous qualifications reduce the number of qualified mediators? Why or why not? If yes, do the benefits of rigorous qualifications outweigh the cost?

3. One way to approach the qualifications debate is to identify what characteristics an effective family mediator should have and what qualifications best reflect those characteristics. In light of that question and in light of the above reading, draft your own qualifications statute. As you do so, describe why you think each qualification is necessary. You might wish to consult examples of mediator qualification statutes included in Appendix A-2.

4. Should there be a mechanism for disciplining otherwise qualified mediators in light of certain misconduct from mediating? If so, what process should there be? What could potential sanctions be?

5. Some have argued that by training and temperament, lawyers are *not* well suited to be mediators. *See* Leonard Riskin, *Mediation and Lawyers*, 43 Ohio St. L.J. 29, 57–59 (1982); Jean Sternlight, *Lawyers' Representation of Clients in Mediation: Using Economics and Psychology to Structure Advocacy in a Nonadversarial Setting*, 14 Ohio St. J. Disp. Resol. 269, 315 (1999). Do you agree? Why or why not?

6. The Model Standards of Practice for Family and Divorce Mediation is included as Appendix C and is discussed in detail in Chapter 12. Standard II describes what a family mediator needs in order to be "qualified by education and training to undertake the mediation" and then sketches out what an effective family mediator should know. Review this Standard in the Appendix. Does this advance your thinking about appropriate qualifications for family mediators?

## D. JUDICIAL REVIEW OF AGREEMENTS IN FAMILY MEDIATION

Are there circumstances when courts should review, modify, or reject agreements reached in mediation? This is an issue that extends to all types of mediation, but two aspects are of particular importance in the context of family mediation. One relates to the independent role, if any, that courts should have in assessing such agreements.

This issue usually, but not always, arises with agreements as to child custody or child support, where courts by law almost always have an obligation to insure that an agreement is consistent with the best interests of children and in accordance with a state's child support guidelines. The other circumstance arises when a participant seeks to abrogate an agreement reached in mediation because of allegations that the mediation was tainted in some way, often as a result of alleged mediator misconduct. The particularly intense emotions that accompany family disputes are more likely to generate such claims than other types of mediation. The following material explores both of these issues.

## 1.   Independent Judicial Review of the Terms of Mediated Agreements

As discussed in Chapter 4, a critical aspect of many family disputes is custody and visitation. Mediation is particularly valuable in resolving these issues given in many instances parents are in a far better position than courts to craft such arrangements. After all, it is difficult, if not impossible, for a court to understand the nuances of parental schedules, modes of communication, personalities and qualities of children, and so on. When parents cannot agree on child access issues the question is then submitted to courts for resolution. What role, however, do courts have when parents do reach an agreement in mediation? The following case addresses this question.

### WAYNO v. WAYNO
District Court of Appeal of Florida, Fifth District
756 So. 2d 1024 (2000)

. . . Appellant asserts the court was bound to accept and ratify by judgment the mediated settlement regarding child custody . . . .

We disagree with appellant's assertion . . . It is axiomatic that only the court can be the final authority regarding child custody and child support and those issues can always be subject to review based on the evidence and, after judgment, upon a showing of a material change in circumstances. It goes without saying that the best interest of the child is the overriding factor to be considered. Even though the judge found in this case that a change in circumstances had occurred, that is not the guiding principle. Although the rule does not explicitly require it, it is at least implicit in the rule and certainly the better practice for the judge to not approve either custody or support before being fully informed about the welfare of the children. Thus, approval should be withheld in those issues until final judgment, or, if not, then the withdrawal of approval must be fully available until judgment . . .

CONCUR: Cobb, J., concurring specially.

I concur with the majority opinion. A trial judge has inherent authority to alter or rescind interlocutory orders prior to entry of final judgment. This authority certainly extends to a court's interlocutory approval of an agreement involving custody of children entered at a point in the case where the evidence has not been presented to the trial court. . . . To construe the rule as does the dissent presents a trap for the unwary and well-intentioned trial judge, and seriously interferes with his obligation to protect the best interest of the child in a custody dispute.

**DISSENT:** Sharp, W., J., dissenting.

I respectfully disagree and would reverse this case. In my view, the trial judge erred when he changed the primary parental residency of the parties' daughter . . .

Dissecting this case to what actually occurred and bypassing the legalese, the trial judge in this case erroneously allowed the former husband to try the issue of child custody in the dissolution case despite the mediated court-approved settlement of this issue, where the former husband neither pled nor proved a substantial change in circumstances and having heard the testimony. The court decided the custody issued *do novo*. This may be proper in cases involving settlement agreements between parties, which have not been court approved. But this is not such a case. . . .

In my view, the rules suggest that mediation agreements . . . are entitled to be treated as final determinations of the issues covered. If not, there is very little incentive for parties to engage in mediation, in the first place. Why should they go to the trouble and expense to mediate if the issues resolved can be freely retried in the dissolution case by a party, belatedly unhappy with the mediated settlement? Parties should be encouraged to mediate family law disputes, and when the process is followed and the agreement is approved by the court they should be bound by their agreement. Otherwise the mediation process is an exercise in futility.

## NOTES AND QUESTIONS

1.   Upon what basis does the dissent disagree with the majority and concurring opinions? With which opinion to you agree?

2.   It is well-established that courts have a responsibility to insure whether an agreement — whether reached in mediation or not — accords with the best interests of a child. That said, though, what should be the nature of judicial review? The *Wayno* majority holds that a court should be "fully informed about the welfare of the children" prior to approving a settlement. What process would this entail? An evidentiary hearing with testimony? A cursory review of the terms of an agreement? Should particular circumstances trigger a more extensive review? If so, what might those be?

3.   *Wayno* is framed exclusively in the context of child access. How about other issues that might arise in family mediation? The following case explores this issue.

### CLOUTIER v. CLOUTIER
Supreme Judicial Court of Maine
814 A.2d 979 (Me. 2003)

Lorenzo and Dawn Cloutier were married on August 29, 1987, and three children were born to the marriage. . . . Dawn filed a complaint for divorce in September of 2000. . . . As a result of a mediation at which both parties were represented, the Cloutiers signed a "points of agreement" form that resolved the majority of the issues in dispute. Among the matters agreed upon was an arrangement for their home to be sold and for the proceeds to be used to satisfy certain debt. The agreement was never incorporated into a court order. Immediately after the mediation session, [a Case Management Officer ("CMO")] held a pretrial conference. In its pretrial order, the CMO listed only a few matters remaining in dispute, including allocation of pension benefits, personal property and debt, and coverage of medical insurance for Dawn.

The District Court began the trial on the 2nd of August. At the beginning of trial, Dawn requested that the court disregard the mediation agreement and award sole possession of the home to her. Initially, the court declined to disregard the agreement and precluded real estate from becoming an issue. As the evidence developed, however, the court concluded that the issue of the disposition of the real estate was intricately intertwined with the resolution of the matters remaining in dispute. Therefore, the court postponed the hearing until October 16 to allow each party to gather more evidence of their financial situations. The court specifically stated at the August 2 hearing and in the resulting order that disposition of the real estate would be an issue to be resolved at the October hearing. Lorenzo objected to the court's ruling and the court overruled this objection. The parties returned to trial on October 16, and the court ultimately awarded the home and all rental income to Dawn. After the court denied Lorenzo's motion for further findings of fact, he appealed the divorce judgment.

Lorenzo argues that the trial court erred when it awarded the home and rental income solely to Dawn and disregarded the mediated "points of agreement," which included a different disposition of the real estate . . . The question presented is whether, and under what circumstances, a judge may set aside a pretrial agreement between parties to a divorce and award an item of property in contravention of that agreement. Preliminarily, we note that the nature of the proceeding is important to the analysis. This is not a general civil matter where the parties are ordinarily free to enter into any agreement so long as it is not coerced. Rather, this is a family matter, where the court is called upon to exercise its authority in equity, and may be required to act as parens patriae if children are involved. Thus a pretrial agreement between parties to a divorce may be treated somewhat differently than a settlement in a civil suit.

Further, the fact that the pretrial agreement was entered into in the context of a court mandated mediation does not give the agreement the imprimatur of a court order. A family matter agreement does not become an order of the court until it is presented to and approved by the court. As is often the case in the progression of divorce proceedings, the mediated partial agreement between the Cloutiers had not been presented to and approved by the court or a CMO prior to trial. Therefore, the agreement in this case was not enforceable as a court order. Nonetheless, an agreement reached prior to trial does represent a method by which the parties may identify matters that are not disputed and by which the parties may be assured that those matters will not be the subject of litigation. Thus, in the normal course, the court should honor an agreement reached by the parties. This assures that mediation is an effective tool for dispute resolution, and prevents the parties from unilaterally reopening matters that have been resolved. Therefore, ordinarily, when the parties have agreed to the resolution of some or all of the matters previously in dispute, the court will not address those matters at any trial on the remaining disputed issues, and will not, without more, allow the agreed upon matter to be litigated. When the court, acting within its discretion, concludes that there is a basis for setting aside an agreement that has not been incorporated in a court order, however, it may do so.

Because the court will not set the agreement aside without cause, we address several factors that may be considered in making the decision to enforce or set aside a pretrial agreement. The court should consider, among other things, whether the parties have agreed to set aside the agreement; whether leaving the agreement in place would result in a significant inequity; whether there has been an unanticipated and substantial change in the parties' circumstances since the creation of the agreement; whether the court can resolve the matters not contained within the agreement in a reasonable manner in light of the parties' agreed upon resolution of the settled matters; and what affect the enforcement or setting aside of the agreement would have on the best interests of the children.

Once the court determines that an agreement must be set aside, there may be delay in resolving the entire matter and there may be further expenses or detriment to the children inherent in returning an issue to disputed status. Thus, in determining whether to reopen a previously agreed upon matter, the court should consider whether the expense and delay occasioned by setting the agreement aside is outweighed by the importance of the issue to be returned to litigation.

In the context of the Cloutiers' disputes regarding the allocation of their debt, particularly regarding the debt related to the marital home, the court did not exceed the bounds of its discretion in setting aside the parties' agreement to sell the home. The court had ample reason to conclude that selling the Cloutiers' home and dividing the profits would be manifestly unjust. The court was concerned that the Cloutiers' equity in the home was not nearly enough to pay off any of their large debt. Since this was the home in which the children have always lived, one of the main reasons for allowing Dawn to retain the house was to keep the children in their current school district. Further, Dawn's ability to pay for alternative housing, in relation to Lorenzo's, was insufficient. Given the limited benefit that selling the house would have had on the debt and the substantial detrimental effect it would have had on the children, the court acted well within the bounds of its discretion when it set aside the parties' agreement to sell the marital home.

## NOTES AND QUESTIONS

1.   The *Cloutier* court notes that unlike a "general civil matter," there is a particular basis for judicial review in a "family matter." This evidently extends to all issues in family disputes, not just child access. Why do you think the Court reaches this conclusion? Do you agree?

2.   Both the *Wayno* dissent and the *Cloutier* court suggest that judicial review would create a disincentive for participants to engage in mediation. Do you agree? Would it make a difference if there were mandatory mediation as opposed to discretionary mediation?

3.   Although *Cloutier* appears on its surface to be about the disposition of the marital home, the court does note the impact that that issue would have on the parents'

children. To what extent does the *Cloutier* court believe courts should review mediated agreements in family disputes apart from child access? Do you think the case would have been decided the same way if the parties did not have children?

## 2.  Judicial Review of Claims of Improprieties in Mediation

The emotional intensity of family conflict might not only lead to second thoughts about an agreement reached in mediation, but also might generate allegations that the mediation process was tainted. The following opinion represents how one court grappled with this issue.

### VITAKIS-VALCHINE v. VALCHINE
District Court of Appeal of Florida, Fourth District
793 So. 2d 1094 (2001)

STEVENSON, J.

This is an appeal from a final judgment of dissolution which was entered pursuant to a mediated settlement agreement. The wife argues that the trial court erred . . . in denying her request to set aside the settlement agreement on the grounds that it was entered into under duress and coercion. We affirm the order to the extent that the trial court concluded that the wife failed to meet her burden of establishing that the marital settlement agreement was reached by duress or coercion on the part of the husband and the husband's attorney. The wife also alleges that the mediator committed misconduct during the mediation session, including but not limited to coercion and improper influence, and that she entered into the settlement agreement as a direct result of this misconduct. For the reasons which follow, we hold that mediator misconduct can be the basis for a trial court refusing to enforce a settlement agreement reached at court-ordered mediation. Because neither the general master nor the trial court made any findings relative to the truth of the allegations of the mediator's alleged misconduct, we remand this case for further findings.

Procedural background

By August of 1999, Kalliope and David Valchine's divorce proceedings to end their near twelve-year marriage had been going on for one and a half to two years. On August 17, 1999, the couple attended court-ordered mediation to attempt to resolve their dispute. At the mediation, both parties were represented by counsel. The mediation lasted seven to eight hours and resulted in a twenty-three page marital settlement agreement. The agreement was comprehensive and dealt with alimony, bank accounts, both parties' IRAs, and the husband's federal customs, postal, and military pensions. The agreement also addressed the disposition of embryos that the couple had frozen during *in vitro fertilization* attempts prior to the divorce. The agreement provided in this regard that "[t]he Wife has expressed her desire to have the frozen embryos, but has reluctantly agreed to provide them to the husband to dispose of."

A month later, the wife filed a *pro se* motion seeking to set aside the mediated settlement agreement, but by the time of the hearing, she was represented by new counsel. The wife's counsel argued two grounds for setting aside the agreement: (1) coercion and duress on the part of the husband, the husband's attorney and the mediator; and (2) the agreement was unfair and unreasonable on its face. The trial court . . . rejected the wife's claim on both grounds. On appeal, the wife attacks only the trial court's refusal to set aside the couple's settlement agreement on the ground that it was reached through duress and coercion.

Third party coercion

As a general rule under Florida law, a contract or settlement may not be set aside on the basis of duress or coercion unless the improper influence emanated from one of the contracting parties-the actions of a third party will not suffice. In this case, the record adequately supports the finding that neither the husband nor the husband's attorney was involved in any duress or coercion and had no knowledge of any improper conduct on the part of the mediator.

Because there was no authority at the time holding that mediator misconduct, including the exertion of duress or coercion, could serve as a basis for overturning the agreement, the general master made no findings relative to the wife's allegations. The mediator's testimony was presented prior to that of the wife, and, consequently, her allegations of potential misconduct were not directly confronted. Here, we must decide whether the wife's claim that the mediator committed misconduct by improperly influencing her and coercing her to enter into the settlement agreement can be an exception to the general rule that coercion and duress by a third party will not suffice to invalidate an agreement between the principals.

The wife testified that the eight-hour mediation, with Mark London as the mediator, began at approximately 10:45 a.m., that both her attorney and her brother attended, and that her husband was there with his counsel. Everyone initially gathered together, the mediator explained the process, and then the wife, her attorney and her brother were left in one room while the husband and his attorney went to another. The mediator then went back and forth between the two rooms during the course of the negotiations in what the mediator described as "Kissinger-style shuttle diplomacy."

With respect to the frozen embryos, which were in the custody of the Fertility Institute of Boca Raton, the wife explained that there were lengthy discussions concerning what was to become of them. The wife was concerned about destroying the embryos and wanted to retain them herself. The wife testified that the mediator told her that the embryos were not "lives in being" and that the court would not require the husband to pay child support if she were impregnated with the embryos after the divorce. According to the wife, the mediator told her that the judge would *never* give her custody of the embryos, but would order them destroyed. The wife said that at one point during the discussion of the frozen embryo issue, the mediator came in, threw the papers on the table, and declared "that's it, I give up." Then, according to the wife, the mediator told her that if no agreement was reached, he (the mediator) would report to the trial judge that the settlement failed because of her. Additionally, the wife testified that the mediator told her that if she signed the agreement at the mediation, she could still protest any provisions she didn't agree with at the final hearing-including her objection to the husband "disposing" of the frozen embryos.

With respect to the distribution of assets, the wife alleges that the mediator told her that she was not entitled to any of the husband's federal pensions. She further testified that the mediator told her that the husband's pensions were only worth about $200 per month and that she would spend at least $70,000 in court litigating entitlement to this relatively modest sum. The wife states that the mediation was conducted with neither her nor the mediator knowing the present value of the husband's pensions or the marital estate itself. The wife testified that she and her new attorney had since constructed a list of assets and liabilities, and that she was shortchanged by approximately $34,000 — not including the husband's pensions. When asked what she would have done if Mr. London had told her that the attorney's fees could have amounted to as little as $15,000, the wife stated, "I would have took [sic] it to trial."

Finally, the wife testified that she signed the agreement in part due to "time pressure" being placed on her by the mediator. She testified that while the final draft was being typed up, the mediator got a call and she heard him say "have a bottle of wine and a glass of drink, and a strong drink ready for me." The wife explained that the mediator had repeatedly stated that his daughter was leaving for law school, and finally said that "you guys have five minutes to hurry up and get out of here because that family is more important to me." The wife testified that she ultimately signed the agreement because

> [I] felt pressured. I felt that I had no other alternative but to accept the Agreement from the things that I was told by Mr. London. I believed everything that he said.

Court-ordered mediation

Mediation is a process whereby a neutral third party, the mediator, assists the principals of a dispute in reaching a complete or partial voluntary resolution of their issues of conflict. Mandatory, court-ordered mediation was officially sanctioned by the Florida legislature in 1987, and since then, mediation has become institutionalized within Florida's court system. The process is meant to be non-adversarial and informal, with the mediator essentially serving as a facilitator for communications between the parties and providing assistance in the identification of issues and the exploration of options to resolve the dispute. Ultimate authority to settle remains with the parties. Mediation, as a method of alternative dispute resolution, potentially saves both the parties and the judicial system time and money while leaving the power to structure the terms of any resolution of the dispute in the hands of the parties themselves.

Mediation, pursuant to chapter 44, is mandatory when ordered by the court. Any court in which a civil action, including a family matter, is pending may refer the case to mediation, with or without the parties' consent. Communications during the mediation sessions are privileged and confidential. During court-ordered mediation conducted pursuant to the statute, the mediator enjoys "judicial immunity in the same manner and to the same extent as a judge." The mediation must be conducted in accordance with rules of practice and procedure adopted by the Florida Supreme Court.

. . . One of the hallmarks of the process of mediation is the empowerment of the parties to resolve their dispute on their own, agreed-upon terms. While parties are required to attend mediation, no party is required to settle at mediation. . . .

[W]hile mediation techniques and practice styles may vary from mediator to mediator and mediation to mediation, a line is crossed and ethical standards are violated when any conduct of the mediator serves to compromise the parties' basic right to agree or not to agree. Special care should be taken to preserve the party's right to self-determination if the mediator provides input to the mediation process.

In keeping with the notion of self-determination and voluntary resolution of the dispute at court-ordered mediation, any improper influence such as coercion or duress on the part of the mediator is expressly prohibited. . . .

Likewise, a mediator may not intentionally misrepresent any material fact in an effort to promote or encourage an agreement . . . [W]hile mediators may call upon their own qualifications and experience to supply information and options, the parties must be given the opportunity to freely decide upon any agreement. Mediators shall not utilize their opinions to decide any aspect of the dispute or to coerce the parties or their representatives to accept any resolution option.

The question we are confronted with in this case is whether a referring court may set aside an agreement reached in court-ordered mediation if the court finds that the agreement was reached as a direct result of the mediator's substantial violation of the rules of conduct for mediators. We believe that it would be unconscionable for a court to enforce a settlement agreement reached through coercion or any other improper tactics utilized by a court-appointed mediator. When a court refers a case to mediation, the mediation must be conducted according to the practices and procedures outlined in the applicable statutes and rules. If the required practices and procedures are not substantially complied with, no party to the mediation can rightfully claim the benefits of an agreement reached in such a way. During a court-ordered mediation, the mediator is no ordinary third party, but is, for all intent and purposes, an agent of the court carrying out an official court-ordered function. We hold that the court may invoke its inherent power to maintain the integrity of the judicial system and its processes by invalidating a court-ordered mediation settlement agreement obtained through violation and abuse of the judicially-prescribed mediation procedures.

. . . In a variety of contexts, it has been held that the courts have the inherent power to protect the integrity of the judicial process from perversion and abuse. While the doctrine of inherent power should be invoked "cautiously" and "only in situations of clear necessity," we have little trouble deciding that the instant case presents a compelling occasion for its use.

We hasten to add that no findings were made as to whether the mediator actually committed the alleged misconduct. Nevertheless, at least some of the wife's claims clearly are sufficient to allege a violation of the applicable rules. On remand, the trial court must determine whether the mediator substantially violated the Rules for Mediators, and whether that misconduct led to the settlement agreement in this case.

## NOTES AND QUESTIONS

1. The mediator's alleged actions are obviously improper. Do allegations of mediator impropriety need to reach a certain threshold to warrant rejection of a mediated agreement? Upon what basis should that threshold be? We will explore bases for mediator ethics in Chapter 12, but these rules regarding proper mediator conduct are not overly explicit. Can you think of rules that are more specific than "I know it when I see it"?

2. What about confidentiality? The wife in *Vitakis-Valchine* must presumably prove mediator misconduct, but how can she prove mediator misconduct without disclosing confidential information from the mediation? If she waives confidentiality, what about the husband? Would he effectively be compelled to waive confidentiality in order to oppose his wife's allegations of mediator misconduct? How should the balance be struck between confidentiality and maintaining the integrity of the mediation process?

3. As discussed in Chapter 11, a vast number of family litigants are *pro se*. In contrast, the wife in *Vitakis-Valchine* had counsel. Should courts feel freer to subject allegations of mediator misconduct to greater scrutiny when one or both of the parties in mediation are *pro se*?

4. The court notes how the mediator in this case was "court-appointed." What if parties hire a private mediator and one party subsequently claims that the mediator engaged in misconduct?

5. Should the wife's allegations against the mediator be found to be true, most would agree that Mr. London should not be mediating. Nevertheless, even if the wife obtains relief in this particular case, the mediator might ask for "a strong drink" when mediating subsequent cases. This implicates how to conduct ongoing assessments of mediators in order to maintain the quality and integrity of the mediation process, let alone identifying outright examples of misconduct. Consider ways to do this.

# Chapter 8

# MEDIATING OTHER FAMILY CONFLICTS

## A.  INTRODUCTION

"Family mediation" encompasses a range of disputes in addition to issues related to divorce and child access. The concepts and practical applications that we have been exploring apply to this wider range of disputes, although each has its own distinctive qualities

This Chapter will offer an overview of a few of these disputes. Coverage is necessarily brief and something of a grab bag, but this is not intended to dismiss the significance of the growing use of mediation in these and other types of disputes in which families are involved.

## B.  CARE OF INFIRM FAMILY MEMBERS

A range of wrenching issues face families who have ill or aging family members. As the population ages, these situations are, unfortunately, becoming increasingly common. They generally fall into two general categories: 1) end of life decisions; and 2) guardianship cases.

### 1.  End of Life Decisions

With an aging population and advances in medical care, issues relating to end of life decisions are common. Sometimes these disputes arise between physicians and family members, while others are among family members. Both may implicate family dynamics, but the latter is more likely to do so. Consider the situation in the following excerpt.

### *MEDIATING LIFE AND DEATH DECISIONS*[1]
#### 36 Ariz. L. Rev. 821, 830–831, 836–38, 873–74 (1994)
#### By Diane E. Hoffman

. . . Joseph R. is a 75 year old male with a history of chronic emphysema who suffered a massive stroke while hospitalized for breathing difficulties. As a result of the stroke, he was initially unable to breathe on his own and experienced considerable loss of brain function. He was supported on a ventilator, underwent surgical drainage of intraventricular cerebrospinal fluid and then placement of a permanent shunt, was

---

[1] Copyright ©1994. Reprinted with permission.

weaned from the ventilator but required a tracheostomy tube. He developed a pneumonia and was being given IV (intravenous) antibiotics to treat the infection. His other medical conditions included diabetes, hypertension, and chronic bronchitis.

The patient's family, his 49 year old son, who is an engineer, and his 42 year old daughter, who is a nurse, disagree about the appropriate course of treatment for him. The daughter wants the attending physician to stop treating the patient with antibiotics and wants only tube feeding and hydration administered. The son disagrees. He bases his decision on the attending physician's remarks that the pneumonia is reversible and would routinely be treated. If the antibiotics are discontinued the patient will likely die from the pneumonia. If the pneumonia is treated, the patient may live more than six months, although he will suffer from the residual effects of the stroke, i.e., diminished mental capacity, and from his other chronic conditions.

In an interview with the chair of the institution's ethics committee, the patient's daughter stated that it seemed to her that the patient was only going "downhill all the way." In particular, she remembered her 19 year old nephew who twice suffered a cardiac arrest and each time was "saved" only to become "blind, demented, and comatose." That, the daughter related, was thought by the patient to be a terrible outcome and something that he wanted to avoid for himself. The patient's son, however, remembered that when their mother died, their father did everything to keep her alive despite the fact that she was bedridden and senile.

The daughter had cared for the father during the previous year in her home and felt that she should make this decision. The son, although close to his father as a younger man, had not seen his father much during the past six years as he had moved across the country to take a new job.

. . . .

In the case of family disputes, disputing parties can include spouses, adult children where the patient has more than one child, a spouse and a child, a spouse and a parent, a parent and a sibling, some other combination of individuals related to the patient, or disputes between blood relatives and domestic partners.

. . . .

What makes disputes among family members unique is the historical relationship of those individuals. Family disputes often come "wrapped in a thick gauze of past relationships." These relationships also tend to be ongoing and are often interdependent. Each family is unique but typically has an established pattern of relating wherein the individuals take on certain roles. These roles, in terms of dominance and dependence are likely to play themselves out in the context of health care decision-making.

For example, there may be power issues at play. Certain family members may have dominated family life years ago and want to continue in that role, e.g., "mom would have wanted me to speak for her, not you." Others may now resent that domination and attempt to assert their more recent status within the family or relationship with the patient, e.g., "I was a better daughter than you, I cared more about mom, you were never good to mom, you never visited mom while she was in the nursing home," etc.

The case of Joseph R. has some of these elements. The patient's daughter seems resentful of the fact that her brother has not participated much in the care of their father or even visited him much during the past six years and now wants to participate in the decision about their father's treatment. . . .

The case of Joseph R. seems to have most of the attributes of the "paradigm" case for mediation. It is likely that the parties — Joseph's 49 year old son and 42 year old daughter — would be willing to mediate their disagreement and, in fact, may prefer it to the "intervention" of an ethics committee. As brother and sister they have an "ongoing" relationship and they probably see this as a private family matter and may be reluctant to disclose these private matters to the scrutiny of a committee of "strangers." Both parties also seem to be "competent" to negotiate. Although they are both dealing with the possible death of their father, the facts indicate that Joseph has been ill for a number of years — his illness was not sudden. Also, it does not appear that there is a significant power imbalance between the parties. Although the son is older, there is no indication of a history of dominance on his part and although the daughter may be somewhat more knowledgeable of the medical issues, given her nursing background, both parties appear to be well educated. There may be some underlying emotional issues influencing their positions, i.e., guilt on the part of the son for not being around more for his father during his illness, and resentment on the part of the daughter towards her brother, yet neither party appears to have any overriding conflict of interest that would prevent him or her from acting in the best interest of their father. Although it may seem fairly narrowly defined, the resolution of the case also does not necessarily rely on a choice between two mutually exclusive options — treatment with antibiotics or no treatment with antibiotics. The options can be expanded to include other types of treatment, e.g., CPR if the patient has a cardiac arrest, ventilatory support if the pneumonia does not respond to the antibiotics, artificial nutrition and hydration, etc.

As mentioned, the Joseph R. case has a host of emotional issues that need to be addressed between the two parties. It is not a case that is purely ethical or legal. Finally, a norm centered approach to the case will not necessarily lead to a single, best outcome. Both results advocated by the parties, treatment and no treatment, are justifiable on ethical or legal grounds. Both ethical and legal norms would support the son and daughter as appropriate decision-makers in this case and there is evidence to support a conclusion that providing or withholding of the antibiotics is consistent with what the patient would have wanted or is in his best interests.

## NOTES AND QUESTIONS

1.  How does the author define "Joseph R." as a case that is appropriate for mediation? What sorts of cases, given her analysis, would not be appropriate for mediation? Does the litigation alternative offer a more effective way to resolve conflicts in this area than mediation?

2.  Institutional "ethics committees" are important entities in reaching decisions about medical care. Should such committees, in appropriate cases, be involved in mediation, even to the extent that they should participate in the mediation itself? In

one famous case involving Karen Ann Quinlan, the New Jersey Supreme Court held that the concurrence of the hospital ethics committee was necessary before Quinlan's feeding tube could be removed. *Matter of Quinlan*, 355 A.2d 647 (N.J. 1976).

3. The morality of end of life decisions is hotly contested and may strike at the core of individual values. Can such differences be mediated? Consider the case of Terri Schiavo. Schiavo was found to be in a persistent vegetative state. Schiavo's husband wanted her feeding tube removed, and her parents did not. The case was litigated but never mediated. Is it in society's interest to privately mediate such disputes or are there advantages to a public adjudication through the courts? For discussions of this issue, see Judith D. Moran, *Families, Courts and the End of Life: Schiavo and Its Implications for the Family Justice System*, 46 FAM. CT. REV. 297 (2008); Robert M. Shafton, *Family Meltdown or Mediation? Schiavo Converges Private and Public ADR Needs*, 23 ALTERNATIVES TO THE HIGH COST OF LIT. 77 (2005).

4. What does end of life mediation have in common with child access mediation?

5. Disputes regarding a family member can continue even after the family member has died. For a discussion of these issues, see Yvonne Oldfield, *Disputes over Interment and Cremation: The Mediation Option*, 45 VICT. U. WELLINGTON U. L. REV. 613 (2014).

## 2. Guardianship

Chapter 5 addresses issues relating to the welfare of children, but guardianship issues frequently arise with adults as well. Adults might be candidates for guardianship due to substance abuse, mental impairments that are congenital or the result of an injury or medical condition such as a stroke, developmental issues, mental illness, and dementia that sometimes accompanies aging. As with end of life issues, there are sometimes disputes as to whether or to what extent there should be a guardian, or who should be appointed guardian.

The following excerpt describes one guardianship situation and traces out how it might be resolved with and without mediation.

### *MEDIATION: A TOOL FOR RESOLUTION OF ADULT GUARDIANSHIP CASES*[2]
14 NAT'L ASS'N OF ELDERLAW ATTORNEYS Q. 4, 6–7 (2001)
By Susan Butterwick & Penelope A. Hommel

Robert Jones is concerned that his sister, Linda Smith, a single working mother, is not giving their mother, Mary Jones, the care she needs and is wasting her assets. Mary Jones has lived in Linda's home for a year.

---

[2] Copyright ©2001. Reprinted with permission.

Take One — without mediation:

Robert files a petition requesting that he be appointed guardian of his mother. Mary and Linda are angry and upset at this action. The matter escalates into litigation in which harsh accusations are exchanged. The judge appoints a third party non-relative as guardian. The guardian moves Mary into an adult care home. All parties end up angry and hurt.

Take Two — with mediation:

The parties meet with a mediator who helps them identify needs and issues. They recognize that Mary enjoys living with Linda, but she is lonely while Linda is at work. They acknowledge that Mary is confused about her finances and Robert is willing to help. With the mediator's help, they agree that Mary will continue to live with Linda; Robert will help Mary with her bills, and Mary will attend a senior center during the week. They agree to meet in three months to review the situation. The parties end up understanding and respecting each other's concerns. And, an unnecessary guardianship is avoided . . .

Mediation can save time in the long-run in cases where the legal issues presented in the petition or motion are not the underlying issues causing the family turmoil and dissension. Complicated family dynamics can be extremely difficult and time-consuming for courts and attorneys to try to unravel and find an equitable solution that meets the needs and interests of the proposed ward as well as other parties. Mediation allows the parties to discuss the underlying interests and needs in a way that more fully addresses some of the real "sticking points" that can make court hearings contentious and sometimes lead to violation of court orders and further hearings. Mediation can also result in a more thorough, personalized, and specific plan that better addresses underlying issues and needs than a court can craft. In the long-run, the more specifically these underlying needs and issues can be addressed at the beginning, the more time is saved in repeated court hearings and even litigation later on, when difficulties arise in contentious cases or in cases involving difficult family relationships . . .

[C]ases [can begin] where disputes arise at the time an initial petition for guardianship is filed. Typically the respondent feels s/he is able to make his or her own decisions and does not need a guardian because a less restrictive alternative is available. Or, the respondent may contest the petition on the grounds that the guardian's powers should be limited, or that someone other than the petitioner should be named guardian. Of course, other interested parties may also raise any of these issues.

Other disputes arise after a guardian has been appointed. These issues, raised either by the ward or by another interested party, may involve accounting for expenditures by the guardian, the need to continue the guardianship, a petition to terminate, limit, or expand the guardian's powers, a petition to remove the guardian and substitute another, or a challenge to an action or proposed action of the guardian.

Disputes may also arise in advance of, or in anticipation of, the filing of a guardianship petition. Issues in these "pre-petition" situations may include such things as whether the person needs a surrogate decision maker (a guardian, conservator, or power of attorney) and who that person would be, what medical care decisions should be made, whether the person needs a change in living arrangements and care facilities, other issues involving autonomy, independence, safety, and decision-making, and how money will be invested or spent and by whom. Often, legal issues are not the ones causing the turmoil, and the parties in mediation may focus on quite different issues from those that would be argued in a legal case or court proceeding. Even when there are no contested legal issues, family disputes may need to be addressed in order to preserve family relations or avoid future litigation.

Cases that are inappropriate for mediation are those where domestic abuse or substance abuse are involved, or where an emergency decision is needed by a court, the parties exhibit volatile or extremely hostile behavior, or when the possibility of coercion or intimidation of a vulnerable party exists. The personal presence of the alleged incapacitated person or ward may not be appropriate if the person is too incapacitated to take part in the mediation and understand and voluntarily make or keep agreements. In such circumstance, nevertheless, mediation may be helpful for the other parties — family members, caregivers, other support persons, who may disagree among themselves over the best course to follow for an incapacitated person.

## NOTES AND QUESTIONS

1.    While family dynamics are at play in guardianship situations such as those involving Robert, Mary, and Linda, there is a unique element here: the "ward" or "alleged incompetent person" — who may or may not be present in the mediation. Moreover, what if this person does not agree that guardianship is warranted? Does this strike you as appropriate for mediation?

2.    As a matter of law, parents or others involved in family mediation are guardians of minors. Does child access mediation have similar characteristics to guardianship mediation? Why or why not?

3.    Expert medical opinion can be crucial in guardianship issues. Should physicians or mental health professionals be formally included in guardianship mediations? If so, how?

## C.   TRUSTS AND ESTATES

Estate planning and administration issues usually implicate families in one form or another. Most estate planning and administration matters are straightforward, but this is not always the case. For example, some family members might resent their share of an estate, or a share of an estate claimed by a second or subsequent spouse will lead to conflict among other family members. Mediation has become increasingly important when disputes such as these arise.

The growth of mediation in this area falls into two categories: 1) anticipating conflict through mediation clauses in estate planning documents; 2) employing mediation to resolve disputes surrounding estates whether or not estate documents contain a mediation clause.[3]

Mediating disputes involving trusts and estates has multiple advantages:

- Litigation is time consuming and expensive, which both dissipates resources of parties who might share in the estate and delays the dispensation of shares of the estate.

- Remedies available through litigation are uncertain and unlikely to satisfy family members in conflict. Disputants can craft creative means to resolve a dispute that would be more satisfying than a win/lose resolution typical of litigation.

- Litigation is more likely to maintain or exacerbate family conflict than mediation. Litigation thus risks permanently damaging family relationships.

- Will contests may ultimately be driven by longstanding conflicts within families. Mediation might allow venting and airing of grievances which has the potential to address underlying causes of conflict.

## D.  EDUCATION AND FAMILIES

At least two areas involving children's education have been the subject of mediation: special education and truancy.

Disputes as to the type of education provided to special needs children are subject to the Individuals with Disabilities Education Act ("IDEA").[4] The core guarantee of the IDEA is that all students receive a "free and appropriate public education." Parents often disagree with a school system's decision as to the nature of the educational services being offered to a child with special needs. A 1997 amendment to the IDEA specifically provides for mediation of such disputes to be conducted by a "certified mediator."[5]

Chronic truancy is another area that has been mediated. Truancy problems are often intertwined with family issues, and thus many believe that a punitive approach to address truancy is ineffective. Mediation has emerged as an alternative that offers an opportunity to explore underlying issues that lead to truancy and thereby address them. Ohio, for example, has developed a mediation program that operates as follows:

> The participating school identifies a child who has a specified number of unexcused absences or tardiness and sends the parent or guardian warning letters. If the problem continues, the school schedules a mediation session at the school and ensures that the parent and teacher, and, if appropriate, the child attend. The job of the mediator, a third-party neutral, is to explain to the parent what the state and local attendance requirements are and the legal

---

[3] For an excellent overview of the role in mediation in estate planning and disputes, see Roslyn L. Friedman & Erica E. Loard, *Using Facilitative Mediation in a Changing Estate Planning Practice*, 32 Est. Plan. 15 (2005).

[4] 20 U.S.C. § 1600.

[5] Pub. L. No. 105-17, 111 Stat. 37 (1997) (codified as amended at 20 U.S.C. § 1415(e)(1)).

consequences of habitual and chronic truancy. The mediator then tries to help the parties identify the issues that are keeping the child away from school and attempts to get an agreement on what steps will be taken by the school and the home to resolve those issues and assure the child's attendance. If an agreement is reached, the mediator crafts the agreement on the spot and the parties sign it. If the parents don't show up for the mediation or no agreement is reached or the agreement is substantially breached, the matter is referred to the pupil personnel office for "fast-tracking" to the Juvenile Court. If there is part-compliance with the agreement, the parties may agree to re-mediate the matter. If there is full compliance, the file is closed.

Michael A. Lindstadt, *Employing Mediation to Approach Truants*, 43 Fam. Ct. Rev. 303, 310 (2005).

## E.  FAMILY BUSINESS DISPUTES

Family businesses are common. They can range from "mom and pop" stores to multinational corporations and everything in between. Disputes regarding family business might be among or between co-owners, or as founders of businesses age or die and spouses, siblings, or other family members dispute management or ownership.

Passion and emotion generated by such disputes can be extraordinarily high. While disputes about business organizations may, at first blush, appear to be only about money, this is rarely the case. Conflicts within family relationships often overlap with business considerations. As a result, exploring family dynamics can be key to a durable and successful resolution of these disputes. There also might be the additional interest in privacy which can be driven by a desire not only to avoid airing embarrassing personal issues, but also to minimize or eliminate the impact that a public airing of family "dirty laundry" can have on the business itself.

Lawyers play a distinctive role in family business disputes. It is highly likely that disputants in this type of conflict have resources and thus almost always have retained an attorney, particularly a lawyer with some experience in litigating general business disputes. While no research and little scholarship have been devoted to this area, some evidence suggests that such lawyers still embrace mediation as preferable to litigation, albeit typically after litigation has been commenced.[6] Lawyers might have a tendency to veer towards evaluative mediation — a commonly employed style in general business mediation — although mediators who are involved in family disputes can engage in the full range of styles, including transformative mediation.

---

[6] James John Jurinski & Gary A. Zwick, *How to Prevent and Solve Operating Problems in Family Business*, 47 No. 2 Prac. Law. 37 (2001).

# Chapter 9

# POWER DIFFERENTIALS AND FAMILY MEDIATION

## A. INTRODUCTION

Commentators and practitioners of family mediation often grapple with the challenges of how to address "power differentials" among participants. Early proponents highlighted mediation's promise as a dispute resolution tool especially suited to disputes where one participant is less powerful. Other commentators, focusing on the informality and privacy of mediation, developed a "power critique" which questions the suitability of mediation when one participant in mediation is less powerful than another participant.

This Chapter will examine "power" and family mediation at several levels. First, power differentials might exist between the parties prior to the start of mediation sessions. Second, power differentials might develop during the course of the mediation itself. Third, when, if at all, should a family mediator seek to "equalize" or minimize power differentials? The tension between such a role for a mediator, if it is appropriate at all, and a mediator's status as a "third party neutral" is not an easy issue to resolve.

One circumstances that has long been a source of controversy involves domestic violence and mediation — a topic which we will explore in Chapter 10. Some commentators, however, have gone further and made broad critiques that mediation disfavors a defined group of people. These debates often focus on family mediation. In this Chapter, we will examine arguments for and against such critiques and review legislation designed to take these critiques into account.

## B. THE ELEMENTS OF POWER

The term "power" often obscures as much as it reveals. Power in mediation broadly means the ability of one party to exert influence to achieve a desired end. While power has negative connotations and appears inconsistent with the spirit of mediation, this need not be the case. Such influence, for example, can be exerted for the good of both parties, or for children, or for the mediation process. Moreover, it is seductive to reduce power to a ledger where one party has all of it and the other party has none of it. While there are certainly instances of very substantial disparities of power, a closer examination of circumstances may reveal that each party might have power over the other party in different ways. To complicate matters further, what power (if any) a party has in family mediation may shift over time. An appreciation of these issues is central to success both as a mediator and as an attorney in family mediation.

## 1.  Preexisting Power Differentials between Parties Prior to Family Mediation

Family mediation occurs in real time between people with a specific history at many levels, including a history of how they have interacted with one another. Here is a partial list of potential sources of power that participants in family mediation might possess:

- **Physical power**: There might be history of threatened or actual physical violence or emotional abuse in a marriage.[1]

- **Financial power**: One party might have substantially more income than the other, or real or personal property, or access to financial resources through family or other connections. Financial power might also be exerted through knowledge. For example, one party might have exclusively or primarily managed family finances.

- **Interpersonal style**: Individuals vary in their willingness to pursue needs and wants. Some might have "strong personalities" or "be aggressive." Others might be "accommodating" or "soft-spoken." These terms, however, do not necessarily mean that individuals who exhibit individual characteristics are successful or unsuccessful in pursuing what they need or want. For example, a person who is soft-spoken but diplomatic might be more likely to achieve desired ends than someone who is aggressive or impetuous. Moreover, in family mediation, individuals with distinct interpersonal styles have often interacted over time, sometimes for very long periods of time, and this personal history often leads to patterns of interacting that might not always mean what they seem to mean.

- **Custody or possession**: The cliché that "possession is nine-tenths of the law" has particular meaning in family mediation. One party might currently have sole custody of children, or of a home, or of personal property. Such possession might generate power in favor of the possessor.

- **Cultural Norms**: Stereotypes and social norms might contribute to possible marginalization of one participant. For example, the disempowerment of women can be an embedded social norm in certain cultures or contexts. We explore this issue more below.

## 2.  Power Differentials at the Mediation Session

While the above list describes power differentials prior to mediation session, these may also be manifested in the mediation itself. Consider the following examples.

- **One participant has an attorney and one participant does not.** The existence of an attorney for only one participant introduces a substantial power differential. Even if the attorney does not attend the mediation, the represented participant has far greater access to an expert source of information about each participant's legal rights and remedies, and the

---

[1] Chapter 10 specifically addresses issues regarding domestic violence and mediation.

participants' chances of success in court. If the attorney actually attends the mediation, the represented participant will have a trained advocate speaking on that participant's behalf. In addition, the prospect of a judicial proceeding might be less daunting to a represented participant and, as a result, that participant might be less willing to resolve a matter in mediation. An empirical study has substantiated these concerns.[2]

- **Time**. Participants in family mediation might have different time constraints. One participant, for example, might earn an hourly wage, or have a significant commute to work, or might have primary or exclusive child care responsibilities. This, in turn, might motivate that spouse to simply get the mediation process over with quickly. The other spouse can use such time limitations to his or her advantage.

- **Location**. The location of the mediation might generate sources of power. The location might be in a setting familiar to one participant and not to the other (say, at the office of a lawyer representing one participant) or the location may be more convenient to one participant than to another.

- **The Law**. The application of family law statutes might mean that one participant has clear legal advantages should the matter be adjudicated.

- **The Mediator**. The gender, race, ethnicity or other characteristics of the mediator may have an impact on the power balance between the participants to the mediation.

## 3.   Power Differentials Due to Ethnicity, Class, and Gender

Power differentials due to ethnicity, class, or gender can arise prior to or during mediation. This set of issues has triggered debate.

Proponents of mediation argue that mediation offers advantages over litigation for all disputants, including women, people of color, immigrants and the poor. They argue that the hierarchical, "winner takes all" approach of the adversary system further disempowers the disempowered. The delays, expense, complexity and inflexibility of litigation make it particularly ill-suited to resolving family disputes. Mediation, on the other hand, with its emphasis on listening, relationships, and problem solving has greater potential to "heal" and "hear" all voices. Its procedural informality, lack of reliance on substantive rules of law, and lower cost might also make it more accessible to those who cannot afford lawyers.

Others take the opposite position. They hold that mediation is inappropriate, even dangerous, in a private setting without meaningful review of both the process and outcome of mediation. This can be especially difficult when a mediator, due to background or experience, unknowingly draws upon stereotypes that do not reflect the lived experience of one or more of the participants. This can also be the case when,

---

[2] Michael M. Pettersen *et al.*, *Representation Disparities and Impartiality: An Empirical Analysis of Party Perception of Fear, Preparation, and Satisfaction in Divorce Mediation When Only One Party Has Counsel*, 48 FAM. CT. REV. 663 (2010).

as noted above, cultural norms disempower a participant in a way that application of law by a judge could remedy.

This critique has tended to focus on disempowerment in the context of divorce.[3] A particularly prominent critique is contained in an article by Professor Trina Grillo called *The Mediation Alternative: Process Dangers for Women*, 100 YALE L.J. 1545 (1991).[4] One of her points draws upon what she sees as how mediation tends to "obscure[] issues of unequal social power and sex role socialization." Consider one story that Grillo tells:

> A woman . . . told me that her husband had told her two days previously that he was leaving her and intended to marry someone else. He told her he wanted to have the divorce mediated and wanted joint custody of the children. He told her she would have to start looking for a job right away. He also told his wife that it would hurt the children if he and she were angry at each other, and that he wanted to retain a friendly, cordial relationship and have a rational, peaceful divorce. She cried into the phone that she felt terrible that she was unable to be rational, and that although she was trying hard to be mature, she still had these angry feelings. She still wanted to blame him, although she realized, she said, that nothing is ever black and white, and no one is at fault when a marriage breaks up.
>
> My acquaintance . . . did not trust her sense that she had been injured, treated in a way that human beings ought not to deal with each other. She did not have the support of a clear set of legal principles to help her define her injury; rather, she had been exposed to a discourse in which faultfinding was impermissible, so that she ended up unable to hold her husband responsible for his actions, and instead felt compelled to share his fault. To the extent that there is something to be gained by the assertion of rights, especially for women and minorities, this is unacceptable. . . . Both the current state of divorce law and the reigning model of mediation were operating to keep her in a position in which she tried not to blame others and, in the process, lost herself.

## NOTES AND QUESTIONS

1.   Do you agree? Would your view change if you set aside Grillo's gender focus and considered her critique more broadly as to other disempowered participants in mediation?

2.   Embedded in the critique that Grillo presents is a vision of how mediation is practiced. Do you think facilitative mediation, as you understand it, would lead to the

---

[3] The critique assumes the divorce involves a man and woman, although, as we discuss in Chapter 15, mediation involving same sex couples is increasingly common.

[4] Another oft-cited critique, albeit one focused on attorney representation of women in mediation, is Penelope Eileen Byant, *Reclaiming Professionalism: The Lawyer's Role in Divorce Mediation*, 28 FAM. L.Q. 177 (1994). For a response, see Margaret F. Brinig, *Does Mediation Systematically Disadvantage Women?*, 2 WM. & MARY J. WOMEN & L. 1 (1995).

consequences that Grillo articulates? Are there ways you, as mediator, would conduct the mediation that would minimize her concerns?

3.    Does litigation do a better job of resolving power differentials? For a critique of the potential of the adversary system to address the needs of women and minorities in resolving disputes, see Carrie Menkel-Meadow, *The Trouble with the Adversary System in a Postmodern, Multicultural World*, 38 WM. & MARY L. REV. 5 (1996).

4.    Grillo's article was written in 1991. Do you believe it is dated? Do you believe feminism or social changes more generally, to the extent you believe they exist, undercut Grillo's arguments?

5.    Researchers have examined levels of satisfaction for women as opposed to men in mediation. The results have been mixed. They depend on, among other things, the type of issues mediated (custody vs. financial issues), whether process or outcomes are being examined, and whether the parties have experienced both litigation and mediation. For a summary of research in this area, see Connie J.A. Beck *et al.*, *Research on the Impact of Family Mediation, in* DIVORCE AND FAMILY MEDIATION 447, 456–57 (Jay Folberg, Ann L. Milne & Peter Salem, eds., 2004) (citing studies that showed, among other things, that women were more satisfied with the process but not the outcome of mediation; another study showed that men were less satisfied than women with litigation outcomes as compared to mediation outcomes).

## C.    THE ROLE OF MEDIATORS IN ADDRESSING POWER DIFFERENTIALS

A mediator has obvious control over a few matters that might lead to a power imbalance, such as where the mediation will take place. In addition, techniques to maintain mediator neutrality, such as those discussed in Chapter 3, serve to encourage a process where each participant has an equal opportunity to engage in the mediation. Such techniques would include "buy in" directed at both parties, allowing each participant an equal opportunity to express themselves, never having one private caucus without having a private caucus with other participants, establishing "ground rules" that would prevent one participant from interrupting the other, carefully thought out seating arrangements, and so on. One way of characterizing these techniques is that they foster a fair *process* — one in which the mediator tries at every turn to encourage full participation.

Fostering a fair process, however, does not mean that one party will not dominate the process. At least in terms of the facilitative model, it would not be appropriate for a mediator to "shut down" one participant because that participate is dominating the mediation. Rather, a favored technique would be to encourage more participation by the apparently less powerful participant. Power differentials, however, are not so easily diminished, especially given how longstanding and complicated they often are.

An even deeper, more difficult issue can arise, however. What if the mediator believes that the *results* of mediation are unfair to the less powerful participant and the unfairness is due to that power differential? This is usually called the question of mediator intervention to insure "substantive fairness." Should (or must) a mediator put a "thumb on the scale" or "level the playing field" to somehow warn or otherwise communicate to the less powerful participant that a possible settlement is unfair? Is such an act anathema to the role of a third-party neutral, or is it exactly what a third-party neutral should do in order to insure the autonomy and self-determination of all participants to the mediation?

## 1.   The Debate

The mediation literature has confronted this question for some time. The following excerpt, written by Robert A. Baruch Bush and Joseph P. Folger — the originators of transformative mediation — traces current thinking on the issue.

### *MEDIATION AND SOCIAL JUSTICE: RISKS AND OPPORTUNITIES*[5]
27 OHIO ST. J. ON DISP. RESOL. 1, 10–13, (2012)
By Robert A. Baruch Bush & Joseph P. Folger

In the earliest years of the modern mediation field, practitioners made no particular claim that mediated agreements were substantively fair by some objective standard. The mediator's duty of impartiality applied to the conduct of the process itself, but the only guarantee regarding outcome was that any agreement would be "mutually acceptable" to the parties. Whether the agreement was substantively fair enough to accept was up to the parties themselves; the mediator had no role in guaranteeing that fairness.

Soon, however, a clear difference of approach emerged between those who felt the mediator bore no responsibility for fairness of outcome and those who felt, to the contrary, that the mediator was indeed "accountable" for a fair and just outcome, not just a mutually acceptable agreement. That difference of opinion first crystallized in an exchange between two major figures in the field's development, both still very influential today-Lawrence Susskind and Joseph Stulberg. Susskind argued that mediators could not ignore the potential for parties to make unwise decisions and therefore agree to unfair deals, and he suggested that the mediator was accountable to intervene in ways that reduced that risk of unfairness. Susskind's argument was specifically addressed to mediators of environmental and other public policy disputes, and he was specifically concerned with impacts on unrepresented and likely disadvantaged groups . . . . Stulberg countered that, whether in policy disputes or any others, substantive intervention to ensure a fair agreement would contradict the mediator's duty of impartiality, and even worse, compromise his or her ability to serve the central function of facilitating a mutually acceptable agreement between the parties. Even with this sharp difference of views, there was an implicit agreement that mediators could shape their interventions to avoid unjust results, even if there was disagreement on whether they should do so.

Over time, the dominant view in the field has moved in the direction of Susskind's "accountability" view of best practices in mediation-that substantive fairness of

---

outcome is indeed one of the mediator's key responsibilities. . . . [A]s the approach is generally understood and practiced by most mediators today, facilitative mediation incorporates the view that the mediator is accountable for outcome fairness. . . . For a facilitative mediator, the aim is not simply an agreement, but an agreement that accounts for the needs and interests of all concerned. Such an agreement must obviously be one that avoids unfairness in the substance of the deal, and it is therefore part of the mediator's job to monitor for and ensure such fairness, through a variety of methods. While not all authorities agree on which methods to use, some of those suggested include: encouraging or steering the parties, through questions or other-wise, to consider the fairness/justice dimensions of issues being discussed or solutions being proposed; advising parties who lack relevant information, regarding legal rights or otherwise, to obtain that information before reaching any agreement (and even providing them with information within the mediator's knowledge); openly discussing the importance of (and asking parties to commit to) achieving just outcomes, in mediators' opening statements on the aims of the process; and directly suggesting or supporting specific proposals aimed at creating a fair outcome. . . .

Beyond the other methods of taking accountability for substantive fairness, one specific method of doing so is emphasized by mediation's defenders, a method commonly referred to as "power-balancing." It is at the heart of best practices, according to most authorities, and they argue that it is a solid guarantee that mediation will not result in micro-level injustice in individual cases.

The mediator's job of power-balancing is recognized as a key part of his or her work by many authoritative sources. For example, Christopher Moore, author of one of the basic and widely used texts on mediation practice, believes that the mediator has substantial tools at his or her disposal that can effectively protect weaker parties from the effects of unequal power in the mediation, and thus prevent unjust outcomes. According to Moore and others, the mediator is expected to use these tools to do just that.[6]

John Haynes, another widely recognized authority and one of the founders of divorce mediation . . . explain[s] that there are multiple strategies by which the mediator can "correct" the power imbalance, including "identifying with the person under attack" and "controlling the communication" between the parties. Regarding the latter strategy, Haynes explains that:

> [T]he mediator intervenes to take charge of the way the couple communicate and reorganizes it to disempower the overly powerful spouse and empower the powerless spouse. . . . Thus the mediator adjusts the power imbalance sufficiently to permit the negotiations to proceed fairly and smoothly.[7]

It is very clear that these well-respected mediation experts regard power-balancing as a key responsibility of the mediator, that they identify practical strategies to

---

[6] CHRISTOPHER W. MOORE, THE MEDIATION PROCESS: PRACTICAL STRATEGIES FOR RESOLVING CONFLICT 391–93 (3d ed. 2003) (quoting in part James A. Wall Jr., *Mediation: An Analysis, Review, and Proposed Research*, 25 J. CONFLICT RESOL. 157, 164 (1981)). [author's footnote]

[7] JOHN HAYNES, POWER BALANCING, DIVORCE MEDIATION 280–82 (1981) (quoting in part JEFFREY Z. RUBIN & BERT R. BROWN, THE SOCIAL PSYCHOLOGY OF BARGAINING AND NEGOTIATION 79 (1975) [authors' footnote].

discharge this responsibility, and that they believe that the mediator's power-balancing can effectively protect weaker parties from stronger ones who could otherwise take advantage of their power to gain unjust and unfair agreements. . . .

However, . . . [t]he best practices commitment to be accountable for substantive fairness faces several daunting obstacles in practice. First, . . . the real world demand of client expectations often leads mediators to privilege settlement per se, with much less attention to the quality of that settlement. This is especially so when "client" means . . . an institutional client like a court, agency, organization or the like, whose primary interest is likely to be the speedy disposition of the case in a way that obviates the need for further, more formal procedures. . . . If so, mediators serving such clients will feel constrained to concentrate on achieving a timely settlement, even if it means attending less to the substantive fairness of the settlement achieved. There is substantial evidence that this is in fact what occurs with mediators operating in such contexts.[8] Couple these findings with the likelihood that cases mediated for such institutional clients often involve parties of unequal power — divorcing husbands and wives, landlords and tenants, businesses and consumers, school officials and parents — and the likelihood emerges that pressured settlements in cases involving unequal parties result in substantively unfair outcomes. . . . Best practices of accountability for outcome fairness . . . often take a back seat in practice to settlement-production demands. . . .

Practical limitations also draw into question the claim of mediation's defenders that mediators can [promote] social justice by . . . power balancing. . . . As Stulberg argues persuasively. . ., power-balancing by the mediator introduces a practical incoherency that is likely to undermine the mediator's ability to facilitate any kind of agreement, fair or otherwise.[9] In effect, the power-balancing mediator becomes an advocate for one party. . .; however, engaging in advocacy for one party risks losing the trust of the other party. Once that trust is lost, the mediator cannot work effectively to do other crucial tasks, including questioning or probing, challenging positions, reality testing, offering options — because one of the parties no longer is confident of the mediator's impartiality or neutral motives. Apart from this practical problem, the one-sided interventions typically involved in power-balancing . . . risk violating ethical standards requiring mediator impartiality and party self-determina-tion. . . . [In sum,] the critics are probably right about the risks posed to social justice by the use of mediation. And the responses of mediation's defenders . . . are not persuasive, given the limits on those practices and approaches when faced with the practical constraints of real-world mediation.

---

[8] Studies of court-referred mediation, for example, document that mediators apply both subtle and overt pressures for settlement, and these same studies suggest that this often comes at the expense of the quality and fairness of the outcome.

[9] Joseph B. Stulberg, *The Theory and Practice of Mediation: A Reply to Professor Susskind*, 6 Vt. L. Rev. 85, 86–87, 91–97 (1981). See also Joseph B. Stulberg, *Mediation and Justice: What Standards Govern?*, 6 Cardozo J. Conflict Resol. 213, 245 (2005) ("[M]ediation . . . powerfully exemplifies those features of a procedure suitably viewed as one of pure procedural justice . . . . [P]arty-acceptability of outcomes is, and should be, the defining feature of justice in mediation. Standards independent of the process are not needed.") [author's footnote]

# NOTES AND QUESTIONS

1.   Do you believe "power balancing" is appropriate for a mediator? Why or why not?

2.   List all of the techniques that Bush and Folger identify as a means to engage in "power balancing." Are any consistent with the different models of mediation described in Chapter 2? Are they consistent with the "norm generating," "norm educating," or "norm advocating" models described by Ellen Waldman in Chapter 2?

3.   As Bush and Folger note, John Haynes was a prominent figure in developing modern family mediation. Haynes was a proponent of a power-balancing role for mediators. Do you believe that family mediation has characteristics that make power-balancing more or less appropriate?

4.   What should the basis be for determining "substantive fairness"? The mediator's knowledge of law? Experience? Knowledge of social science? Is one of these a more legitimate basis to measure "fairness" than others?

5.   Can a mediator accurately gauge power differentials? Even if a mediator intervenes in order to redress power imbalances, can a mediator misinterpret what is fair or not? Is this an argument against the legitimacy of mediator "power balancing"?

## 2.   Power Differentials and Child Access

Consider child access issues in the context of a mediator's role, if any, in diminishing power differentials. Children have no power to approve child access arrangements even though they are the ones that the entire issue is about.

In thinking through this circumstance, assume that parents agree to a child access arrangement. Setting aside the issue of potential child abuse or neglect or domestic violence, the mediator does not believe that the arrangement the parents agree to is in the best interests of the child. Should the mediator intervene in some subtle or more direct way? Consider the following scenario.

*A Scenario*

You are mediating a divorce involving Ben and Lisa. The couple has one child — Emily — who is 4 years old.

Ben works from 8:30 to 4:30 as a sales representative. Lisa works as a security guard from 3:00 pm to 10:00 pm. Lisa is not able to get home until 11:00 pm at the earliest. Lisa has asked her supervisor if she would be able to change her shift, but her supervisor has told her that would not be possible for the foreseeable future. Neither Ben nor Lisa work weekends. Emily is in day care from 8:00 am to 5:00 pm during the week.

Lisa and Ben agree that they should both spend time with Emily. They agree as follows: Lisa will drop Emily off at day care in the morning, and Ben will pick Emily up from day care in the afternoon. Ben will then drop Emily off at 11:30 pm at Lisa's, and Lisa will then drop Emily off at day care the following morning. This arrangement necessitates that Emily would need to be woken up at about 11:00 pm to go from Ben's house to Lisa's.

## NOTES AND QUESTIONS

1.   Do you think that this arrangement is in the best interests of Emily? Why or why not?

2.   As a parent, would you agree to waking up a 4-year-old every evening? Does this question matter if you are acting as a mediator if the parents agree that this is the best arrangement for them and Emily?

3.   Assume that as a mediator you believe that this arrangement is not in Emily's best interest. Consider the following sequence of options:

- Do not share your opinion about their arrangement or offer alternatives.

- Consider alternative arrangements and suggest them without offering your opinion about the appropriateness of what Lisa and Ben are about to agree to.

- Assume that you do share potential alternatives and Lisa and Ben still want to maintain their original agreement. You then share your opinion that this arrangement is not in Emily's best interests.

- Assume that Lisa and Ben still want to maintain their original agreement. The mediation concludes and you hope that the judge, who will review the arrangement, does not approve it, although your knowledge of the judge is that he rarely scrutinizes child access arrangements that parents agree to.

Which option or sequence of options do you feel is most appropriate? Assuming that you believe that at least the second option is warranted, how exactly would you implement a given option? Write what you would say or do in role.

4.   Consider Standard VIII of the Model Standards of Practice for Family and Divorce Mediation in Appendix C. This Standard appears to adopt a more active role for mediators regarding child access issues than for other issues in family mediation. Do you agree?

## D.   TERMINATING THE MEDIATION DUE TO POWER DIFFERENTIALS

There might come a time when a mediator believes that power differentials make mediation inappropriate. As we will see in the next Chapter, this is a particularly difficult issue with domestic violence. There are other relatively straightforward examples that might warrant termination, such as a risk to the safety of the participants, or child abuse or neglect. In addition, some ethics issues, such as the presence of conflicts of interest, might also require termination.

Are there other less extreme circumstances that might render family mediation inappropriate, especially given power differentials? Standard XI of the Model Standards of Practice for Family Mediation in Appendix C suggests the answer is yes in two situations. One is when "the participants are about to enter an agreement that the mediator believes to be unconscionable." The other is when "a participant is using the mediation process to gain unfair advantage." The Standards, however, do not define these terms. For example, what is the basis for characterizing an agreement as "unconscionable"? This is a term in contract law which is sometimes defined as an agreement that "shocks the conscience" or is "grossly unfair." Does this mean that a mediator would need to apply the legal definition? Would terminating the mediation on that basis mean that a mediator would be acting as a judge — precisely what the mediator role is *not* supposed to be? Can non-lawyer mediators reach a legal conclusion? Gaining an "unfair advantage" seems to set a lower threshold with even less to go on in terms of what it means.

# NOTES AND QUESTIONS

1.    Should a mediator have the power to take away a party's ability to mediate? Would not this be inconsistent with the value of self-determination in mediation?

2.    If a mediator terminates a mediation, should the mediator tell participants why? Would characterizing an agreement as "unconscionable" or accusing one participant of taking an "unfair advantage" destroy a mediator's neutrality? If the mediator says nothing, however, it would leave participants guessing as to what is going on. Is that fair?

3.    Does terminating mediation really make a difference? Perhaps it would be with child access issues, where a court has an independent obligation to assess whether an agreement is in the best interests of a child, but participants might still agree to settle on other matters which might be subject to little or no judicial scrutiny. Would not that mean that the "unconscionability" or "unfair advantage" remain unredressed?

4.    Does it make a difference if both parties are represented? What if one only one party is represented? What if, in the mediator's judgment, one or both attorneys are incompetent?

5.    Should a meditator feel more free to suspend or terminate mediation because of issues relating to child access as opposed to other issues, such as the division of property?

6.    Review the "Elements of Power" material earlier in this chapter. Do any of these elements individually or collectively warrant suspension or termination of mediation?

# Chapter 10

# FAMILY VIOLENCE AND MEDIATION

## A. INTRODUCTION

Perhaps no question has engendered as much controversy in family mediation as the issue of whether mediation is appropriate in cases involving family violence. Most would agree that mediating custody and visitation decisions where one parent has engaged in child abuse or intimate partner violence raises issues that require special treatment in mediation. Some argue that mediation should never happen when there are allegations of child abuse or domestic violence. Others feel, given appropriate protections, mediation is an acceptable or even preferred alternative to litigation. As with many such questions, the answer depends on a deeper examination of the circumstances in each case. What do we mean by domestic violence or child abuse in this context? What does the mediation process being considered look like? Who is the mediator and what approach will be taken? How does mediation compare to the alternative — most likely litigation — in serving the needs of the participants?

The Chapter begins with a primer for identifying intimate partner violence. Later excerpts address the complex question of when mediation is an appropriate option when some level of abuse is present, how it compares to the litigation alternative and the challenges of lawyers, courts, and mediators screening cases for special treatment. Finally, the Chapter concludes by briefly addressing the special circumstances of child abuse.

## B. WHAT IS DOMESTIC VIOLENCE?

### SCREENING FOR DOMESTIC VIOLENCE: MEETING THE CHALLENGE OF IDENTIFYING DOMESTIC RELATIONS CASES INVOLVING DOMESTIC VIOLENCE AND DEVELOPING STRATEGIES FOR THOSE CASES[1]
39 COURT REVIEW 4, 4–6 (2002)
By Julie Kunce Field

Domestic violence is a pattern of assault and coercion, often including physical, sexual, and psychological attacks, as well as economic coercion, that adults and adolescents use against their intimate partners. The key factor characterizing domestic abuse is one partner's need to control the other. The most recent, reliable and

---

[1] Copyright ©2002. Reprinted with permission.

comprehensive studies of violence find that:

- Women are more likely than men to be victimized by intimate partners; women are harmed more severely in those assaults; and males who are victims of assault are generally assaulted by other males.

- More than 50 percent of abusers will be abusive of their partners in a subsequent relationship.

- Nearly 100 percent of children in violent homes hear or see the abuse.

- False allegations of domestic violence occur infrequently, and there is in fact a significant *underreporting* of domestic violence.

- Consequently, the great majority of cases where there is domestic violence will have female victims and male perpetrators.

The Family Violence Prevention Fund has identified five central characteristics of domestic violence:

## 1. Domestic violence is learned behavior.

Domestic violence perpetrators use domestic violence because it works: it serves to maintain power over the battered woman and to cause her to do what the batterer wants. Domestic violence is learned behavior that batterers perfect through observation, experience, reinforcement, culture, family, and community. The batterer learns what works, and what doesn't, to cause his victim to do his will.

## 2. Domestic violence typically involves repetitive behavior encompassing different types of abuse.

The key factor characterizing domestic abuse is one partner's need to control the other. The methods of control include using economic abuse, isolation, intimidation, emotional abuse, and sexual abuse. Children become pawns that the abuser may use to continue his control over his partner's actions. Each method of control may be enforced — and reinforced — with the use or threat of physical violence.

## 3. The batterer — not substance abuse, the battered woman, or the relationship causes domestic violence.

Rarely do substance abuse, genetics, stress, illness, or problems in the relationship cause domestic violence, though these conditions are often used as excuses for the violence, and they may exacerbate violent behavior.

## 4. Danger to the battered woman and children is likely to increase at the time of separation. . . .

Notably, leaving the home or the relationship breaks all of the universal rules of batterers. So, far from guaranteeing safety, when the battered woman attempts to leave, the violence against her and the children is likely to increase. To the batterer, leaving or attempting to leave can represent his ultimate loss of control over his victim and can lead to lethal violence.

5. The victim's behavior is often a way of ensuring survival.

The conduct of domestic violence victims may sometimes seem counterintuitive — the victim fails to leave the situation, even though it may objectively appear to be intolerable. Her failure to leave doesn't necessarily indicate a lack of desire to do so, but rather that she is afraid, doesn't have resources, fears that he will become lethal if she leaves, or for some other reasons, leaving is not a viable option.

## C.   IS IT APPROPRIATE TO CONDUCT MEDIATION IN THE PRESENCE OF DOMESTIC VIOLENCE?

The following excerpt recognizes the complexity embedded in the question: Should domestic violence cases be mediated? Rather than taking a rigid position on one side of the debate, Professor Ver Steegh undertakes the challenging task of identifying when mediation should never be used, when it might be the best alternative and the many cases that fall between these ends of the spectrum. She provides an analysis of factors that are particularly relevant to this decision making. In this way, she provides mediators, lawyers, and most importantly, domestic violence survivors, with the tools to make informed decisions about whether to participate in mediation and what to expect from the mediation process.

### YES, NO, AND MAYBE: INFORMED DECISION MAKING ABOUT DIVORCE MEDIATION IN THE PRESENCE OF DOMESTIC VIOLENCE[2]
9 WM. & MARY J. WOMEN & L. 145, 180–81, 184–86, 195–98 (2003)
By Nancy Ver Steegh

Although mediation provides a desirable alternative for many families, there are serious concerns about its use in cases of domestic violence. Some of these concerns arise from the mediation process itself and others stem from the varying quality of the conducted mediation.

A. Reasons Why Mediation Might Never Be Appropriate

1. Is Mediation Too Private?

Privacy and confidentiality are critical aspects of the mediation process. Both are necessary to encourage full disclosure and candid problem solving. Some women's advocates, however, are troubled by the private nature of mediation. After years of working to have domestic violence dealt with as a crime, they see mediation as potentially returning the issue "back into the shadows." Because criminal prosecution

---

sends a public message to the abuser that his behavior is unacceptable, advocates fear that the abusers in mediation will not be held accountable for the abuse. Similarly, they fear that if these cases are removed from the courts, new favorable legal precedents will not be established. Two factors mitigate these concerns. First, divorce mediation need not supplant the use of the criminal system. If an abuse survivor chooses to do so, she can file criminal charges, pursue a protective order, and mediate the divorce. Use of the criminal courts is not an exclusive remedy. Second, a growing body of evidence suggests that applying criminal sanctions may not deter further abuse. Rather, in some cases, criminal charges have been correlated with an increased likelihood of a recurrence of abuse. Consequently, each victim must make an individual assessment of whether the abuser will be deterred from further violence by criminal prosecution. Either way, she could proceed with mediation.

. . . .

### b. The Problem of Power Imbalance in Cases of Domestic Violence

In cases where domestic violence has taken place, there has already been a severe abuse of power and the consequent power imbalance can make mediation impossible. Barbara Hart argues that cooperation between spouses when domestic abuse had occurred is "an oxymoron." Others agree that especially where there has been a culture of battering coupled with severe abuse, the power imbalance is too great to be overcome in mediation. Victims may fear retaliatory violence if they disagree with the abuser, thus making negotiation impossible.

. . . .

Research does bear out some of these concerns. A 1995 study found that abused women perceive themselves as having less power than women who have not been abused; they were more likely to think that the abuser could "out-talk" them, had "gotten back at them" previously, and said they were afraid to "openly disagree" for fear of retaliation. Interestingly, the authors also made some contrary discoveries as well.

However, there were no significant differences for abused and nonabused women on four personal empowerment items: (a) giving in just to stop dealing with the abuser, (b) feeling guilty for asking for the custody and visitation that they wanted, (c) perceived ability to speak up for themselves about custody and visitation wishes, and (d) getting what they wanted in disagreements.

Other studies report that abuse survivors are able to negotiate effectively and are not at a disadvantage in mediation because of power imbalances. These favorable findings may be related to the mediator screening for abuse and carefully monitoring relative power levels.

Despite the contrary indications found in the research, power imbalance is an important consideration in deciding whether mediation is appropriate. The extent of the problem varies with the individual couple. As discussed previously, women who are dealing with ongoing and episodic male battering or psychotic and paranoid reactions as defined by Johnston and Campbell, may have more difficulty mediating. Similarly, women suffering from "battered women's syndrome" or PTSD may have difficulty standing up for themselves. However, some abuse survivors are able to state their own needs and problem solve effectively.

. . . .

Each couple differs with respect to power imbalance and relative power levels may change throughout the relationship. The power imbalance inherent in domestic violence will render some abuse survivors unable to mediate. However, this assumption cannot be made for all couples who have had violent incidents. Capacity to mediate can only be assessed on an individual level. However, if the couple and the mediator proceed with the mediation, the mediator needs to remain especially alert for power imbalances and be prepared to deal with them. In addition to viewing each couple as unique when deciding whether the mediation process is appropriate, it is important to ask, as Folberg and Milne do, "Compared to what?"

c. Dealing with Power Imbalances

In some cases, the power imbalance is too severe for mediation to take place. However, in less extreme cases, skilled mediators are equipped to deal with moderate power differentials. One way that mediators deal with power imbalance is through their own exercise of power. The mediator controls the process by:

1. Creating the ground rules.
2. Choosing the topic.
3. Deciding who may speak.
4. Controlling the length of time each person may speak.
5. Allowing and timing the person's response.
6. Determining which spouse may present a proposal to the other.
7. Presenting an interpretation of what the spouse said.
8. Ending the discussion.
9. Writing down the agreement.

The mediator gradually transfers power from himself or herself to the divorcing couple as they become able to use it appropriately. If the mediator retains too much power the couple will not "own" the agreement, but if the mediator relinquishes power prematurely, sessions are unproductive and, in the case of domestic violence, potentially dangerous. Because knowledge is a form of power, special care is taken to share information and verify facts. Power can also be balanced in a neutral fashion by asking probing questions and validating the concerns of the less powerful party. Separate caucuses give the mediator a chance to obtain direct feedback on power and safety issues. Mediators watch for specific behaviors that indicate power imbalances. These include but are not limited to tone of voice, glaring, insults, passivity, threats, outbursts, and refusal to speak. In addition to behavioral cues, mediators watch for lopsided agreements. "Even if we concede that a mediator will not be able to see how the husband is maneuvering his wife to where he wants to get her, it is simply impossible for the mediator not to see where her husband has brought her."

Additional safeguards in such situations include independent legal advice and, to some extent, judicial review. If necessary, the mediator can end the mediation "on behalf" of the less empowered person. Some have argued that mediators cannot deal with power imbalance without jeopardizing their neutrality and impartiality. Mediators do remain neutral with respect to the outcome of the mediation but they are not "value-free" with respect to the process and the safety of the participants. For example, as a part of the process of balancing power, mediators ask probing questions and suggest that legal counsel be sought to ensure that the parties are equally informed and fully understand the implications of agreements being considered. The alternative to ignoring power imbalances would essentially amount to siding with the more powerful party. Obviously, the experience of the mediator is key.

Mediation Triage

As noted previously, mediation should never proceed against the wishes of the abuse survivor. However, even when the victim wants to mediate, there are some conditions under which many mediators will not agree to mediate. For this reason, the Model Standards specifically state that some domestic violence situations "are not suitable for mediation because of safety, control, or intimidation issues."

Experts agree that some categories of domestic violence cases should never be mediated. Erickson and McKnight find mediation inappropriate when (1) the abuser discounts the victim and refuses to acknowledge how his behavior affects her, (2) abuse is ongoing between mediation sessions, (3) either client is carrying a weapon or attempts to mediate while drinking or using drugs, or (4) either party continues to violate the mediation ground rules.

Linda Girdner writes that cases should be excluded from mediation when abuse and/or control are central to the relationship to such an extent that the parties are unable to differentiate their interests, the abuser does not accept responsibility for his behavior, and the victim fears retribution. These conditions render the couple unable to negotiate. In addition, Girdner cautions against mediation when weapons are involved and/or the abuser has fantasies of killing the victim and children or committing suicide. . . . In a similar vein, Elizabeth Ellis suggests that mediation may go forward if the violence has been brief, was instigated by the wife, and/or began only after the separation.

Because abuse can differ widely in "form, duration, and severity," the existence of violence creates a red flag for the mediator signaling a need for a closer look at the victim's ability to negotiate and the level of the abuser's denial and control.

If there has been abuse but the identified prohibitions are absent, mediation might proceed, but only under stringent conditions. These include use of a specially trained mediator, a specialized process, and agreed upon safety protocols.

Context and Making Informed Decisions

The abuse survivor is more familiar with her situation than anyone. Consequently, all process decision-making should start and end with her. She will have the best information on the following topics and should consider the following questions.

The Abuse. As discussed previously, there is a continuum of abuse and the experience of each victim is unique. What is the history with respect to the severity, frequency, and amount of abuse? How recently has the abuse occurred? Is there a pattern? Is there a culture of battering with systematic domination and control by the batterer?

Immediate Safety Issues. The abuse survivor cannot make any decisions until she is safe. Has the couple separated? Is the abuse ongoing? If so, referrals should be made to community resources and the victim should consider pursuing a protective order and/or pressing criminal charges.

Status of the Abuse Survivor. Is she ready and able to make decisions? What does she want to happen? Is she interested in counseling? Does she need medical treatment for PTSD?

Likely Behavior of the Abuser. The abuse survivor is usually very knowledgeable about how the abuser is likely to respond to a protective order, criminal charges, and/or mediation. The point of this discussion is not to put his needs before hers, but to anticipate and avoid future abuse.

Need for Future Contact. If the couple has children, especially young ones, there will be some form of future contact that must be carefully structured.

Resources. What resources does the victim have? Can she afford to be represented by an attorney? Is she connected to an advocate or other support system? Are there other time and cost issues?

All of these factors can point in different directions and this makes decision-making difficult. For example, if the abuse survivor is seriously traumatized, has no children, and can afford an attorney, she may elect to proceed through the court system. On the other hand, if the abuse has been less severe and only took place around the time of the separation, if she has small children, and if she cannot afford an attorney, exploring mediation might make sense. Most abuse survivors will fall between these two scenarios and their decisions will be more complex.

Beyond individual considerations, divorce process decisions must be made within a larger context. Ideally the abuse survivor should have access to information about the quality and approach of the court system as well as the particular mediation process. Whatever process is chosen, state law will inform the ultimate outcome. The abuse survivor should be aware of whether the law provides a rebuttable presumption against custody awards to batterers or whether custody decisions are made in accordance with the "best interests" standard. The survivor might also want to consider whether joint custody is the norm.

If the abuse survivor enters the adversarial system, she should know whether the judge is likely to be informed about domestic violence issues. If she enters mediation, she might consider whether she will have access to a mediator or co-mediators who are experienced and specially trained to mediate domestic violence cases. The survivor should also learn whether the mediation will cover all topics and involve multiple sessions.

The quality of the process may be of more significance than the process itself. Poorly conducted mediation could be more dangerous than when unrepresented parties appear before a well-trained and sensitive judge. In reality, there is not always a clear choice between mediation and the adversarial process. For example, a well-structured, cooperative two-attorney negotiation is more like mediation than a contested trial. Consequently, each abuse survivor must individually evaluate her actual options.

Other commentators have addressed the question of whether to mediate cases where domestic violence is present by comparing it to the most common dispute resolution alternative, litigation. The following excerpt makes this comparison and concludes that mediation may, in many cases, be a better alternative for participants experiencing domestic violence.

## MOVING OUT OF THE 1990s: AN ARGUMENT FOR UPDATING PROTOCOL ON DIVORCE MEDIATION IN DOMESTIC ABUSE CASES[3]
22 Yale J.L. & Feminism 97, 117–122 (2010).
By Mary Adkins

. . . [I]t is important to compare the nature and current practice of the two possible proceedings in the family court context — mediation and litigation — before determining that one poses a greater risk to victims' interests. Are DV victims more likely to raise their concerns before a judge than they are before a court mediator?

Formally, the two processes differ fundamentally in that litigation is a rights-based process, while mediation emerged as and remains an interests-based process, largely in reaction to feminist qualms with a rights-based approach. This dichotomous understanding of the two processes has led to criticism on both sides. Critics of ADR processes, which include mediation, argue that justice is lost in the settlement process. ADR advocates believe that imposing an adversarial, zero-sum approach on an idiosyncratic conflict can entrench false notions of diametrically opposed positions, making mutually beneficial outcomes nearly impossible.

There is growing support for the idea that this dichotomous understanding presents an inaccurate picture of both litigation and ADR. In reality, judges, particularly in the family law context, are frequently managerial, becoming immersed in the interests of the parties as those interests are advanced and dealing with rights only when they come into conflict. Likewise, mediators in court settings conduct mediation in the "shadow of the law," with individual mediators and programs varying in the degree to which they respond, both by policy and by discretion, to legal influence.

In a "norm-advocating model" of mediation, the mediator will not only educate the parties about legal and ethical norms but will insist on incorporating them into the agreement. But even court mediators who do not advocate norms are likely to ensure that the parties are informed of legal norms — what Ellen Waldman distinguishes as the "norm-educating model."

---

[3] Copyright 2010. Reprinted with permission.

Robert Mnookin describes how two parties negotiating, after the mediator or their attorneys have educated them about their legal entitlements and advised them on the strength of their cases, will bargain within a range of outcomes that is limited to those leaving both as well off as they would be or would likely be if they were to proceed through litigation. He provides an example of a custody case in which both parents have a sense of the realm of possible trial outcomes and are therefore able to "negotiate some outcome that makes both better off" (based on idiosyncratic tastes within that range) but still falls within the scope of judicially feasible outcomes. It is important to keep in mind that court-mediated agreements remain subject to approval by a judge for them to be entered as court orders.

Finally, court mediators are most often judicial employees under the supervision of a director who reports to the chief judge. They have been described as having a "symbiotic [relationship] with the court system." Like judges, they operate under the pressure of limited resources. Efficiency is necessary, hence the heavy evaluative component of mediation in a court setting.

Because judges behave managerially and mediators behave judicially, the discussion of legal entitlements becomes more integrated into mediation and the discussion of interests more integrated into litigation. Consider the following examples.

A pro se divorcing couple with children appears before a judge. Several financial issues are being contested, as is visitation, but not custody. There are many other litigants sitting in the courtroom or hovering in the hall, waiting to be called. The parties petition the court, each explaining their reasons for requesting certain orders — how debt should be divided, when the house must be sold, and what visitation schedule is most convenient. Resolving these issues is almost certain to become a discussion between both parties and the judge about interests, not rights. The judge will say, "Mr. X wants Fridays and every other Saturday. Is this okay with you, Ms. X? No, you're busy? Mr. X, how about Fridays and every other Sunday? Now, when can we get this house sold? . . . "

The parties will attempt to reach an agreement in discussion with the judge; only if and when they do not agree will the judge impose applicable law against the interests of one or both parties. This moment of transition may be the fundamental distinction between the contemporary family courtroom and many contemporary family court mediation rooms. The infrequency with which such transitions occur, combined with the potential benefits of mediation as chronicled in current research and the unique risks posed by litigation (discussed below), suggests that the extent to which litigation has been upheld in the relevant literature and the Model Code as the preferable process for DV victims is no longer justifiable.

Suppose in a mediation that is not norm-advocating, the same pro se DV victim decides she is willing to assume all marital debt, wishes to waive any entitlement she may have to alimony, and holds no desire for equity in the marital home or any marital property. She makes these concessions because she is intimidated by the abuser and frightened to voice her true wishes. In any court-sponsored mediation program, the agreement will be subject to mandatory judicial review. A judge will ask, "Did you agree to these concessions freely and voluntarily? Are you sure? Do you realize that by waiving alimony now, you are making yourself ineligible to return and ask for alimony at any time in the future [in some states]?"

This sample inquisition also illustrates what would likely occur in a courtroom where there had been no mediation if a DV victim stated before a judge that she wished to relinquish all entitlements to marital property and alimony, for a judge is unlikely to impose alimony on an unwilling beneficiary. Even if the judge were to do so, it would become the victim's responsibility in most cases to report noncompliance if she wished for the order to be enforced. Notably, compliance rates for child support orders are worse for couples with a history of DV than those without DV.

The comparability of the two proceedings is enough to cast doubt on the idea that mediation inherently poses a greater risk to the victim's interests based on the respective roles played by the judge and mediator. Perhaps the risk then can be found in the victim's greater willingness to express her interests in the courtroom than in mediation. The hypothetical above illustrates the realm of interests-based litigation, in which parties are responsible for ensuring that their interests are represented to the court. Again, a judge retains the authority to impose rights, but as a neutral arbiter he or she must not advocate for one party over the other to the extent of imposing interests on one party. Within this realm, the victim must voice her interests just as she must in the mediation room.

There are many reasons to question the assumption that a victim is more likely to express her interests to a judge than to a mediator. First, the ability of an abuser to intimidate through "face-to-face" interaction is by definition greater in a courtroom than it is in a shuttling mediation in which the couple never actually participates in face-to-face engagement. Indeed, the abuser, a named party, is entitled to be heard, to "have his day in court." This is particularly true where both parties are, or even the alleged abuser alone is, pro se, a situation that applies in the majority of divorce filings. Under these circumstances, if the victim wishes to allege DV in order to establish fault, which depending on the jurisdiction could be grounds for divorce or alimony, she must testify that the violence occurred, which then allows for her to be cross-examined by the pro se alleged abuser himself. The abuser may challenge her, question her, and imply she is to blame in open court.

The rules of adjudication that entitle a pro se litigant abuser to personally cross-examine a victim may in themselves intimidate that victim into shying away from advancing her true interests. At the very least, it is impossible to conclude that litigation, with its particular procedural and evidentiary requirements and public forums, is less likely to silence a victim litigant than mediation sessions, particularly with shuttling and/or a mediator attuned to the risk of intimidation.

Feminist theory on domestic violence has recognized the importance of investigating how the unique interests of minority groups are addressed by socioeconomic and political structures. Though one could devote extensive discussion to this topic, I will briefly offer several examples of specific minority populations that may face special disadvantages under the presumption against mediation.

Designing effective policy means understanding that in particular ethnic communities, a victim may experience tension between her identity as a victim of abuse and her identity as a community member with communal commitments and values. For example, although many victims have reasons to remain silent about their abuse, it has been suggested that black women may harbor the fear that "to break the silence is to bring further shame and disapprobation on African American men from the wider society." In Orthodox Jewish communities, a woman who seeks divorce must acquire a get, a Jewish divorce decree, from her husband who retains exclusive power to give or refuse it. Forcing the husband to give the get may invalidate the divorce. In practice, this often means the husband retains the exclusive power to grant or deny the divorce, even in abuse cases. Victims in the Orthodox Jewish community sometimes prefer to deal with the violence privately rather than publicly.

In these and similar instances, the choice between mediation and litigation can mean the difference between staying in the relationship, even if it means further abuse, and seeking a divorce, which requires involving the state. In the former example, the victim who is free to mediate has the option of choosing not to expose or vilify her abusive spouse in open court. Rather, she may enter into an agreement in the privacy of the mediation room, where the violence can be taken into account, but not under the watchful eyes of the public and not on the record. In the latter example, the mediation option is one that can be used to bargain for the get (by agreeing not to litigate in open court and expose the abuse, if the abuser will grant her the get) and one that may be preferable to both parties if they prefer a private negotiation to a public one. New approaches to addressing domestic violence in the Orthodox Jewish community have had notable success, suggesting exciting potential for the further development of similar models.

Fear of outcomes could motivate litigants who lack immigration status as well. Consider an undocumented immigrant victim who is financially dependent on her abuser. He is also undocumented and working illegally. Afraid to involve the state in their lives for fear of exposing her or her abuser's lack of immigration status, the victim is cautious in her approach to seeking a divorce. It is quite conceivable that to petition for a support order before the court in an antagonistic proceeding with her spouse — exposing both of them to questioning on their ability to earn income and their means of support, which are actions both are undertaking illegally — is more daunting than to enter into a facilitated agreement of support through mediation. The latter is subject to judicial review, but the scope of questioning involves the voluntariness of the agreement, not the means by which the parties will comply with its terms. Whether or not the fear that a family court judge will alert the federal government of violations of immigration law is well founded, it is a rational concern that may encourage inaction. The option to mediate could assuage such a fear.

Finally, the degree to which litigants are confused and intimidated by the formality of court hearings contrasted with their reported comfort and satisfaction with mediation, also calls into question the claim that a victim is more likely to voice her interests in the courtroom. Participants in mediation report that they generally find mediators to be "impartial, sensitive and skilled." In part because most court mediators work in mandatory mediation programs, they often have expertise beyond the scope of standard training programs for private mediation. Most are licensed mental health professionals with over five years of court experience, and forty-four percent have over ten years court experience. Most have been trained specifically in dealing with DV issues which, while part of my argument is that this training is also misguided, demonstrates that courts are at least recognizing and responding to the unique challenges presented by DV cases.

## NOTES AND QUESTIONS

1.   How does Mary Adkins describe court based mediation? How does she describe litigation of family disputes? How do her descriptions compare with your observations or experiences in litigation and mediation in family court?

2.   Both Ver Steegh's and Adkin's analyses offer alternatives to earlier scholars and practitioners who argued that mediation should never be used when there are allegations of domestic violence. After reading these excerpts, who do you think should make the decision about whether to use mediation as a dispute resolution option in a given case — the judge, the mediator, or the participants? If you were making the decision, what information would you need? Consider these questions as you read about various approaches taken by courts and legislatures in court based mediation and the efforts to develop screening tools to help inform decisions about domestic violence and mediation.

## D.   LEGISLATIVE AND JUDICIAL RESPONSES TO DOMESTIC VIOLENCE AND MEDIATION

Courts and legislatures have responded to the consensus that domestic violence cases should be given special treatment in mediation by enacting a variety of rules and statutes to achieve that goal. As discussed in Chapter 7, nearly all states have enacted statewide statutes or court rules authorizing mandatory, discretionary, or voluntary court-sponsored mediation programs of selected family law disputes. A few statutes make mediation mandatory, even in the presence of domestic violence. *See* Cal. Fam. Code § 3181(a) (mediator shall meet with parties separately and at separate times, if history of domestic abuse, if a protective order is in effect or if a party alleges under penalty of perjury that domestic violence occurred and party alleging the abuse so requests); Utah Code Ann. § 30-3-38(4)(c) (mandatory mediation of visitation disputes under pilot program may continue notwithstanding an allegation of physical or sexual abuse of a child, unless otherwise ordered by a court). In the majority of these states, however, the statutes or rules create some kind of exception to the court's authority to order mediation when domestic violence and/or child abuse are present or prohibit mediation entirely under these circumstances.[4]

The threshold determination under these statutes is whether domestic violence is present; the statutes vary widely in determining the level and type of proof that is required to establish that abuse exists. A handful of statutes require the court or mediator to screen for domestic violence. *See, e.g.*, Haw. Rev. Stat. § 580-41.5 (b) ("a mediator who receives a referral or order from a court to conduct mediation shall screen for the occurrence of family violence between the parties"); W. Va. Code

---

[4] For a compilation of these rules and statutes, see http://www.americanbar.org/content/dam/aba/administrative/domestic_violence1/Charts/2014%20Mediation%20Statutory%20Chart.authcheckdam.pdf (last visited Jan. 7, 2015).

§ 48-9-202 (requiring the highest court of the state to develop rules for premediation screening procedures to determine whether domestic violence would adversely affect the safety of a party). Most other states leave it to the parties to raise the issue with a range of evidentiary requirements. *See, e.g.*, Ala. Code 6-6-20 (d) (allegations of domestic violence); Ind. Code 34-26-5-15 (existence of a civil protection order); Ohio Rev. Code Ann. § 3109.052(a) (one party was convicted or pled guilty to a crime of domestic violence involving the other party or their children); Minn. Stat. Ann. § 518.619, subd. (2) (probable cause that one party has sexually or physically abused the other party or child).

Once it is established that domestic violence is present, statutes and rules generally take one of three approaches to exempting cases. Some prohibit mediation, regardless of participant preferences, whenever domestic violence is present. *See, e.g.*, Mont. Code Ann. § 40-4-301 (court may not authorize . . . mediated negotiations if . . . reason to suspect that one of the parties or a child of a party has been physically, sexually, or emotionally abused by the other party). Other statutes permit mediation if appropriate procedural and substantive safeguards exist. These include representation of the victim by counsel. *See e.g.*, Del. Code Ann. tit. 13 § 711A (2001) (mediation is prohibited if domestic violence has occurred . . . unless the victim is represented by counsel.).

Finally, some statutes leave the choice to participate in mediation to the victim who is most knowledgeable about her circumstances. *See e.g.*, Tenn. Code Ann. 36-6-107 (a) (if an order of protection has been issued . . . or if there is a court finding of domestic abuse . . . the court may order mediation . . . only if victim agrees). For a discussion on the pros and cons of giving victims of domestic violence the right to consent to mediation, compare Leigh Goodmark, *Autonomy Feminism: An Anti-Essentialist Critique*, 37 FLA. ST. U. L. REV. 1, 35–36 (arguing that women who have experienced domestic violence should always have the choice to participate in mediation) with Douglas D. Knowlton & Tara Lea Muhlhauser, *Mediation in the Presence of Domestic Violence: Is It the Light at the End of the Tunnel or Is a Train on the Track?*, 70 N.D. L. REV. 255, 267 (1994) (arguing that "Mediation is unequivocally wrong when the dynamics of violence exist in a relationship.") Of course, the right to consent or object to mediation domestic violence is only an effective protection if participants are aware of the right and know how to communicate their preferences to the court. For an example of the challenges of doing so, particularly where the participant is unrepresented, see *Adolphson v. Yourzak*, 2008 Minn. App. Unpub. LEXIS 1228 (Oct. 21, 2008).

A number of major professional organizations have also weighed in on the need to provide special treatment for family violence cases in mediation. The Model Standards of Practice for Family and Divorce Mediation (Appendix C in this book) and endorsed by the American Bar Association and the Association of Family and Conciliation Courts, among others, includes provisions defining domestic violence, requiring domestic violence training for mediators, screening, and setting forth steps to ensure safety during mediation. The Model Standards also recognize that some cases should not be mediated "because of safety, control or intimidation issues. A mediator should make a reasonable effort to screen for the existence of domestic abuse prior to entering into an agreement to mediate. The mediator should continue to assess for domestic abuse throughout the mediation process." Another group of distinguished academics, judges, and practicing lawyers, the American Law Institute (ALI), has also addressed the issue of mediating family disputes where domestic violence is present. In its Principles of the Law of Family Dissolution, the ALI takes the position that the risks of coercion and intimidation in mediation for victims of domestic violence require that all mediation programs be voluntary. In order to protect victims in parent education and the development of parenting plans, the ALI would require courts to develop a screening process to identify cases in which there is "credible" evidence that domestic violence has occurred and to conduct evidentiary hearings to evaluate such evidence. The ALI, then, takes the position that the best way to address the risks of domestic violence and mediation is to make certain such cases are identified in the courts and to use mediation only when both parties agree to it.

For a broader discussion of family mediation statutes and rules, see Chapter 7. *supra.*

## E. SCREENING FOR DOMESTIC VIOLENCE

Despite the consensus that domestic violence cases require special treatment in mediation, few statutes or rules provide guidance to courts about their obligation to identify domestic violence cases before an order to mediate is issued. As a result, both attorneys of clients in mediation and family mediators have an important role to play in screening cases for domestic violence. The following excerpt provides some guidance as to the role of both these players in mediation.

### *DOMESTIC VIOLENCE AND MEDIATION: RESPONDING TO THE CHALLENGES OF CRAFTING EFFECTIVE SCREENS*[5]
39 FAM. L.Q. 53, 65–67, 69–70 (2005)
By Jane C. Murphy & Robert Rubinson

Best Practices in Screening for Domestic Violence

Screening for domestic violence is not a one-step process. Indeed, many individuals — both lawyers when parties are represented and a wide range of court personnel-can help to narrow the gap between theory and practice in protecting domestic violence victims in the mediation process.

A. *The Role of Attorneys*

An initial problem in approaching the role of lawyers in protecting victims of domestic violence is that the vast majority of such victims cannot obtain counsel. As addressed below, this common situation vastly enhances the responsibilities of the judicial system — both administrators and judges — to protect victims through appropriate screening protocols.

---

[5] Copyright ©2005. Reprinted with permission.

A second problem is when the abuser — sometimes the party with greater economic resources — is represented and the victim is not. Such an instance intensifies an inherent power imbalance, and such an imbalance would, in virtually all circumstances, render the case inappropriate for mediation. In other instances, however, all parties are represented by counsel or the victim is represented and the abuser is not. In such cases, lawyers have a crucial and positive role to play.

First, lawyers are exceptionally well positioned to act as screeners themselves. By learning and understanding the specific circumstances surrounding domestic violence and by knowing and understanding how mediation is likely to be conducted in a given jurisdiction, lawyers can counsel clients about whether or not mediation is an appropriate process. Moreover, lawyers' relationships with their clients enable them to conclude that mediation would not be appropriate as events unfold and more information is gathered. As a result, lawyers can act as screeners at all points in their representation, up to and including the mediation session itself.

Second, lawyers can advise their clients about other potential remedies and, if appropriate, pursue them. For example, pursuing mediation does not preclude seeking a protective order or pressing criminal charges against an abuser. The advisability of such actions, in turn, might influence whether or not mediation is an appropriate alternative.

Third, when possible, lawyers can assess the qualifications and competence of potential mediators. As "repeat players" in the mediation process, lawyers are in a far better position than parties to help insure the choice of a sensitive and sophisticated mediator.

Fourth, lawyers can have a crucial role to play in preparing for and attending the mediation sessions themselves. In so doing, lawyers act as power enhancers and equalizers: they can speak on behalf of clients, evaluate proposed solutions in light of applicable legal norms and the specific experiences of the client, and, if necessary, suggest opting out of the mediation itself if it is not serving the interests of clients.

These constructive roles for attorneys presuppose, of course, effective lawyering. In the context of a case involving a client who has experienced domestic violence, this means attorneys who are sophisticated in their understanding of the special needs and experiences of such clients, are rigorous in their fact investigation, and understand the possibilities and shortcomings of mediation in resolving specific issues facing individual clients.

## B. *The Role of the Courts*

Because so many family law litigants are unrepresented, courts must play the primary role in screening cases for mediation. The obligation to screen should be made explicit in the governing statute or court rule. This shifts the burden of raising domestic violence issues from the victim to the court and lays the groundwork for courts to lobby for appropriate resources for effective screening. In addition, courts, by rule or other directive from the chief judge of the highest court, should provide mediation programs with a protocol defining the obligations of each player in the system. Because there are many points of entry into the family justice system, and because domestic violence issues are often difficult to identify, cases should be screened at several different points in the court system. . . .

## Mediation

Despite multiple efforts to screen for domestic violence cases prior to mediation, cases involving abusive relationships will still get to mediation. It is, therefore, critical that mediators are properly trained to identify domestic violence and conduct their own screenings. This is required by mediator's ethical standards and is an essential part of an effective screening system. Mediators have developed a number of their own screening tools for this purpose. To insure quality and consistency, courts may want to prescribe the use of a uniform screening tool to be used by all mediators. A variety of professional organizations have developed lists of questions for mediators and others to use to elicit information to evaluate for the presence of domestic violence in premediation meetings with participants See e.g., Katherine Waits, *Battered Women and Their Children: Lessons from One Woman's Story*, 35 HOUSTON L. REV. 30 (1998) (reprinting screening tool from the American Medical Association); The Impact of Domestic Violence on Your Legal Practice: A Lawyer's Handbook 2-1-2-11 (Goelman, et al. eds. 1996). Even if screening occurs at multiple levels, cases involving abusive relationships will still find their way into mediation. Experts have developed checklists for mediators of behaviors that may be observed in mediation that suggest a power imbalance resulting from domestic violence. These behaviors look at tone of voice, facial expressions, willingness to express needs, outbursts and lopsided agreements. See e.g. Lenard Marlow, *Sampson and Delilah in Divorce Mediation*, 38 Fam. and Conciliation Courts Review 224 (2000). Mediators who observe such behaviors can conduct private caucusing and other screening techniques to determine whether to exclude the case from mediation or implement appropriate power balancing or safety measures if the mediation is to continue.

## NOTES AND QUESTIONS

1.   Assume you are a legislator in a state in which the family mediation statute simply provides: "In cases involving custody and mediation disputes, the court shall order the parties to attend a minimum of two sessions of mediation before a court certified mediator." In response to requests from domestic violence advocates, you are considering amendments to the statute to give special treatment to victims of domestic violence. What are your options? Do you provide an exception for cases in which domestic violence is present? Why or why not? If you decide to include an exception, how do you establish the presence of domestic violence? Do you make the decision to order mediation in the presence of domestic violence discretionary with the court or make the exception absolute? If you decide to permit discretion, what factors should guide the court's discretion?

2.   Since the publication of the Murphy & Rubinson article, a number of new screening tools have been developed to assist attorneys, mediators, and courts in identifying potential domestic violence victims. Many are single page instruments that can be used to assess relative risk for potential mediation participants by adding up a

score based on a series of questions. *See e.g., Women's Experience with Battering* http://www.parentsasteachers.org/images/stories/documents/ Guidance_for_DOVE_Screening_2-28-12.pdf (last visited January 6, 2015); Noreen Stuckless, *Domestic Violence, DOVE, and Divorce Mediation*, 44 FAM. CT. REV. 658 (2006). There are also more complex tools that not only identify potential risk but also identify what strategies will be most effective if mediation is undertaken. *See e.g.,* Connie J. A. Beck, Michele E. Walsh, Robin H. Ballard, Amy Holtzworth-Munroe, Amy G. Applegate, John W. Putz, *Divorce Mediation with and Without Legal Representation: A Focus on Intimate Partner Violence and Abuse*, 48 FAM. CT. REV. 631–642 (2010). (MASIC screening tool available at http://info.law.indianan.edu/faculty-research/faculty-saff/profiles/faculy/applegate-amy-g.shtml) (last visited February 6, 2015).

3.   Substance abuse problems affect large numbers of families facing divorce, separation, or other family disputes. While many believe substance abuse and family violence are connected, most experts agree that family violence is not *caused* by the substance abuse. Rather, the cause is the abuser's need for power and control. Nevertheless, substance abuse and family violence often occur in the same families. The National Center on Addiction and Substance Abuse has concluded that "[c]hildren whose parents abuse drugs and alcohol are almost three times . . . likelier to be physically or sexually assaulted and more than four times . . . likelier to be neglected than children of parents who are not substance abusers." *No Safe Haven: Children of Substance Abusing Parents* ii (1999). Drug and alcohol problems in a couple, however, interfere with that couple's ability to communicate and make meaningful decisions in mediation. As a result, some family mediation statutes and rules provide exceptions to court ordered mediation where there are allegations of substance abuse. *See, e.g.,* N.C. Unif. Rules Cust. and Mediation Program Rule 8 (court may waive mediation where there are allegations of alcoholism or drug abuse); S.C. Rules Fam. Ct. Rule 2 (2004) (a court may defer or dispense with mediation upon a showing of substance abuse.)

4.   Once potential mediation participants have been screened and identified as experiencing domestic violence at some level, checklists like the one below help mediators develop strategies when the decision is made to proceed with mediation.

### Strategies for Different Levels of Domestic Violence Risk[*]

### LOW RISK

1.   Clearly stated written "rules of civility" that encourage respectful communications and specifically exclude coercive conduct during and between mediation sessions.

2.   Parties agree in writing to terminate mediation if the mediator obtains credible evidence of threatened or actual violence and/or abuse.

---

[*] Level of risk determined by DOVE, a 19-item instrument designed to assess and manage the risk of domestic violence between partners during and following their participation in divorce mediation. This Instrument and these risk categories can be found in Desmond Ellis and Noreen Stuckless, *Domestic Violence, DOVE, and Divorce Mediation*, 44 FAM. CT. REV. 658 (2006).

3.  Face-to-face mediation.

4.  Referrals to appropriate treatment interventions.

## MODERATE RISK

5.  Mediator carefully monitors compliance with violence/abuse prevention rules during private interviews with partners, and/or by communicating with third parties identified as trusted contact persons by partners.

6.  Partners arrive and leave at different times or routes and do not wait in the same room.

7.  Mediators provide both partners with a list of community resources such as shelters, men's programs, health services, male and female support groups, and legal information.

8.  Face-to-face mediation with advocate or supporter present, or shuttle mediation.

9.  Referrals to appropriate treatment interventions.

## HIGH RISK

10.  Partners given safety warnings in writing.

11.  Interpersonal contact only takes place in public places, or with trusted third parties present.

12.  Arrange for third party to be present during exchanges of children, or third party transports children.

13.  Communication only through trusted third parties or through journals exchanged with children and subject to monitoring by mediator.

14.  Partners escorted to and from premises where mediation is being conducted.

15.  Shuttle, telephone, or on-line mediation.

16.  Referral to appropriate treatment Interventions.

## VERY HIGH RISK

17.  Referral to appropriate treatment Interventions.

18.  Telephone or on-line mediation if referrals produce credible evidence of positive personal and/or situational change.

## F.  CHILD ABUSE AND MEDIATION

Family violence may also involve child abuse. Research demonstrates that domestic violence and child abuse often overlap. Children exposed to domestic violence are at an increased risk of being abused or neglected. A variety of studies reveal there are both adult and child victims in 30 to 60 percent of families experiencing domestic violence. Most statutes and rules creating exceptions from court ordered mediation treat domestic violence and child abuse in the same way, permitting the victim or parent to opt out of mediation upon a satisfactory showing of abuse. Despite the lumping together of these two issues, allegations of child abuse in a family experiencing separation or divorce raise additional issues for the mediator. While screening for intimate partner violence is challenging, the mediator may be even less likely to be able to identify child abuse in a family through interviews with parents. The following excerpt provides valuable information about the incidence of child abuse for attorneys and mediators involved in these cases.

## CHILDREN, COURTS AND CUSTODY: INTERDISCIPLINARY MODELS FOR DIVORCING FAMILIES
### 94; 96–97 (2004)[6]
### By Andrew Schepard

Parents are the principal perpetrators of child maltreatment. Mothers and fathers tend to commit different types of child abuse and neglect. Mothers are significantly less likely than fathers to physically abuse their children. The role of mothers in physical abuse tends to be limited to tolerating and sometimes facilitating abuse by male partners. Mothers, however, are more likely to neglect children than fathers. Mothers tend to be the children's primary care-takers and thus are the parents primarily held accountable for any omissions and or failures in care-taking. Females are thus more often guilty of neglect than men (87 percent to 43 percent). In contrast, men more often than women physically abuse children (67 percent to 40 percent) and are far more likely to commit sexual abuse.

Child abuse has devastating consequences for children — acts of abuse are likely to continue after first being committed, victims are likely to be repeatedly abused, and the longer the abusive behavior continues, the more severe the damage to the child.

There are many different kinds of child abuse, and thus the practice has many different negative effects on children, too many to summarize here. Perhaps the most critical fact is that violence begets violence — child abuse, like domestic violence, replicates itself across generations. Children who are abused are much more likely to be abusers themselves when they grow up than children who are not abused. Intervention to treat both the abuser and the abused is critical to break the intergenerational cycle . . .

. . . Most sex abusers of children are not strangers but fathers and men in long-term relationships with their mothers, and the risk of abuse, particularly of girls, significantly increases following divorce.

The child custody court faces significant coordination problems when an allegation of family violence is made in a dispute before it, as those same allegations can be the basis of a criminal prosecution or a child protection proceeding. A father who has a sexual relationship with a minor child, for example, commits a serious crime for which he may be prosecuted. Allegations of child abuse and neglect can also trigger an investigation by a state's child protective services (CPS). CPS can initiate a child protection proceeding against the offending parent to terminate that parent's custody rights if it believes the violence allegations are true. To conserve scarce resources,

---

prosecutors and CPS often count on the child custody court to determine the truth and make appropriate orders.

"True" and "False" Accusations

Accusations of being an abuser or a batterer made in a child custody dispute are extremely serious. As one state Supreme Court has noted, "a parent's reputation, access to the custody of her children and even liberty may be lost over a false accusation." There are documented instances in which children have made allegations of child abuse that later turned out to be false. The focus on false claims that follows must be placed in context. The problem of family violence is very serious, and a focus on false claims should not be taken to minimize it. "We must always temper the incidence of true disclosures with the possibility of false ones."

Child custody disputes create a particularly troublesome setting for accusations of family violence. Divorce is often a time for disclosure of violence that was previously hidden from public view. Parents may leave the marriage to protect the child and themselves from further violence. On the one hand, parents must be encouraged to bring allegations of violence to the attention of authorities who have the power to provide protection to the vulnerable. On the other hand, parents in a custody dispute are often very angry at each other, misinterpret each other's behavior, and have an incentive to disclose previously unreported child abuse to the court, as the court is more likely to award the non-violent parent greater rights. This constellation of factors leads to some false or exaggerated allegations of violence or abuse.

Different definitions of "false" allegations cloud the question of whether false allegations of child abuse are more common in child custody disputes than allegations made against parents who are not involved in custody disputes. False allegations should not be confused with "unsubstantiated" or "unfounded" allegations as determined by a child protection agency. When a child protection agency finds an allegation to be unsubstantiated, it means only that the agency is of the opinion that there is not enough evidence to continue investigation and file an action in court. A child custody court is not bound by that finding, as it is possible that with further investigation and evaluation, some unsubstantiated allegations might eventually be validated. False allegations, furthermore, can encompass a variety of kinds of behavior ranging from deliberate, malicious false reports to misinterpretation of events and intentional or unintentional coaching of children.

## NOTES AND QUESTIONS

1.   Detecting child abuse or evaluating claims of such abuse by others is beyond the expertise of most family mediators. But given the rate of incidence described in the Schepard article, family mediators mediating child access disputes should have some training in this area. The Schepard excerpt provides a starting point. *See also* Robin Fretwell Wilson, *Children at Risk: The Sexual Exploitation of Female Children After Divorce*, 86 CORNELL L. REV. 251(2001) (noting the substantial social science research demonstrating that girls are at an elevated risk for sexual abuse after divorce by a parent, step-parent or other person).

2.   As with intimate partner violence, uncovering child abuse is just the first issue a family mediator must deal with. Assuming it is not a case where the child abuse has already been discovered and adjudicated in some way, mediator suspicions of child abuse, party allegations, or party admissions raise a variety of questions for the mediator. As discussed more fully in Chapter 12, most ethical rules governing family mediation obligate mediators to keep matters discussed in mediation confidential. *See, e.g.*, Model Standards for Divorce and Family Mediation Standard VII. This promise of confidentiality, however, does not extend to threats of future violence of adults or children made during mediation. In the case of child abuse, child protection laws may *require* the mediator to report to appropriate state agencies allegations or admissions about both past and ongoing child abuse disclosed in mediation. *See, e.g.*, MD. FAM. LAW ART. 5-704. If a mediator has reasonable grounds to suspect child abuse, she is required to report it and will, as a result, most likely withdraw from the mediation. Many cases, however, may raise suspicions or concerns but not reach the "reasonable grounds" to believe abuse or neglect is occurring to warrant a formal report. These cases raise the difficult ethical and professional issues for family mediators.

3.   Assume you are mediating a child access case. The parties get into a heated argument after the husband/father states that the wife/mother "is a lousy mother who can't take care of herself let alone a child," referring to the parties' 5-year-old daughter, Clare. You suggest a private caucus with each of the parties to cool things down and give the mother a chance to talk uninterrupted about whether she is, indeed, overwhelmed in her current role as primary caretaker. During the private caucus with the mother, you learn that Clare stays with her 10-year-old cousin when the after school program is unavailable. He lives in the same apartment building as the mother and daughter and stays by himself after school. About once a week, he walks home with his cousin and they stay at his apartment unattended for about three hours until his mother or Clare's mother comes home.

Putting aside specific statutory-or rule-based ethical mandates (until we get to Chapter 12), what do you think your next step should be as a mediator? Do you tell the husband/father? Do you step out of your role as mediator to "advise" the mother? Do you bring in any third parties? Do you continue to mediate the case?

# Chapter 11

# UNREPRESENTED PARTIES AND FAMILY MEDIATION

## A. INTRODUCTION

The composition and structure of the families who appear in family court has changed dramatically in recent decades. In addition to resolving conflicts between divorcing parents, mediators now deal routinely with child-related disputes involving unmarried parents, stepfamilies, gay and lesbian families, and third-party caregivers. Not only have disputing families become more complicated and diverse, but the way those families interact with the legal system has also changed. The number of pro se or unrepresented litigants in family court has skyrocketed. Recent statistics from state courts across the country demonstrate that family law cases constitute 25 percent of trial court civil dockets. NATIONAL CENTER FOR STATE COURTS, EXAMINING THE WORK OF STATE COURTS: A NATIONAL PERSPECTIVE FROM THE COURT STATISTICS PROJECTS 33 (2006). The majority of such cases involve one or both parties who do not have counsel. Although comprehensive nationwide statistics do not exist, studies have indicated that between 55 and 90 percent of family cases involve at least one self-represented party. In many large urban jurisdictions, a substantial majority of family law cases proceed entirely without lawyers. Thus, far from being exceptional, pro se litigants are now the norm in family courts across the country. Indeed, experts have called the rise in unrepresented litigants the single most important issue facing family courts today.

There are a number of reasons why parties in family cases represent themselves. Some disputants believe their cases are simple and they can handle the issues on their own. The widespread availability of legal information on the Internet has encouraged some consumers to bypass lawyers and other professionals. Others distrust lawyers and worry that lawyers will exacerbate conflict or create unnecessary issues in order to enhance their fees. But most individuals, particularly those with low or modest incomes, cannot afford legal representation. *See e.g.*, Julie Macfarlane, *Time to Shatter the Stereotype of the Self-Represented Litigants*, ABA DISPUTE RESOLUTION MAGAZINE (Fall 2013) 14 (summarizing her research and finding that "this research makes it clear beyond doubt that the most significant reason for joining the ranks of the pro se litigants, who now constitute the majority in some family courts, is the high cost of legal services."). Even where parties' incomes are low enough to be eligible for free legal assistance, existing legal aid and legal services offices can only meet a fraction of the need.

Unrepresented parties pose particular challenges in family mediation. Some family mediation rules exclude cases with unrepresented parties from court-based mandatory mediation but most do not. This has a number of consequences for participants and mediators. This Chapter explores the benefits and risks mediation poses for unrepresented parties and mediators and highlights some of the solutions proposed by scholars and practitioners.

## B.  BENEFITS OF MEDIATION FOR UNREPRESENTED PARTIES

Some argue that one of mediation's principle benefits is that it improves access to family dispute resolution for unrepresented litigants. For low and moderate income families, it is usually a less costly and quicker alternative than litigation. While legal rules may constrain mediation in limited areas such as child support, parties are largely encouraged to generate their own norms. Even in evaluative mediation, which uses legal norms to inform agreements, the sessions are private and informal with few rules governing the scope of discussions or exchange of information, other than mediator-developed rules of courtesy. As two mediation scholars explain:

> The ultimate authority in mediation belongs to the parties themselves and they may fashion a unique solution that will work for them without being governed by precedent or by concern for the precedent they may set for others. The parents may, with the help of the mediator, consider a comprehensive mix of their children's needs, their interests and whatever else they deem relevant, regardless of rules of evidence or strict adherence to substantive law.

Leonard Marlow and S. Richard Sauber, *The Handbook of Divorce Mediation* (New York: Plenum Press, 1990)

Under this conception, lawyers have little or no role to play in mediation. Without complex rules of procedure and evidence and governing substantive law, many parties feel mediation can save them the cost of lawyers and the delays of court proceedings and craft resolutions themselves. Research supports this claim in cases where the mediation is successful. Jessica Pearson, *Family Mediation: A Report on Current Research Findings: Implications for Courts and Future Research Needs* 53–75 (1994).

Many mediators have also endorsed the view that attorneys are not needed in the mediation room and can, indeed, impede the mediation process. *See e.g.*, Mark C. Rutherford, *Lawyers and Divorce Mediation: Designing the Role of "Outside Counsel,"* 12 MEDIATION Q., June 1986, at 17, 27 ("For mediation to succeed as a profession and to reach its highest objectives, advocacy has no place in any part of the process. For outside counsel to advocate a client's interests contradicts the very essence of mediation and can produce inequitable results."). This view that attorneys have little or no role to play during the mediation process is being challenged on a number of fronts, however, and "mediation advocacy" is becoming an important part of a lawyer's training.

## C.   RISKS TO UNREPRESENTED PARTIES AND MEDIATORS

Other commentators believe that family mediation programs may create dangers for unrepresented participants and ethical risks for mediators. With regard to participants, many scholars argue that reliance on informal processes and non-legal staff increases the danger that parties will leave the court system without the legal remedies they need and are entitled to under existing law.

When formal procedures and legal rules are jettisoned in favor of consensus and party self-determination, parties risk entering agreements that waive important rights. The risk increases when parties lack information about legal norms that may govern if their efforts to reach agreement fail. One scholar described the potential harm for unrepresented litigants in court-sponsored mediation programs:

> From an unrepresented litigant's point of view, however, the effect of the [mediation] rules can be devastating. The pressure exerted by courts to send cases to mediation and the lack of explanation of the mediation process raise serious questions about the "voluntary" nature of the decision to mediate. Once in mediation, the pressures on mediators to obtain settlements are immense. With a large number of unrepresented litigants, this pressure guarantees that mediators will rarely, if ever, exercise the option to terminate the mediation due to the incapacity of an unrepresented litigant to participate. . . . In theory, judges could provide a check on the dangers identified above in mediation, because mediated agreements are usually sent to them for approval. In reality, judges typically rubber-stamp agreements reached in mediation.

Russell Engler, *And Justice for All — Including the Unrepresented Poor: Revisiting the Roles of the Judges, Mediators, and Clerks*, 67 FORDHAM L. REV. 1987, 2010–2011 (1999)

Some commentators have also raised concerns about the impact of cost on mediation. The first concern is about the risk that mediation will become justice "on the cheap" for the poor. While the "second class" justice concerns usually focus on court-ordered mediation versus litigation, there is growing concern that vast differences in quality may develop between private, voluntary mediation and public, court ordered mediation. To the extent parties have resources, they will tend to choose their own mediators and opt out of court-based programs. The remaining cases sent to mediation from the ever expanding family law docket will be predominately poor, unrepresented litigants who have no choices and will experience the mediation equivalent of the "mass justice" of low-income courts. *See* Robert Rubinson, *A Theory of Access to Justice*, 29 J. LEGAL PROF. 89 (2005).

A second concern about costs and access to justice is that when parties have to pay for mediation it can add to the costs. This is a particular problem when parties are required to attempt mediation as a prerequisite to litigation or perceive it as such. As one commentator has put it:

> Programs mandating or encouraging divorcing parties to mediate and pay for the service raise significant legal and policy questions concerning access to

justice. Mandatory referral schemes, in which divorcing parties are ordered to attend mediation and pay the costs, are certainly effective in increasing the use of mediation while holding down court expenditures. If mediation is not voluntary, and parties are required to attend and are obligated to pay the mediator, constitutional due process and equal protection issues may be implicated. Further, as a practical matter, parties may be denied access to adjudication of their cases because they lack the funds to pay for the prerequisite mediation. Particularly in divorce cases, when partners are setting up two households on the same income that formerly supported only one, money is tight. Divorcing parties who are mandated to use and pay for mediation services may be unduly pressured to settle on unacceptable terms because they cannot afford to pay lawyers' fees for trial or further negotiation, in addition to the fees they have been forced to spend for mediation.

Carol J. King, *Burdening Access to Justice: The Cost of Divorce Mediation on the Cheap*, 73 St. John's L. Rev. 375, 381–382 (1999).

Some courts do waive costs for indigent litigants, have a sliding scale fee system or excuse parties who cannot pay from the mediation requirement. *See, e.g.*, Colo. Rev. Stat. Ann. § 13-22-311(1) (2000) (party can be excused for a compelling reason including costs of mediation and lack of success in previous mediation).

There are also risks to mediators when working with participants without access to legal representation or even legal advice. As discussed in earlier Chapters, neutrality is a core element of the mediator's role. This neutrality is viewed as both central to the legitimacy and effectiveness of mediation, and critical for maintaining ethical standards for mediators. As a result, even mediators with legal expertise are generally constrained from opining about the merits of either party's positions or predicting a likely outcome if the disputed matters were litigated. Yet mediators who work with unrepresented parties are often put in the position of providing information about legal standards (which may sound very much like legal advice to the lay person). If a mediator declines to provide such information, she risks having uninformed parties reach agreements that the parties may not understand or are contrary to their interests. The concerns about uninformed decision making are particularly acute when the mediation is court ordered, as it is in many child access cases. By contrast, if a mediator provides legal information related to the disputants' situation, she risks crossing the line from facilitation to evaluation — a move that many mediators reject.

While many have recognized this conflict for mediators, few agree on the appropriate response. Some believe providing traditional legal representation to parties participating in mediation would address the concerns and improve the process, but they recognize that state budget constraints make this solution unlikely. Others argue for responses that would fundamentally change the mediation process — building in more formality to the process, or reconceiving the mediator's role to include providing legal education when mediating cases with unrepresented parties, particularly in a court-based setting. Others have discussed the importance of simply "providing clearer guidance for mediators working with self-represented parties, considering the special needs of parties without attorneys." These changes will require rethinking some of the rules and standards governing mediator and lawyer conduct as well as rules governing unauthorized practice. The following excerpt explores these dilemmas and offers some proposals to responding to the challenge of mediation with unrepresented participants.

## *SELF-REPRESENTED PARTIES IN MEDIATION: FIFTY YEARS LATER IT REMAINS THE ELEPHANT IN THE ROOM*
51 Fam. Ct. Rev. 87, 89–93, 96–100 (2013)
By Amy G. Applegate and Connie J.A. Beck

### III. CONSIDERATIONS FROM THE PARTY PERSPECTIVE

As compared to parties with attorneys, parties without attorneys who mediate their family law disputes are potentially disadvantaged in several ways, including lack of legal knowledge, lack of personal competence to proceed in mediation, and lack of knowledge about the mediation process.

### A. LEGAL KNOWLEDGE

Perhaps the most significant disadvantage to a self-represented party is his or her potential lack of knowledge about the law and the judicial process, and the advantages and risks to settling or not settling a dispute. Without attorney representation, parties who settle in mediation may be giving up legal rights to which they may be entitled. For example, in mediation programs that only address custody and parenting time issues, a self-represented parent who makes significant concessions in parenting time may not understand the effect those concessions may have on child support. Likewise, in mediation programs that address all issues, a self-represented party may make concessions about property division without understanding what he or she would be entitled to under applicable law. Additionally, parties who settle in mediation may be putting themselves at risks that they do not understand (e.g., tax consequences from property division or the effect of releases from claims). Conversely, the attorney-represented party is significantly advantaged by having an attorney who can provide legal advice necessary to make informed, long-term legal decisions concerning custody, parenting time, and financial matters. For example, an attorney can advise the party on the applicable law, how the court would likely apply the law to the specific facts of the case, whether it is in the party's interest to settle and on what terms, and provide support beyond legal advice. The attorney can also push harder in testing the party's expectations regarding what is possible in a settlement, thus creating more realistic expectations about settlement and the possible outcome of litigation. Finally, the attorney can assist the party in preparing for the mediation session by constructing a narrative of the party's interests and concerns for the mediation session or, if allowed, speak on the party's behalf. . . . Ensuring that mediation parties are competent is essential because the goal of court-ordered mediation is to produce legally binding contracts (e.g., agreements). Once drafted, signed by the parties, and approved by the judge, these agreements may be difficult to modify.

## C. MEDIATION PROCESS

A self-represented party may be confused about the mediation process, the mediator's role in that process, and the party's relationship with the mediator. The party's confusion may be particularly acute when the matter was court-ordered to mediation and the party has no prior mediation experience. Considering the emotional and financial stresses often involved in divorce or separation, the party may have difficulty understanding what the mediator can and cannot do for the parties in mediation. These potential problems may be less serious for attorney- represented parties, as attorneys can (and often do) explain these issues to their clients prior to the mediation. Mediators do often explain their roles but their explanations may not be sufficient.

In sum, compared to attorney-represented parties, there are several important ways in which self-represented parties may be at a significant disadvantage in mediation. These particular disadvantages may also interact with problems created for the mediator in attempting to create a fair process for self-represented clients.

## IV. CONSIDERATIONS FROM THE MEDIATOR PERSPECTIVE

## A. UNAUTHORIZED PRACTICE OF LAW (UPL) OR CONFLICTING REPRESENTATION

. . . When the parties do not have attorneys, the mediator must proceed cautiously in providing information to the parties and conducting certain activities for the parties, in order to avoid providing legal advice or taking on an attorney representational role with the parties, thus implicating UPL [author's note: Unauthorized Practice of Law] and/or conflicting representation issues. The nonattorney mediator, as well as the attorney-mediator who is not admitted to practice law in a jurisdiction in which the mediator mediates, must consider the possibility of UPL issues. The attorney-mediator, admitted to practice law in the jurisdiction in which the mediator is mediating, must also be concerned about the possibility of conflicting representation, which may implicate violation of attorney ethical rules of conduct.

In a world of increasing self-representation, some parties look to their mediator for all necessary legal information and document preparation. However, as outlined in the sections below, in certain jurisdictions and under certain conditions, a mediator may be deemed to be engaged in UPL or conflicting representation when the mediator discusses with self-represented parties the applicable law, the court's application of the law to the facts, or whether to make or accept an offer, and tests reality based on the law. Additionally, a mediator may be deemed to be engaged in UPL or conflicting representation when the mediator drafts the parties' memorandum of understanding (mediation agreement), and any documents beyond the mediation agreement, or files these documents with the court.

## B. ONE PARTY SELF-REPRESENTED

When only one party to the mediation is self-represented, there are additional concerns that include an imbalance of power and knowledge between the parties. Both the parties in these cases are more likely to report concern, fear, unpreparedness, and lower levels of satisfaction in mediation. The mediator must also be careful in how to structure the mediation process and dispense information to the self-represented party to avoid compromising the mediator's impartiality and/or neutrality.

. . . .

## VI. STATE REGULATION OF MEDIATION WITH SELF-REPRESENTED PARTIES

Though mediation is commonly utilized in family law cases where the parties are represented by attorneys, there is considerable uncertainty about the parameters of the role of the mediator when mediating cases with one or more self-represented parties. . . . [I]t appears universally accepted that providing mediation services is not the practice of law. However, depending on the jurisdiction, certain activities may be deemed to be or become the practice of law, especially when the parties are self-represented. These activities include the mediator discussing the law with the self-represented party(ies); drafting the mediation agreement; drafting other documents needed to resolve (or at times, initiate) the family law case; and filing documents for self-represented parties.

## VII. OUR PROPOSAL

Courts and mediators should provide appropriate mediation services to self-represented parties based on the premise that regardless of representation status, all parties who want to mediate and could benefit from mediation should be permitted to participate in mediation. However, the needs of self-represented parties differ in some significant ways from parties represented by attorneys. Accordingly, we propose that states, through their highest courts, follow the lead of Virginia and Indiana, and adopt statewide rules (or guidelines) that clarify appropriate mediation practice involving self-represented parties. A particular state's prior ethical opinions, guidelines, or rules may need to be revisited, but the highest court is in the best and most appropriate position to have this task done.

In addition, it is important for each state to affirm (if the state has not done so) that mediation is not the practice of law, and clarify which activities in mediation do not transform the practice of mediation into the practice of law. Specifically, each state should adopt the rules or guidelines that address at least the following issues for mediators working with self-represented parties.

## A. ADDRESSING THE NEEDS OF SELF-REPRESENTED PARTIES

Though the emphasis in the past has been on the challenges for the *mediator* who works with self-represented parties, states should focus at the outset on protecting the *self-represented party* in mediation. In doing so, states should seek guidance from the Virginia and Indiana rules, and the California guidelines.

First, unless the case has already been prescreened by court personnel, the mediator should determine that mediation is an appropriate process for the parties and that each party is able to participate effectively within the context of the mediation process. The mediator should conduct an intake process that includes identifying the issues the parties want to mediate, the issues the parties may need to address (e.g., if they wish to finalize a divorce outside of court), careful screening for domestic violence, as well as party competence and capacity to mediate. The mediator should use case-specific approaches, including whether and when the parties should be mediating together in the same room or separately, planned and implemented after a thorough intake procedure is completed.

Second, the mediator should avoid pressuring the parties to settle. Consistent with our belief in the importance of case-specific approaches, we are uncomfortable recommending that the mediator should use a particular style of mediation. Assisting the parties in generating and evaluating possible resolutions should be more empowering to parties than urging them to reach terms suggested by the mediator. However, Virginia's rules permitting the attorney-mediator to offer evaluation services are intriguing and indeed empowering, as evaluative mediation may well be what some self-represented parties want. At the same time, it seems likely that such evaluation could interfere with the mediator's impartiality and/or the parties' self-determination.

Third, mediators should be prepared to provide legal education and information. . . . This information is often a necessity for parties who do not have the benefit of attorney representation and can be provided ethically with guidance by the state's highest court.

Fourth, mediators should be permitted to draft the parties' mediation agreement and other related documents. These services are often a necessity for parties who do not have the benefit of attorney representation and can be done ethically with guidance by the state's highest court. . . . If the parties do not reach an agreement, then the mediator should assist them in understanding the steps that need to be taken to resolve their dispute.

Fifth, appropriate disclosures are also essential when mediating with self-represented parties. In addition to standard disclosures in mediation (voluntary agreements only, confidentiality of the process, etc.), the following should also be discussed: (1) the difference between a mediator's role and a lawyer's role; (2) that the mediator can provide legal information or education, but not legal advice (see below for definition); (3) that the mediator's role is to assist both (or all) parties and that the mediator does not represent either (or any) party; (4) that the mediator can assist with drafting and filing mediation agreements and related documents as permitted by the rules, so long as the parties want the mediator to do this; (5) that the mediator recommends that the parties seek or consult with their own legal counsel as needed and before finalizing any written documents; and (6) without their own legal counsel, the parties may be giving up legal rights to which they are entitled, or running certain risks of which they may not be aware.

Sixth, although confidentiality of the process is a standard mediation disclosure, it is particularly important that self-represented parties be fully informed about confidentiality and any limits on confidentiality. Parties should understand what mediators are required to report to authorities (e.g., unreported child abuse or neglect, or imminent harm to anyone) and any circumstances under which the mediator or others may be providing information or testifying to a court about what was said in mediation. For example, in some jurisdictions in California, mediators working with parties who do not reach agreement in mediation make written recommendations to the courts regarding resolution of disputed issues. It is critical that parties understand this prior to mediating.

## B. IDENTIFYING PERMISSIBLE INFORMATION ABOUT THE LAW AND LEGAL PROCESS

Although the boundaries between legal information and legal advice can be hazy, the Virginia guidelines and the Indiana ADR rule provide helpful guidance that states should consider when addressing mediation with self-represented parties. Each state's highest court should define permissible legal information that mediators can provide to self-represented parties. Depending on prior state law, this information can include legal sources such as statutes, rules, guidelines, and settled case law. The mediator should also be permitted to make accurate statements about the law (e.g., descriptions of applicable statutes, rules, guidelines, and settled case law). The mediator should further be permitted to ask reality-testing questions that may raise legal issues for the parties to consider (e.g., how the party thinks that the judge would react to what the party is seeking, based on the facts as described by the party(ies)). Additionally, the mediator should be able to discuss the mediator's past experiences and observations of the court's resolution of cases. Finally, the mediator should be allowed to provide information about the enforceability of a mediation agreement. For example, in Indiana, an agreement reached in a family law case is only enforceable after it has been signed by all parties (and any attorneys), and is reviewed and approved by the judge. If the parties do not wish to submit their mediated agreement to the court, the mediator should be able to explain the enforceability issue (and, of course, encourage the parties to get legal advice about the issue). Or the parties may wish to agree to an automatic change in custody if a contingency takes place; again, in Indiana that would raise an enforceability issue, which the mediator should be able to address with the parties.

When providing any information or education, the mediator should include a disclaimer that the mediator cannot assure how the court would apply the law in the parties' case or the outcome of the dispute. The mediator should also recommend that the parties seek or consult with their own legal counsel. Further, the mediator should not advise a party what to do in a specific case or whether to accept an offer, as these would constitute attorney representational activities.

## C. ATTORNEY AND NONATTORNEY MEDIATORS

Whether requirements should be different for attorney and nonattorney mediators in providing legal information and drafting documents is a difficult question that does not lend itself to a simple answer. Unfortunately, the vast majority of jurisdictions across the United States separate child custody and parenting time issues from financial issues in court-mandated mediation. If disputed, the former are mandated to court-sponsored mediation for resolution with mostly mental health trained mediators, while the latter are left for the couples to resolve some other way. Agreements negotiated in child custody and parenting time mediations may have financial repercussions which are not addressed in the mediation. A self-represented litigant may not understand that this is the case. For example, a self-represented parent may negotiate a parenting time arrangement that leaves them unable to pay for the basic necessities for the children. Regardless of the original intention in separating these issues, this does not appear to serve the best interests of self-represented mediation parties. Putting aside the question of mandated separation of custody and parenting time issues from financial issues, the mediator, as a professional, must be competent to provide whatever services he or she is offering. On the one hand, a nonattorney mediator, without appropriate skills, training, and experience, may not be competent to draft agreements concerning financial issues or ancillary documents needed to finalize a divorce for self-represented parties. On the other hand, a nonattorney mediator may well be highly competent to draft agreements reached in mediation, at least as to parenting arrangements and perhaps child support. Some attorney-mediators may not be competent to mediate or prepare documentation for complex financial settlements.

We recommend that states resolve this issue by requiring all mediators to have the appropriate skills, training, and experience to prepare the mediation agreement and other documents memorializing the issues addressed and agreed to in the mediation. For example, if custody and parenting time are addressed in mediation, the mediator would need the requisite training and skills to create such a mediation agreement. If the mediation addresses financial issues, the mediator would then need the requisite skills and training to draft any documents needed for self-represented parties in this mediation. We also recommend that the states adopt a more unified mediation process, and consider including in mandated mediation all, rather than some, of the issues that need to be resolved.

## D. IDENTIFYING APPROPRIATE DOCUMENT PREPARATION AND RE-LATED ACTIVITIES

Based on the needs of self-represented parties, each state, through its highest court, should identify permissible document preparation by the mediator. The state's highest court defines practice of law issues and thus could rely in part on the Maine ethics opinion and professional conduct rule and in larger part on the Indiana ADR rule to construct this type of rule. Mediators in family law cases, who are trained and competent to do so, should be permitted to prepare documents such as the parties' mediation agreement, and ancillary documents such as an order approving the mediation agreement (if used in a particular jurisdiction), a summary decree of dissolution, a verified waiver of final hearing, a child support calculation, and an income withholding order, as long as each of these documents represent the parties' agreement and the mediator uses court-accepted or adopted forms. Other ancillary documents, such as quitclaim deeds, transfers of title, separate releases of claims, and qualified domestic relations orders, represent more legally-based content, and accordingly may be more problematic for mediator preparation. Importantly, mediators are not mere scriveners and state authorities that characterize the mediator role as such misunderstand the mediation process. The mediation process is an interactive process that involves parties reaching agreements through interactions with each other and the mediator. As noted by the ABA, it is unlikely that a mediator can serve as a scrivener given the complexities of the divorce-related and mediation processes.

It is also important that the mediator review each document drafted during mediation with any self-represented parties, and explain that the parties should not rely on language in documents prepared by the mediator as legal advice. It is also important to disclose to parties that any agreement signed by the parties constitutes evidence that may be introduced in litigation. Finally, the mediator should be allowed to tender to, or file with the court any documents prepared by the mediator, along with the mediator's report, which most jurisdictions require after completion of mediation.

## E. CONCLUSION

If access to justice is to have real meaning, then parties in family law cases without attorney representation should be able to participate in ADR processes available to parties represented by attorneys, especially when the processes may be beneficial. ADR processes may reduce conflict, reduce legal costs, permit the parties to address important issues that might not be addressed by the court, and serve the best interests of the children by quickly (and it is hoped, appropriately) resolving disputed issues. Our proposal is intended to help provide needed guidance to mediators, while also considering the needs of, and challenges posed by, this population of litigants. We urge the AFCC and the ABA to consider drafting Model Rules of Practice for Mediating with Self-Represented Parties to assist the states in undertaking this task and implementing appropriate rule changes.

## NOTES AND QUESTIONS

1.    Only a handful of family mediation statutes or rules currently address the need for representation during court-ordered family mediation. *See, e.g.*, Ala. Code § 6-6-20 (any party not represented by an attorney may be assisted in mediation by a person of his choice); Cal. Fam. Code §§ 3170–3185 (mediator may recommend to court that counsel be appointed for child in custody mediation); Mich. C.R. 3.216(D)(3)(c) (cases may be exempt from mediation if one or both parties are unable to negotiate for themselves at mediation). Which, if any, of these approaches do you think offers the greatest safeguards to parties and mediators? Who might be an appropriate substitute for counsel under Alabama's statute? How would a court determine whether a party is able to negotiate for themselves at mediation under Michigan's statute?

2.    Do family mediation statutes or rules that make mediation voluntary and allow parties to "opt out" respond to the concerns identified in the reading for unrepresented parties? Why or why not?

3.   What are the ethical risks for mediators when facilitating dispute resolution with two unrepresented parties? Does the level of risks change depending upon the nature of the dispute — i.e., whether the dispute relates to financial issues or child access?

4.   Do Applegate and Beck's proposals for addressing the risks to mediators and unrepresented parties have the potential to change either the mediator's role or the mediation process? If so, in what way(s)?

# Chapter 12

# ETHICAL ISSUES IN FAMILY MEDIATION

## A.  INTRODUCTION

The study of ethics in family mediation has several dimensions. First, there are conventional "doctrinal" issues such as conflicts of interest, confidentiality, and the importance of mediator neutrality. A more difficult issue is the application of these standards when circumstances are uncertain, especially in the emotionally-charged world of family disputes. This Chapter seeks to offer insights into the law as well as offer a taste of the difficulty of applying standards in actual mediation.

## B.  SOURCES OF FAMILY MEDIATION ETHICS

### 1.  General Sources of Standards Governing Mediation

Family mediators are subject to statutes and standards governing the general practice of mediation. Whether these sources have the force of law depends on the jurisdiction. In addition to rules relating to mediator qualifications, which we have already explored in Chapter 7, these standards typically address confidentiality, conflicts of interest, and mediator "neutrality" or "impartiality."

The following represents primary sources of standards governing mediators generally:

- *The Uniform Mediation Act*: The National Conference of Commissioners on Uniform State Laws promulgated this Act in 2001. As of this writing, 11 states and the District of Columbia have adopted it.[1] The Act is under consideration in several other states and is likely to become more widely adopted in the coming years.

- *The Model Standards of Conduct for Mediators*: First adopted in 1994 and revised in 2005, the Model Standards are promulgated by the American Arbitration Association, the American Bar Association, and the Association for Conflict Resolution. This is the preeminent unified set of standards governing mediation. While influential, these standards, unless a jurisdiction's law provides otherwise, do not have the force of law.

- *State statutes and rules*: As we have seen previously, both mediation and family mediation are subject to an ever-changing array of state law and rules

---

[1] The Uniform Law Commission monitors when the Act is enacted or under consideration for adoption. Its findings can be found at http://www.uniformlaws.org/Act.aspx?title=Mediation%20Act.

that vary from jurisdiction to jurisdiction. An influential set of guidelines for states is the *National Standards for Court-Connected Mediation Programs* issued by the Center for Dispute Settlement and the Institute of Judicial Administration.

## 2.   Model Standards of Practice for Family and Divorce Mediation

The *Model Standards of Practice for Family and Divorce Mediation*, Appendix C in this book, is, by its terms, "aspirational in character" and thus do not have the force of law. They are nevertheless the most recent and influential set of ethical standards specifically addressing family mediation.

The history of its adoption shows both the every-increasing intensity of focus on family mediation and how interdisciplinary the field is. The following excerpt traces this history.

### *FOREWORD TO THE MODEL STANDARDS OF PRACTICE FOR FAMILY AND DIVORCE MEDIATION* (2000)
#### By Andrew Schepard

The *Model Standards of Practice for Family and Divorce Mediation ("Model Standards")* are the family mediation community's definition of the role of mediation in the dispute resolution system in the twenty-first century. . . .

Between 1982 and 1984 [the Association of Family and Conciliation Courts ("AFCC")] convened three national symposia on divorce mediation standards. Over forty individuals from thirty organizations attended to explore issues of certification, licensure and standards of practice. Drafts were distributed to over one hundred thirty individuals and organizations for comment and review. The result of the efforts was the 1984 *Model Standards of Practice for Family and Divorce Mediation ("1984 Model Standards")* which have served as a resource document for state and national mediation organizations.

In tandem with the process convened by AFCC, the American Bar Association's Family Law Section drafted *Standards of Practice for Lawyer Mediators in Family Law Disputes* (1984) *("1984 ABA Standards")*. . . . [which] were basically compatible with the *1984 Model Standards*.

In 1996, the Family Law Section of the American Bar Association came to the conclusion that interest in and knowledge about family mediation had expanded dramatically since the *1984 ABA Standards* were promulgated and a fresh look at that effort was required. . . .

First, the *1984 ABA Standards* did not address many critical issues in mediation practice that have been identified since they were initially promulgated. They did not deal with domestic violence and child abuse. The *1984 ABA Standards* also did not address the mediator's role in helping parents define the best interests of their children in their post-divorce parenting arrangements. They made no mention of the need for special expertise and training in mediation or family violence.

Second, the *1984 ABA Standards* were inconsistent with other guidelines for the conduct of mediation subsequently promulgated. The ABA Committee believed that uniformity of mediation standards among interested groups is highly desirable to provide clear guidance for family mediators and for the public. . . .

[T]he ABA Committee examined all available standards of practice, conducted research, and consulted with a number of experts on family and divorce mediation. It particularly focused on consultations with experts in domestic violence and child abuse about the appropriate role for mediation when family situations involved violence or the allegations thereof. . . .

The *Model Standards* . . . are thus the result of extensive and thoughtful deliberation by the family mediation community with wide input from a variety of voices. Nonetheless, they should not be thought of as a final product but more like a panoramic snapshot of what is important to the family mediation community at the beginning of the new Millennium. . . .

## NOTES AND QUESTIONS

1.  Review the *Model Standards*. Given your current understanding of family mediation, are there issues that you believe need to be addressed now that the "new millennium" has passed?

2.  Professor Schepard notes that the *Model Standards* are the result of "wide input from a variety of voices" within the "family mediation community." The "family mediation community," however, has distinct sub-communities. These distinctions might arise from professional background (such as lawyers as opposed to mental health professionals), from adherence to different models of mediation (such as to evaluative, facilitative, and transformative mediation), or from the context in which mediators practice (such as private mediators whose mediations involve participants with resources as opposed "public" mediators with participants who are primarily low-income in court-connected programs). Do you think these different "voices" might lead to different views on the issues that the *Model Standards* seek to address? Does this have an impact on the specificity of the *Model Standards*?

## C.  CONFIDENTIALITY AND ITS EXCEPTIONS

### 1.  Overview

Confidentiality is fundamental to mediation. A number of rationales have been set forth explaining why this is the case: 1) it enhances candor by creating a "safe space" for participants to speak without fear that it will be used against them in court; 2) it makes mediation more attractive to participants by insuring that "dirty laundry" will not be disclosed publicly — a particularly important factor in family mediation; 3) it protects the integrity of the process by minimizing the risk that the mediation will be used as "free discovery" in litigation; 4) it makes practicing mediation more appealing by limiting the possibility that a mediator will be subpoenaed or otherwise compelled to discuss what happened in mediation. Although, as we will see shortly, other interests might sometimes trump mediation confidentiality, confidentiality remains a powerful norm in mediation. Virtually no description of mediation omits it as a core component of what mediation is.

The application of confidentiality in family mediation can be complex. The following is an overview of the sources of the principles of confidentiality in mediation. Note that special issues regarding disclosure obligations in the context of child abuse are explored separately below.

- *Rules of Evidence.* Federal Rule of Evidence 408 and similar state evidentiary rules protect the confidentiality of settlement discussions. Mediation would usually qualify as a "settlement discussion" for purposes of Rule 408 and similar state provisions.

- *Uniform Mediation Act.* This Act establishes an evidentiary privilege for communications in mediation.[2] Such rules of evidence limit the admissibility of evidence at trial. They do not, however, address voluntary disclosure of information outside of litigation.

- *State Statutes.* Most states have adopted confidentiality provisions relating to mediation, a selection of which is included in Appendix A-3. For example, Maryland prohibits the "mediator and participants requested by the mediator" as well as "parties or participants requested by parties" from being compelled to disclose mediation communications.[3] As in most other states, there are exceptions "provided by law" or to "prevent bodily harm or death."[4] In the family mediation context, this is particularly important given the possibility of domestic violence and mandatory reporting for child abuse or neglect. Some statutes apply only to mediation conducted in connection with a court or administrative body, and some apply to both "public" and private mediation.

- *Contract.* Mediators and mediation programs often require mediation participants to execute agreements that prohibit participants from disclosing mediation communications or subpoenaing the mediator to testify at a trial or hearing. The remedy for breach of such agreements would be a lawsuit for breach of contract. It is questionable whether such a remedy is likely to be pursued and, if so, how successful it would be. The purpose of such contracts, then, can be seen primarily as a means to educate and emphasize to participants the importance of confidentiality in mediation.

- *Non-Binding Family Mediation and General Mediation Guidelines.* The primary example is the *Model Standards of Practice for Family and Divorce Mediation* included as Appendix C. The *Model Standards* provide the following guidelines regarding confidentiality:

  > A family mediator shall maintain the confidentiality of all information acquired in the mediation process, unless the mediator is permitted or

---

[2] Unif. Mediation Act §§ 4, 5, 6.

[3] Md. Cts. & Jud. Proc. § 3-1803.

[4] Md. Cts. & Jud. Proc. § 1805(b).

required to reveal the information by law or agreement of the parties.[5]

## 2. Judicial Enforcement of Confidentiality in Mediation

Mediation participants sometimes seek a court order to permit disclosure of information from mediation. Courts usually decide these cases based upon individual state statutes. Here are three situations where these issues have arisen:

- *Can a mediator be subpoenaed to testify about whether a written agreement accurately reflected an agreement reached in mediation?* One court found that evidence regarding mediation-related communications remains confidential in these circumstances absent a waiver. *Eisendrath v. The Superior Court of Los Angeles County*, 109 Cal. App. 4th 351 (2003).

- *Can evidence regarding the terms and enforceability of an oral agreement reached in mediation be admissible?* One court found that such evidence is inadmissible. The evidence included a written statement from the mediator that an unsigned document from the mediation reflected the parties' actual agreement. *Hudson v. Hudson*, 600 So. 2d 7 (Fla. Dist. Ct. App. 1992).

- *Is evidence from mediation admissible to show that an agreement should not be enforced due to emotional distress or mediator misconduct?* One court found that a mediator can be called to testify about a claim that a written agreement should not be enforced due to "severe emotional distress," "duress," and "intimidation." The court concluded that the party alleging misconduct had "opened the door" to such testimony and the other party should be given an opportunity to rebut such evidence with otherwise confidential information from the mediation. *McKinlay v. McKinlay*, 648 So. 2d 806 (Fla. Dist. Ct. App. 1995).[6]

## NOTES AND QUESTIONS

1.   Courts in these cases reached decisions based on statutes and factual details not included here. That said, do you believe confidentiality, as a policy matter, should potentially give way in any or all of these situations? Why?

2.   Do you think there should be less confidentiality protection when the best interests of a child are at stake as opposed to the division of property or alimony? To what extent should a court, when conducting an independent inquiry as to what custody or visitation arrangements are in the best interest of a child, be able to inquire into what happened in mediation?

3.   Recall that "recommending" jurisdictions described in Chapter 7 provide that a mediator can become a fact-finder who recommends child access arrangements to a court if the participants themselves do not reach an agreement in mediation. The mediator can draw upon what the mediator has learned in the mediation in making this recommendation. This structure seems to value confidentiality as a means to reach an

---

[5] *Model Standards*, Standard VII.

[6] Chapter 7 addresses judicial enforcement of claims regarding allegations of mediator misconduct.

agreement, but then views other interests as trumping confidentiality should partici-pants not reach an agreement. What do you think of this structure?

4.　Consider the situation presented in the *McKinlay* case. What should happen to confidentiality should a participant claim mediator misconduct? If confidentiality is preserved, how can a participant ever prove mediator misconduct? If confidentiality is not preserved, it seems that other participants, perhaps including the mediator, would be forced to disclose otherwise confidential information in order to rebut allegations of misconduct. Is this fair?

## 3.　Duties to Report Child Abuse or Neglect

Unfortunately issues regarding child abuse arise regularly in family mediation. Most mediators, when faced with plausible allegations of child abuse, would not agree to mediate the matter or, if the mediation had already begun, would immediately terminate the mediation. A related but distinct issue — and the one that the following materials will explore — addresses whether, how, and when mediators must disclose the possibility of child abuse.

### *MEDIATORS AS MANDATORY REPORTERS OF CHILD ABUSE: PRESERVING MEDIATION'S CORE VALUES*
34 FLA. ST. U. L. REV. 271, 292–299, 302–308 (2007)
By Art Hinshaw

Consider the following: During a joint session of a child custody mediation one parent says to the other, "The children are afraid of spending time with you. Let's just put it on the table, your disciplining of the children is nothing short of abuse!" Following a predictable response that the discipline situation is being blown out of proportion, the accusing parent describes three episodes of apparently abusive behavior. What responsibilities does the mediator have once the information is divulged? Should the mediator immediately contact the state Child Protection Services and report the alleged abuse? What happens if the mediator does not make a report? The answers to these questions depend on several factors, but should they?

Scenarios like the one described above are not far-fetched because mediation has become a vital component of the litigation process for divorce and child custody matters. In fact, it is difficult to proceed to a hearing on the merits of a child custody case without being required to attend at least one mediation session. With mandatory mediation so prevalent in child custody cases, it stands to reason that mediators may be the first to hear allegations of child abuse. Surprisingly, however, child abuse issues are rarely discussed in the mediation literature.

### [Standards for Reporting]

One of the most confusing facets of mandatory reporting for all reporters is the reporting standard itself. Mandatory reporters are required to report when they have a "reason to believe" or when they have a "reasonable cause to suspect or believe" child abuse has occurred or is occurring. In addition, a small number of states look to the potential of abuse, requiring a report of observed conditions or circumstances that "would reasonably result" in abuse.

Unlike the "reason to suspect standard," the "reasonable cause to suspect" standard is an objective one: Would a reasonable person in similar circumstances believe abuse has occurred or is occurring? In other words, the reasonable cause standard is a totality of the circumstances test. Reporters have violated this standard when failing to report abuse after observing a child's physical injuries, hearing first person accounts of abuse, or having witnesses provide accounts of another's abusive conduct.

Because of the wide range of information that may prompt the need for a report, the "reasonable cause" standard has been criticized for being "subjective and undefined" and for providing little guidance to practitioners as to when a report should be made. . . . Requiring reports based on information that simply indicates or suggests child abuse constitutes a low standard indeed. However, it is not an invitation to report whenever one has a vague, amorphous, or unspecified concern for a child's welfare.

## [Mediators as Mandatory Reporters]

Mandatory reporting laws vary by state; thus, the status of mediators as mandatory reporters for child abuse also varies by state. In twenty-two states, mediators are mandatory reporters. Of those states, only four expressly include mediators in the class of professions identified as mandatory reporters. The remaining eighteen states indirectly require mediators to be mandatory reporters because "any person" who reasonably suspects abuse is designated a mandatory reporter.

In the remaining twenty-eight states, the inquiry goes a step further. Because mediation is a secondary profession for most mediators, one must first determine the reporting status of the mediator's other profession. Indeed, mediators in family matters are drawn from a variety of primary professions, including social work, psychology, counseling, and law, and many of these professions are classified as mandatory reporters. This raises an issue: are reporting responsibilities a function of the reporter's professional role or do they follow a reporter from one professional role to another? . . . .

In states where mediators are not mandatory reporters by statute, mediators must look closely to the reporting statutes to determine if their primary or secondary profession is listed among those professions mandated to be reporters. If that profession is listed as a mandatory reporter, the mediator should determine whether role and services that mediators provide are subsumed into the reporting profession's role and services. If that is the case, the individual should be considered a mandatory reporter when acting as a mediator. If that is not the case, the person should not be a mandatory reporter when acting as a mediator. . . .

Even though every state has at least some mediators who are mandatory reporters, the question remains whether having mediators serve as mandatory reporters makes sense from a policy perspective. Persuasive arguments exist on both sides of the issue.

## Arguments in Favor of Mandatory Reporting

The complementary policy goals of family mediation and mandatory reporting are synergized when mediators are mandatory reporters. Mandatory reporting laws "expedite the identification of abused children . . . to prevent further abuse," and mediation strives to produce better results for children than those provided through the adversarial process when the family structure is being reorganized through judicial proceedings. Improved outcomes for children who are victims of abuse are encompassed in both of these goals. Because mediators may be the first to hear reports of child abuse, getting such cases into the child protection system more quickly should result in the earlier provision of needed social or therapeutic services and thus provide better results for children in need of such services.

Currently, family mediators are advised to take the "best interests of the child" into account in their mediations and thus would be expected to ensure a child's safety in abusive situations. The Model Family Standards specifically advise mediators to "assist participants in determining how to promote the best interests of children." Also, some state custody mediation statutes require mediators to act in the child's best interests.

Mandatory reporting requirements also prevent the possibility of mediators failing to act. . . . Absent a statutory duty to report, some mediators may believe that their commitment to general notions of mediation confidentiality and promises of confidentiality to mediating parties is more important than reporting a reasonable suspicion or even a strong intuition of abuse.

Mandatory reporting also furthers the goal of consistency in mediation. The lack of consensus regarding whether mediators should be mandatory reporters divides the mediation profession into groups of mandatory reporters and permissive reporters. . . . [I]nconsistent reporting requirements may be confusing to family mediation participants when they try to understand the process, select mediators, and use different mediators at various times in the family dispute. Indeed, it could potentially lead to a situation where mediating parties may refuse to accept mediators who are mandatory reporters in favor of mediators who are not mandatory reporters.

## Arguments against Mandatory Reporting

In the absence of mandatory reporting requirements, other avenues are available for mediators to report child abuse. For instance, people who are not mandatory reporters are encouraged to report abuse as permissive reporters. . . . [I]n those cases where reporting would do more harm to the child and the family, allowing mediators the discretion to refrain from reporting is consistent with mediation's policy of arriving at outcomes that serve mediation parties better than court adjudication. . . .

Mandatory reporting may also have the unintended consequence of inviting abuse of the mediation process. Because legal standards for awarding child custody take into account and penalize poor parenting, parents often compete with each other as to who is the "better" parent, which can generate claims that the other parent is less qualified to care for the children. In an environment of pervasive competition and distrust, certain incidents may be misconstrued or exaggerated, resulting in unwarranted reports from mediators who misunderstand the reporting standard. Because the subsequent investigation can be quite stressful and unpleasant, such improper reports constitute objectionable infringements on party self-determination. Furthermore, the competitive environment may also result in dubious abuse allegations where a malicious or desperate parent may make a deliberately false accusation of abuse against the other parent simply to invoke the mediator's reporting requirement. Thus, mediators may become unwitting conduits for dubious or fraudulent allegations of abuse.

Dubious or fraudulent abuse allegations present a problem for mediators, as they do with other mandatory reporters, because reporters are routinely advised to refrain from conducting in-depth investigations into allegations of abuse and to simply report reasonable suspicions of abuse. Mediators may probe an allegation or a revelation to confirm a reasonable suspicion, yet a malicious but credible allegation must be reported. In such instances the false allegation destroys the integrity of the mediation process.

Mandatory reporting also has a negative impact on mediation's core values. Of course, the most dramatic impacts occur when a report is made. Expectations of mediation confidentiality are dashed, an accused party is likely to believe the mediator is biased, and the parties are at the mercy of what CPS determines should happen next. But even when reporting is not necessary, mediation's core values can be affected. For example, what are mediators to do when they have a sneaking suspicion of abuse? If mediators are to take the best interests of the child into account, they should follow up on the issue to determine whether there is reasonable suspicion or not. No matter whether that sneaking suspicion turns into something more, the parties' self-determination has been compromised to some extent because the mediator has moved from discussion facilitator to discussion leader.

Even routine mediator behavior may result in unintended consequences during mediation. Standard mediation protocol dictates that mediators disclose their status as mandatory reporters of child abuse in their opening remarks in the mediation. Although this disclosure serves many important purposes, it may prevent discussion of issues needed to maximize the parties' self-determination. One purpose of disclosure is an implicit warning that disclosure may lead to the loss of custody of the children and/or criminal penalties against one or both of the parties. Thus, fearing the consequences of speaking freely, some parties may entirely avoid speaking of legitimate child abuse issues. Parties may withhold information for a variety of reasons, but the fact that self-censorship may occur as a result of requiring mediators to be mandatory reporters is troubling because it compromises one of mediation's primary benefits-increasing the quality of the parties' communication to address emotionally charged issues. . . .

The ultimate question to ask when determining whether mediators should be mandatory reporters is: Are the benefits from mandatory reporting worth the burdens it places on mediating parties and the mediation process? Because child protection is such a compelling state interest, the need for "private" conversations in mediation must be quite high to overcome that state interest. . . . When child abuse comes to light in mediation, it is neither in the child's best interests nor in society's best interests to allow the abuse to continue. Forbidding mediators from refusing to act when told of horrific acts of abuse is a hole in the reporting system. Requiring mediators to act as mandatory reporters of abuse is sound public policy. . . .

### Minimizing Reporting's Impact on Mediation's Core Values

[P]rotecting and supporting mediation's core values as much as possible in a mandatory reporting environment is essential for mediation's continued vitality in family matters. This section is intended to assist mediators with reporting requirements to minimize the impact of mandatory reporting on mediation's core values.

### 1. Party Self-Determination

Party self-determination is the most vulnerable mediation core value when mediators are mandatory reporters. This is because once a report is made to CPS, the mediation parties cannot control the outcome of the upcoming CPS investigation. While the loss of self-determination is socially acceptable when reporting is warranted, it is an objectionable infringement when reporting is unwarranted.

Minimizing mandatory reporting's effect on party self-determination is largely an educational task-making sure mediators understand what mandatory reporting requires of them. For example, some mediators may become overzealous in their capacity as mandatory reporters, inquiring about or steering the parties' conversation to issues of potential child abuse, even in cases where there are no indications that abuse is an issue. Other than disclosing their status as mandatory reporters, mediators should not inject the issue of child abuse into mediation without a party somehow leading the discussion to the topic. While it may seem obvious, mediators should remember that their primary role, facilitating the parties' resolution of their dispute, should not take a back seat to abstract worries of potential child abuse.

Mediators must also have a good understanding of when reporting is necessary so they can preserve the parties' self-determination by refusing to report when reporting is not required. No matter which reporting standard a mediator is operating under, the mediator should report when she feels there is enough evidence to support a belief of abuse regardless of whether there is proof of abuse. To help mediators conceptualize the reporting standard, some general guidelines are in order. When mediators hear remarks that rise only to the level of innuendo, allusions, hints, or other indirect references to potential child abuse, the reporting obligation has not been triggered. By definition, remarks of this type are indeterminate and are not capable of clear interpretation. Similarly, patently false accusations of child abuse should not be reported.

The situation becomes more complex as the mediator's beliefs about abuse develop into a reasonable suspicion. If the mediator's beliefs fall into the gray area of a hunch or sneaking suspicion of abuse, the mediator's reporting requirement is not directly affected. However, the mediator's focus must become the best interests of the child. Thus, the stronger the suspicion, the greater the mediator's need to probe the issue of abuse. A fleeting suspicion need not be pursued.

If these suspicions do not go away, mediators should remind the parties of their status as mandatory reporters of abuse. While a gentle warning may suppress party self-determination in certain ways, it can also be reasonably expected to enhance party self-determination. In response to the reminder, the parties may choose to address the mediator's sneaking suspicions, confirm the suspicions, or even decide to terminate the mediation, the ultimate act of party self-determination.

Once the reporting standard is met and a report must be made, it is inappropriate to continue the mediation. Doing so would lead the parties to believe that their self-determination remains intact, when, in fact, it is extremely limited. Thus, the mediator should begin terminating the mediation session. However, before terminating the mediation, mediators can encourage limited instances of party self-determination. For example, if allegations of child abuse are made in caucus, the mediator may have a conversation with the accuser about the best way to disclose the information to the accused. The mediator may also encourage the parties to visit family service agencies and help the parties understand how to pursue their legal rights and responsibilities in light of the report. In some cases, mediators may ask the parties if there is any information that they would like to have included in the report, such as a rebuttal to an accusation of abuse. . . .

## 2. Mediator Neutrality

The true test of a mediator's neutrality in a mandatory reporting environment comes when the issue of abuse unexpectedly surfaces. These situations are among the most difficult professional and ethical circumstances mediators face. A mediator's initial act of either minimizing or legitimizing allegations of abuse may appear hostile to either or both parties and may compromise the mediator's appearance of neutrality. Recognizing that an initial allegation or admission standing alone may not necessarily meet the reporting standard, mediators should first attempt to confirm or deny a reasonable suspicion of abuse by gaining a better understanding of the revelation. For example, statements that could lead to an unreasonable suspicion of abuse may be based on a mistaken idea of what constitutes child abuse, an attempt to find out additional information to either confirm or deny a suspicion, or part of a strategy of bad-faith bargaining to gain negotiation leverage.

To determine if any of these possibilities apply, mediators should focus the conversation on specific acts and actions instead of conclusory statements. Mediators should remember that trying to confirm a reasonable suspicion to determine whether to make a report is not the same as investigating whether or not abuse occurred. In the appropriate situation, mediators may act as educators on the law and facts, clarifying mistaken terms.

Once the mediator confirms a reasonable suspicion of child abuse, the mediator's utmost task is to safely terminate the mediation session. Rather than abruptly calling the mediation to a halt, mediators should do their best to maintain the integrity of the process, primarily by maintaining their neutrality. This can be difficult and may seem counterintuitive, but it is the best mediator strategy for managing the difficult emotions associated with being accused of abuse. Maintaining mediator neutrality is also important because, due to the low reporting standard, it is possible that the subsequent investigation may come back as inconclusive or unfounded. Thus, it is possible, albeit unlikely, that the parties may work with the mediator again once the investigation is completed. Maintaining mediator neutrality keeps that possibility open.

Part of terminating the session, barring compelling circumstances, is informing the parties of the need for a report. There is no one correct method for doing so. . . .

One method is to use the need for a report as a measured conversation winding down the mediation. For example, after reminding the parties of the mediator's status as a mandatory reporter of child abuse and acknowledging that he or she is required by law to make the report, a mediator should disclose the accusation or other information without being accusatory. At this point, the mediator has the opportunity to let the parties know that no one has been convicted of any crime, because no proof of the alleged abuse has yet been established. Alternatively, the mediator may educate the parties about the institutions that will become involved once the report is made and what actions they are likely to take as part of the investigation. . . .

## 3. Confidentiality

The pressures mandatory reporting places on confidentiality arise once a mediator's reporting requirement is triggered, because at that point there is no choice but to disclose mediation communications. . . . In making a report, a mediator's difficulty lies with knowing the contours of what is confidential and what is not. A mediator's goal in complying with the reporting requirement and mediation confidentiality statutes should be to provide enough information to maximize the possibility of child protection while minimizing the breach of confidentiality. Since the purpose of the disclosure is to protect children, only information that assists CPS in making its determination of whether the child needs state protection should be disclosed. Appropriate disclosures include:

- the identity of the child,
- the identity of the child's parents or persons responsible for the child's care,
- the suspected perpetrator's name and relationship to the child (if any),
- a description of the abuse or neglect, and
- the identity of other people who have knowledge of the abuse.

Thus, when describing the circumstances of suspected abuse, mediators should limit their disclosures to the parties' disclosures that support the suspicion of abuse and subsequently led to the reporting decision. . . . Information not germane to child protection maintains its mediation confidentiality protection and should not be disclosed.

# NOTES AND QUESTIONS

1.   Should mediators be mandatory reporters of child abuse? In thinking this through, list out each of the reasons for or against mentioned by Hinshaw as well as others that you can think of.

2.   Consider the possible levels of proof necessary to trigger either mandatory or discretionary reporting. Which of the options mentioned by Hinshaw make the most sense? Is one more "objective" than another? Which, if any, do you think gives the most guidance to a mediator?

3.   Hinshaw discusses three ways to identify the duties mediators have as reporters of child abuse: 1) rules that explicitly designate mediators as reporters; 2) rules that mandate "all persons" as reporters, which would, of course, include mediators; 3) rules that require a mediator to determine reporting obligations in their "primary or secondary" professions. Which model do you prefer?

4.   Hinshaw identifies approaches to the mandatory reporting debate from a distinct angle: Does mandatory reporting actually reduce incidences of child abuse? What points does Hinshaw make regarding this argument? Do you agree or disagree?

5.   How does a mediator assess whether there is enough evidence to meet whatever the legal standard is that would trigger mandatory reporting? Does a mediator become an investigator instead of a facilitator? Are these roles consistent? If they are not, are there ways that a mediator can diminish the inconsistency? Consider the suggestions Hinshaw makes in this regard.

6.   What should a mediator say to participants and to a child protection agency should the mediator report? Do you agree with Hinshaw's list?

7.   Assume you are in a mandatory reporting jurisdiction that, as most jurisdictions do, have a "reasonable cause to suspect" child abuse standard.

You are mediating a divorce involving John Davis and Diane Davis. The only issue is child access. The couple have one child, Jeffrey, who is 7 years old. Neither party is represented at the time of the mediation.

You conduct the mediation and the couple is about to reach an agreement regarding child access. John will pick up Jeffrey Friday evening and will drop him off at Diane's house on Saturday evening. The parties have also agreed to split holidays and to permit John to take Jeffrey for an additional two weeks during the summer. John and Diane also agree to joint legal custody.

During the mediation, you observe that John is prone to extreme, unpredictable outbursts of anger. These outbursts include pounding on the table and shouting. At one point, John also shouts how Diane is too "soft" with Jeffrey and that he, John, believes in "tough discipline." When he says "tough discipline," he pounds his right fist several times into the palm of his left hand. You have never seen someone as volatile and unpredictable as John and you would never leave a child alone with him.

- Do you continue with the mediation? If so, do you believe it is part of your role to undertake further investigation as to whether the child is at risk?

- Assume you believe further investigation is warranted. What options do you have? Which would you choose? Why?

- Assume that as a result of your investigation, you have concluded that the reporting standard has been met.

    o  What would you say to the participants?

    o  What would you say to an agency responsible for investigating allegations of child abuse?

    o  What would you say to a judge if the mediation is referred by the court?

## 4. Death or Substantial Bodily Harm

Many standards and rules governing confidentiality in mediation permit or require a mediator to disclose information about death or bodily harm. For example, the *Standards of Practice for Family and Divorce Mediation* require disclosure of "a participant's threat of suicide or violence against any person to the threatened person and the appropriate authorities if the mediator believes such threat is likely to be acted upon as permitted by law."[7] Most statutes, however, provide that such reports are discretionary.

It is relatively rare for this exception to arise in family mediation with one exception: domestic violence. As discussed in Chapter 10, a core issue surrounding domestic violence and mediation is whether mediation is appropriate in the presence of domestic violence and how domestic violence can be detected prior to or during the mediation. There is also discussion of mediators' role in referring victims of domestic violence to programs that could provide support. There tends to be less discussion about whether a mediator should report domestic violence to an appropriate agency that could address it, including law enforcement agencies.

### NOTES AND QUESTIONS

1. Is there a difference in public policy regarding preventing child abuse as opposed to preventing domestic violence? If so, do you agree that disclosure for the latter should be discretionary? As a mediator, would you be more or less inclined to undertake an investigation regarding child abuse as opposed to domestic violence?

2. Consider the issue of suicide. How and when does a mediator conclude that a threat is "likely to be acted upon?" Consider issues relating to mediator expertise. A mediator who is a mental health professional might be better suited to assess how serious threats of suicide might be. In light of this, should an attorney-mediator be more or less reluctant to report the possibility of suicide?

---

[7] *Model Standards*, Standard VII.

## 5.  Speaking to Parties About Confidentiality

In Chapter 3 we explored how a Mediator's Opening Introduction typically includes a discussion of confidentiality. Needing to discuss confidentiality, however, only takes us so far. Given the relative complexity of confidentiality and its exceptions, there are decisions to be made about how detailed this discussion should be.

The *Model Standards* offer the following guidance: "Prior to undertaking the mediation the mediator should inform the participants of the limitations of confidentiality such as statutory, judicially, or ethically mandated reporting."[8] In addition, whatever the content of a discussion of confidentiality, the *manner* of the mediator — how the mediator exudes discretion and professionalism when discussing confidentiality — is just as important.

It is crucial to think through in detail how to discuss confidentiality. Consider some of the decisions to be made:

- Would you follow the advice of the *Model Standards* and discuss the possibility of "mandatory reporting?" If so, how explicit would you be? Would you, for example, mention mandatory reporting generally or would you mention child abuse specifically?

- Would you discuss exceptions that are typically discretionary, such as for a threat of "substantial bodily harm?" Would you be explicit as to domestic violence?

- To what extent do you need to be detailed about the law that would trigger mandatory or discretionary reporting? The more detailed you are, the more extended your discussion will be and the more likely your discussion will omit details. The less detailed you are, the more likely that the participants will not understand the nature of the exceptions. How would you strike a balance?

- Apart from decisions about the level of detail, consider that a mediator can mention the possibility of disclosure in passing, or emphasize it as a separate issue. This can be the result of tone as well as content. What choice would you make?

## QUESTION

Consider these bullet points. Write exactly what you might say in an Opening Introduction about confidentiality in a family mediation case involving child access. Read aloud what you have written and reflect upon the choices you have made. Would you make further changes in light of your reflection?

---

[8] *Model Standards*, Standard VII B.

## D.   CONFLICTS OF INTEREST IN FAMILY MEDIATION

As opposed to exceptions regarding confidentiality, ethical norms governing mediation and conflicts of interest are relatively straightforward. Standard IV of the *Model Standards* succinctly expresses the consensus in the family mediation community about the issue:

> A family mediator shall disclose all actual and potential grounds of bias and conflicts of interest reasonably known to the mediator. The participants shall be free to retain the mediator by an informed, written waiver of the conflict of interest. However, if a bias or conflict of interest clearly impairs a mediator's impartiality, the mediator shall withdraw regardless of the express agreement of the participants.[9]

Standard IV imposes on the mediator an obligation to "disclose all actual or potential grounds of bias and conflicts of interest reasonably known to the mediator." Thus, a mediator must disclose to the parties any potential conflict *of which the mediator is aware*. An obvious example would be if a mediator knows one or more of the participants, including attorneys, either professionally or personally. The mediator would then ask the participants if it would still be acceptable to them to continue with the mediation with that mediator.

A second possibility is that there might be conflicts of which the mediator is not aware. To explore this possibility, some mediators will, as part of their Introductory Statement, ask mediation participants if they know the mediator (or co-mediators) or if they have any reason to believe that the mediator could not be fair and impartial. Again, if the answer is yes the mediator would inquire as to whether it is acceptable to participants to continue with the mediation. A side benefit of such inquiries is that it demonstrates to participants that they control the mediation process.

The *Standards*, however, also identify another type of conflict. These are conflicts that are so severe that that even participant consent would still not cure the conflict. This is a relatively uncommon circumstance. One example might be a mediator's friendship — not acquaintanceship — with a participant, although in such an instance it is hard to conceive why the other party would consent. In these situations it is the mediator's obligation to inform the parties that it would not be appropriate for the mediator to continue to act as mediator. There would ordinarily be no obligation to detail the reasons why, although it might be prudent for a mediator to stress that this has nothing to do with the participants individually or (if appropriate) whether the matter should be mediated. Assuming that the mediator believes the matter is appropriate for mediation, the mediator might use her best efforts to secure a replacement mediator.

Knowing a mediation participant is an easy case of a potential or actual conflict. There are more subtle situations, however. What if, for some reason, a mediator has an aversion to a mediation participant or to issues that are presented in the mediation? Can such feelings impair a mediator's neutrality? The following article tackles these questions.

---

[9] *Model Standards*, Standard IV.

## PRACTICAL AND ETHICAL CONCERNS IN DIVORCE MEDIATION: ATTENDING TO EMOTIONAL FACTORS AFFECTING MEDIATOR JUDGMENT

13 MEDIATION QUARTERLY 193, 222–226 (1996)

By Robert A. deMayo

Divorce mediation is frequently an emotion-laden experience for all involved. The process often requires painful decisions regarding living arrangements, assets, child custody, and so forth . . . Given this emotional context, it is easy to see that only the most unempathic mediator is likely to be untouched by the pain and suffering of the involved parties. However, the potential for emotional reaction goes well beyond exposure to people in pain, for the mediator is not simply a passive observer of the process. Rather, the mediator's role is more appropriately conceptualized as that of a *participant-observer:* one who actively participates in an event while making professional observations of those at the center of the action.

[W]hen the mediator accepts an empathic position, the participants' words are more likely to touch a responsive chord, particularly when a client describes an emotion that resonates with the mediator's personal experience. In other words, engaging in empathic listening potentially brings more of the mediator's emotional self — including feelings, identifications, values, and needs — into the mediation room.

Thus, one client may stimulate nurturing and protective attitudes in the mediator, while another may stimulate mistrust and defensiveness. In either case, the process potentially stimulates the emotions of the mediator in a way that influences cognitive processes such as judgment and decision making. . . . For example, as a husband argues that he should have primary custody of his teenage son because of the adolescent's need for a strong role model, a male mediator's experiences of his own adolescence, parenting experiences, and so on are likely to be stimulated, and potentially play a role in the approach he takes to the discussion. As the mediator attempts to facilitate a fair resolution of issues, elements of his subjective life experiences may profoundly influence the way he conducts the mediation session.

### CASE EXAMPLE

Joseph Smith, a family law attorney with over twenty years' experience practicing law and six years conducting divorce mediations, undertook the divorce mediation of Mr. and Mrs. W. Mr. W. was forty-seven years old; Mrs. W. thirty-eight. Both were born in the Middle East and emigrated to this country twenty years earlier. They had been married for nineteen years and had three children, ages seventeen, fourteen, and eleven.

The mediation proceeded rapidly in the first two sessions. The couple agreed that it would be best for Mr. W. to assume primary legal and physical custody of the children and to remain in the family home while Mrs. W. moved to an apartment. They agreed to use Mr. W.'s estimate of the value of his retail business for the purpose of division of assets, and Mrs. W. expressed little interest in the notion of obtaining independent appraisals. Mr. Smith expressed his concerns to the couple that the rapid pace of their sessions was creating an unfair mediation process and a substantially unfair agreement at odds with prevailing legal standards, but they seemed to dismiss his expressions of caution. Feeling frustrated with their unresponsiveness, Mr. Smith deviated from his usual practice and suggested an individual caucus with each member.

The caucus with the husband was brief and uninformative. Mr. W. was polite but firm in his statements that the children belonged with him. He considered himself the head of the household who could best make decisions for adolescent children. He informed the mediator that he did not personally believe in the notion of community property, but he accepted that it was the prevailing law and was prepared to pay his wife a fair share of the business, the value to be determined by him. Although Mr. Smith was not fully aware of the extent of his reaction at the time, he felt offended by and judgmental toward Mr. W's views.

The caucus with Mrs. W. was quite different. In contrast with his negative reaction to her husband, he felt protective and nurturing toward Mrs. W. In response to several uncomfortable silences, Mr. Smith naturally began to use his active listening skills to facilitate conversation with his reticent client. To the mediator's surprise she then vehemently began to disclose the emotional history of the relationship. While she assumed the majority of parenting tasks, her husband's contacts with the children were dominated by his extravagant gifts to them. She did not really wish her marriage to end, but her husband had discovered that she was having an affair with a member of their religious community and had demanded a divorce. Mrs. W. was tearful throughout her disclosure, and as Mr. Smith listened empathically, he noticed that in contrast to his lack of emotional connection with Mr. W., he felt touched by Mrs. W.'s profound sadness.

As he had with many clients, Mr. Smith recommended that she seek counseling for her emotional troubles. He reminded her that he was not a therapist, and that his role as a mediator demanded neutrality. Mrs. W. thanked him for his sympathy, but declined his referral to therapy.

At the next session, Mrs. W. asked for a caucus with Mr. Smith. Although it was not his practice to caucus under these circumstances, his irritation with the husband and the protectiveness he felt toward the wife led him to say yes without full consideration of what this might or might not accomplish. She then went into further details about the emotional history of her marriage. Although Mr. Smith was an experienced mediator, he felt cruel interrupting Mrs. W. He decided at this point to raise again his concerns about the fairness of the mediation with both members present. Both members dismissed this concern, and stated that if Mr. Smith were to terminate the mediation, they would simply find another mediator. Feeling concerned for Mrs. W. and hoping that he could steer the mediation in a helpful direction, Mr. Smith agreed to continue the mediation.

The following day, Mr. Smith's receptionist informed him that an obviously distraught Mrs. W. had arrived at the office without an appointment requesting to see him immediately. Upon entering his office, Mrs. W. confided that as she thought about life without her children, she saw no reason to go on living, and was planning to take her life. Again, he suggested emphatically that she seek psychological treatment. Believing that she was serious about her intentions, and despite some internal misgivings, Mr. Smith found himself agreeing not to tell her husband of the visit, if she agreed ·to see a therapist. Two days later, Mr. Smith received a phone call from an enraged Mr. W., who reported that his wife had told him that she had changed her mind about conceding custody of the children to him. In the midst of arguing about this, Mrs. W. informed him of her private visit to Mr. Smith, and how the mediator had "given me the courage to stand up for myself." Mr. W. complained on the phone that he sensed that the mediator did not like him, and questioned the mediator's intentions. Furthermore, he advised Mr. Smith that he had discussed the matter with his business attorney, who expressed concern about the propriety of the individual meeting with Mrs. W. Mr. Smith never saw the couple again. Several weeks after the phone conversation, Mr. W. filed legal action to recover the costs of the mediation and filed a complaint with the state bar association.

It is traditional in discussions of standards of practice to focus on the abstract principles involved. For example, was the mediator's conduct in violation of the Academy of Family Mediator's standards of practice? The standard regarding impartiality and neutrality states, "If the mediator feels, or any one of the participants states, that the mediator's background or personal experiences would prejudice the mediator's performance, the mediator should withdraw from mediation unless all agree to proceed." These discussions often rest on the assumption that the mediator is aware of the potential conflict, and is therefore making a rational decision about how to proceed. However, as the case described in this article illustrates, emotional responses can supersede rational decision making and disrupt the ordinarily sound practice of experienced, well-trained mediators. . . .

[I] is useful to keep the intersubjective perspective in mind-in all human interactions, each person subtly or overtly influences the other. In the case presented here, none of the mediator's mistakes can be attributed to ignorance, sociopathy, or bad intentions. The problems described in the case example arose directly from the mediator's inability to sufficiently manage his emotional reaction to the participants so as to prevent it from influencing his on-the-spot decisions in the case. Because divorce mediation involves working with individuals who are experiencing many of the deepest of human emotions, the potential for emotional reaction is great. The case example illustrates that many of the decisions that we make may be influenced by subtle emotional factors, and that lack of awareness of these factors can compromise our standards of practice.

### Recommendations

The problems described in this article cannot be solved simply by disseminating more explicit standards of practice or rules of conduct for mediators, nor can they be prevented by mandating that mediators maintain emotional distance from the situation. Even the most experienced and professional mediators may encounter cases that touch them in ways of which they are unaware. Consequently, the solution lies in understanding that the potential for intense emotional responses is inherent to the process of divorce mediation, and then in proactively taking steps to maintain standards of practice in light of this phenomenon. In other words, emotional responses are not an aberration or something that only happens to people with poor boundaries, but rather are commonly present and need to be addressed in divorce mediation training and professional practice. The recommendations presented in this article outline six steps that can help maintain sound divorce mediation practices and prevent ethical mistakes.

- *A mediator must acknowledge the emotional biases and vulnerabilities that he or she brings to the mediation process.* For example, it is helpful to be aware of the types of people, situations, ethnic groups, gender roles, and so on that generate negative reactions such as antipathy and rejection. Conversely, one must acknowledge those types that produce sympathy, caretaking, and other nurturing responses. It should be noted that positive feelings can be just as much of an impediment to objective professional decision making as negative ones. Awareness of biases can prevent acting upon them. . . .

- *A mediator should pay close attention to those situations in which he or she is experiencing widely divergent emotional responses to the two parties . . .* The nature of their personalities and communication styles may elicit profoundly different responses in the mediator. Any time one notices this type of marked divergence in emotional reactions, one must be particularly attentive to issues of bias and neutrality.

- *A mediator should attend to the level of emotional reaction he or she is experiencing in the mediation sessions.* From the intersubjective perspective, those mediations that stimulate intense emotional reactions during the session, or lingering thoughts, feelings, and concerns after the session, are worthy of additional reflection. In this regard, in response to intense feelings about a particular mediation, the mediator should attend to how the parties' conflicts parallel the mediator's own current or past life circumstances. Conflicts that closely parallel one's own warrant particular consideration. In addition, one might need to reflect on the possibility that one is experiencing a positive or negative identification with a participant; that is, viewing that person as containing a positive quality, such as assertiveness, or a negative quality, such as pushiness, that one likes or dislikes about oneself . . .

- *A mediator may wish to attend to even subtle deviations in standard operating procedures.* While mediation frequently requires flexibility and creativity on the mediator's part, changes in standard procedures may be the initial warning signs of emotions impinging upon judgment . . .

- *A mediator should know that relying solely upon oneself to identify potential problems as they arise might be dangerous.* Even the most insightful mediator can be unaware of the subtle and gradual process of emotional involvement. Outside consultation may be as valuable for the mediator as for the clients, who are often counseled to seek it. It is encouraging to note that many local mediation societies recognize the value of consultation groups, peer supervision mentoring, and so forth. Through this growing movement, a mediator may avoid isolation and receive the feedback necessary to prevent some of the problems this article has discussed.

- *A mediator must acknowledge that despite our best efforts, some mediations may be too emotionally provocative for one to proceed as the mediator.* This requires an acknowledgment that each of us has limitations that prevent us from being the right mediator for every situation. Sometimes good intentions, such as the wish to help, cause us to ignore our best judgments in this regard. At other times, less noble concerns, such as financial considerations or difficulty acknowledging our biases, may cause us to proceed despite significant concern There is no universal guideline that one can use to determine whether a mediation is too emotionally provocative to proceed. Perhaps a useful rule of thumb is that if one has gone through the five steps outlined above and there remain significant questions about one's impartiality and neutrality, one should carefully review the Academy of Family Mediators' *Standards of Practice for Family and Divorce Mediation* (1995) and seriously consider one's ethical responsibility to withdraw if the situation warrants. . . .

## NOTES AND QUESTIONS

1.   Should Mr. Smith have terminated Mr. and Mrs. W's mediation? Why or why not?

2.   DeMayo suggests that a mediator's emotional involvement with mediation participants is inevitable. Do you agree?

3.   Mrs. W. threatens suicide when speaking to Mr. Smith alone, and Mr. Smith concludes that Mrs. W is "serious about her intentions." Does Mr. Smith respond appropriately to Mrs. W's threat? Could or must Mr. Smith have taken other actions? In answering this question, consider the prior discussion of exceptions for confidentiality if there might be death or substantial bodily harm.

4.   Do the *Model Standards* shed light on the issues deMayo identifies?

5.   DeMayo suggests that a mediator's emotional response to participants can be "subtle" and, perhaps below the level of a mediator's consciousness. Do you believe this to be the case? Why? Assuming your answer is yes, how might a mediator address this issue in the context of the practice of mediation?

6.   Do you find any or all of deMayo's recommendations convincing? Why or why not? Can you think of other recommendations?

## E.   SPECIAL ETHICAL CONSIDERATIONS FOR LAWYER-MEDIATORS

### 1.   Introduction

Puzzling issues sometimes arise for lawyers who mediate. Consider this conundrum: A lawyer who is mediating is a mediator who happens to be a lawyer just like a psychologist who is mediating is a mediator who happens to be a psychologist. At the same time, however, this is a simplification: some professional obligations of a lawyer might continue to apply even while the lawyer is mediating.[10]

Consider, for example, the following: A lawyer acting as a mediator observes a lawyer committing a substantial breach of professional ethics while the lawyer is representing a participant in mediation. Does the lawyer have an obligation to report the lawyer to appropriate disciplinary authorities, or is she prohibited by obligations to confidentiality in mediation? Answers remain unclear.

Another issue is when attorneys wish to incorporate mediation into their practice by formally associating with non-lawyers. This has arisen particularly in the area of family law practitioners. This scenario potentially conflicts with prohibitions against fee splitting between lawyers and non-lawyers. Answers to this question also remain unclear. For an ethics opinion addressing — and ultimately sidestepping — "ethical implications of system to provide family law mediation," see MSBA Comm. on Ethics, Op. 97-7.

## 2.   Clarifying Confusion about the Role of Lawyer-Mediators

An important development directed to lawyer-mediators is the adoption in 2002 of Rule 2.4 of *The ABA Model Rules of Professional Responsibility*. This Rule, for the first time in lawyer's ethics, explicitly addresses ethical considerations when lawyers act as "third party neutrals." The Rule is primarily concerned with potential confusion on the part of pro se parties about what role a lawyer-mediator has undertaken in mediation. Given the "pro se" crisis in family mediation that we discussed in Chapter 11, Rule 2.4 has particular importance for family mediators, especially those mediating in court-annexed programs.

Rule 2.4 sets forth two principles. First, the Rule mandates that a "lawyer serving as a third-party neutral shall inform unrepresented parties that the lawyer is not representing them." Second, where parties to mediation are unclear as to whether the lawyer-mediator is acting as a lawyer or as a mediator, "the lawyer shall explain the difference between the lawyer's role as a third-party neutral and a lawyer's role as one who represents a client."

Model Rule 2.4 is only binding in jurisdictions that have adopted it. Nevertheless, it is worth considering whether its provisions reflect good mediation practice even in jurisdictions that have not done so.

---

[10] Richard E. Crouch, *Divorce Mediation and Legal Ethics*, 16 FAM. L. Q. 219 (1982); Robert Rubinson, *The New Maryland Rules of Professional Conduct and Mediation: Perplexing Questions Answered and Perplexing Questions That Remain*, 36 U. BALT. L.F. 1 (2005).

# Chapter 13

# REPRESENTING CLIENTS IN FAMILY MEDIATION

## A. INTRODUCTION

Representing clients in family mediation is a subject distinct from how to mediate family disputes. At the heart of the problem is how the norms of family mediation — a collaborative process which often hopes to preserve relationships — squares with the norms of lawyering. Problems multiply because the norms of lawyering themselves are shifting: for example, notions of lawyers as "problem solvers" as opposed to "advocates" are becoming more commonplace. Given the unique qualities of family disputes, this "problem solving" orientation has blossomed into a full-fledged movement in which lawyers who practice family law are engaged in what they call "collaborative lawyering" — a subject we will explore in later in Chapter 14.

This is an area very much in flux. It is nevertheless of extraordinary importance as the legal profession increasingly recognizes that mediation is a fundamental element of what it means to practice of law in the 21st century. Nowhere is this more the case than in family law.

## B. CONCEPTUALIZING AN ATTORNEY'S ROLE IN FAMILY MEDIATION

Conceptions of lawyers as "hired guns" persist. Consider a classic statement of this view expressed by English Barrister Lord Brougham in 1820:

> [A]n advocate, in the discharge of his duty, knows but one person in all the world, and that person is his client. To save that client by all means and expedients, and at all hazards and costs to other persons . . . is his first and only duty; and in performing this duty he must not regard the alarm, the torments, the destruction which he may bring upon others.[1]

Few modern lawyers would subscribe to this view in its pure form. The ABA Model Rules of Professional Conduct offers a more measured consensus:

> A lawyer should . . . take whatever lawful means and ethical measures are required to vindicate a client's cause or endeavor. A lawyer must also act with commitment and dedication to the interests of the client and with zeal in

---

[1] Monroe H. Freedman, Understanding Lawyers Ethics 71 (3d ed. 2004).

advocacy upon the client's behalf. A lawyer is not bound, however, to press for every advantage that might be realized for a client . . ."[2]

Some family law practitioners refine this conception even further. For example, a set of rules entitled the "Bounds of Advocacy" issued by the American Academy of Matrimonial Lawyers provides for the following:

> Some clients expect and want the matrimonial lawyer to reflect the highly emotional, vengeful personal relationship between spouses. The attorney should counsel the client that discourteous and retaliatory conduct is inappropriate and counterproductive, that the measures of respect are consistent with competent and ethical representation of the client, and that it is unprofessional for the attorney to act otherwise . . . The matrimonial lawyer should make every effort to lower the emotional level of the interaction among parties and counsel. Some dissension and bad feelings can be avoided by a frank discussion with the client at the outset of how the attorney handles cases, including what the attorney will and will not do regarding vindictive conduct or actions likely to adversely affect the children's interests. If the client is unwilling to accept the attorney's limitation on objectives or means, the attorney should decline the representation.[3]

There are also, at times, explicit limitations on particular strategies that clients may suggest or demand. A core example is using child access claims as a "bargaining chip." If a client wants to persist in this strategy even after the lawyer counsels otherwise, the Bounds of Advocacy recommends that the attorney withdraw from representing the client.[4]

Even in light of these recommendations, however, consider the challenges facing a lawyer representing a client in mediation. The oft-stated goal of law school is to train law students to "think like a lawyer." With an eye towards this goal, the curriculum of law school involves identifying issues, distinguishing cases, learning legal rules, "arguing" points of law. All of these reflect a norm of the adversary system. Once in practice, litigators become immersed even more in the norms of litigation. Consider how one scholar has described this tendency:

> [L]awyers gravitate toward an adversarial approach. The reason may seem simplistic, if not superficially glib: lawyers are too preoccupied with litigating . . . Legal training and experience teach lawyers to view legal disputes as zero-sum or distributive conflicts about money in which one party wins and the other one loses . . . The litigator's mindset is also molded by the only too familiar routine for pursuing litigation. . . . As the attorneys and parties become consumed by these litigation tactics, the litigation and related negotiation become sharply adversarial . . .[5]

---

[2] ABA Model Rules of Professional Conduct 1.3 Comment [1].

[3] American Academy of Matrimonial Lawyers, BOUNDS OF ADVOCACY Rule 1.3 Comment (2000).

[4] *Id.* at Rule 5.2, Comment.

[5] Harold Abramson, *Problem-Solving Advocacy in Mediations: A Model of Client Representation*, 10 HARV. NEGOT. L. REV. 103, 114–117 (2005).

Consider one dimension of the how profoundly different a lawyer's role might be in mediation as opposed to litigation. Aside from pro se litigants and formal testimony, only lawyers — not clients — can address a judge. Lawyers also directly negotiate with one another on behalf of clients. In contrast, mediation is about self-determination, and participants' direct engagement in the process is not only a way to vindicate this value, but also a means to enhance the quality of participants' communication. Can mediation be a participant's process when an attorney speaks on behalf of the participant/client?

## NOTES AND QUESTIONS

1.    Reflect on your own conceptions of what lawyers do. Does a "lawyer's mindset" resonate with you? To what extent do you think such a "mindset" might impede effective lawyering in the context of mediation?

2.    Is there such a thing as "mediation advocacy" or is that an oxymoron?

3.    Consider the conceptions of a lawyer's role as articulated by Lord Brougham, the ABA Model Rules of Professional Conduct, and the Bounds of Advocacy. Do you believe any are compatible with how you conceptualize what an attorney's role should be when representing clients in mediation?

## C.   LAWYERS' ROLES PRIOR TO AND DURING FAMILY MEDIATION

What role or roles should lawyers perform in relation to the mediation process itself? There are numerous variables that go into answering this question: the nature of and complexity of the issues in dispute, the nature of the planned mediation (including whether it is "court annexed" or not), whether or not a client has had experience with mediation before, and so forth. The following examines these issues in chronological order: counseling clients before mediation, preparing clients for mediation, representing clients in mediation, and activities after the conclusion of mediation.

### 1.   Counseling Clients About the Mediation Option

Assuming mediation is not mandated or otherwise court-ordered, clients can choose whether to pursue mediation or not. Increasingly, lawyers' ethical rules have begun to address lawyers' obligations to discuss with clients the option of pursuing ADR processes, including mediation. For example, the ABA Model Rules of Professional Conduct provides that "when a matter is likely to involve litigation, it may be necessary . . . to inform the client of forms of dispute resolution that might constitute reasonable alternatives to litigation."[6] This amendment generated and continues to generate a lively debate about whether it should *mandate* counseling about the availability of ADR[7]: its "may be necessary" language melds the mandatory

---

[6]   ABA Model Rules of Professional Conduct Rule 2.1 Comment [5].

[7]   Andrew Schepard, *Kramer vs. Kramer Revisited: A Comment on the Miller Commission Report and*

with the discretionary with no guidance as to which should apply. In any event, this new Rule does reflect a growing consensus that lawyers should be aware of and counsel clients about non-adversarial processes to resolve a dispute.

## Assessing Options

What factors might go into assessing whether mediation is appropriate? Consider the following possibilities:

- Are there power differentials?
- Is there actual or suspected child abuse or domestic violence?
- Would either or both parties be open to a collaborative process?
- Will the resources of a client facilitate meaningful time to mediate or, if the possible mediation will be court-annexed, does the structure or resources allocated to the program offer the possibility of a successful mediation? Whether mediation is mandatory is also relevant in considering this question.
- What are the legal issues involved and how might they be resolved in adjudication?

## Presenting Options

If counseling clients about the mediation option is ethically mandated or appropriate, consider options in how an attorney might approach the task:

- Assuming a lawyer believes mediation is a good alternative, should a lawyer "advocate" for mediation?
- Should a lawyer present mediation as one of several options without trying to "convince" a client that she should choose mediation?
- If a client decides that litigation is what she wants to pursue, should a lawyer seek to "convince" her otherwise?

Can you think of other factors that might be explored?

## Word Choice

As with issues relating to confidentiality discussed in Chapter 12, consider what words to use when describing mediation.[8] In thinking through this issue, consider how clients have likely internalized the norms of adjudication and what lawyers do. Virtually all family disputes portrayed in movies, television shows, and high profile divorces present dramatic and confrontational advocacy. After all, has there been a portrayal in popular culture about family mediation?

Given this reality, consider the following word choices a lawyer might choose to use or avoid:

---

the Obligation of Divorce Lawyers for Parents to Discuss Alternative Dispute Resolution with Their Clients, 27 PACE L. REV. 677 (2007).

[8] See Robert Rubinson, Client Counseling, Mediation, and Alternative Narratives of Dispute Resolution, 10 CLINICAL L. REV. 833 (2004).

- Avoid "win the case" or "get what you want." Characterize options as "managing controversy" or "resolving the case."

- Avoid language that reflects the process of litigation, such as "claim," "defend," "argue," "present evidence," and "testifies." Consider substituting "discuss," "problem-solve," and "resolve."

- Avoid characterizing disputes solely in terms of "custody" and "visitation." Consider "co-parenting" instead and, if applicable, mention a potential parenting plan.

## 2.  Preparing Clients for Family Mediation

Assume that a client chooses mediation and the other party agrees, or that mediation is mandated or court-ordered. How should a lawyer should prepare a client for mediation?

An initial issue relates to goals in mediation. The openness of mediation should not mask that a lawyer still must work intensively with the client to establish and assess a range of goals and interests, as well as identifying probable goals and interests of the other party. Increasing the range of settlement alternatives facilitates reaching a mutually satisfactory agreement in mediation. When a client is aware of this feature of mediation, she may see the generation and development of alternatives not as a retreat from achieving a particular outcome, but as the means of potentially achieving a satisfactory resolution of the dispute. As a result, she is more likely to engage thoughtfully prior to and during mediation.

Moreover, as we have seen in Chapter 3, "facts" in mediation is a much broader concept than in adjudication. Preparing a client for mediation is thus much more than a "tell me what happened" dialogue. Given that mediation promotes dialogue among participants themselves, a lawyer should seek to understand who the parties are and how they typically interact. Further questions might be as follows: Is the parents' relationship such that one party will unfairly dominate in a more open process? Is it a goal of one or more parties to continue the relationship in some form? What sorts of non-either/or ideas might be available regarding financial issues or child access?

Yet another challenge is for a lawyer to move away from the "admit and deny" pattern of other forms of dispute resolution. Rather, a lawyer might consider that a crucial aspect of the attorney role prior to and during mediation is to collaborate with a client to insure that the client's "frame" or narrative is what is meaningful to the client even if it is not, strictly speaking, a "response" to another party's position.

## 3.  The Lawyer's Role During Mediation

An issue that should be explored prior to mediation is how the attorney should act during mediation.

In considering who should do what at mediation, lawyers should first consider the options that are available. In litigation, arbitration, and negotiation, the lawyer's formal communications are directed almost exclusively to the decision-maker or opposing counsel. In mediation, however, the lawyer can communicate with multiple audiences: client(s), other mediation participants, opposing counsel (assuming the other party is represented), and the mediator(s).

An attorney should also consider the characteristics of the client and any barriers that are likely to prevent a case from being resolved. Not all clients are the same. Some are shy and some are more than willing to communicate. Some might be knowledgeable about legal forums and processes and others might have little or no experience with them. Some might make good impressions and others less so. Some are even-tempered and others are quick to anger. It is important to take the client's personality and presentation into account in exploring with the client what role the client and lawyer should play at mediation.

In addition, an attorney should consider the attorney's own tendencies. Some attorneys have more experience and facility at collaborative forms of bargaining, including mediation. For lawyers accustomed to the highly adversarial litigation process, adjusting to the interest-based, collaborative nature of mediation can be a new, challenging, and disconcerting experience. For lawyers whose usual goal in litigation or negotiation is to wrest and maintain as much control over the flow of information and outcome as possible, relinquishing control to the parties and the mediator may seem counterintuitive. Nevertheless, such lawyers — as all lawyers in mediation — should strive to facilitate settlement by framing and complementing the client's voice rather than by acting as the client's "mouthpiece."

In light of these variables, consider the three "models" presented in the following excerpt.

## MODELS OF CLIENT INTERACTION WITH ATTORNEYS IN MEDIATION
### (2002)[9]
### By Jonathan Hyman

Here are three models of how a lawyer can interact with a client during mediation.

*The (substantive) counselor* The client negotiates in the mediation. The lawyer only provides advice to the client about the risks and benefits of adjudication . . . and reviews the terms of agreement to avoid any hidden traps or unforeseen gaps. Under this model the lawyer need not even attend.

*The (positional) negotiator.* The lawyer does most of the negotiating at the mediation, and mostly in the positional mode. That is, the lawyer uses the mediation primarily as an opportunity to manage the concealment/disclosure game, trying to extract information from the other side that helps assess the value of the case and the other side's willingness to settle, and trying to conceal harmful information from the other side, and also to convey information that will cause the other side to see their own case in a less favorable light . . . The client decides on the goals, and the lawyer decides on the means . . .

*The (negotiation) counselor.* This approach is more complex. The lawyer and client

---

[9] Copyright ©2002. Reprinted with permission.

both participate in the mediation, with the lawyer continually assessing the information exchange, the proposals, and the dynamics of the negotiation. It requires ongoing dialogue with the client about how the negotiation is going, and how to increase the chances of a good outcome with the client. But it also entails some independent action by the lawyer, that can't be subject to dialogue with the client. For instance, the lawyer might see how the various cognitive and affective obstacles to agreement are affecting the client, something the client, almost by definition, can't see. A lawyer might be able to see, in a way the client can't, why the other side isn't effectively communicating [with] the client (and vice versa). The lawyer then has some obligation to try to overcome those obstacles, without the luxury of extended dialogue with . . . the client . . . At the same time, the lawyer should know when the client may have a better chance of getting a good result, either because the client knows the other side better than the lawyer . . . or because it's important for the other side to relate to the client, not the lawyer . . . .

## NOTES AND QUESTIONS

1.   Do you see additional "models" that Hyman does not describe? What would such a model or models look like? Consider, for example, whether there might be a role that is even less active than Hyman's "(negotiation) counselor"?

2.   Do you believe one or more "models" is particularly appropriate for certain issues in family mediation? For example, would the answer to this question turn on whether the mediation is addressing child access issues or financial issues?

3.   Do you believe attorneys should adhere to different models if the mediator's orientation is evaluative, facilitative, or transformative?

4.   There is little uniformity in how mediators and attorneys behave in actual mediation sessions. Temperaments, sophistication, and understanding of mediation vary. Can you conceive of being prepared to undertake different roles at different points in a mediation session? What might trigger a change in "model" in the midst of a mediation session?

How about details regarding the respective roles of attorney and client during the mediation itself? The following excerpt discusses this issue.

### *LAWYER'S REPRESENTATION OF CLIENTS IN MEDIATION: USING ECONOMIC AND PSYCHOLOGY TO STRUCTURE ADVOCACY IN A NONADVERSARIAL SETTING*[10]
14 Ohio St. J. On Disp. Resol. 269, 274, 345–349, 353–354, 356, 365 (1999)
### By Jean R. Sternlight

. . . While no single lawyer's role in mediation is always proper, lawyers need to be particularly vigilant in guarding against their own tendencies to behave in mediation exactly as they would in litigation. Instead, to serve their clients' interests, and in light of the conflicts of interest and perception between lawyers and their own clients,

---

[10] Copyright © 1999. Reprinted with permission.

attorneys should often encourage their clients to play an active role in the mediation, allow the discussion to focus on emotional as well as legal concerns, and work toward mutually beneficial rather than win-or-lose solutions. Those lawyers who, seeking to advocate strongly on behalf of their clients, take steps to dominate the mediation, focus exclusively on legal issues, and minimize their clients' direct participation, will often ill serve their clients' true needs and interests. Such overly zealous advocates are frequently poor advocates. . . .

Some clients undoubtedly prefer to have their attorneys take a dominant role during the mediation. . . . Such clients may be shy; they may believe that their attorneys could express their positions more articulately and cogently than they could; they may fear that a stronger or better educated opponent may take advantage of them if they represent themselves in the mediation; they may worry that they would make an inappropriate admission; they may fear that they would cry or get angry if they had to speak; or they may believe that their speech would anger or upset the opposing party and thereby bring about physical or emotional harm or derail the negotiations. From a strategic standpoint, a party that wishes to settle the dispute but does not want to admit fault may also find it desirable to be represented in the negotiation.

As well, some clients prefer to have their lawyers serve as buffers, limiting the clients' direct confrontations with either the opposing parties, the opposing parties' attorneys, or even the mediators. For example, some clients have been emotionally or even physically abused or harassed by the opposing parties and would find future confrontations emotionally distressing and perhaps physically threatening. Certain clients may also recognize that they would be subject to coercion or be outmatched if they had to go head-to-head with the opposing party or attorney. Mediation may not be an appropriate dispute resolution device for many parties who have such concerns. Or, if the dispute is to be mediated, such clients may prefer to stay home (if this is allowed by the jurisdiction rules) and allow their attorneys to represent them in mediation. At times, a client who has these concerns may choose to attend the mediation but request that the attorney do all or most of the talking and also ensure that neither the opposing side nor the mediator engages in conduct that would be painful or detrimental to the client.

In other cases the client may desire to play an active role in the mediation, but the attorney may believe that such active participation would not serve the client's best interests. For example, the client may desire to speak out but the lawyer may fear that the client would not be a good advocate of her own position, that she would make damaging admissions, or that she would either get mad or make the other side mad, thereby disrupting the negotiation process. Similarly, the client may express a desire to participate actively in the mediation, and perhaps to have the attorney stay home, but the attorney may fear that the client would be bullied or tricked by the opposing party or simply settle the case for less than the attorney might have obtained. Or, the attorney may fear that the client is not up to the emotional stress that will occur if the attorney does not participate actively in the mediation.

All of these concerns of both client and attorney are potentially legitimate. While some, and particularly some mediators, may believe that all attorney participation in mediation intrudes inappropriately into what should be a client-oriented process, situations do exist in which attorneys need to serve as their clients' protectors and spokespersons. It is crucial to consider these important interests in devising guidelines for attorneys' roles in mediation . . .

The worst mistake one can make in determining the appropriate roles of lawyer and client in a mediation is to refuse to see the issue and simply operate out of habit. Too many lawyers and clients have never thought seriously about how the lawyer-client relationship should work in the context of a mediation. Many lawyers, particularly those with extensive deposition or trial experience, have simply transferred their assumptions and behavior from those areas to the mediation forum without thinking through the differences between a trial or a deposition and a mediation. Such lawyers often instinctively try to do all the talking for the client, tell the client not to volunteer anything, try to stifle emotional outbursts, and focus primarily on establishing the superiority of their clients' legal positions rather than on a problem-solving approach. While this dominating approach may be appropriate in certain mediations, adopting it as a general rule will prevent the use of mediation to overcome the various barriers to negotiation.

Equally inappropriately, some lawyers, like some mediators, assume that mediation is exclusively the clients' process and either fail to attend altogether or do attend but act as the much discussed "potted plant." Such a lawyer may figure that because comments made in mediation are protected by confidentiality, and because no settlement can be reached without her client's agreement, the lawyer need not worry much, if at all, about protecting her client's interests. Again, while this approach may sometimes be appropriate, adopting it unthinkingly in every case is a mistake which may subject certain clients to coercion and abuse and ultimately cause them to accept a settlement which is unfair.

Instead of exclusively taking one approach or the other, lawyers and their clients should divide their responsibilities on a case-by-case basis after taking into account such factors as the nature of the clients and their attorneys, the respective goals of these participants, and the nature of the dispute . . . [A]ttorneys should consult extensively with their clients not only as to what position should be taken in a negotiation and as to whether the case should be mediated, but also as to the respective roles to be taken by lawyer and client in the mediation. . . . [S]uch consultation is desirable as a matter of good practice for several reasons. First, the determination of roles may well implicate important substantive concerns. For example, a client may wish to give her own opening in the mediation because one of her substantive goals is to be able to explain how she feels directly to the opposing party [or] a client may wish to have her attorney handle all of the questions because the client feels it would be emotionally damaging to attempt to confront the opposing party or her attorney directly . . . .

Second, the client likely has more information regarding the client's aptitudes and abilities than does the attorney. If the attorney does not discuss participation issues with her client, she may make false assumptions regarding the client's interest or ability in participating actively in the mediation. A client who appears articulate may for emotional reasons nonetheless be ineffective in certain mediation contexts.

Alternatively, a client who appears very shy or inarticulate may be capable of making a very moving and personal opening statement.

Third . . . [w]here the attorney makes choices about the respective roles of client and attorney in mediation, she is likely, at least unwittingly, to make a decision that is biased in favor of her own economic and psychological interests. In cases where such conflicts are possible, it is particularly important that an attorney should consult with her client.

. . . .

Of course, when the attorney consults with the client, the client will sometimes throw the question of roles back to the attorney and ask the attorney to make the decision. It would be preferable to have the attorney outline the pros and cons of various options to the client and let the client make the call. However, if having heard all the options the client still requests that the attorney decide who should make the opening or how it should be structured, the attorney should go ahead and make these decisions.

. . . .

As well, the attorney should ask herself whether the client would benefit by having the attorney protect her from the opposing party. Although, ideally, mediation should be an opportunity for clients to communicate directly with one another, sometimes such direct communication by clients or their attorneys may be undesirable . . . [I]f the client has been subjected to domestic abuse by the opposing party, it may be not only emotionally distressing but also coercive and even unsafe for the victim to converse directly with her abuser. . . .

Anyone who says they have a simple answer to the question of how lawyers and clients should divide their responsibilities in a mediation must be wrong. Either their answer is not simple or their answer is not right. The answer is complicated because the division of responsibilities should vary substantially depending upon who the client is, who the lawyer is, and what factors appear to be blocking a reasonable and fair settlement of the dispute . . . In determining her role in a mediation, a lawyer should do the following: (1) serve as her client's advocate, (2) consult with her client regarding the division of responsibilities, (3) consider who her client is, and (4) take into account whether she or her client is best situated to help to overcome the extant economic, psychological, and principal-agent barriers to a fair negotiated agreement. . . .

## NOTES AND QUESTIONS

1. Is Sternlight's approach *too* contextual, that is, should an attorney operate from an initial assumption of minimal participation as opposed to fashioning her role through the analysis Sternlight suggests?

2. Consider how the unfolding of mediation might change plans as to the respective roles of attorney and client. Consider the following examples:

- Opposing counsel approaches mediation as if it were litigation. She is aggressive and her client does not speak.

- Your assessment prior to the mediation is that your client is well able to communicate in the mediation on her own. Nevertheless, as the mediation continues, you sense her getting increasingly uncomfortable.

- Your client is agreeing to things that she told you emphatically that she would not agree to when you had met her before the mediation.

- The mediator acts like a judge and appears not to understand fundamentals of mediation,

How would you handle these situations?

3.    Sternlight's discussion is not focused on family mediation. Do family conflicts warrant a different approach to attorney representation in mediation than other types of disputes?

## 4.   Lawyers and Mediation: An Example

The following is a narrative of one person's experience in a family mediation. As you will see, the narrative is framed as a critique of mediation. In light of the above material, as well as prior chapters, do you believe the critique is well taken or, at least, a prudent warning about the risks of attorney representation in mediation?

## RECLAIMING PROFESSIONALISM: THE LAWYER'S ROLE IN DIVORCE MEDIATION[11]
### 28 Fam. L.Q. 177 (1994)
### By Penelope Eileen Bryan

Gayle's Story

When I [married] Warren, he was an elected county official . . . Warren [then] ran a successful campaign and began his long tenure as a state legislator. Then came the children. First Stephanie, then Josh, and finally Julie. Years passed. At first I enjoyed being the wife of a popular public official. . . . Over the years, though, some troublesome patterns emerged . . . Warren took almost exclusive control of family finances. Toward the end of our marriage, my weekly allowance was $200. From this amount Warren deducted any amount I spent on my own needs, such as shoes, clothing, cosmetics, haircuts, or lunches with friends. Warren also gave me a credit card, but he deducted any charge related to my personal needs from my weekly allowance.

In addition to my allowance, Warren deposited $400 a week into my checking account for family expenses. This money was to be spent exclusively on groceries and on the children. Each week Warren required me to justify each expenditure I made from my checking account . . .

Troubling incidents occurred with increasing frequency. For instance, dinner time became a nightmare. Warren insisted that the children eat efficiently — nothing put

---

[11]   Copyright ©1994 by the American Bar Association. Reprinted with permission.

on their plates was to be wasted. Warren also maintained that Josh was too self-indulgent and that he needed more discipline. To correct Josh's failings, Warren required me each day to cook one dish Josh disliked. At dinner Warren, with a broad smile, would serve Josh a large portion of this dish. When he was young Josh simply hung his head and quietly ate what his father put before him. As he grew older and bigger, however, Josh's anger frequently flared.

During one angry exchange, Warren lifted Josh's plate that was piled high with lima beans and smashed it on the table. The beans went everywhere. He then towered over Josh and made him eat the beans without using utensils, one at a time, from the table and the floor. Warren yelled at and berated Josh until he had finished . . .

Control and derision were not the only problems in Warren's interactions with the children. His violent anger frequently led to his use of excessive physical force. During one angry outburst, Warren threw eight-year-old Julie against the wall, almost causing her to faint . . .

Tension had been mounting in the house and Warren was drinking heavily. The children and I were in the kitchen. I was putting the finishing touches on a Saturday morning breakfast. Warren entered just as Josh reached into the ceramic cookie jar. Warren yelled that Josh would ruin his appetite. Josh glared, extracted a cookie, and took a bite. Warren tried to hit the cookie out of Josh's hand while he grabbed the ceramic jar. Josh retreated to the other side of the room near his sisters. While staring at his father, Josh took another bite from the forbidden cookie. Warren lost it. He hurled the ceramic jar at Josh's head. Fortunately the bloody-marys he had consumed that morning impaired his accuracy. But the ceramic jar caught Stephanie, leaving a two inch split in her cheek. Trembling, I quickly ushered the children out of the house and into the car . . . I announced that I wanted a divorce and I asked Warren to leave the marital home. He refused. Since I wanted the divorce and he did not, he insisted that I and the children should be the ones to leave.

Not knowing where we should go or what we should do, I called Melinda to represent me. I chose Melinda because I knew several other politicians' wives who had used Melinda for their divorces. I explained that the children and I had nowhere to go. Melinda agreed to see me immediately. With the children sitting in the waiting room, Melinda and I had our first conference. Knowing Warren's political and financial status, Melinda told me to rent an apartment for the family until she could work things out with Warren's lawyer.

I left Melinda's office and began a futile search for housing. Landlords would not accept my credit card for rent and I had no cash or money in my checking account. I called Warren. He refused to give me money for housing. He told me to get a job. I felt frightened. Growing desperate, I turned to my friend Marty and asked if we could stay with her for a day or two. Although Marty had three children of her own, she agreed. The "day-or-two" extended to ten. I again called Warren, explaining that living in another person's house was becoming extremely stressful. After a day and a half of negotiation, Warren agreed that we could live in his motorhome if he could park it in Marty's driveway. With no other alternative available, the children and I moved to Marty's driveway. . . . The motorhome's heating and cooling units could not be used. Whenever they were turned on, all the circuits in Marty's house blew. Ventilation and temperature control became oppressive problems, especially with our unstable fall weather . . .

I began calling Melinda almost daily, asking whether something could be done. Finally my psychologist Paul called her and insisted that my living situation had to change. Melinda told him that Warren had been more difficult about paying temporary support than she had expected and that she intended to request a temporary support hearing. She explained that first, however, the law required me to mediate with Warren. Paul expressed his concern about my ability to negotiate with Warren. Melinda assured him that mediation was just a hoop that had to be jumped through to get to court. Melinda and Warren's attorney scheduled a mediation session.

I met with Melinda once before the mediation. I explained that I knew nothing about mediation and that, whatever it was, I did not want to do it with Warren. She insisted that the law required mediation before a temporary support hearing. I should not worry — nothing would happen and she would be there with me. After the mediation we could get our hearing before a judge . . .

The entire week before the mediation I was a wreck. I slept little and cried frequently. I chain smoked. My hands constantly shook. I met with my psychologist several times. He helped calm my nerves — but only temporarily. When I left his office my anxiety resurfaced. Worse — I was embarrassed and angry with myself. I could remember a time in my life when I had felt strong and competent. I had trouble believing that I had become this nervous wreck and that my life and my children's lives seemed so vulnerable to Warren's whims . . .

The day of the mediation I went to Melinda's office. Soon afterwards Warren and his attorney arrived. To my chagrin, I was shaking and close to tears. I told my attorney's receptionist I had arrived. She nodded briefly and told me to have a seat. Melinda would be out in a moment. I sat as far away from Warren as I could and tried not to look at him or his attorney. The receptionist asked whether Warren would like coffee. She referred to him as "senator." He thanked her for her attentiveness. His old seductive charm was in full-swing. No one asked whether I wanted coffee. Other attorneys in the firm wandered through the waiting room. They each spoke deferentially to Warren, ignoring me completely — even though several of them knew me socially. I began to feel apologetic — uncomfortable with the awkwardness my presence seemed to cause. I went to the bathroom, looked in the mirror and tried to convince myself that I was being overly sensitive. Yet I was becoming apprehensive and I worried whether I could control my tears.

Finally Melinda appeared. She engaged in a casual chat with Warren. Both of them acted as though nothing unusual were happening. I wondered whether I was the only person there who understood the significance of the divorce and the desperateness I felt. I felt extremely anxious and unable to concentrate. Melinda ended her conversation with Warren and called me into her office, explaining there was no need for me to sit in the waiting room with Warren.

Settling into her chair, Melinda told me that the mediator was an attorney named Frank and that they had decided I should not confront Warren directly during the mediation. But first we all had to meet with Frank in Melinda's conference room. I was relieved that I did not have to deal with Warren . . . Frank . . . explained the mediation process to all of us, but I could not listen. In Warren's presence, I was too emotionally agitated to listen. Besides Melinda had assured me she would protect me. I was there so that I could get to a judge and get the children and me out of the motorhome. At the end of Frank's talk, Melinda and I left the conference room and returned to her office.

On the way to the office, Melinda's receptionist stopped me and asked that I return the key to the bathroom. Frowning, she told me that my taking the bathroom key into the conference room had caused considerable difficulty for others in the office. I felt ashamed — like a bad child. I started to cry.

After Melinda and I were back in her office and I had calmed down, Frank entered. I told him of the family's need to get out of the motorhome and find suitable housing. I explained what living in the motorhome had been like. He seemed genuinely concerned and he promised that I would get out of the motorhome. I cried again — this time with relief. Regaining my composure, I relaxed some and allowed myself to imagine having easy access to a bathroom. My positive feelings proved premature.

Melinda and Frank left to talk with Warren and his attorney. My first few minutes alone were fine, but as time passed I became anxious — wondering what was taking so long. My imagination conjured up negative images — Warren's refusing to pay support, Warren's deciding that he wanted custody of the children, Warren's convincing everyone that I was malingering. The comfort I experienced earlier gave way to feelings of insecurity and dread. I began pacing. By the time Frank and Melinda returned I had convinced myself that I was in trouble. I was right. Melinda seemed excited and she told me progress had been made. Warren was willing to leave the marital home and allow me and the children to return. I again cried with relief. Melinda also explained that Warren had offered me ownership of the marital home. She could not believe my good fortune. She had not anticipated ANY reasonable offer — certainly not one as generous as this. No court, she assured me, would award me $500,000.

My relief immediately gave way to panic. I felt numb. I had many jumbled thoughts. I paced the room, trying to calm myself so that I could explain. I did not want the marital home. In order to get any money out of it, I would have to sell it. The real estate market was depressed. I had heard of people who had walked away from their homes because there were no buyers. The house was not worth $500,000. The house needed work before it could be sold. I knew of two leaks in the roof. I could not afford repairs. I did not have any money! Had she forgotten that? Melinda left the room to confer with Warren and his attorney. She returned and stated that "the senator" said the roof did not leak. That seemed to close the topic.

I asked about financial support. Melinda said that Warren would not pay spousal maintenance — it was "absolutely out of the question." I sank into confused anxiety. I needed spousal maintenance. I could not afford to live in the house without it. Melinda, who knew this, blankly stared at me during my attempt to explain. I could not comprehend what was happening. When I first hired Melinda, she indicated that I was entitled to maintenance. I again explained, as thoroughly as I could, the expenses of maintaining the house and the children, my lack of recent work experience, and my limited ability to work. At a brave moment, looking straight at Melinda, I told her I HAD to have spousal support. Melinda flinched. Frank frowned and explained that courts disapprove of spousal maintenance, making it difficult to get. I felt light-headed. I sensed I was losing control.

I protested. I thought nothing was going to happen today. Mediation was just a hoop. I could not do this. I was not ready. Frank asked Melinda how long it would take to get a temporary support hearing. Melinda replied it would take five or six weeks. I was shocked. If I did not agree, the children and I would spend another six weeks in the motorhome! It would be winter! I had to breathe deeply to keep from getting dizzy. I began to cry.

The pressure increased. Melinda said I could invest $150,000 in another house and then I could live nicely off the interest on $350,000. If I invested the money at 10 percent, she explained, I would have a $35,000 a year income. I did not think to challenge her, even though I knew interest rates had fallen. I did, however, express my belief that the house was not worth $500,000 — so her calculations were inaccurate. We had not even had an appraisal done! I felt ambushed.

Frank then pulled up a chair right in front of me, put his elbows on his knees, and cupped his chin in his hands. Sitting there knee to knee with me, he asked me to tell him about the house. I told him what I already had told Melinda. He asked if the acreage we owned could be subdivided. I said no-the community restrictions would not allow it. After listening to me, he talked about how valuable ten acre home sites were, how people valued space and privacy, and how people were moving to our state because our economy was on the up-swing. Surely the house would sell for $500,000 — perhaps much more. I would be a wealthy woman. He told a story of how his friend's home had sold quickly. Surely mine also would sell quickly. Frank then stated that, in his experience as a lawyer, Warren's offer was generous. He and Melinda suggested that I should be grateful. I wondered if we lived on the same planet. Melinda repeated that no court would give me $500,000. I was wearing out — but I tried again. I did not want the house. I did not know its worth. I was not sure I could sell it . . . Why did no one understand these things?

Melinda responded that I was being unreasonable — I obviously did not understand the offer — I should stop whining about petty details. If I would just agree I would be a half-millionaire. Her tone became cold and authoritative. I again felt like a "bad child" . . .

Soon we all went into the conference room to sign a typed agreement. Melinda explained that she would draft another agreement in the morning, but it would be wise to get something signed now. She handed me the agreement, asking me to read through it. I flipped the pages without much comprehension. . . . I could no longer concentrate. I asked whether she was sure I should sign. She was sure. I signed.

I have no memory of my drive "home" to the motorhome. Soon after my arrival I told Marty what had happened. She was surprised I had accepted the marital home because I earlier had told her that I did not want the house . . . She doubted that my house could be sold quickly and that it was worth half a million dollars.

After calling two other friends who shared Marty's opinion, I began to panic. I realized I had to make some changes in the final agreement that Melinda was preparing. I never thought the paper I signed in Melinda's office immediately after the mediation was a "final" agreement. I thought a second agreement was coming — that changes could be made.

The next morning I called Melinda. I told her I wanted . . . him to guarantee that I would realize at least half a million dollars from the sale of the house. Melinda told me Warren would not sign the agreement if she made the changes. I said that was okay, because I did not intend to sign it unless those provisions were included. Melinda was furious with me. She told me . . . that I was going to screw up the whole deal. I was shocked by the way she spoke to me and I retreated, insisting only that she insert a clause about the roof. She then told me she could not insert such a clause — that the agreement I had signed the day before was a binding contract. I could not change its provisions. I had to sign the final copy. I told her I would wait and see what the judge had to say. She told me there would be no temporary support hearing — no judge — the contract I had signed took care of everything. I was stunned. I hung up on Melinda and began to weep. It seemed I had sold myself down the river . . .

More than a year has passed since the mediation. My new lawyer and I are in the middle of a legal fight with Warren who, understandably, wants the agreement to stand and shows no willingness to compromise . . . I am glad I decided to fight. When I look back on the mediation I feel very angry. I cannot believe that I was forced into that experience, that my lawyer abandoned me, and that I almost gave up what I think I deserve after over twenty years of service to my husband and family — a chance for a decent life.

## NOTES AND QUESTIONS

1.   Consider the actions of Melinda. List out what she did and how you think you could have handled it differently prior to, during, and after the mediation. Consider the ideas of Professor Sternlight in the earlier excerpt from her article.

2.   Do you think Gayle's story is a warning against the role of attorneys in mediation? If so, do you think the warning is realistic?

3.   Is there a power differential between Gayle and Warren? In what way(s)?

4.   It appears from the excerpt that the mediation was court-mandated. Assume, however, that it was not and that Gayle had the option of participating in mediation or not. If you were representing Gayle, how would you have counseled her about the mediation option?

5.   Are there incentives for an attorney to act, at least in part, the way that Melinda acted in this narrative? What might those be?

6.   While the focus of this article is on the lawyer's role, consider also how the mediator performed. If you were mediating this dispute, what would you have done differently?

## D.   SPECIAL ETHICAL CONSIDERATIONS FOR LAWYERS REPRESENTING CLIENTS IN MEDIATION

There are a few ethical restrictions worth noting when lawyers are representing clients in mediation.

First, unless a rule explicitly provides otherwise, a jurisdiction's rules of professional conduct apply to lawyers representing clients in mediation.[12] This is true even given the different conceptions of representing clients in advocacy discussed in this Chapter.

Second, ethical rules governing lawyers strictly limit the degree to which mediators can represent a party before or after mediation. Rule 1.12 of the ABA Model Rules of Professional Conduct provides that (1) "a lawyer shall not represent anyone in connection with a matter" in which the lawyer had acted as a mediator "unless all parties to the proceeding give informed consent, confirmed in writing"; and (2) a lawyer-mediator shall not negotiate "for employment with any person involved as a party or lawyer" in the mediation.

Third, both mediator ethics and legal ethics would prohibit a lawyer representing a party from later acting as a mediator in a dispute relating to that representation. Such a situation would constitute one of the "non-consentable" conflicts described by Standard IV of the *Model Standards* (*see* Appendix C) given that the lawyer-mediator's prior role as advocate would certainly "impair a mediator's impartiality."

---

[12] One exception is Rule 3.3 — "Candor to the Tribunal" — where the definition of "Tribunal" in Rule 1.0(m) does not include mediation. Note, however, that Rule 4.1, which articulates some of the basic principles of Rule 3.3, does apply to representation in mediation.

# Chapter 14

# BEYOND MEDIATION: COLLABORATIVE PRACTICE AND OTHER FORMS OF ADR IN FAMILY LAW

## A. INTRODUCTION

The success of mediation in family law has given rise to range of other non-litigation dispute resolution options. Mediation continues to dominate, particularly in court settings, but lawyers and court reformers are beginning to conclude that a "one size fits all" approach to ADR does not serve all families. *See, e.g.*, Peter Salem, *The Emergence of Triage in Family Court Services: The Beginning of the End of Mandatory Mediation?* 47 FAM. CT. REV. 371 (2009). As a result, options such as collaborative practice, cooperative law and family arbitration have become available as dispute resolution options in private settings. Others, such as early neutral evaluation and parenting coordination, have been offered more widely as court based services. This Chapter briefly explores these other options, giving particular emphasis to Collaborative Practice.

## B. COLLABORATIVE PRACTICE AND COOPERATIVE LAW

### 1. Collaborative Practice

Collaborative Practice is a dispute resolution model that embodies many of the client-centered, interest based negotiation principles that are at the core of the mediation process. The primary difference is that lawyers are central to the collaborative process working with clients to create agreements outside of court. Stuart Webb, a Minnesota family lawyer, is often described as the founder of the collaborative law movement. In the early 1990s, he sought an alternative to the adversarial approach due to the impact it had on divorcing parties, their children, and the lawyers who represented them. The central features of collaborative practice are the parties' and lawyers' agreement that they will not take their cases to court; if an agreement is not reached the attorneys are "disqualified" from litigating the case. The parties and attorneys also agree that they will retain and share experts, including mental health and financial "neutrals" to approach problems holistically, and that they will disclose all relevant information with everyone on the "team."

Because the collaborative approach is so different from the adversarial model, scholars and practitioners raised issues from the beginning about the ethical implications of the practice under current ethical rules and standards. Can a client waive the right to litigate with the attorney of her choice? If so, what constitutes informed consent in this context? Are agreements truly "voluntary" if the consequence of not reaching an agreement is the loss of your attorney and the need to begin work with another attorney? How do the traditional guarantees of confidentiality and privileged communications for attorneys and other professionals operate when the attorneys and parties have entered into an agreement providing for full disclosure of relevant information?

Attempting to respond to these questions and provide uniformity and predictability from state to state, the Uniform Law Commission (ULC) drafted the Uniform Collaborative Law Act (UCLA) in 2009 and amended it in 2010. The model statute attempts to standardize the practice of collaborative law, while securing the benefits of collaborative law and providing ethical safeguards. To date, some version of the UCLA has been adopted in eleven jurisdictions and introduced in several others. *Legislative Fact Sheet — Collaborative Law Act*, UNIFORM LAW COMMISSION, http://www.uniformlaws.org/LegislativeFactSheet.aspx?title=Collaborative%20Law%20Act (last visited January 5, 2015). The following excerpt from the Prefatory Note to the UCLA provides an overview of the collaborative process and the issues addressed by the statute:

Collaborative law is a voluntary, contractually based alternative dispute resolution process for parties who seek to negotiate a resolution to their matter rather than having a ruling imposed upon them by a court or arbitrator. The distinctive feature of collaborative law, as compared to other forms of alternative dispute resolution such as mediation, is that parties that are represented by lawyers ("collaborative lawyers") during negotiations. Collaborative lawyers do not represent the party in court, but only for the purposes of negotiating agreements. The parties agree in advance that their lawyers are disqualified from further representing parties by appearing before a tribunal if the collaborative law process ends without complete agreement ("disqualification requirement"). Parties thus retain collaborative lawyers for the limited purpose of acting as advocates and counselors during the negotiation process.

The basic ground rules for collaborative law are set forth in a written agreement ("collaborative law participation agreement") in which parties designate collaborative lawyers and agree not to seek tribunal (usually judicial) resolution of a dispute during the collaborative law process. The participation agreement also provides that if a party seeks judicial intervention, or otherwise terminates the collaborative law process, the disqualification requirement takes effect. Parties agree that they have a mutual right to terminate collaborative law at any time without giving a reason.

The goal of collaborative law is to encourage parties to engage in "problem-solving" rather than "positional" negotiations. . . .

Lawyers can and do, of course, encourage clients to engage in problem-solving negotiations without formally labeling the process collaborative law. The distinctive feature of collaborative law is, however, the disqualification requirement — the enforcement mechanism that parties create by contract to ensure that problem-solving negotiations actually occur. The disqualification requirement enables each party to penalize the other party for unacceptable negotiation behavior if the party who wants to end the collaborative law process is willing to assume the costs of engaging new counsel. Each side knows at the start that the other has similarly tied its own hands by making litigation expensive. By hiring two Collaborative Law practitioners, the parties send a powerful signal to each other that they truly intend to work together to resolve their differences amicably through settlement. . . .

To encourage problem-solving negotiations, collaborative lawyers emphasize that no threats of litigation should be made during a collaborative law process and the need to maintain respectful dialogue. . . .

Both collaborative law and mediation offer parties the benefits of a process to promote agreement through private, confidential negotiations, the promise of cost reduction, and the potential for better relationships. . . .

Mediation and collaboration law do, however, have differences which might make collaborative law more or less attractive to some parties as a dispute resolution option. A neutral is not present during collaborative law process negotiation sessions unless agreed to by the parties, while mediation sessions are facilitated by a neutral third party. . . . Despite their limited purpose of representation in negotiating a resolution of a dispute, collaborative lawyers are not neutrals but are advocates for their clients.

-------

### Middle and Low Income Families and Collaborative Practice.

One of the criticisms of collaborative practice is that, because of the need for attorneys as well as other experts, it is too expensive for most family law disputants. *See e.g.*, Susan Daicoff, *Collaborative Law: A New Tool for the Lawyer's Toolkit*, 20 U. FLA. J.L. & PUB. POL'Y 113, 130 (2009). But there is also research showing that the cost of litigating a case is higher than resolving the dispute through the collaborative process. The initial costs of retaining attorneys and experts are, of course, substantial in collaborative practice. But, if successful in reaching an agreement, the costs to parties in a collaborative case may ultimately be less than if that case were litigated to its conclusion or a settled through traditional lawyer led negotiations. *See generally* Kathryn S. Lazar, *Comparing the Costs of Divorce: Mediation vs. Collaborative vs. Litigation*, MH MEDIATION, http://www.mhmediation.com/news/comparing-the-costs-of-divorce-mediation-vs-collaborative-vs-litigation/ (Last visited Jan. 5, 2015).

Nevertheless the collaborative model of dispute resolution continues to be unavailable for low income parties who cannot afford attorneys. Even for the small percentage of the poor who can secure a free attorney from a legal services organization, collaborative practice is not likely to be an option. *See e.g.*, Lawrence P. McLellan, *Expanding the Use of Collaborative Law: Consideration of Its Use in a Legal Aid Program for Resolving Family Law Disputes*, J. DISP. RESOL. 465, 467 (2008). Legal service providers typically do not offer this option either because of lack of training or because of concerns about the disqualification provision in the "four way agreement." These attorneys understand that their clients may lose the benefit of a free attorney in the event an agreement is not reached because under current ethical rules the disqualification of the attorney will be imputed to other members of the firm or Legal Aid office. Rule 1.10 Model Rules of Professional Conduct. Responding to this concern, the drafters of the Uniform Collaborative Law Act (UCLA) created an exception to the imputation of conflicts rule for legal service providers engaging in collaborative practice:

> Rule 10 creates an exception to the disqualification for lawyers representing low-income parties in a legal aid office, law school clinic, or a law firm providing free legal services to low-income parties. If the process terminates without settlement, a lawyer in the organization or law firm with which the Collaborative lawyer is associated may represent the low income party in an adjudicatory proceeding involving the matter in the Collaborative law process, provided that the participation agreement so provides, the representation is without fee, and the individual Collaborative lawyer is appropriately isolated from any participation in the Collaborative matter before a tribunal.

Uniform Laws Commission, Collaborative Law Act Summary, Rule 10

## 2.   Cooperative Law

Concerned about the limitations imposed by the "disqualification clause" in collaborative practice requiring attorneys to withdraw from a case if settlement is not reached, some lawyers began practicing under a "cooperative law" model. Cooperative lawyers practice much like collaborative lawyers except they do not obligate themselves to withdraw from representation if settlement fails and the participants must litigate. The following case compares collaborative and cooperative law in one of the first jurisdictions to adopt the Uniform Collaborative Law Act, Texas.

### IN RE MABRAY
Court of Appeals of Texas
355 S.W.3d 16 (2010)

. . . After 35 years of marriage, Mary discovered her husband Gary's alleged ongoing infidelity and sought a divorce. . . . On February 12, 2009, the parties and their counsel signed a four page document titled "Cooperative Law Dispute Resolution Agreement" ("the Agreement"). The Agreement states that the parties agreed to "effectively and honestly communicate with each other with the goal of efficiently and economically settling the terms of the dissolution of the marriage." The Agreement forbids formal discovery unless agreed upon, relying instead on "good faith" informal discovery. Specifically, the Agreement provides:

> No formal discovery procedure will be used unless specifically agreed to in advance. The parties will be required to sign a sworn inventory and appraisement if requested by the other party.

We acknowledge that, by using informal discovery, we are giving up certain investigative procedures and methods that would be available to us in the litigation process. We give up these measures with the specific understanding that the parties will make to each other a complete and accurate disclosure of all assets, income, debts, and other information necessary for us to reach a fair settlement. Participation in this process is based on the assumptions that we have acted in good faith and that the parties have provided complete and accurate information to the best of their ability.

Neither party requested a sworn inventory and appraisement.

The Agreement also provides that, if the divorce was not settled by April 30, 2009, the cooperative law process would cease and the parties agreed to submit the divorce to arbitration. Specifically, the Agreement provides:

> The parties further agree that if this case has not been settled by negotiation and an Agreed Final Decree of Divorce has not been submitted to and signed by the Court before April 30, 2009 then this matter will be submitted to binding arbitration pursuant to the Joint Motion for Referral to Arbitration and Agreed Order of Referral to Arbitration attached hereto and made a part hereof.

\* \* \* \*

The case before us concerns the legitimacy of cooperative law. Because cooperative law is untreated in Texas case law, and its more established cousin, collaborative law, only receives minor treatment, a brief exposition of each is warranted.

Collaborative law is codified in the Texas Family Code, which provides, in part:

(a)   On a written agreement of the parties and their attorneys, a dissolution of marriage proceeding may be conducted under collaborative law procedures.

(b)   Collaborative law is a procedure in which the parties and their counsel agree in writing to use their best efforts and make a good faith attempt to resolve their dissolution of marriage dispute on an agreed basis without resorting to judicial intervention except to have the court approve the settlement agreement, make the legal pronouncements, and sign the orders required by law to effectuate the agreement of the parties as the court determines appropriate. The parties' counsel may not serve as litigation counsel except to ask the court to approve the settlement agreement.

(c)   A collaborative law agreement must include provisions for:

(1)   full and candid exchange of information between parties and their attorneys as necessary to make a proper evaluation of the case;

(2)   suspending court intervention in the dispute while the parties are using collaborative law procedures;

(3)   hiring experts, as jointly agreed, to be used in the procedure

(4)   *withdrawal of all counsel involved in the collaborative law procedure if the collaborative law procedure does not result in settlement of the dispute;* and

(5)   other provisions as agreed to by the parties consistent with a good faith effort to collaboratively settle the matter.

TEX. FAM.CODE ANN. § 6.603 (Vernon 2006) (emphasis added).

\* \* \* \*

The presence of a disqualification agreement is widely held to be the minimum qualification for calling a practice collaborative law. Specifically, collaborative law attorneys cannot represent their collaborative clients in litigation if the collaborative process fails, but collaborative law clients retain their right to pursue litigation with new counsel. In some jurisdictions, collaborative law attorneys may continue to represent their clients in arbitration if the parties agree to arbitration in the collaborative law agreement. *See, e.g.,* N.C. GEN.STAT. § 50-78 (2007) (providing, "The parties' attorneys for the collaborative law proceeding may also serve as counsel for any form of alternate dispute resolution pursued as part of the collaborative law agreement"). Although case law has not addressed the issue, Texas appears to preclude a collaborative-law attorney's representation of a collaborative-law client in arbitration. *See* TEX. FAM.CODE ANN. § 6.603(c)(4).

Akin to collaborative law, cooperative law "is a process which incorporates many of the hallmarks of Collaborative Law but does not require the lawyer to enter into a contract with the opposing party providing for the lawyer's disqualification." Smith and Martinez, 14 HARV. NEGOT. L. REV. at 166. "Cooperative law includes a written agreement to make full, voluntary disclosure of all financial information, avoid formal discovery procedures, utilize joint rather than unilateral appraisals, and use interest-based negotiation." Put simply, cooperative law agreements mirror collaborative law agreements in spirit and objective, but lack the disqualification clause unique to collaborative law agreements.

Mary portrays cooperative law as an illegitimate aberration of collaborative law, and asks that the Agreement be interpreted by the statutory standards of a collaborative law agreement. However, it is noteworthy that at least one legal association has determined that cooperative law passes ethical muster while collaborative law does not. The Ethics Committee for the Colorado Bar Association states:

> [T]he practice of Collaborative Law violates Rule 1.7(b) of Colorado Rules of Professional Conduct insofar as a lawyer participating in the process enters into a contractual agreement with the opposing party requiring the lawyer to withdraw in the event that the process is unsuccessful. The Committee further concludes that pursuant to Colo. RPC 1.7(c) the client's consent to waive this conflict cannot be validly obtained. Because Cooperative Law lacks the disqualification agreement found in Collaborative Law, the practice of Cooperative Law is not per se unethical.

Colo. Bar Ass'n Ethics Comm., Formal Op. 115 (Feb. 24, 2007).

Here, we do not weigh the legitimacy of collaborative law; it already has been adopted in Texas. Instead, we examine whether the collaborative law statute excludes the use of cooperative agreements and whether Texas public policy permits cooperative law, a matter of first impression in this court. According to experts, cooperative law is a small but legitimate movement akin to collaborative law. . . .Like collaborative law, it possesses both benefits and detriments. For example, the absence of a disqualification agreement offers advantages but also poses disadvantages. Specifically, "parties and lawyers may act reasonably only if they face a credible threat of litigation."

[citations omitted]. Additionally, cooperative law clients are less likely to feel mired in the cooperative process because they need not hire and educate new lawyers should litigation ensue. Conversely, collaborative law clients may feel unduly pressured to complete the collaborative process rather than pursue litigation because of the cost and inconvenience of hiring and educating a new attorney. . . .

While we have not encountered cooperative law's codification in any state's code, neither have we encountered its prohibition. In fact, as we have observed, it has been found to be a better system in at least one jurisdiction. *See* Colo. Bar Ass'n Ethics Comm., Formal Op. 115.

Against this general backdrop, we must determine whether the collaborative law statute controls this agreement and, if not, whether a cooperative law agreement is void as a matter of public policy within the State of Texas. We will first consider whether the collaborative law statute controls before determining whether cooperative law agreements violate public policy.

### Applicability of the Collaborative Law Statute

. . . Mary asserts that Keen [husband's attorney] must be disqualified because Keen's continued representation of Gary violates the Texas collaborative law statute. Specifically, Mary contends that "[u]sing a slightly different title for the ADR agreement does not avoid the protections of the statute." Gary responds that the collaborative law statute is inapplicable to a cooperative law agreement.

The trial court determined that the Agreement is a cooperative law agreement, not a collaborative law agreement, and therefore need not conform to Texas's collaborative law statute. The Agreement does not suffer from a crisis of identity; it does not reference collaborative law or the collaborative law statute.

Mary contends that "leaving out a required element does not avoid a statute; it violates it." In order for this to be true, however, the statute would either have to mandate its application or forbid the use of cooperative law agreements. We hold that it does neither. It is clear by its plain language that the collaborative law statute is elective, not mandatory. Subsection (a) of the statute explicitly provides that "a dissolution of marriage proceeding *may* be conducted under collaborative law procedures." TEX FAM.CODE ANN. § 6.603(a) (emphasis added). Nothing in the statute mandates its usage. Instead, parties that elect to follow its procedures obtain certain benefits from the trial court. The parties can obtain a judgment on their collaborative law agreement by signing the settlement agreement and including a boldfaced, capitalized, or underlined statement that the agreement is not subject to revocation. *Id.* § 6.603(d). If the parties provide proper notice to the trial court, the court is precluded from setting a hearing or trial in the case, imposing discovery deadlines, requiring compliance with scheduling orders, or dismissing the case while the parties are using the process. *Id.* § 6.603(e). Additionally, the statute incorporates the provisions for confidentiality of alternative dispute resolution procedures as provided in Chapter 154 of the Civil Practices and Remedies Code for collaborative law procedures. *Id.* § 6.603(h).

In order to obtain these benefits, the parties must enter into an agreement providing for (1) a full and candid exchange of information; (2) suspending court intervention in the dispute while the parties are using collaborative law procedures; (3) hiring any experts jointly; (4) withdrawal of all counsel in the collaborative law procedure if the collaborative law procedure does not result in settlement of the dispute; and (5) other provisions agreed to by the parties that are consistent with a good faith effort to collaboratively settle the suit. *Id.* § 6.603(c). The Agreement signed by Mary and Gary does not require the withdrawal of counsel if settlement is not obtained, the fourth requirement for application of the collaborative law statute. Accordingly, by the plain language of the statute, the collaborative law procedures and resulting benefits do not apply to the Agreement.

Additionally, nothing in the statute or in its legislative history leads us to the conclusion that the collaborative law statute forbids parties in Texas from entering into cooperative law agreements. It has been the stated policy of Texas from at least 1987 "to encourage the peaceable resolution of disputes . . . and the early settlement of pending litigation through voluntary settlement procedures." TEX CIV. PRAC. & REM.CODE ANN. § 154.002 (Vernon 2005). There is no statute or case law in Texas that explicitly prohibits any specific form of alternative dispute resolution.

The collaborative law statute is one of four alternative dispute resolution processes that the Texas legislature specifically encourages parties in divorce proceedings to utilize. The four processes are arbitration, mediation, collaborative law, and informal settlement conferences. TEX FAM.CODE ANN. §§ 6.601–.604 (Vernon 2006). Nothing in these statutes states that they are the exclusive forms of alternative dispute resolution available to parties to a divorce.

Even if these were the exclusive forms of alternative dispute resolution available to parties to a divorce, the Agreement specifically cites to sections 6.601 and 6.604 of the Family Code. Those are the arbitration and informal settlement conference provisions, respectively. . . . In an informal settlement conference, "[t]he parties to a suit for dissolution of a marriage may agree to one or more informal settlement conferences and may agree that the settlement conferences may be conducted with or without the presence of the parties' attorneys, if any." TEX FAM.CODE ANN. § 6.604(a). The legislature did not in any other way limit or constrict the parties' abilities to determine how informal settlement conferences would be conducted. Because this statute is deliberately silent as to the procedures that can be used in informal settlement conferences, we must conclude that the legislature meant to cast a wide net and give the parties wide latitude in deciding how to structure them, including structuring them through a cooperative law agreement.

The dissent argues that the legislature's enacting of the collaborative law statute is proof that they meant to exclude cooperative law agreements. We cannot agree. The legislature knows how to conscribe permissible actions when other related actions would be in violation of public policy. *See, e.g.,* TEX BUS. & COM.CODE ANN. § 15.05 (Vernon 2002) (mandating every contract in restraint of trade is unlawful), § 15.50 (Vernon Supp. 2009) (providing strict requirements for covenants not to compete to avoid violation of public policy). The legislature has taken no such action here. Instead, it has determined that alternative dispute resolution is beneficial and encourages it. TEX CIV. PRAC. & REM.CODE ANN. § 154.002. Given the legislature's broad approval of alternative dispute resolution, we find no reason to determine that it meant to prohibit parties from entering into cooperative law agreements.

We overrule Mary's first point of error.

———————

## C.  ARBITRATION

Arbitration is a form of ADR in which parties agree, usually in a written contract, to resolve a current or future dispute without resort to the courts. Instead, the parties agree that they will choose an arbitrator who will review the evidence and reach a decision. In most instances that decision will be binding and not subject to judicial review except in narrow circumstances where fraud or corruption is alleged. Arbitration has most commonly been used in business disputes and most states have statutes governing this process based on the model Uniform Arbitration Act. Because arbitration is gaining popularity in family law, the Uniform Laws Commission has developed a model Uniform Family Arbitration Act and states are starting to enact legislation to regulate family arbitration. *See generally* Lynn P. Burleson, *Family Law Arbitration: Third Party Alternative Dispute Resolution*, 30 CAMPBELL L. REV. 297 (2008). *See e.g.*, Conn. Gen. Stat. §§ 46b-66(c) (2010); Ind. Code Ann. §§ 34-57-5-1 to - 13 ; Mich. Comp. Laws Serv. §§ 600.5070–600.5081 ; N.H. Rev. Stat. Ann § 542:11 (2010); N.M. Stat. Ann. § 40-4-7.2 .

Parties have begun to regularly include provisions in agreements on family issues that provide that all future disputes will be submitted to arbitration. In this way, the parties seek to avoid the delays and expense of litigation to enforce agreements. Courts have generally upheld these arbitration clauses, including the non-reviewability provisions, on issues relating to marital property and, in some cases, spousal support. *See e.g.*, *In Re Marriage of Pascale*, 295 P.3d 836 (Wash. Ct. App. 2013) (where parties' included an arbitration clause in their agreement, parties' dispute regarding the substance and enforceability of a spousal support provision was a matter for the arbitrator, not the court). There are, however, limits on parties' ability to avoid judicial review of provisions related to children. The Model Uniform Act permits judicial appeals of substantive issues of law and modification of child custody, child support and spousal support to the extent those issues are modifiable under state law. The Model Act also provides for de novo judicial review of child custody and child support arbitration awards. Various state statutes address these issues in different ways. For example, Colorado's family law arbitration statute law permits arbitration of child custody, visitation and child support but the court retains jurisdiction over the issues to review them de novo upon either party's request. Col. Rev. Stat. Annotated. § 14-10-128.5. Connecticut's statute takes a narrower approach to what's arbitrable and states that arbitration agreements shall not include issues related to child support, visitation and custody. Conn. Gen. Stat. § 46b-66(c).

# NOTES AND QUESTIONS

1.   What are the primary differences between meditation, collaborative, and cooperative practice? Assume you are meeting with a client and are describing the range of dispute resolution options available to resolve child access and financial issues in a divorce case. How would you describe these alternatives to litigation? Which process do you think you would most often recommend? Why? Does the nature of the dispute and the level of conflict between the couple affect your recommendation?

2.   What are the ethical issues raised by collaborative practice? Are they present in cooperative practice? Are you concerned about them? One of the reasons that advocates for collaborative practice have supported passage of the UCLA is that it addresses some of these issues. Has a version of the UCLA been passed in your jurisdiction? If so, does it respond to the ethical concerns? If not, are there ethical or court opinions in your jurisdiction that respond to any of these issues?

3.   The Prefatory Note to the Uniform Collaborative Law Act states: While the Act does not limit the reach of collaborative law to divorce and family disputes, it does systematically address the problem of domestic violence. The most significant provision of the Act's approach to domestic violence is the obligation it places on collaborative lawyers to make "reasonable inquiry whether the [party or] prospective party has a history of a coercive or violent relationship with another [party or] prospective party." § 15(a). If the lawyer "reasonably believes" the party the lawyer represents has such a history, the lawyer may not begin or continue a collaborative law process unless the party so requests and the lawyer "reasonably believes" the party's safety "can be protected adequately during the collaborative law process." *See infra* § 15(c). Uniform Collaborative Law Act, 38 HOFSTRA L. REV. 421, 459 (2009). Are the potential risks of informal dispute resolution greater in mediation or in collaborative practice? Why?

4.   Regardless of what parties include in the scope of issues to be arbitrated, most courts and the Model Uniform Family Arbitration Act, preserve judicial review of child access agreements. *See e.g. Fawzy v. Fawzy*, 973 A.2d 347 (N.J. 2009) (arbitration awards regarding child custody are subject to judicial review). Why is this?

# Chapter 15

# COMPARATIVE, CROSS CULTURAL, AND INTERNATIONAL PERSPECTIVES IN FAMILY MEDIATION

## A. INTRODUCTION

Developing an understanding of the way mediation is experienced in and by different cultures will add depth to your understanding of how to be an effective mediator and lawyer in mediation. This Chapter introduces multicultural dimensions of mediation by examining how mediation has developed in other cultures, the impact of culture on participants and mediators in mediation, challenging legal issues in mediating international family disputes, and issues regarding LGBT mediation.

## B. COMPARATIVE PERSPECTIVES IN MEDIATION

### 1. Family Mediation: A Cross-Cultural Example

Family mediation as practiced in the 21st century United States has roots in a variety of formal and informal dispute resolution systems in both this country and others. Modern western mediation has adopted elements of dispute resolution practices from both ancient Chinese and Native American cultures. The following excerpt describes one example: the peacemaking model of mediation practiced by the Navajo Nation.

### PEACEMAKING AS CEREMONY: THE MEDIATION MODEL OF THE NAVAJO NATION[1]
11 INT'L. J. OF CONFLICT MGMT. 267–68, 274–79, 284 (2000)
By Jeanmarie Pinto

. . . Before 1868 the Navajos settled disputes by mediation. Navajos have always understood these concepts. We could have taught the Anglos these things one hundred and fifty years ago.

The Navajo philosophy and system of justice focuses on healing both the wrongdoer and all the people that may have been affected — directly and indirectly. Navajo justice does not try to punish anyone. The focus of Navajo conflict resolution is on *healing* everyone that has been touched by the conflict. Navajo justice listens to

---

[1] Copyright ©2000. Reprinted with permission.

everyone who may have been affected and seeks a solution that helps not only those who have been wronged but also the wrongdoer. The philosophy of Navajo *beehaz' aanii* teaches that everyone and everything is connected, so that the actions of one individual affect many others. Punishment of the individual not only does not help him or her — it also does nothing to help the community . . . That sense of relationship of one thing to another is evident in the process of the Peacemaker Ceremony because it promotes the balance of one person to another, one person to the group, and the group to the larger community. It also aids in restoring the balance of body, mind, and spirit within the individual.

Furthermore, the Peacemaker Ceremony illustrates the Navajo perception of connection between spiritual beliefs and the law. The law then becomes more than maxims applied in certain situations — it is a way of conducting oneself in day-to-day activities. The success of the Peacemaker Division is dependent on a shared conception of this sense of interconnectedness in all things. In this way, the application of the Navajo common law using the Peacemaker process transcends the notion of a method of resolving disputes and becomes a powerful tool for healing the inner processes of the individual and the group that contribute to the production of conflict. Presently, the Navajo Nation Courts are operated in a similar fashion to those in mainstream Anglo-American society. The Peacemaker Division, however, is founded and operates solely in traditional Navajo philosophy. The concepts and foundations are taken from the Navajo Creation and Journey Narratives, which give order and meaning to the Peacemaker system.

The Navajo have found a creative way to use their traditional system of justice and integrate some of the methods of the Anglo-American court system to create a new way to resolve conflicts. The Peacemaker Division stands as an example of the usefulness of learning from other cultures while keeping one's own cultural perspective . . . [It] revolves around the idea of "talking things out". This Navajo concept of "talking things out" is not as simplistic as it sounds. It involves the interconnectedness of the participants, thereby creating equality by allowing everyone a voice, and addressing all three levels of human beings: body, mind, and spirit. When there is balance within the individual, then balance can be attained in relationships with others.

At first glance, the Peacemaker process appears to be similar to Western mainstream mediation or arbitration — but the similarity ends with appearances. Although the *naat' aanii* (Peacemaker) may appear to be acting as a Western styled mediator, in actuality this person has a much more interactive role with the participants. Neutrality is thought to be an unattainable and undesirable goal and therefore does not have a place in Navajo Peacemaking. Furthermore, the *naat' aanii* is usually known to the disputing parties, either on a personal level or by reputation . . . The ultimate aim of peacemaking is *hozho nahasdlii*, which generally translated into English as "now that we have done these things we are again in good relations" . . .

### The Case of the Families Who Weren't Fooled

A young Navajo woman sued a man for paternity. When they got into court, the woman said, "He's the father." The man said, "No. I'm not." The judge sent the case to Navajo Peacemaker Court.

The peacemaker sent notice to the man's and woman's families, and they went to the peacemaking. During the peacemaking, they stopped the "He is/I'm not" talk. The families knew what had been going on all the time and said, "We're going to talk about what to do about *our* child."

The young man didn't have a job, and couldn't afford to pay child support. The woman, who lived in a rural area, relied on firewood for heat and cooking fuel. The families agreed that the young man should supply firewood to the woman until he could pay child support.

By involving the child's family, the discussion turned from paternity to a practical discussion of how to solve a problem. There was no question about paternity — and no need for blood tests — because Navajo families know what their children are doing. They also know what is best for their grandchildren
. . .

Navajo justice and peacemaking are concerned with healing on all levels so that the conflict does not erupt again. Peacemaking travels to where a problem actually starts — inside a person — maybe due to alcoholism or to a recent or past traumatic event. Chief Justice Robert Yazzie describes this attention to the inner cause of conflict in this way: [p]eacemaking gets below the surface of a problem and leads people to the heart of the matter. Speaking of hearts, it uses emotions and the whole person to solve the problem . . .

Navajo style mediation relies on the objectivity — not the neutrality — of the peacemaker. Very often, the parties may choose the *naat' aanii* from their own community, clan, immediate family, or church. The characteristics of wisdom, knowledge, honesty, and leadership are most important for a *naat' aanii*. A peacemaker is a person who thinks well, speaks well, shows a strong reverence for the basic teachings of life, and has respect for himself or herself and others in personal conduct. A *naat' aanii* functions as a guide, and views everyone — rich or poor, high or low, educated or not — as an equal. A *naat' aanii* is chosen for knowledge, and knowledge is the power which creates the ability to persuade others.

Through the telling of Sacred Navajo Narratives, and in relating wisdom grained though personal experience, the peacemaker teaches basic Navajo principles and guides the participants from a negative frame of mind to one that is positive enough to promote problem solving. The *naat' aanii* aids the healing process through *persuasion*, no coercion. Navajo morality and Navajo common law do not allow for the use of coercive force. Freedom and equality are fundamental to Navajo thought, and the phrase "it's up to him" (or her) is illustrative of the belief that no one makes decisions for another. Therefore, the *naat'aanii* may use many techniques to show peacemaking participants where their thinking has gone astray or suggest actions to bring about a resolution — but may not use coercion or authoritarianism. The participants make the final decisions, based on their sense of respect, responsibility, and relationships. . . .

### The Peacemaking Journey: Steps of the Process

The steps of the peacemaker process are similar to those followed by Western mediators. However, the Navajo peacemaker session begins and ends with a prayer, and the focus is on finding solutions that are grounded in Navajo philosophy. Additionally, the unique relationships that are a result of the clan system . . . provide a different emphasis than that of Western mediation. Finally, where some Western mediators utilize storytelling as a part of the process, Navajo peacemakers draw their stories from Navajo Narratives, which most participants grew up hearing.

It may seem to some that the biggest value in this merging of traditional conflict resolution beliefs and practices with those of the dominant society is most relevant to non-Western cultures, the theory could be applied to any close-knit community. Every neighborhood has its own climate; unwritten rules about what is acceptable and what is not. The climate may or may not be cultural, in the sense that everyone shares the same country or culture of origin. However, it may be possible to go into a neighborhood, apartment building, or area and assist in identifying what the values, more, and practices of that group are, in order to design a peacemaking method based on that particular "culture." . . . While it may be true that in much of American mainstream society there is little sense of community, spirituality, or even relationship, there is nothing to say that a peacemaking system — based on the Navajo model — could not work . . .

The Navajo Peacemaker process provides a model that recognizes the fears that we all have and offers a pragmatic and spiritual method for dealing with those fears. This model is flexible enough to be adapted for use by any group of people who have the courage to strive to find a more effective way of gaining control over the "Mutations and Monsters" that plague human life.

## NOTES AND QUESTIONS

1.   Prof. Harold Abramson has summarized some of the dominant features of the mediation model practiced in the United States:

> U.S. practices reflect a culturally shaped view of mediation . . . Mediation is a process in which an impartial third party — a mediator — facilitates the resolution of a dispute by promoting voluntary agreement (or "self-determination") by the parties to the dispute. A Mediator facilitates communications, promotes understanding, focuses the parties on their interests, and seeks creative problem solving to enable the parties to reach their own agreement. These standards give meaning to this definition of mediation. This definition, however, has been modified in the recent changes to the Model Standards to reflect a momentous broadening of the term mediation to encompass different "styles." The revised definition provides that: "Mediation is a process in which an impartial third party facilitates communication and negotiation and promotes voluntary decision making by the parties to the

dispute." According to the Reporter's Notes "It [the new definition of mediation] is not designed to exclude any mediation style or approach consistent with Standard I's commitment to support and respect the parties' decision-making roles in the process." Therefore, this ostensibly broader definition has a firm limit. It only welcomes those styles of mediation that comport with the Westernized fundamental principle of party self-determination.

Harold Abramson, *Selecting Mediators and Representing Clients in Cross-Cultural Disputes*, 7 CARDOZO J. CONFLICT RESOL. 253, 262 (2006). In light of this quote, consider the three "styles" of mediation discussed in Chapter 2 — evaluative, facilitative, and transformative. Compare each of these styles to the Navajo peacemaker process. What are the similarities and differences?

2.    The Chinese, another ancient culture with a long history of dispute resolution, emphasize the Confucian values of harmony and community over the individual. Like the Navajos, the Chinese also contemplate a different role for the mediator, one that includes the roles of counselor, educator, and problem solver. J.A. Wall, Jr., *Community Mediation in China and Korea: Some Similarities and Differences*, 9 NEGOT. J. 141, 141–42 (1993). This conception of the role of the mediator is common in a number of non-Western nations. *See, e.g.,* Amr Abdalla, *Principles of Islamic Interpersonal Conflict Intervention: A Search Within Islam and Western Literature*, 15 J.L. & RELATIONS 151, 161–62, 165, 176 (2000–2001). How does this differ from the role of mediator described in U.S. family mediation? What are the advantages and disadvantages of the different approaches?

3.    Some scholars have advocated for the use of the Navajo Peacemaking model in conflicts involving domestic violence. *See, e.g.,* Donna Coker, *Enhancing Autonomy for Battered Women: Lessons from Navajo Peacemaking*, 47 UCLA L. REV. 1 (1999). Based on your reading of domestic violence and mediation, what, if any, benefits do you see for this model of dispute resolution in claims involving domestic violence? Are there any potential dangers?

## 2.   Learning from International Models

The American approach to mediation has also adopted elements from a variety of European and other western nations with longer histories of using alternative dispute resolution to resolve family conflicts. The excerpt below describes mediation and its part of a larger structure the Family Courts in Australia — a country long regarded as a leader in innovation in family conflict resolution.

### *AUSTRALIAN FAMILY LAW AND THE FAMILY COURT — A PERSPECTIVE FROM THE BENCH*
40 FAM. CT. REV. 279, 280, 285–87, 293, 295 (2002)
By Alastair Nicholson

The Family Court of Australia . . . has fifty-three judges, approximately two hundred registrars and mediators, and approximately six hundred other administrative and support staff. It serves 250,000 new clients each year through twenty-two major locations and a large number of rural and provincial circuit locations. It is a self-managed court that receives appropriated revenues of around $110 million per year.

The challenges [faced by the Court] are linked to the nature and volume of the workload and are magnified by the geographical and cultural diversity of the Australian landscape. By way of example, Australian Bureau of Statistics figures indicate that 48 percent of all Australians were either born overseas or have one overseas-born parent, and of those, 26 percent are people from non-English-speaking backgrounds. Australia is second in the world to Israel in its cultural and linguistic diversity. Thirteen percent of recently divorcing couples were born in the same overseas country, and 29 percent of divorcing couples involved one partner who was born in a different country. The impact of these statistics on the provision of services by the court is that cultural diversity is a mainstream issue. . . .

## PRIMARY DISPUTE RESOLUTION SERVICES

A distinctive feature of the Family Court is its provision of free, in-house conciliation services by staff who have either legal or social science qualifications and experience. The Family Law Act requires the court to provide a range of both voluntary and mandatory non-therapeutic services to help separating couples and their children resolve their disputes without recourse to litigation. . . . Currently, the act requires the court to offer the following . . . services:

- conciliation conferences in financial matters conducted by a legally qualified registrar,
- conciliation counseling in children's matters conducted by a counselor qualified in either psychology or social work,
- joint conciliation conferences conducted by a registrar and a counselor in enmeshed matters, and
- pre-filing mediation (or post-filing by consent of the parties) in financial and children's matters conducted by a registrar and/or a counselor.

Neither reconciliation nor relationship counseling is offered, but clients seeking such assistance are referred out to appropriate community agencies. . . .

In a contested children's matter, the court may direct a court counselor to provide it with information and expert advice in a report on matters relevant to the proceedings, and the court counselor may include any additional matters that relate to the welfare of the child. These family reports frequently involve a number of interviews with the child and with people relevant to his or her best interests, such as family members and teachers. The judge may direct that a particular aspect (such as the child's wishes or relationship with a stepparent) be explored in the report. The report is released to the parties before the hearing, and its contents frequently provide a sound basis for the settlement of the dispute. . . .

[C]hildren may be separately represented. . . . [I]t is now generally accepted that the role of [a] separate representative is to investigate matters that he or she considers are relevant to the best interests of the child, to convey to the court (but not necessarily to endorse) any wishes expressed by a child . . . [T]he child's representative provides the court with a perspective that may otherwise not otherwise be available to it or that may be distorted by a parent who is seeking a particular outcome that may not coincide with the child's best interests. . . .

The act requires court counselors or other members of the court staff who have reasonable grounds for suspecting that a child has been abused, or is at risk of being abused, to notify the state child welfare authority of their suspicions and the basis for them. Where a member of staff suspects that the child has been ill-treated or exposed to behavior that psychologically harms the child, or that the child is in threat of either ill treatment or psychological harm, he or she may notify that authority of his or her suspicions and the basis for the suspicion.

Mediation was introduced as a separate primary dispute resolution stream in 1991, and until 1999, a co-mediation model involving a staff lawyer (registrar) and a counselor was employed. Subsequently, two changes were made. First, due to shrinking resources, the mediation was limited to a single mediator (except in enmeshed children's and property matters); and second, mediation was integrated with the range of services offered by the court when all these services were put under the single banner of mediation. . . .

One area of the court's awareness that has increased over the years is that of family violence. The unsuitability of mediation in circumstances of power imbalance is well recognized, and the court has a family violence policy and guidelines for staff (currently being reviewed) that acknowledge the importance of comprehensive intake procedures for identifying the appropriateness of intervention. The use of separate rooms, and telephone and/or video conferencing where necessary, is also catered for. In addition, indigenous family consultants provide an important liaison between counselor and client where one or both parties are Aboriginal or Torres Strait Islanders. . . .

We are also working toward a comprehensive overhaul of our services to culturally diverse clients. The court already produces a wide range of written and audio materials in a large number of languages, conducts training programs on family law issues to community workers specializing in working with ethnic communities, and provides funded interpreter services for all court events. . . .

. . . As all aspects of our lives have become less insular and more global in outlook, and as mobility increases, family law generally and the Family Court of Australia specifically have become integral parts of a wider family law system. This is partly due to the ratification of international instruments such as The Hague International Abduction Convention and the Convention on the Rights of the Child. It is also the result of the less formal but significant links that are forged at conferences, both within and outside Australia.

From an international point of view, this court is regarded as a model that has been used to provide assistance to other countries considering changes to their family law systems. . . . As in the past, family law and the Family Court will continue to be the subject of controversy. But the court will continue to be at the forefront of innovation in the area of family law and in the wider arena of courts generally with respect to case management, court governance, and information technology. . . .

## NOTES AND QUESTIONS

1.   Do you see the Australian model as something the United States can or should emulate?

2.   Australia continues to expand and refine the services it provides to families. In 2006, Australia established "Family Relationship Centres" ("FRCs"). FRCs provide mediation as part of a comprehensive set of services for families. The role of FRCs is to assist:

- Couples about to be married to get information about pre-marriage education.

- Families wanting to improve their relationships to get information about family relationship education and other services that can help strengthen relationships.

- Families having relationship difficulties to get information about other services that help to prevent separation.

- Separated parents to resolve disputes and reach agreement on parenting arrangements outside the court system through child-focused information, advice and family dispute resolution, or referral to other services.

- Separated parents whose arrangements have broken down or whose court orders have been breached, to resolve the issue outside the court system, through information, advice, referral, and family dispute resolution.

- Other people who deal with families, such as teachers or doctors.

- Grandparents and other extended family members affected by a family separation through information, advice, referral, or dispute resolution services.

Patrick Parkinson, *The Idea of Family Relationship Centres in Australia*, 51 FAM. CT. REV. 195, 201–202 (2013). FRC's provide three sessions of mediation either free of charge or with low fees. *Id.* at 204–205. What do you think of FRC's as compared to the more typical "court-annexed mediation" that we have discussed previously? How about in conjunction with Australia's "Family Court"? Do you believe FRC's are a good idea for the United States?

3.   You might recall an example of an international model from Chapter 5 that has taken hold in the United States: Family Group Conferencing. Family Group Conferencing originated in New Zealand where it, in turn, drew upon the culture of the Maori Tribe and other native peoples.

## C.   CROSS-CULTURAL MEDIATION: CHALLENGES FOR MEDIATORS

Family mediators regularly encounter families of diverse racial, religious, and ethnic composition. Some may come from backgrounds with different cultural and legal norms than the mediator. Some families have members who have emigrated from different countries or who share different religious beliefs. Accommodating diverse family traditions is a challenge to mediators. Nevertheless, the informality and flexibility that mediation affords offers mediators an opportunity to address cultural differences more effectively than in litigation.

Drawing on both her own experience and others' research, Allison Taylor has developed a list of factors that a family mediator may want to explore to identify potential barriers to understanding in mediations involving participants from different cultures.

## *ASSESSMENT OF CULTURAL FACTORS*

*from* The Handbook of Family Dispute Resolution: Mediation Theory and Practice 234–236 (2002)[2]

### By Alison Taylor

. . . Irving and Benjamin (1995) summarize the recent tidal wave of information to find the features within each particular sociocultural, ethnic, or racial group that most relate to . . . family identity and patterns that can be cross-compared. They list six such factors that should be taken into consideration when analyzing, understanding, or working with a family's identity. Together, these factors form a pattern of interaction that can be observed and handled across families of different cultural backgrounds.

- Modal social class, based on education and income level. This affects the family's resources and opportunities for basic needs and aspirational wants.

- Definition of the family, based on the cultural expectations of who is in and who is out of the socially constructed family expectations.

- Life cycle, based on the stage of development that the family as a whole is experiencing, such as "newly formed couple," or the phase of development of the individuals, such as "young adult." This designation influences and sets the expectations for the behavior of each participant in the different stages.

- Marital relations, based on the cultural expectations of how husband and wife can and should relate, and the acceptable range of variation, regarding their power and decision-making dimensions, the relationship of the marriage to the parent-child responsibilities, and the requirement for commitment to each other under circumstances such as problems and other affiliations.

- Parent-child relations, based on the level of autonomy and deference required between parents and their children, the basic system as democratic or despotic, and the gender differentiation of authority, obedience, and duty.

- Perspective on treatment, based on how culturally consistent it is to have the mediator function as expert, decision maker, helper, or analyst and how open the family should and can be regarding the full dimensions of the problem or its solution.

Missing from this schema are other important cultural factors that a family

---

mediator may want to ask about or understand for the family they are working with — for example,

- The relationship to time orientation, where certain cultures have different understandings of the meaning of timeliness and duration of a problem. Does their lateness for an appointment mean a lack of interest, or is it an expression of their culture, where things happen as they do and being late is acceptable?

- The urge for social or economic mobility, which can lead to stronger bargaining, hardened positions, or a refusal to consider options. Are the participants bargaining from hopes to gain or not to fall back in economic class?

- Hierarchy within the family, both between the generations and interpersonally within the generations. Is the paternal grandmother the real head of the family, or is it the father or the mother who must be listened to and obeyed?

- Common emotional and psychological states, which are not personal pathology but culturally acceptable and predictable behavior and feelings. For example, in Mexican families, those who believe they have been touched by a folk illness such as the evil eye may exhibit symptoms that could appear to be a diagnosable mental health condition to those from a Western medical model of mental health.

- Language capacity — that is, their ability to understand the social and interpersonal discussion and context of mediation efforts with nuances of meaning that convey more than the basics. This is one of the issues in having an interpreter.

- Culturally consistent responses to stress — that is, what people are allowed or expected to do in their culture when experiencing distress. Some cultures have elaborate grief patterns that mimic mental breakdown.

- Communication patterns or requirements, such as directness, the use of intermediaries, the lack of voice, speaking for the entire family unit, or taboo topics within the culture. Asian cultures often have very different communication issues from Western cultures.

- Migration and acculturation issues, or the level at which this process has affected each member of the family. Do they all want to acculturate?

- Dimensions of face, such as typical insults to face, face-saving behaviors, and face-maintenance strategies. This factor is usually associated with high-context cultures.

- Understandings of pain and suffering and mental and emotional illness. In some cultures, stress and problems are more or less manifested as somatic complaints and symptoms; in others, a person who is "crazy" has heightened or lowered status and expectations for his behavior.

- The relationship to problems and self-efficacy, such as beliefs that make certain conditions intolerable or unchangeable by people because they believe it was willed by God and therefore unchangeable.

The reading below gives concrete example of the way in which some of the factors identified in the preceding excerpt may affect party decision making in family mediation. It also offers practical suggestions for mediators to become more culturally responsive.

## CROSSING BORDERS INTO NEW ETHICAL TERRITORY: ETHICAL CHALLENGES WHEN MEDIATING CROSS-CULTURALLY[3]
### 49 S. Tex. L. Rev. 921, 922–37, 942 (2008)
### By Harold Abramson

. . . A Muslim woman asked her Imam at her Mosque for advice on obtaining a divorce from her husband. As part of the process of counseling, the Imam met with both spouses and advised them about the principles of Islamic law that they should follow in dissolving their marriage contract or nikkah. Both spouses want to resolve their conflicts Islamically and in accordance with Quranic principles.

Their Imam advised them that a husband can ask for and obtain a divorce for any reason (talaq). However, he is obliged to support his children until they reach the age of majority and provide for the wife's needs for a "waiting period" of seclusion, if the wife remains in the husband's home to observe the waiting period (the iddath, which lasts three menstrual cycles to check that the wife is not pregnant). In addition he is obliged to pay his wife the amount stipulated in the marriage contract (the mahr) that she must receive if the marriage ends. The marriage contract provided for $40,000.

A wife cannot receive a divorce without her husband's consent. If she initiates the divorce, she forfeits her right to the mahr although the obligation of the husband to support his children continues until each child reaches eighteen years old.

The Wife is pressing for divorce and the Husband is resisting giving consent. The Wife, who has little means to support herself, is deeply unhappy in the relationship, especially since her Husband took a second wife, which he is entitled to do Islamically. The Imam advised them that the husband cannot force his wife to continue with him and should not unreasonably withhold his consent — but that giving consent would release him from any obligation to pay his wife the mahr.

The Wife, who is distraught and humiliated, says that she wants permission for an Islamic divorce from her Husband in order to move on with her life. The Husband says that he will not grant her request unless she forfeits her mahr and any other financial support for herself and agrees to give up custody of each child at puberty. The Husband insists that he wants custody of their six-year-old son when he turns seven years old. He wants custody of their thirteen-year-old daughter when she turns fifteen years old. When reaching the stated age, the Husband told the Wife that the child would be taken into the care of the Husband's female relatives.

At the mediation, the Wife capitulates and says she will waive all rights to financial support and agree to his requests regarding the transfer of custody at the given ages

---

so long as the Husband grants her request for a divorce. Having extracted these concessions, the Husband seems pacified. The Wife and Husband are heading toward this agreement. Such an agreement would be broadly supportable under Islamic law principles and within the norms of the Iranian community in which the parties live. What should a western mediator do?

For the mediator, this is a cross-cultural conflict with a twist. Instead of the cultural conflict arising between the parties, the conflict arises between the mediator and the parties. It is in this peculiar context that this hypothetical presents one overarching and challenging feature: The parties agree to a Rule that when applied by these parties results in a mediated agreement that is unfair based on the Mediator's westernized values and may even violate western domestic law. Consider the way the Husband's power over granting a divorce was being used to extort a one-sided agreement, at least from a westernized point-of-view. A western Mediator would likely view such an agreement as grossly unfair where the unemployed Mother waives needed financial support and relinquishes rights to her children in return for the Husband consenting to the divorce. Under westernized common law and statutory laws, such a one-sided agreement also is likely to be invalid and unenforceable due to the unclean hands of the withholding Husband and the duress suffered by the Mother who wants the divorce.

This culturally shaped family mediation starkly raises an old issue in new packaging: Should a mediator withdraw when the mediator encounters a rule, practice, or emerging agreement that the mediator thinks is unfair? In this dispute, the new packaging entails an objectionable foreign cultural rule and its impact on the resulting mediated agreement. Without this cultural overlay shaping the parties' behavior and resulting agreement, I suspect that many western mediators would withdraw from the mediation, as will be explored later. With the cultural overlay, however, it is less clear what a mediator might do. In analyzing what a mediator might do, I will suggest a four step approach for proceeding ethically and for avoiding the charge of cultural imperialism.

Bridging Cultural Conflicts between Mediator and Parties: A Methodology

Cross-cultural mediators live under the constant threat of cultural imperialism charges. Mediators do not want to be guilty of parochial ignorance and arrogance when objecting to what might be a cultural practice. Mediators want to avoid claiming that they are right and the parties wrong. In order to reduce this risk, cross-cultural mediators should approach mediations with a healthy respect for cultural pluralism and a clear understanding of the other cultural practice. This sequence of four initiatives is designed to guide mediators along this pathway. . . .

A. Understand Own Culture

A mediator inescapably views a dispute through his or her culturally shaped lens, whether conscious of it or not. And, a mediator must be self-aware of this perspective in order to distinguish universal behavior and other cultural behavior from the mediator's own cultural views when reading a dispute. Developing self-awareness requires doing some research. I have found it helpful to read articles and books that describe cultural categories like forms of communicating in different cultures and describe American culture for foreigners (and it is especially fascinating to read how others view your own culture). . . .

The Model Standards of Conduct for Mediators . . . establish[] as the primary obligation of mediators to tenaciously preserve party self-determination as to process and outcome. The Model Standards define self-determination as "the act of coming to a voluntary, uncoerced decision in which each party makes free and informed choices as to process and outcome." In support of this obligation, the Standards further oblige mediators to conduct an impartial and quality process that includes promoting procedural fairness and party competency. In short, as long as mediators follow these ethical standards, the parties can arrive at whatever result that they choose to adopt.

These principles reflect the values of the mediation culture in the United States. These principles give mediators a rationale for avoiding becoming entangled in judging the fairness of the result. However, these principles of party self-determination, impartiality, and quality process still offer much for mediators to ponder and evaluate, as this hypothetical illustrates.

In view of these principles and without the cultural overlay, the mediator might withdraw from the mediation. The one-sided agreement is unlikely to be viewed as an agreement that the wife entered into voluntarily, consistent with the principle of party self-determination. The agreement is so problematic that it would likely be held invalid and unenforceable because of the unequal bargaining relationship. This westernized view of the emerging agreement may also poison the mediator's view of the Husband, and as a result, compromise the mediator's ability to maintain his or her impartiality. Further, the combination of these two possibilities may make it difficult for the mediator to meet his or her obligation to conduct a quality process. In the face of these types of problems, the Model Standards instruct the mediator to "take appropriate steps including, if necessary, postponing, withdrawing from or terminating the mediation" . . . The Model Standards of Practice for Family and Divorce Mediation adopted by the ABA require a mediator to "consider suspending or terminating the mediation" when the mediator "reasonably believes" the agreement to be "unconscionable" or when parties are using the mediation to "further illegal conduct" or to "gain an unfair advantage."

Therefore, both of these model ethical codes provide ample justifications for a mediator to withdraw. But, in a dispute laden with non-westernized practices and behavior, the mediator should take additional steps before deciding whether to withdraw. The mediator needs to research the other culture and try to bridge any cultural gaps, if the mediator wants to avoid the charge of cultural imperialism.

## B. Research Other Culture

A mediator cannot help bridge a cultural gap without learning and understanding the cultural practices of the parties. Researching culture is not easy to do, as anyone who has tried knows only too well. In the face of sometimes difficult to find materials that may reveal amorphous, as well as conflicting information, the mediator needs to become acquainted with the terms of a practice as well as its rationale. Learning about someone else's culture can be a treacherous inquiry because the mediator is trying to understand a practice that not only might be contrary to his or her own, but also abhorrent — based on the mediator's cultural upbringing. This inquiry is vital if the mediator wants to avoid the charges of ethnocentrism and cultural imperialism. The inquiry can be an uncomfortable, if not repulsive, one however, because the mediator must be open to the possibility that what appears, in abstract, to be an offensive practice, may turn out to be tolerable when understood in context.

For example, it may feel offensive to be open to investigating a practice of arranged marriages involving payment, a practice apparently condemned in the United Nations Report of the Committee on the Elimination of Discrimination Against Women, but you might find it helpful to learn a justification for the payment practice as explained by one commentator: "The payment of mahr (dower), which involves payment or preferment, is a central feature of the marriage contract in Islam and, as a measure intended to safeguard [a woman's] economic position after marriage, [the mahr is offered to the bride]."

It also may feel repugnant to be open to investigating a practice that gives men a right to a greater share of property, a practice also apparently condemned in the Convention on the Elimination of All Forms of Discrimination Against Women. But you might find it helpful to learn how it is justified, as the same commentator explained that in Islam, men have financial obligations to others that are not shared with women so men need a disproportionate amount of assets to meet those other obligations.

Of course, neither of these explanations provides the final word. These explanations offer leads that can give the mediator a line of challenging research to pursue.


## C. Bridge Any Cultural Gap

With some understanding of the cultural context of the practice, the mediator should next proceed with a sophisticated party self-determination inquiry. As a threshold matter, I assume that the parties have legal counsel. I also assume that the parties were encouraged to seek counsel from a trusted family member or friend so that each party has the benefit of a support system that each party trusts.

The mediator might give the Wife and Husband an opportunity to express their reactions to the Rule and to consider its rationale, benefits, and drawbacks. Then, the mediator might follow-up with clarifying and reality-testing questions. This is not a simple inquiry, giving rise to the old adage that it can be easier to describe what to do than to actually do it. But, it is an essential inquiry if mediators want to seriously pursue party-self-determination. One of two basic scenarios might emerge for the mediator to pursue: the Wife accepts the Rule or the Wife objects to it.

Under the first scenario, if the Wife understands and accepts the Rule despite the disadvantageous trade-offs that it can produce when dissolving the marriage, at least she is making an informed choice to follow the Rule and live with its consequences. Formal consent under these circumstances, however, should not end the inquiry as succinctly emphasized by one insightful commentator on culture and international human rights. She explained that the most difficult situation is when those who do it and those who endure it offer no objection. But this surely does not mean that nothing may be done. First, there is an abiding suspicion that things are not what they seem in such examples. Are they really just as happy? Does the fact that they have no other way of life open to them make a difference? In short, a good deal more information is needed about the conditions those persons face and the sources of our knowledge about those conditions. Second, intervention comes in degrees, not wholesale. [Look for ways to] increase their range of choice. It is one thing to embrace a way of life when none other is available, an entirely different one to cling to it when alternatives present themselves.

The mediator can test consent by tempting the Wife with options. It turns out that the Wife has an alternative if the mediation is taking place in New York State. There is a state law designed to diminish the ability of a husband to extort an unduly favorable settlement under a religious rule that gives the power to divorce to the husband. The mediator might inquire whether the parties or attorneys are aware of the applicable law. (How a mediator might delicately initiate this inquiry is beyond the scope of this article.) Through their attorneys, the parties would learn that New York law authorizes a court to consider whether the Husband exploited a barrier to remarriage when the court determines the distribution of marital property and appropriate maintenance. Therefore, the Wife would have an option for ameliorating the influence of the Rule and a choice to make. She could agree to the onerous terms, or to turn to or threaten to turn to the secular courts to reduce her unequal bargaining power. This may not seem like a real choice for someone who wants to preserve her standing in her own religious community. But it gives the Wife an opportunity to choose which value is more important to her — preserving her standing in her community or improving the terms of divorce.

. . . .

I was unexpectedly aided in my journey by a visit to my office by a bright, articulate, reflective, and extremely distraught female law student. She wanted to talk about her separation and divorce. Her arranged marriage was a disaster; after less than a year, she had moved out the day before. As a practicing Muslim woman born in the U.S. who is determined to live within the customs and practices of her religion, she was deeply upset. To proceed with the divorce would make it difficult to remarry within her Muslim community and to continue with the marriage would make her life painfully miserable — a reality that even her parents recognized. As she told me her choice, I was starkly reminded about our limited role as mediators who persevere to honor the principle of party self-determination. All mediators can do is conduct a process where the parties can make an informed choice, regardless of how personally painful the choice may be to one of the parties and how unfair the result may seem to the mediator.

Under the second scenario, if the Wife, a dedicated member of her religious community, objects to the Rule and its consequences, then the conflicting values between the mediator and one of the parties disappear. The mediator can no longer be accused of imposing his or her values on the parties when those values are being asserted by one of the parties. The cultural values now coincide between the mediator and the Wife, giving the mediator a shield from the charge of cultural imperialism, although not from the charge of partiality. The mediator no longer needs to bridge a cultural conflict between the mediator and the parties. The mediator can now return to the familiar territory of trying to bridge a gap between the parties.

## D. Assess Whether to Withdraw

Even in the face of the parties consent or apparent consent, the mediator may still find the practice so personally abhorrent that the mediator may want to withdraw. But, how can a mediator withdraw and avoid the charge of cultural imperialism?

## 1. Assess Whether Cultural Practice Violates Internationally Recognized Norms

I . . . pursued the grand inquiry in cultural studies — the search for universal norms, against which the mediator could judge the practice . . . I started researching international treaties, reading articles on international human rights, and consulting with human rights professors. I quickly learned about two international treaties with surprisingly relevant and specific provisions. First, I read the Universal Declaration of Human Rights that was adopted by the United Nations General Assembly and learned that even Iran among other Muslim countries voted for it. And it gets even better because Article 16 (1) is right on point. It provides that, "they [men and women] are entitled to equal rights as to marriage, during marriage and at its dissolution." But, then this pathway turned bumpy. The Universal Declaration turns out not to be a treaty ratified by member nations. It is more of an enabling legislation. Fortunately, it led to an impressive treaty on point.

In the Convention on the Elimination of All Forms of Discrimination Against Women, Article 16 provides that the "States Parties shall take all appropriate measures to eliminate discrimination against women in all matters relating to marriage and family relations and in particular shall ensure, on a basis of equality of men and women: . . . (c) The same rights and responsibilities during marriage and at its dissolution." This treaty was ratified by one hundred and eighty-five countries. Now, that is an impressive level of agreement — except, unfortunately, Iran did not ratify the treaty nor did the United States! Not ready to give up, I next checked to see if any countries in Iran's neighborhood had ratified the treaty and discovered that many did, including Egypt, Iraq, Jordon, Lebanon, Saudi Arabia, and Syria. New hope! But then I noticed these small footnotes called reservations and quickly secured copies of each footnote. Each of these countries either generally or specifically opted out of Article 16(c). The reservations opted out, for example, when the terms violated "norms of Islamic Law" (Saudi Arabia) or were "incompatible with the provisions of the Islamic Shariah" (Syria). This promising pathway failed. It did not reveal universal norms, but instead, revealed unambiguously the lack of universal agreement for the principle of equality in the dissolution of marriage. This inquiry failed to discover a principled source of internationally recognized standards that could be the basis for withdrawing from the mediation.

2. Assess Whether Still Impartial or Conducting a Quality Process

At last, I reached the final step in this journey. If the Rule does not violate a universal standard, is there any other principled basis for withdrawing? A mediator might withdraw . . . if the mediator could no longer be impartial because the mediation is being conducted under a Rule that violates the mediator's personal values. Threats to impartiality arise anytime the mediator becomes conscious of something unfair in the mediation that is impacting on one of the parties. This is familiar territory for mediators, and mediators know to withdraw when the mediator thinks he or she can no longer be evenhanded. The mediator also might withdraw . . . if the mediator feels that this unfair Rule compromises the quality of the mediation process. Of course, if the mediator's decision to withdraw is based on his or her own cultural value, the decision would expose the mediator to the ultimate charge of cultural imperialism — the charge that the mediator is claiming that "my cultural value is better than your cultural value." . . .

Despite these concerns, I suspect that many westernized mediators would not withdraw. Instead, they would likely rely on the common refrain that "it is the parties' process" — as I and others have often declared — "so we should defer to their choice." Nevertheless, in this particular case, I would likely withdraw, so I thought.

Withdrawal was the direction I was going until my research assistant innocently asked what would happen next. "Would what would happen after withdrawal be better than the mediator continuing," she inquired. Yes. She queried what their BATNA [Best Alternative to a Negotiated Agreement] would be if the negotiation in the mediation was prematurely halted.

To work through her inquiry, I ventured down two different pathways. I first wondered whether the BATNA would provide a fair (or at least a fairer) process. If it would, a decision to withdraw would seem easy to make. The parties would be relegated to a better process, and the Wife would have the opportunity to possibly improve her situation.

The second pathway entailed the opposite inquiry — whether the BATNA would not likely lead to a better process. If it would not, a decision to withdraw would negatively impact on the disadvantaged party. If the mediator withdraws, the wife would lose access to help by a third party with expertise in dispute resolution, a third party who might be culturally sensitive to this unequal power dynamic, and who might be able to help the parents negotiate further details within the parameters of the agreement. A mediator who continues with the mediation might be able to help the parties negotiate valuable details that might benefit the children including addressing such issues as visitation by the non-custodial parent and education plans for the children.

This was the most difficult decision moment for me. After trying to research the wife's BATNA and much cogitating, I thought I still would withdraw if faced with this dilemma. I would not want the mediation process (or me) to be associated with such an unfair mediated result. I would want to avoid conferring the imprimatur of mediation on a process and result that violated such a core value of fairness — even when my definition of fairness was shaped by distinctively westernized values. . . .

Thanks to challenges by colleagues and friends, however, I discovered that I was so determined to withdraw that I had become blinded to the significant benefits of continuing for the parties. I am now inclined to continue to mediate. If both parties want to continue with me and the mediation, I think I should try to mediate the best agreement which the parties are willing to enter into so long as the agreement is not illegal.

Conclusion

[M]ediators need to be aware of their own culturally shaped behavior and perspective and be open-minded and nonjudgmental when proactively learning about other ways of behaving. And, mediators should diligently search for ways to bridge any gaps between the mediator and the parties before confronting the difficult possibility of withdrawing. By conscientiously following the four steps outlined in this article, mediators should be able to avoid the charge of cultural imperialism, except when the mediator decides to be imperialistic.

## NOTES AND QUESTIONS

1.    Differences in racial, religious, or ethnic backgrounds are the primary way we think of multiculturalism. Reviewing the list of behaviors that might be culturally shaped in the Taylor excerpt, can you identify differences that might be grounded in factors unrelated to race, ethnicity, or religion? What other life circumstances create "cultural" differences?

2.    Professor Abramson identifies four steps to become a more culturally sensitive and ethical mediator: (a) understand your own cultural identity; (b) research the culture of the mediation participants; (c) attempt to bridge cultural gaps by promoting an informed and voluntary decision making; and (d) consider withdrawing as mediator if cultural barriers or agreements compromise mediator impartiality or the mediation process.

While the first step may appear the easiest to accomplish, understanding one's own culturally shaped behavior is challenging. Practice this skill by identifying yourself culturally (or by home region or other identifiable group). Behaviors or values that may be shaped by culture include: appropriate spatial distance between people talking with one another; conventional gender roles including those related to child rearing and "breadwinning"; meaning of nonverbal behavior (including the appropriateness of eye contact); relationship of individual to family (as in the value of individualism as opposed to communitarianism); deference to authority in a private or public context. Using these examples and others listed by Taylor, identify cultural characteristics of the group with which you identify. Which are grounded in stereotypes and which are rooted in your own behavior or preferences?

For an analysis of cultural characteristics of particular ethnic or racial groups, see Cynthia R. Mabry, *African Americans "Are Not Carbon Copies" of White Americans — The Role of African American Culture in Mediation of Family Disputes*, 13 Ohio St. J. on Disp. Resol. 405 (1998); Jessica R. Dominguez, *The Role of Latino Culture in*

*Mediation of Family Disputes*, 1 J. LEGAL ADVOC. & PRAC. 154 (1999).

3.   Professor Abramson assumes "as a threshold matter" that "the parties have legal counsel." Assume instead the parties are unrepresented. How, if at all, would this change your analysis of how a mediator should handle the dispute Professor Abramson describes?

4.   Consider your role as a family mediator in the following case:

A third party child custody complaint has been filed by Bob and Mary Rose seeking custody of 7-year-old Prosper. Prosper's mother was killed in his home country, Rwanda, and his father, Gaheej, has struggled since coming to the United States. Bob Rose is a Boy Scout leader who has helped Prosper and for the last three months he and his wife have taken him in when Gaheej had moved to a shelter. Gaheej has bouts of depression when he remembers how his wife and other children were killed during his country's civil war. He has trouble keeping jobs because he is unskilled, does not speak English, and misses work because of his untreated depression. At a hearing shortly after the custody case was filed, the Roses were given temporary custody, Gaheej was referred for psychiatric counseling and given a specific visitation schedule at the Roses' home, and the case was referred to court sponsored mediation. If mediation fails, the court has set the date for trial in three months.

At the mediation, the Roses are the first to accept your invitation to make an opening statement. They explain that they took Prosper in at Gaheej's request, that Gaheej has not moved from the shelter, and that he cannot hold a job. He visits Prosper irregularly and when he does, he seems more distant and polite with Prosper than affectionate and loving. The court records also reveal that Gaheej has not attended any sessions with the court psychiatrist. When it is Gaheej's turn to speak he is reserved and formal, and simply says, "Sometime from now I will be well. I will take care of my son."

(a) What, if any, conclusions do you draw about the desires of each side to provide primary care for Prosper?

(b) What, if any, conclusions do you draw about what custody arrangement would be in the best interest of Prosper? Is this relevant to your role as mediator?

(c) Assume that the Roses, responding to Prosper's pleas, have agreed to allow Prosper to move back with Gaheej and limit their contact to monthly visits. In addition to the above facts, you have learned during the mediation that Gaheej believes seeking public assistance will bring shame to him and his son. He plans to move out of the shelter as soon as he can but has no plans to find employment or seek public assistance. You fear allowing the parties to reach an agreement giving Gaheej primary custody will be harmful to Prosper. Use the approach outlined in the Abramson excerpt to determine how to proceed.

For a variation of this approach focused on steps mediators can take when facing cultural conflicts between the disputing parties (rather than between mediator and parties), see HAROLD I. ABRAMSON, MEDIATION REPRESENTATION: ADVOCATING IN A PROBLEM-SOLVING PROCESS 173–81 (2004).

## D.  MEDIATING INTERNATIONAL FAMILY DISPUTES

A byproduct of our growing global society is an increase in family disputes that involve multinational parties. It is important, therefore, to have some understanding of the limits foreign law may place on parties' freedom to enter into agreements. These limits often depend on the specific facts of a case. In such cases, an analysis of facts will produce no clear answers. The following material offers a brief overview of these issues.

### 1.  Prenuptial Agreements

Mediators often see parties planning to marry who seek to mediate an agreement about how financial or other issues should be resolved should they divorce, commonly called a prenuptial agreement. Where one or both parties may return to a foreign country, mediators should inform parties that the enforceability of such agreements varies considerably from country to country. Most states will now enforce prenuptial agreements so long as certain criteria are met. Some non-U.S. jurisdictions — Hong Kong, for example — still view such agreements as against public policy and are unenforceable.

### 2.  Divorce

Mediating agreements predicated on the validity of a foreign divorce might raise legal issues. Foreign divorces are regularly enforced on principles of comity, even where the divorce is granted by a religious authority. The primary requirement for recognition in this country is that the foreign divorce proceeding embody basic U.S. norms of due process. It is usually sufficient that one of the parties is domiciled in the country granting the divorce and that the defendant has had notice and an opportunity to be heard. This norm is also embodied in the Hague Convention on the Recognition of Divorces and Legal Separations (in effect in 17 countries).

Jeremy Morely, a noted international family law attorney, identifies divorces that might not be recognized:

- Religious divorces, such as (a) Islamic "talaq," which in traditional Islamic law is simply the husband's triple declaration of divorce; (b) Jewish rabbinic divorce ("get"), which has recognized civil law authority in Israel, and varying degrees of recognition elsewhere in the world; and (c) divorces in Cyprus, which, under Cypriot law, for members of the Greek Orthodox Church can usually only be issued by a church tribunal.

- Registry office divorces, such as in Japan and Taiwan (and, with certain variations, in China and Korea), whereby both spouses merely file a paper in a local registry office and are promptly divorced.

- "Quickie" divorces, such as in the Dominican Republic, whereby one party typically travels there for a couple of days with a consent paper signed by the other spouse, and a court issues a divorce decree quickly thereafter.

Jeremy D. Morely, *International Family Law*, N.Y.L.J., November 24, 2004.

## E.  ISSUES IN FAMILY MEDIATION INVOLVING LESBIAN, GAY, BISEXUAL, AND TRANSGENDER PARTICIPANTS

Individuals in the lesbian, gay, bisexual, and transgender community often participate in family mediation. Some mediators are particularly active in mediating LGBT family disputes. The legal status of LGBT couples, however, is changing radically, and the role and practice of mediation involving these participants might be changing along with it.

Until recently, all jurisdictions did not accord same-sex couples legal status. Indeed, legislation and judicial decisions often reflected a bias against such couples. This non-status generated numerous complications in many areas of life that married couples take for granted, including division of property and child access. Same-sex couples were thus left with legal rules that did not recognize and distorted the reality of their relationships.

In the face of such social stigma and legal barriers, mediation has held certain advantages for the LGBT community. The privacy of mediation can be appealing to LGBT individuals who do not public identify as LGBT. Participants in mediation could set aside a body of law that did not legally recognize the nature of their union, and instead pursue arrangements that reflected how they lived and the norms that they adhered to. Perhaps ironically, this state of affairs meant that "[i]nstead of the lack of access to state courts being a disadvantage for LGBT couples, mediation has given LGBT couples an advantage over couples whose disputes fall under the province of the courts."[4]

The legal terrain in this area, however, has undergone vast changes in recent years. While social stigma endures, legal non-recognition of same-sex couples has receded. As of this writing many states have recognized same-sex marriage either through judicial decision, popular vote, or legislative action.

Little has been written about the impact that these rapid changes will have on family mediation. If, as is now largely the case, family law recognizes marriage regardless of sexual orientation, mediation involving same-sex couples may more closely track mediation involving the marriage of a woman and man. Nevertheless, opinions do differ as to whether social and psychological issues in LGBT mediations are different from other mediations whatever the legal status of same-sex relationships. Some see little or no difference between LGBT and non-LGBT family mediations. Others argue that mediators may face distinct challenges in light of the mediator's own sexuality, or in light of how LGBT couples might have children who are biologically related to only one partner. Moreover and perhaps surprisingly, one commentator argues that legal recognition of same-sex marriage actually presents challenges because "many same-sex couples are not accustomed to this way of thinking."[5] It remains to be seen, then, how legal changes regarding same-sex

---

[4] Mark J. Hanson, *Moving Forward Together: The LGBT Community and the Family Mediation Field*, 6 Pepp. Disp. Resol. L.J. 296, 302 (2006).

[5] Frederick Hertz *et al*, *Integrated Approaches to Resolving Same-Sex Dissolutions*, 27 Conf. Resol. Q. 123, 135 (2009).

marriage will play out in family mediation.

## NOTES AND QUESTIONS

1.   How do you believe legal recognition of same sex marriage will have an impact on mediation involving LGBT individuals?

2.   Do you believe a mediator's identification as LGBT makes the mediator more effective in mediating these disputes?

3.   Consider the articles by Taylor and Abramson regarding "cross-cultural" mediation and how a mediator can address cultural differences. Do these analyses apply when a mediator is not LGBT and participants are? Why or why not?

# APPENDIX A

## APPENDIX A-1
### Selected Statutes and Rules Governing Court-Sponsored Family Mediation

## 1) CALIFORNIA

### FAMILY CODE § 3170: Setting Matters for Mediation

(a)  If it appears on the face of a petition, application, or other pleading to obtain or modify a temporary or permanent custody or visitation order that custody, visitation, or both are contested, the court shall set the contested issues for mediation.

(b)  Domestic violence cases shall be handled by Family Court Services in accordance with a separate written protocol approved by the Judicial Council. The Judicial Council shall adopt guidelines for services, other than services provided under this chapter, that courts or counties may offer to parents who have been unable to resolve their disputes. These services may include, but are not limited to, parent education programs, booklets, video recordings, or referrals to additional community resources.

## 2) MARYLAND

### RULE OF PROCEDURE Family Law Actions 9-205: Mediation of Child Custody and Visitation Disputes

(a)  Scope of Rule. This Rule applies to any action or proceeding under this Chapter in which the custody of or visitation with a minor child is an issue, including:

   (1)  An initial action to determine custody or visitation;

   (2)  An action to modify an existing order or judgment as to custody or visitation, and

   (3)  A petition for contempt by reason of non-compliance with an order or judgment governing custody or visitation.

(b)  Duty of Court.

   (1)  Promptly after an action subject to this Rule is at issue, the court shall determine whether:

      (A)  Mediation of the dispute as to custody or visitation is appropriate and would likely be beneficial to the parties or the child; and

      (B)  A mediator possessing the qualifications set forth in section (c) of this Rule is available to mediate the dispute.

(2) If a party or a child represents to the court in good faith that there is a genuine issue of abuse, as defined in Code, Family Law Article § 4-501, of the party or child, and that, as a result, mediation would be inappropriate, the court may not order mediation.

(3) If the court concludes that mediation is appropriate and likely to be beneficial to the parties or the child and that a qualified mediator is available, it shall enter an order requiring the parties to mediate the custody or visitation dispute. The order may stay some or all further proceedings in the action pending the mediation on terms and conditions set forth in the order.

\* \* \*

(e) Role of Mediator. The role of a mediator designated by the court or agreed upon by the parties is as set forth in Rule 17-103.

\* \* \*

## RULE OF PROCEDURE Alternative Dispute Resolution 17-103

Role of a Mediator. A mediator may help identify issues and options, assist the parties and their attorneys in exploring the needs underlying their respective positions, and, upon request, record points of agreement expressed and adopted by the parties. While acting as a mediator, the mediator does not engage in any other ADR process and does not recommend the terms of an agreement.

## 3) MISSOURI

## SUPREME COURT RULE 88.03: Mediation of Child Custody and Visitation — Mediation Defined

Mediation under this Rule 88 is the process by which a neutral mediator appointed by the court assists the parties in reaching a mutually acceptable agreement as to issues of child custody and visitation. The role of the mediator is to assist the parties in identifying the issues, reducing misunderstanding, clarifying priorities, exploring areas of compromise, and finding points of agreement. An agreement reached by the parties is to be based on the decisions of the parties and not the decisions of the mediator. The agreement reached can resolve all or only some of the disputed issues.

## SUPREME COURT RULE 88.04: Mediation — When Ordered — Appointment of Mediators

(a) The court may order mediation of any contested issue of child custody or visitation, at any times, upon the motion of a party or the court's own motion.

(b) No investigation and report will be ordered by the court during the pendency of the mediation.

(c) If the court orders mediation under Rule 88.04(a), then the mediator shall meet the minimum qualifications required under Rule 88.05.

(d)  The court may appoint a mediator agreed upon by the parties. If the parties cannot agree, or if the court does not approve the agreed-upon mediator, the court may select the mediator.

## APPENDIX A-2

## SELECTED FAMILY MEDIATION STATUTES AND RULES ON MEDIATOR QUALIFICATIONS

### 1) CALIFORNIA

### FAMILY CODE § 3164: Qualifications of Mediators

(a)  The mediator may be a member of the professional staff of a family conciliation court, probation department, or mental health services agency, or may be any other person or agency designated by the court.

(b)  The mediator shall meet the minimum qualifications required of a counselor of conciliation as provided in Section 1815.

### FAMILY CODE § 1815: Supervising and Associate Counselors; Qualifications

(a)  A person employed as a supervising counselor of conciliation or as an associate counselor of conciliation shall have all of the following minimum qualifications:

(1)  A master's degree in psychology, social work, marriage, family and child counseling, or other behavioral science substantially related to marriage and family interpersonal relationships.

(2)  At least two years of experience in counseling or psychotherapy, or both, preferably in a setting related to the areas of responsibility of the family conciliation court and with the ethnic population to be served.

(3)  Knowledge of the court system of California and the procedures used in family law cases.

(4)  Knowledge of other resources in the community that clients can be referred to for assistance.

(5)  Knowledge of adult psychopathology and the psychology of families.

(6)  Knowledge of child development, child abuse, clinical issues relating to children, the effects of divorce on children, the effects of domestic violence on children, and child custody research sufficient to enable a counselor to assess the mental health needs of children.

(7)  Training in domestic violence issues as described in Section 1816.

(b)  The family conciliation court may substitute additional experience for a portion of the education, or additional education for a portion of the experience, required under subdivision (a).

(b)   This section does not apply to any supervising counselor of conciliation who was in office on March 27, 1980.

## 2) MARYLAND

### RULES OF PROCEDURE Alternative Dispute Resolution 17-104: Basic Mediation Training Programs

To qualify under Rule 17-205 or 17-304 [court-designed mediation], a basic mediation training program shall include the following:

(a)   Conflict resolution and mediation theory, including causes of conflict, interest-based versus positional bargaining, and models of conflict resolution;

(b)   Mediation skills and techniques, including information-gathering skills; communication skills; problem-solving skills; interaction skills; conflict management skills; negotiation techniques; caucusing; cultural, ethnic, and gender issues; and strategies to (1) identify and respond to power imbalances, intimidation, and the presence and effects of domestic violence, and (2) safely terminate a mediation when such action is warranted;

(c)   Mediator conduct, including conflicts of interest, confidentiality, neutrality, ethics, and standards of practice; and

(d)   Simulations and role-playing, monitored and critiqued by experienced mediator trainers.

### RULES OF PROCEDURE ALTERNATIVE DISPUTE RESOLUTION 17-205: QUALIFICATIONS OF COURT-DESIGNATED MEDIATORS

(a)   Basic Qualifications. A mediator designated by the court shall:

(1)   Unless waived by the parties, be at least 21 years old;

(2)   Have completed at least 40 hours of basic mediation training in a program meeting the requirements of Rule 17-104 or, for individuals trained prior to January 1, 2013, former Rule 17-106;

(3)   Be familiar with the rules, statutes, and practices governing mediation in the circuit courts;

(4)   Have mediated or co-mediated at least two civil cases;

(5)   Complete in each calendar year four hours of continuing mediation-related education in one or more of the topics set forth in Rule 17-104;

(6)   Abide by any mediation standards adopted by the Court of Appeals;

(7)   Submit to periodic monitoring of court-ordered mediations by a qualified mediator designated by the county administrative judge; and

(8)   Comply with procedures and requirements prescribed in the court's case management plan filed under Rule 16-202 b. relating to diligence, quality assurance, and a willingness to accept, upon request by the court, a reasonable number of referrals at a reduced-fee or pro bono.

\* \* \*

(c) Economic Issues in Divorce and Annulment Cases. A mediator designated by the court for issues in divorce or annulment cases other than those subject to Rule 9-205 shall:

    (1) Have the qualifications prescribed in section (a) of this Rule;

    (2) Have completed at least 20 hours of skill-based training in mediation of economic issues in divorce and annulment cases; and

    (3) Have served as a mediator or co-mediator in at least two mediations involving marital economic issues.

\* \* \*

## RULES OF PROCEDURE Family Law Actions 9-205: Qualifications

(c) Qualifications of Court-Designated Mediator. To be eligible for designation as a mediator by the court, an individual shall:

    (1) Have the basic qualifications set forth in Rule 17-205 (a);

    (2) Have completed at least 20 hours of training in a family mediation training program that includes:

        (A) Maryland law relating to separation, divorce, annulment, child custody and visitation, and child and spousal support;

        (B) The emotional aspects of separation and divorce on adults and children;

        (C) An introduction to family systems and child development theory;

        (D) The interrelationship of custody, visitation, and child support; and

        (E) If the training program is given after January 1, 2013, strategies to (i) identify and respond to power imbalances, intimidation, and the presence and effects of domestic violence, and (ii) safely terminate a mediation when termination is warranted; and

    (3) Have co-mediated at least eight hours of child access mediation sessions with an individual approved by the county administrative judge, or, in addition to any observations during the training program, have observed at least eight hours of such mediation sessions.

## 3) MISSOURI

## SUPREME COURT RULE 88.05: Mediation — Qualifications of the Mediator

(a) A mediator who performs mediation in a contested child custody matter pursuant to this Rule 88 shall be a person who has stated by affidavit that he or she:

    (1) Is an attorney or a person who possesses a graduate degree in a field that includes the study of psychiatry, psychology, social work, counseling or other behavioral science substantially related to marriage and family

interpersonal relationships; and

(2) Has received a minimum of twenty hours of child custody mediation training in a program approved by the court.

(b) The court may maintain a list of mediators meeting the requirement of Rule 88.05(a) or rely on such list maintained by a bar organization.

(c) In appointing a mediator, the court shall consider:

(1) The nature and extent of any relationship the mediator may have with the parties and any personal, financial, or other interests the mediator may have that could result in bias or conflict of interest; and

(2) The mediator's knowledge of: (A) the Missouri judicial system and the procedures used in domestic relations cases, (B) other resources in the community to which parties can be referred for assistance, (C) child development, (D) clinical issues relating to children, (E) the effects of the dissolution of marriage on children, (F) family systems theory, and (G) mediation and conflict resolution.

## APPENDIX A-3
## SELECTED STATUTES AND RULES GOVERNING MEDIATOR CONFIDEN-TIALITY

### 1) CALIFORNIA

### EVIDENCE CODE § 1119: Written or Oral Communications During Mediation Process; Admissibility

Except as otherwise provided in this chapter:

(a) No evidence of anything said or any admission made for the purpose of, in the course of, or pursuant to, a mediation or a mediation consultation is admissible or subject to discovery, and disclosure of the evidence shall not be compelled, in any arbitration, administrative adjudication, civil action, or other noncriminal proceeding in which, pursuant to law, testimony can be compelled to be given.

(b) No writing, as defined in Section 250, that is prepared for the purpose of, in the course of, or pursuant to, a mediation or a mediation consultation, is admissible or subject to discovery, and disclosure of the writing shall not be compelled, in any arbitration, administrative adjudication, civil action, or other noncriminal proceeding in which, pursuant to law, testimony can be compelled to be given.

(c) All communications, negotiations, or settlement discussions by and between participants in the course of a mediation or a mediation consultation shall remain confidential.

## FAMILY CODE § 3177: Confidentiality of Proceedings

Mediation proceedings pursuant to this chapter shall be held in private and shall be confidential. All communications, verbal or written, from the parties to the mediator made in the proceeding are official information within the meaning of Section 1040 of the Evidence Code. [Editors note: The Evidence Code defines "official information" as "information acquired in confidence by a public employee in the course of his or her duty and not open, or officially disclosed, to the public prior to the time the claim of privilege is made."]

## 2) MARYLAND

## RULE OF PROCEDURE 17-105 Alternative Dispute Resolution: Mediation Confidentiality

(a) **Mediator.** Except as provided in sections (c) and (d) of this Rule, a mediator and any person present or otherwise participating in the mediation at the request of the mediator shall maintain the confidentiality of all mediation communications and may not disclose or be compelled to disclose mediation communications in any judicial, administrative, or other proceeding.

(b) **Parties.** Except as provided in sections (c) and (d) of this Rule:

(1) A party to a mediation and any person present or who otherwise participates in a mediation at the request of a party may not disclose or be compelled to disclose a mediation communication in any judicial, administrative, or other proceeding; and

(2) The parties may enter into a written agreement to maintain the confidentiality of mediation communications and to require all persons who are present or who otherwise participate in a mediation to join in that agreement.

(c) **Signed Document.** A document signed by the parties that records points of agreement expressed and adopted by the parties or that constitutes an agreement reached by the parties as a result of mediation is not confidential, unless the parties agree otherwise in writing.

(d) **Permitted Disclosures.** In addition to any disclosures required by law, a mediator, a party, and a person who was present or who otherwise participated in a mediation may disclose or report mediation communications:

(1) To a potential victim or to the appropriate authorities to the extent they reasonably believe necessary to help prevent serious bodily harm or death to the potential victim;

(2) When relevant to the assertion of or defense against allegations of mediator misconduct or negligence; or

(3) When relevant to a claim or defense that an agreement arising out of a mediation should be rescinded because of fraud, duress, or misrepresentation.

**(e) Discovery; Admissibility of Information.** Mediation communications that are confidential under this Rule are not subject to discovery, but information that is otherwise admissible or subject to discovery does not become inadmissible or protected from disclosure solely by reason of its use in mediation.

## MD CODE, COURTS AND JUDICIAL PROCEEDINGS § 3-1803: Confidentiality of Mediation Communications

Mediators or persons participating in mediation at request of mediator

(a) Except as provided in § 3-1804 of this subtitle, a mediator or any person present or otherwise participating in a mediation at the request of a mediator:

    (1) Shall maintain the confidentiality of all mediation communications; and

    (2) May not disclose or be compelled to disclose mediation communications in any judicial, administrative, or other proceeding.

Parties or persons participating in mediation at request of parties

(b) Except as provided in § 3-1804 of this subtitle:

    (1) A party to a mediation and any person present or otherwise participating in the mediation at the request of a party may not disclose or be compelled to disclose mediation communications in any judicial, administrative, or other proceeding; and

    (2) The parties may enter into a written agreement to maintain the confidentiality of all mediation communications and may require any person present or otherwise participating in the mediation at the request of a party to maintain the confidentiality of all mediation communications.

## MD CODE, COURTS AND JUDICIAL PROCEEDINGS § 3-1804: Documents Recording Points of Agreement and Other Permissible Disclosures of Mediation Communications

Documents which record points of agreement

(a) A document signed by the parties that records points of agreement expressed by the parties or that constitutes an agreement reached by the parties as a result of mediation is not confidential unless the parties agree otherwise in writing.

Disclosure of communications necessary to prevent bodily harm or death

(b) In addition to any other disclosure required by law, a mediator, a party, or a person who was present or who otherwise participated in a mediation at the request of the mediator or a party may disclose mediation communications:

    (1) To a potential victim or to the appropriate law enforcement authority to the extent that the mediator, party, or person reasonably believes the disclosure is necessary to prevent bodily harm or death to the potential victim;

(2) To the extent necessary to assert or defend against allegations of mediator misconduct or negligence;

(3) To the extent necessary to assert or defend against allegations of professional misconduct or malpractice by a party or any person who was present or who otherwise participated in the mediation at the request of a party, except that a mediator may not be compelled to participate in a proceeding arising out of the disclosure; or

(4) To the extent necessary to assert or defend against a claim or defense that, because of fraud, duress, or misrepresentation, a contract arising out of a mediation should be rescinded or damages should be awarded.

Disclosure of communications by court order

(c) A court may order mediation communications to be disclosed only to the extent that the court determines that the disclosure is necessary to prevent an injustice or harm to the public interest that is of sufficient magnitude in the particular case to outweigh the integrity of mediation proceedings.

## MD CODE, COURTS AND JUDICIAL PROCEEDINGS § 3-1805: Confidential Mediation Communications Not Subject to Discovery

Mediation communications that are confidential under this subtitle are not subject to discovery, but information that is otherwise admissible or subject to discovery does not become inadmissible or protected from disclosure solely by reason of its use in mediation.

## 3) MISSOURI

### SUPREME COURT RULE 88.08: Confidentiality

(a) Mediation proceedings shall be regarded as settlement proceedings. With the exception of information released pursuant to subdivision 88.06(a)(6), any communication relating to the subject matter of such disputes made during the mediation by any participant, mediator, or any other person present at the mediation shall be a confidential communication. No admission, representation, statement or other confidential communication made in setting up or conducting such proceedings not otherwise discoverable or obtainable shall be admissible as evidence or subject to discovery.

(b) No person who serves as a mediator, nor any agent or employee of that person, shall be subpoenaed or otherwise compelled to disclose any matter disclosed in the process of setting up or conducting the mediation.

### SUPREME COURT RULE 88.06: Mediation: Duties of the Mediator

(a) The mediator in writing shall:

(1) Inform the parties of the costs of mediation;

(2) Advise the parties that the mediator does not represent either or both of the parties;

(3)  Define and describe the process of mediation to the parties;

(4)  Disclose the nature and extent of any relationships with the parties and any personal, financial, or other interests that could result in a bias or a conflict of interest;

(5)  Advise each of the parties to obtain independent legal advice;

(6)  Disclose to the parties' attorneys any factual documentation revealed during the mediation if at the end of the mediation process the disclosure is agreed to by the parties;

(7)  Ensure that the parties consider fully the best interests of the children and that the parties understand the consequences of any decision they reach concerning the children.

* * *

# APPENDIX B

## SAMPLE PARENTING PLANS

### I. AGREEMENT USED AT THE ERICKSON MEDIATION INSTITUTE[1]

The following Parenting Plan language has been developed from our experiences with clients as well as our work with mediators throughout the United States. This Parenting Plan includes the best of what we have learned from, and shared with, parents and mediators. The Parenting Plan is presented first with an explanation of some of the topics, followed by optional language (in *italics*) to be used by our fictional parents, John and Mary Doe.

#### Agreements Regarding Parental Responsibilities

#### *Custody Options*

In developing a Parenting Plan, parents have many choices about the legal definitions of their arrangement. They may choose to use custody labels that are consistent with the laws of their state, or they may choose not to use any such labels. When they are deciding whether or not to use the labels, their most important consideration is the legal consequence of the labels. In those states that designate two gradations of custody, *legal custody* relates to the legal incidents of parenthood, such as access to school records, signing for medical emergencies, and other legal rights; *Physical custody* generally relates to parental control of the children, which parent is presumed to be in charge, who will receive child support, and what kind of a visitation schedule will be imposed upon the parent losing custody.

#### *Legal Custody*

The label of *legal custody* relates to the legal rights and responsibilities of parents. Generally, most states encourage both parents to continue to have joint legal custody of their children after a divorce. This gives them the same legal rights and responsibilities that they had while married. In those cases where a parent does not have legal custody, that parent relinquishes the right to share in the major decision making concerning the children's education, medical care, and religious upbringing. When creating a Parenting Plan, almost all parents consider these important decisions as their joint responsibility. Legal custody language in a Parenting Plan varies from state to state but generally follows language that, in this case, incorporates much of the Minnesota statute with a presumption in favor of joint legal custody.

---

[1] Copyright ©2004. Reprinted with permission.

273

### *Joint Legal Custody*

John and Mary have agreed that they will share joint legal custody of their children. Joint legal custody means that John and Mary both have equal rights and responsibilities regarding their children's upbringing, including education, health care, and religious training. Neither of their rights is superior to those of the other parent. Neither John nor Mary will do anything that would lead to estrangement between their children and the other parent, nor will either parent perform any act that would interfere with the natural development of love and affection between the children and either of them. Both John and Mary recognize that children have emotional and psychological needs to establish a healthy and satisfying relationship with both parents.

**_Major decision making._** *On important matters relating to the health, welfare, and/or education of the minor children, John and Mary will discuss and work toward a mutually acceptable determination of the issues, including, for example, but not limited to, the following:*

- *In the event of illness or injury to the children, the parent first learning of the illness or injury will notify the other parent immediately.*

- *The parents will consult with each other regarding the schooling of the children.*

- *Each parent will promptly inform or consult with the other in the event of any serious medical problem of the children.*

- *Each parent will have equal access to the information relating to the children, including but not limited to, access to school, governmental, law enforcement, and medical records, and access to all teachers, governmental officials and officers, doctors, and other professionals having contact with the children.*

- *Both parents may participate, individually or jointly, with the children in special activities including, but not limited to, Scouts, music, sports, school conferences and other activities, etc. Such information and contacts will be available to each parent without notice or any further consent of the other parent.*

- *Each parent is authorized to consent to emergency medical care for the children at the time when the other parent is not easily accessible to give such consent.*

- *Each parent will continue to play a full and active role in providing a sound moral, social, economic, religious, and educational environment for the children. Each parent will inform the other of the children's social and educational activities and appointments, so that both parents might participate, when possible and appropriate, and each parent will further advise the other of the children's emergency situations, illnesses, and problems which may occur when the children are in his or her care.*

- *Both parents agree to resolve all conflicts in a manner consistent with the best interests of the children and, when necessary, to use the conflict resolution mechanisms described in this Parenting Plan.*

### Physical Custody

The *physical custody* label described earlier creates difficulties for parents building a Parenting Plan. Parents generally remove the contest assumption of this label in their Parenting Plan by choosing Joint Physical Custody. This choice nullifies the power of the label and frees parents to make practical, workable decisions about how they will address specific concerns in the future, should they present themselves:

### Sole Physical Custody

*John and Mary agree that [one of them] will have sole physical custody of their children.*

### Joint Legal Custody

*John and Mary have agreed that they will share joint legal custody of their children.*

### No Designation of Physical Custody

Parenting Plan laws in Minnesota have provided parents with the opportunity to refrain from designating the physical custody of their children in a divorce. Many parents choose not to designate a custodial parent and use the following language:

### No Designation of Physical Custody

*John and Mary agree not to designate a Physical custodian of the minor children. For purposes of travel to states or countries that do not recognize Parenting Plans, this arrangement may be considered Joint Legal and Joint Physical Custody.*

The following paragraphs are examples of the form and language of a Parenting Plan for parents to consider as they create their own plan. Not all of these topics are included by parents in their Parenting Plans, of course, but we offer them here as language that other parents have used for their situations.

General Understandings

*As parents, John and Mary are committed to cooperating with each other to provide future parenting of their children that is in the children's best interests. They recognize that they are each very important to the physical, social, and psychological development of their children and that their children need each of them to be actively involved in their lives in the future. John and Mary agree to respect each other's individual parenting role with the children and to be supportive of each other as parents.*

*John and Mary further understand that sending messages to the other parent through the children places the children in the middle of their conflict and that it is their responsibility to communicate with each other directly. They also know that disrespecting the other parent is harmful to the children's sense of self, and so they each agree to refrain from these behaviors. Instead, they will encourage the children's relationship with the other parent and give each child clear permission to love, and be proud of, the other parent.*

## Separate Parenting

*John and Mary agree that they no longer have a relationship as marriage partners and that they have only a relationship as separate parents with separate lives and homes. As separate parents, they agree to the following:*

- *The children will have a meaningful relationship with each of them.*

- *They will communicate with each other directly — either verbally, in writing, or by e-mail and will refrain from sending any messages to each other through the children.*

- *When the children complain to one of them about the other parent, the parent receiving the complaint will ask the child(ren) to discuss it with the other parent. If the child is uncomfortable doing so, the parent receiving the complaint will help the child(ren) communicate with the other parent. Each parent will try to understand the complaint without making a judgment, interfering, or taking sides.*

- *They each understand that their parenting styles may be different and that the differences will enhance their children's growth. They each agree to accept and respect each other's differences.*

- *They will each be supportive of the other's parenting and positively encourage the children in their relationship with the other parent.*

- *When parenting problems arise, they agree that they will deal with the problems as parents, just between them.*

- *They agree that they will refrain from discussing their personal lives and parenting problems or differences with the children.*

- *When they have parenting problems between them that they are unable to resolve, they will seek the services of a professional family mediator, or a professional neutral expert in family and/or child therapy, to assist them in resolving the matter.*

- *They agree to respect each other's boundaries. They agree that their separate lives and private lives are no longer joined. They each agree not to enter the other parent's home or private space without being invited.*

- *Finally, they agree that if either of them enters a new significant relationship that may affect the children, each will inform the other parent of this new relationship. They further agree that they will each assist the children in understanding and adjusting to the new relationship.*

## Residential Arrangements

The first question parents ask when divorcing is "Where will the children live?" This issue is at the core of the Parenting Plan. The answer is that the children will live with each parent at separate times. The best way to determine these times is for parents to develop a schedule of times the children will spend at each of their homes and when the children will move from one home to the other.

The earliest type of schedule that was commonly used by courts in the United States before the introduction of joint physical custody statutes was a very unequal schedule that assumed children would remain with their custodial parent in the family home and the other parent would have the privilege of having the children visit every other weekend, from Friday evening to Sunday evening, and every other Wednesday from 5:00 to 7:00 P.M.

States began to legislate the concept of joint custody at the same time divorce mediation was beginning to be offered, and more and more parents began to consider different ways they could both be more involved with their children after divorce. Parents in mediation often chose to create more equivalent time-sharing schedules of when the children would be with each parent. This was especially appealing to parents who chose to continue to reside in close proximity after the divorce. In our practices, parents have designed a variety of schedules that meet the needs of the children, their activities, and the parents' work schedules. We found that most parents wanted to have equal time with the children on weekends, and so they alternated weekends routinely. They would often, however, add Sunday night as an overnight; in this event, children would be exchanged at school or at after-school programs on Fridays and at school or at before-school programs on Mondays. Some parents then added the Monday and Tuesday nights to the schedule, creating a half-time parenting schedule, in which one parent has the children overnight on Mondays and Tuesdays and the other parent has them overnight Wednesdays and Thursdays:

(M, Mom; D, Dad)

|        | Mon. | Tues. | Wed. | Thurs. | Fri. | Sat. | Sun. |
|--------|------|-------|------|--------|------|------|------|
| Wk. 1  | D/M  | M     | M/D  | D      | D/M  | M    | M    |
| Wk. 2  | M    | M     | M/D  | D      | D    | D    | D    |
| Wk. 3  | D/M  | M     | M/D  | D      | D/M  | M    | M    |
| Wk. 4  | M    | M     | M/D  | D      | D    | D    | D    |

For infants and toddlers, who need more frequent contact with each parent, parents have used the above schedule and added "touch-base" times when the other parent would spend time with children over a meal to break up the longer periods of time.

Some parents wanted longer periods of time, especially with teenage children. These parents frequently chose I-week periods of time with and without the children, with the exchange time being Fridays after school:

(M, Mom; D, Dad)

|        | Mon. | Tues. | Wed. | Thurs. | Fri. | Sat. | Sun. |
|--------|------|-------|------|--------|------|------|------|
| Wk. 1  | D    | D     | D    | D      | D/M  | M    | M    |
| Wk. 2  | M    | M     | M    | M      | M/D  | D    | D    |

|        | Mon. | Tues. | Wed. | Thurs. | Fri. | Sat. | Sun. |
|--------|------|-------|------|--------|------|------|------|
| Wk. 3  | D    | D     | D    | D      | D/M  | M    | M    |
| Wk. 4  | M    | M     | M    | M      | M/D  | D    | D    |

Many parents find that they have to help each other out because of their unique work schedules. Pilots, flight attendants, air traffic controllers, physicians, nurses, U.S. armed services personnel, servers, and professional athletes, are examples of parents who find that they have to create unique parenting schedules and plan them out a year in advance. They also need to build flexibility into their agreements, so that either parent can make changes, as necessary, while not misusing the flexibility as a means to manipulate a schedule for other than parenting purposes.

Some parents chose to have special one-on-one time between a child and a parent and scheduled this into their Parenting Plan so that it would occur regularly. This "one-on-one time" may also be scheduled for a period of time, based on a special need of a child.

Parents often begin this approach by trying out a parenting schedule for a few months to see how it works for themselves and the children. They may find it necessary to make adjustments to the schedule so that both parents can make a commitment to maintain it. Parents find that the parenting schedules tend to keep the separate homes organized around the children. When a parenting schedule is part of an entire Parenting Plan, the parents make agreements that enhance the entire parenting experience for them and their children. Children generally like parenting schedules once they have adjusted to residing in two homes with separate parents. Children also like to have the parenting calendar displayed where they have access to it at each home. Once the family has adjusted to a parenting schedule, the arrangements tend to go quite smoothly for everyone.

Residential Arrangements

*John and Mary realize that their children's needs play a most important role in how they plan their living arrangements, and also that those needs will change as the children grow older. John and Mary will be sensitive to each child's process of adjusting to their divorce and separate parenting in the future. They recognize that their children will adjust better to the changes if they know what will be happening and the schedule of when they will be with each parent. Therefore, John and Mary will clearly communicate to their children the regular schedule for spending time with each parent and the schedule for their holidays. They will make the schedule available to the children at each of their homes or on the Internet.*

*John and Mary will try to keep the schedules predictable, specific, and routine, and when either of them needs to make an exception to the normal schedule, he or she will first ask the other parent to care for the children. They will give each other as much advance notice as possible about a need to make a schedule change. If the other parent is unable to care for the children, the scheduled parent will make other arrangements.*

*From time to time, John and Mary may experiment with different schedules in order to try to find an exchange routine that does not unduly disrupt the children's daily schedule and still allows for significant parenting involvement by each of them. They will follow an initial parenting schedule, as follows:*

(M, Mom; D, Dad)

|       | Mon.  | Tues. | Wed.  | Thurs. | Fri.  | Sat. | Sun. |
|-------|-------|-------|-------|--------|-------|------|------|
| Wk. 1 | M/D/M | M     | MID   | D      | D/M/D | D    | D    |
| Wk. 2 | DIM   | M     | MID   | D      | DIM   | M    | M    |
| Wk. 3 | M/D/M | M     | MID   | D      | D/M/D | D    | D    |
| Wk. 4 | DIM   | M     | MID   | D      | DIM   | M    | M    |

\* Touch-base time from 5:00 to 7:00 P.M. for dinner.

### Summer Parenting and Vacations — Options

- *During the summer, John and Mary may make different parenting arrangements. They will agree on a summer schedule at least a month prior to the end of the school year.*

- *John and Mary will have a preliminary discussion about summer plans, camps, and vacations each year by February with the final plans being decided upon by May.*

- *John and Mary agree that they may each have up to 2 weeks of vacation with the children each year. This time may be in 1-week blocks or a full 2-week block. They agree to discuss their vacation plans with the other parent as soon as each is considering vacation times.*

### Holiday Schedule

A few decades ago it would have seemed strange to have to create a schedule of when children would be with their parents on holidays. Now it is commonly known as an area of great conflict for divorced parents. Parents understand that when they make a holiday schedule, they are engaging their best effort to plan how the holidays with the children will be celebrated in the future. It also gives parents time to consider how they might create new traditions with their children after divorce. We make an assumption that all families celebrate holidays, though by no means the same holidays. A holiday schedule must be based upon the family's beliefs and traditions. A typical holiday schedule follows.

### Holiday Schedule

*John and Mary agree to the following holiday schedule, in which holidays will be treated as an exception to the regular weekly parenting schedule, without the need to have makeup time. The children will spend holidays as follows:*

| Holiday | Even-numbered years | Odd-numbered years |
|---|---|---|
| Spring break | | |
| Passover | | |
| Easter | | |
| Memorial Day | | |
| Fourth of July | | |
| Labor Day | | |
| Rosh Hashanah | | |
| Yom Kippur | | |
| Sukkoth | | |
| Teachers' convention | | |
| Halloween | | |
| Thanksgiving | | |
| Thanksgiving Fri.–Sun. | | |
| Chanukah | | |
| First half-winter break | | |
| Christmas Eve | | |
| Christmas Morning | | |
| Christmas Day | | |
| Second half-winter break | | |
| New Year's Eve | | |
| New Year's Day | | |
| Children's birthdays | According to schedule, and the other parent may have some contact as requested by that parent. | |
| Parents' birthdays | Time to celebrate with each parent | |
| Mother's Day | Mom | Mom |
| Father's Day | Dad | Dad |
| *Spring break* | Dad | Mom |
| *Easter* | Dad | Mom |
| *Memorial Day* | Mom | Dad |
| *Fourth of July* | Mom | Dad |
| *Labor Day* | Dad | Mom |
| *Teachers' convention* | Mom | Dad |
| *Halloween* | Dad | Mom |
| *Thanksgiving* | Mom | Dad |
| *Thanksgiving Fri.–Sun.* | Mom | Dad |
| *First half-winter break* | Dad | Dad |
| *Christmas Eve* | Dad | Dad |
| *Christmas Morning* | Mom | Dad |
| *Christmas Day* | Mom | Mom |
| *Second half-winter break* | Mom | Mom |
| *New Year's Eve* | Dad | Mom |
| *New Year's Day* | Mom | Dad |

| Holiday | Even-numbered years | Odd-numbered years |
|---------|---------------------|--------------------|
| *Children's birthdays* | *According to schedule, and the other parent will have some contact as requested by that parent* | |
| *Parents' birthdays* | *Time to celebrate with each parent* | |
| *Mother's Day* | *Mom* | *Mom* |
| *Father's Day* | *Dad* | *Dad* |

Some parents make some special agreements about Monday holidays, adding the Monday holiday to the on-duty parent's weekend, thereby extending it through Monday. Others acknowledge that the parent normally scheduled for the Monday of the holiday will be responsible for planning the children's activities on that day.

### *Monday Holidays*

*When Mondays are a holiday, John and Mary agree that the parent on duty on the Sunday before the holiday may have the children for an extended weekend.*

### *Optional Parenting Agreements*

### *Conflict Resolution about Parenting Schedules*

If John and Mary disagree about scheduling changes or have disputes about the holiday schedule, they agree to first try to resolve such disagreements on their own but will return to mediation if they have difficulties in resolving these new issues on their own. The future costs of returning to mediation will be shared equally.

### *On-Duty, Off Duty Parenting*

*John and Mary recognize that decision making is an important part of their parenting role. They agree that the parent with whom the children are residing on a particular day will be the on-duty parent and, in that capacity, will make decisions about the care and control of the children on that day.*

*This means that if the children are ill, or either parent had other obligations during their on-duty time with the children, it will be the responsibility of the on-duty parent to make arrangements for the care of the children. John and Mary each expect the on-duty parent to first request assistance from the off duty parent, but they both understand that if the off duty parent is not able to assist the on-duty parent during the scheduled time, it will be the responsibility of the on-duty parent to make alternative arrangements for the children.*

### *Relationships Important to the Children*

*John and Mary recognize that the children will benefit from maintaining their ties with grandparents, relatives, and people important to them. They will each help the children maintain their relationships with these people and spend time with them periodically. John and Mary further agree that they will ask their friends and relatives to refrain from saying negative or disrespectful things about the children's other parent in the presence of the children or within their range of hearing such remarks.*

## Education

*John and Mary agree that unless the present school boundaries change, the children will continue to attend Washington Elementary School, Jefferson Junior High, and Lincoln High School. Mary and John will each reside within easy access of the schools. They will each attend school conferences and will receive copies of report cards. Each parent will communicate with the children's schools to remain informed about each child's needs, progress, and pertinent special events, including parent-teacher conferences. John and Mary also agree to share with each other any information they receive separately about the children's school progress, behavior, and events.*

## Higher Education

*John and Mary further agree that college or technical training is important for their children, and they will encourage and support each child's efforts for further education. Costs associated with pre-college expenses will be shared. These costs include books, field trips, school supplies, and miscellaneous fees, as well as trips to visit campuses and application fees. Both will jointly share in transportation of the children and are committed to strong support of and involvement in, the children's education.*

## Removal from School

*John and Mary agree to obtain the other parent's advance approval if the wish to remove the children from a day of school. They agree that it is acceptable for the children to miss occasional elementary school days for a special event; however, they also agree that at middle and high school levels, the children may not miss school except for family emergencies or for some very special reason to which they each agree in advance.*

## Religious Training and Religious Activities

*John and Mary agree that the children will continue to be raised in the Presbyterian Church, even though John is Muslim. They will each be supportive of the children's religious upbringing and "agree to agree" regarding all religious activities in advance. All costs associated with religious activities that are agreed to in advance will be shared. While each parent will be respectful of the children's wishes, John and Mary will first agree on travel costs and other matters that require cooperation. Since each parent will have the children for half of the weekends, they agree to communicate frequently about organized religious activities, so that each parent may be aware of the children's schedule. Mary and John agree that John may introduce the children to his religious faith; however, both agree that John will not indoctrinate the children in his own particular religious beliefs.*

## *Communication*

*When the children are with one parent, John and Mary agree that the children will have open access to the parent with whom they are not staying. They will each also encourage and help the children communicate frequently with the other parent. They agree to give the other parent the address and phone number where the children can be reached any time they are away from home for more than 24 hours.*

## *Sunday Night Phone Call*

*John and Mary agree that they will talk to each other every Sunday evening at 9 P.M. to discuss the children. The parent who is on duty with the children will initiate the phone call. They will only discuss issues regarding the children. If either John or Mary becomes uncomfortable with the conversation, that parent has only to say that he or she is uncomfortable with the conversation, that they will need to resume it next Sunday, and then gently hang up the phone. The other parent will respect that response, and they will talk to each other the following Sunday evening at 9 P.M.*

## *Safety*

*John and Mary each agree not to compromise the safety of the children. They will not leave a child unattended for more than 2 hours, until each child is 12 years old.*

## *Special Safety Concerns*

*Swimming, jet skiing, and snowmobiling activities require the constant supervision of a parent. John and Mary agree to prohibit the children from riding all ATVs and motorcycles. Both recognize the special danger to children from jet skis and snowmobiles. John and Mary agree that they will each closely monitor and supervise the children's use of jet skis or snowmobiles.*

## *Alcohol or Chemical Abuse*

*John and Mary agree that neither of them will ever care for the children nor transport them while impaired. If either of them believes that the other parent is about to, or has violated, this agreement, that parent may ask for an immediate chemical dependency test for drugs or alcohol. This test may be requested up to two times per month. Should the test result not show impairment, as defined by the state's DUI laws, the parent requesting the test will pay for the cost of the test. However, should the test show impairment, that parent will enter a 3-day inpatient chemical dependency treatment program and follow the recommendations for aftercare. The parenting schedule will be altered temporarily during the treatment program. The other parent will cooperate with requests by the chemical dependency treatment program for participation of the children in the program. The regular parenting schedule will resume immediately upon the recommendation of the chemical dependency treatment program.*

### *Authorized Caregivers*

*John and Mary will exchange a list of authorized caregivers for the children, and both agree that they will not allow any babysitters or child-care workers to provide care for the children who are not on the list without the prior consent of each.*

### **Transportation for the Exchanges of the Children**

*John and Mary each agree that the parent whose home the children are coming to will pick them up. That parent will pick up the children's belongings at the same time he or she picks up the children. In addition, John and Mary will cooperate to help the children remember to take their belongings with them, so each child will have the personal belongings and school supplies they need.*

### *Joint Rules at Each Home*

*John and Mary recognize that they have different parenting styles and agree that the children will be enhanced by the different experiences at each home. However, they agree there are certain ground rules that should be enforced at both homes. Therefore, they agree to the following:*

1. *Bedtimes at both homes will be between 8:30 and 9:30 P.M. on school nights and 10:00 and 11:00 P.M. on weekends.*

2. *Curfew at both homes on weeknights will be 9:30 P.M., and on weekends curfew will be 11:30 P.M., unless there is a special event to which both parents agree in advance.*

3. *Discipline for minor problems will be limited to time-outs and withdrawal of a privilege. Discipline for more serious problems will be limited to greater lack of privilege or grounding; still more serious problems will require consultation between John and Mary. They will cooperate with and support the other in carrying out discipline at each of their homes for serious infractions.*

4. *Mary and John will support each other when a child calls to complain about the other parent. They will help the child discuss the matter, but they will support the other parent and encourage the child to work out the problem with the other parent.*

5. *John and Mary agree that the goal is for the children's entertainment to be beneficial, safe, educational, and expansive. If either is unsure about any entertainment, they agree to consult the other parent in advance. There will be no PG-13 movies allowed for a child until age 13, or any R movies for a child unless one parent is supervising the viewing of the movie.*

6. *John and Mary agree that, in general, the on-duty parent is responsible for the supervision of children's activities and entertainment, and he or she will ensure safety, cleanliness, and appropriate behavior.*

7. *John and Mary will each encourage healthy activities for the children, including attendance at children's museums, reading clubs, Scouts, and*

*church youth groups, and once the specifics are agreed upon, each of them will share in the associated costs. If no agreement can be reached concerning the activity, the initiating parent may enroll the child in the activity and pay for and arrange the transportation. If the activity impacts the other parent's schedule with the children, John and Mary agree to consult and obtain agreement from the other parent before enrolling the child in the activity.*

### Location of Parents' Homes

*John and Mary agree to reside no more than 10 miles from the other parent's home. As the children reach school age, they will attend the school that serves Mary's residence, and each parent will be responsible for transporting the children to school when they are on duty.*

### Parent's Move from Current Home

*If John or Mary anticipates a move from a current residence that will make it impossible to continue the parenting schedule, John and Mary agree to renegotiate the parenting schedules prior to a move. They will focus on how they can still be significantly involved as parents in a way that would meet the needs of the children.*

### Travel Out of the Country

*John and Mary agree to not take the children out of the country without prior written agreement of the other parent. Each will respond reasonably when the other parent requests to take the children out of the country for vacations or travel. They will keep the children's passports in a safe deposit box, with joint access by Mary and John.*

### Access to Information about the Children

*John and Mary agree that they will each have access to information about the children, either through the use of* The Children's Book *[Erickson & McKnight Erickson, 1992], a notebook, ourfamilywizzard.com, or another means to record all information necessary to meet the needs of the children (i.e., medical records, doctors' and dentists' names and phone numbers, medical J.D. cards, names and Phone numbers of the children's teachers, coaches, friends, the parenting and holiday schedules, and any other information they may need to effectively and efficiently meet the children's needs at any given time the children are with them). They will exchange the information with the children. They will also write notes to each other about the children. John and Mary further agree that the comments contained in their information or notes may not be admissible in any court proceeding in the future.*

### *Duration of the Parenting Plan*

*John and Mary understand that this Parenting Plan will be in effect until they make changes to it, and the court subsequently issues a new court order reflecting the new changes. They agree that all changes to the Parenting Plan will be in writing and dated and signed by both of them. Until their divorce decree is amended to reflect written changes, they realize agreements made in this Parenting Plan will legally govern any dispute.*

### *Future Conflict Resolution*

*In the future, John and Mary agree to behave flexibly and cooperatively, and to communicate with each other in order to meet the changing needs of their children. When John and Mary cannot agree about the meaning of a part of the Parenting Plan, or if a significant change (such as a move or remarriage) causes conflict, they will make a good faith effort to resolve their differences through mediation, before petitioning the court. Should they be unable to resolve their differences in mediation, they will select and share the cost of a neutral child expert who will meet with the children and with each parent. Then, the neutral expert will present a plan in mediation that will allow the parents to overcome their differences. The costs of the neutral party shall be shared, and the neutral party may not be called as a witness in any court proceeding.*

[Financial Support of Children Sections Omitted].

## II. MODEL PARENTING PLAN USED IN THE CIRCUIT COURT FOR BALTIMORE CITY

| | |
|---|---|
| _____ | |
| _____ | IN THE |
| _____ | CIRCUIT COURT |
| PLAINTIFF | FOR |
| V. | BALTIMORE CITY |
| _____ | Case No.: _____ |
| _____ | |
| DEFENDANT | |

PARENTING PLAN

### GENERAL INFORMATION

1.1 This parenting plan is:

[ ]    A final parenting plan ordered by the court.

[ ]    A temporary parenting plan.

1.2 This parenting plan applies to the following child(ren):

| Name(s) | Birthdate |
|---------|-----------|
| _____ | _____ |
| _____ | _____ |
| _____ | _____ |
| _____ | _____ |
| _____ | _____ |
| _____ | _____ |

## AFFIRMATION

We, _____ and _____ affirm that we are the parents of the above-named child(ren) regardless of our marital status.

2.1 Voluntary Agreement

[ ]   We enter into this agreement in order to better meet our responsibilities as parents and to safeguard our child(ren)'s future development and well-being regardless of any conflicts that we may have. We recognize that the child(ren)'s welfare can best be served by our mutual cooperation as partners in parenting and by each of us providing a home in which they are loved, and to which they belong — their mother's home and their father's home.

2.2 Good Faith

[ ]   We agree that we have developed this parenting plan with the assistance of, in good faith and on behalf of the best interest of our child(ren).

2.3 Type of Agreement

[ ]   We acknowledge that this is a temporary agreement which is binding upon us and enforceable by either of us after it is submitted to the Court for approval and entered as an Order and signed by a Judge.

[ ]   We acknowledge that this is our final agreement and that it will be binding upon us and enforceable by either of us after it is submitted to the Court for approval and entered as an Order and signed by a Judge.

Review of Mediation

[ ]   The parties agree and understand that their mediators, _____, and _____, and the University of Baltimore School of Law Family Mediation Clinic, have acted as neutral third parties. The parties agree that each will consult their own attorney to review this Agreement, if they so desire. Upon legal review, any recommendation for substantial change or restructuring of this Agreement shall be referred back to mediation.

## I. COMMUNICATION

3.1 Access to Information

[ ]   Does not apply.

[ ]   Both parents will have equal access to all information pertaining to the child(ren)'s:

    [ ]   Health care

    [ ]   Education

    [ ]   School events and extra-curricular activities

[ ]   Other: _____

[ ]   Each parent will be entitled to duplicate information from either the third
      party provider or the other parent, if the provider will not provide duplicate
      information pertaining to the child(ren)'s:

    [ ]   Health care

    [ ]   Education

    [ ]   School events and extra-curricular activities

    [ ]   Other:_____

[ ]   Each parent may initiate contact with:

    [ ]   Heath care providers

    [ ]   Teacher and school personnel

    [ ]   Other: _____

[ ]   Each parent shall provide any information regarding the child(ren) and/or his/
      her/their activities to the other parent immediately upon receipt of such
      information.

    3.2 Communication between Parents

[ ]   Does not apply.

[ ]   Each parent will keep the other informed of a current residential address,
      mailing address (if different), home and work telephone numbers (or other
      numbers at which the parent may be reached during the day or at night).

[ ]   Both parties agree that if either of them has any knowledge of any illness,
      accident, incident or other circumstances seriously affecting the health and/or
      welfare of their child(ren), he/she will promptly notify the other of such
      circumstances.

[ ]   All court related and financial discussions shall occur at a time when the
      child(ren) is/are not present. These discussions shall not occur at times of
      exchange of the child(ren) or during telephone visits with the child(ren).

[ ]   The parents shall communicate with each other as follows:

[ ]   Set schedule as follows: _____

      _____

      _____

    [ ] Mother may communicate with the father by [ ]Phone [ ]Email [ ]Written

    [ ] Father may communicate with the mother by [ ]Phone [ ]Email [ ]Written

    3.3 Communication with the Children

[ ]   Does not apply.

[ ]   The parent with whom the child(ren) is not residing shall have telephone
      access with the child(ren) as follows:

    [ ]   Set schedule as follows:_____

    [ ]   Parent may call child(ren) at any time.

    [ ]   Child(ren) may call parent at any time.

[ ]   In the event that a parent incurs long distance telephone charges as a result
      of calls from the child(ren) to the other parent, the costs shall be split as
      follows:

[ ] Does not apply.

[ ] Parent receiving call from child(ren) shall be responsible for all charges.

[ ] Parents will evenly split costs.

[ ] Other:_____

## II. RESIDENTIAL SCHEDULE

These provisions set forth where the child(ren) shall reside each day of the year and what contact the child(ren) shall have with each parent.

This parenting plan shall begin on the following date:

4.1 Pre-School Schedule

[ ] There are no children of preschool age.

[ ] Prior to enrollment in school, the child(ren) shall reside with the [ ] mother [ ] father, except for the following days and times when the child(ren) will reside with or be with the other parent:_____

_____

_____

_____

4.2 School Schedule

[ ] Does not apply.

[ ] Upon enrollment in school, the child(ren) shall reside with the [ ] mother [ ] father, except for the following days and times when the child(ren) will reside with or be with the other parent:_____

_____

_____

_____

4.3 Schedule for Holidays

[ ] Does not apply.

| | With Mother (Specify Whether (Odd/Even/Every or Other) | With Father (Specify Whether Odd/Even/Every or Other) |
|---|---|---|
| New Year's Eve | | |
| New Year's Day | | |
| Martin Luther King Day | | |
| President's Day | | |
| Easter | | |
| Memorial Day | | |
| Mother's Day | | |
| July 4th | | |
| Father's Day | | |
| Labor Day | | |
| Halloween | | |

| | With Mother (Specify Whether (Odd/Even/Every or Other) | With Father (Specify Whether Odd/Even/Every or Other) |
|---|---|---|
| Veteran's Day | | |
| Thanksgiving Day | | |
| Christmas Eve | | |
| Christmas Day | | |
| Religious Holidays (as follows): | | |
| | | |
| | | |
| | | |
| Mother's Birthday | | |
| Father's Birthday | | |
| Child's Birthday | | |
| Child's Birthday | | |
| Child's Birthday | | |

[ ]   For purposes of this parenting plan, a holiday shall begin and end as follows (set forth times):_____

_____

[ ]   Holidays which fall on a Friday or a Monday shall include Saturday and Sunday.

4.4 Schedule for Winter Vacation

[ ]   Does not apply.

The child(ren) shall reside with the [ ] mother [ ] father during winter vacation, except for the following days and times when the child(ren) will reside with or be with the other parent:_____

_____

_____

_____

4.5 Schedule for Spring Vacation

[ ]   Does not apply.

The child(ren) shall reside with the [ ] mother [ ] father during spring vacation, except for the following days and times when the child(ren) will reside with or be with the other parent:_____

_____

_____

_____

4.6 Schedule for Summer

[ ]   Does not apply.

Upon completion of the school year, the child(ren) shall reside with [ ] mother [ ] father, except for the following days and times when the child(ren) will reside with or be with the other parent:_____

_____

_____

4.7 Vacation with Parents

[ ]   Does not apply.

[ ]   The schedule for vacation with the parents is as follows:_____

_____

_____

[ ]   Each parent to notify the other of their respective vacation plans with the
      child(ren)_____

4.8 Priorities under the Residential Schedule

[ ]   Does not apply.

      [ ]   Neither parent shall schedule activities for the child(ren) during the
            other parent's scheduled residential time, unless the parents agree in
            advance to include the activity in the child(ren)'s schedule.

[ ]   For purposes of this parenting plan the following days have priority:

      [ ]   Vacations and holidays shall have priority over the residential schedule.

      [ ]   Other:_____

            _____

            _____

4.9 Restrictions

[ ]   Does not apply.

[ ]   The following restrictions shall apply when the child(ren) spend(s) time with
      the

            [ ] mother [ ] father:

            _____

            _____

      [ ]   _____

4.10 Transportation Arrangements

[ ]   Does not apply.

      Transportation arrangements for the child(ren), other than costs, between
      parents shall be as follows: _____

[ ]   _____

4.11 Changes to Residential Schedule

[ ]   Does not apply.

[ ]   Requests to change the residential schedule shall be submitted by the parent
      requesting the change to the other parent:

      [ ]   In writing

      [ ]   In person

      [ ]   By telephone

            Other:_____

[ ]   Requests shall be made at least:

[ ]   24 hours in advance

[ ]   One week in advance

[ ]   Two weeks in advance

[ ]   Other:_____

[ ]   Response to the request shall be made by the parent receiving the request:

[ ]   In writing

[ ]   In person

[ ]   By telephone

[ ]   Other:_____

[ ]   Response shall be made within:

[ ]   24 hours

[ ]   One week

[ ]   Two weeks

[ ]   Other:_____

4.12 Additional Care

[ ]   Does not apply.

[ ]   The parent requesting the change shall first contact the other parent who will have the first right of care for the child but is not obligated for such care as a result of the change of schedule.

[ ]   The parenting requesting the change shall be responsible for any additional child related expenses (for example, day care) incurred by the other parent as a result of the change of schedule.

[ ]   Other:_____

### III. DECISION MAKING

5.1 Day-to-Day Decisions

[ ]   Does not apply.

Each parent shall make decisions regarding the day-to-day care and control of each child while the child(ren) is/are residing with that parent, except as provided below. Examples of day-to-day decisions include treatment of minor health problems, injuries, diet, TV, house rules and discipline.

[ ]   We agree to refrain from doing anything to undermine the other parent's household rules and instead, we agree to support the other parent's rules in their household by explaining to our child(ren) that they are expected to follow rules in each parent's household.

5.2 Major Decisions regarding each child shall be made as follows:

|                              | Mother | Father | Joint |
|------------------------------|--------|--------|-------|
| Education Decisions          |        |        |       |
| Extra-curricular activities  |        |        |       |
| Child care                   |        |        |       |
| Associations                 |        |        |       |

| | Mother | Father | Joint |
|---|---|---|---|
| Non-emergency health care | | | |
| Mental Health treatment | | | |
| Religious upbringing | | | |
| Other: | | | |

5.3 Emergencies

[ ] Does not apply.

[ ] If the child(ren) require(s) emergency care, the parent who is responsible for them at that time will immediately arrange for that care and then notify the other parent immediately thereafter.

## IV. FURTHER DISPUTE RESOLUTION

6.1 Dispute Process

[ ] Does not apply.

[ ] No dispute resolution process, except court action, shall be ordered because of limiting factors.

[ ] Disputes between the parties shall be submitted to (list person or agency):

[ ] Counseling by _____

[ ] Mediation by _____

[ ] Other: _____

6.2 Cost of Process

[ ] Does not apply.

The cost of this process shall be allocated between the parties as follows:

[ ] _____ % mother _____ % father.

[ ] based on each party's proportional share of income per the child support guideline worksheets, if available.

[ ] as determined in the dispute resolution process.

6.3 Initiation of Process

[ ] Does not apply.

The counseling and/or mediation process shall be commence by notifying the other party by [ ] written request [ ] certified mail [ ] other:_____

6.4 Procedures to be Used

[ ] Does not apply.

In the dispute resolution process:

[ ] Preference shall be given to carrying out this Parenting Plan.

[ ] Unless and emergency exists, the parents shall use the designated process to resolve disputes relating to implementation of the plan, except those related to financial support.

[ ] A written record shall be prepared of any agreement reached in counseling or mediation and shall be provided to each party.

[ ] If the court finds that a parent has used or frustrated the dispute resolution

process without good reason, the court may award attorney's fees and financial sanctions to the other parent.

[ ]   The parties have the right of review of the dispute resolution process to the Circuit Court.

7.1 Independent Counsel, Parties Fully Informed, Fairness of Terms

[ ]   Does not apply.

[ ]   The parties mutually agree that in entering into this Agreement, each party signs this Agreement freely and voluntarily for the purpose, and with the intent of determining and permanently / temporarily settling the issues of custody and visitation relating to the child(ren). The parties acknowledge that this Agreement is a fair and reasonable agreement, and that it is not the result of any fraud, duress, or undue influence exercised by either party upon the other, or any person or persons upon either party.

8.1 Further Assurances

[ ]   Does not apply.

[ ]   Each of the parties agree to sign such other and further documents and to perform such acts as may be reasonably required to effectuate the purpose of this Agreement.

I (We) declare that this plan has been submitted in good faith.

_____          _____
Mother                           Date

_____          _____
Father                           Date

# APPENDIX C

# MODEL STANDARDS OF PRACTICE FOR FAMILY AND DIVORCE MEDIATION

## Overview and Definitions

Family and divorce mediation ("family mediation" or "mediation") is a process in which a mediator, an impartial third party, facilitates the resolution of family disputes by promoting the participants' voluntary agreement. The family mediator assists communication, encourages understanding and focuses the participants on their individual and common interests. The family mediator works with the participants to explore options, make decisions and reach their own agreements.

Family mediation is not a substitute for the need for family members to obtain independent legal advice or counseling or therapy. Nor is it appropriate for all families. However, experience has established that family mediation is a valuable option for many families because it can:

1. increase the self-determination of participants and their ability to communicate;

2. promote the best interests of children; and

3. reduce the economic and emotional costs associated with the resolution of family disputes.

Effective mediation requires that the family mediator be qualified by training, experience and temperament; that the mediator be impartial; that the participants reach their decisions voluntarily; that their decisions be based on sufficient factual data; that the mediator be aware of the impact of culture and diversity; and that the best interests of children be taken into account. Further, the mediator should also be prepared to identify families whose history includes domestic abuse or child abuse.

These *Model Standards of Practice for Family and Divorce Mediation ("Model Standards")* aim to perform three major functions:

1. to serve as a guide for the conduct of family mediators;

2. to inform the mediating participants of what they can expect; and

3. to promote public confidence in mediation as a process for resolving family disputes.

The *Model Standards* are aspirational in character. They describe good practices for family mediators. They are not intended to create legal rules or standards of liability.

The *Model Standards* include different levels of guidance:

1. Use of the term "may" in *a Standard* is the lowest strength of guidance and indicates a practice that the family mediator should consider adopting but

which can be deviated from in the exercise of good professional judgment.

2. Most of the *Standards* employ the term "should" which indicates that the practice described in the *Standard* is highly desirable and should be departed from only with very strong reason.

3. The rarer use of the term "shall" in a *Standard is* a higher level of guidance to the family mediator, indicating that the mediator should not have discretion to depart from the practice described.

## Standard I

A family mediator shall recognize that mediation is based on the principle of self-determination by the participants.

  A. Self-determination is the fundamental principle of family mediation. The mediation process relies upon the ability of participants to make their own voluntary and informed decisions.

  B. The primary role of a family mediator is to assist the participants to gain a better understanding of their own needs and interests and the needs and interests of others and to facilitate agreement among the participants.

  C. A family mediator should inform the participants that they may seek information and advice from a variety of sources during the mediation process.

  D. A family mediator shall inform the participants that they may withdraw from family mediation at any time and are not required to reach an agreement in mediation.

  E. The family mediator's commitment shall be to the participants and the process. Pressure from outside of the mediation process shall never influence the mediator to coerce participants to settle.

## Standard II

A family mediator shall be qualified by education and training to undertake the mediation.

  A. To perform the family mediator's role, a mediator should:

    1. have knowledge of family law;

    2. have knowledge of and training in the impact of family conflict on parents, children and other participants, including knowledge of child development, domestic abuse and child abuse and neglect;

    3. have education and training specific to the process of mediation;

    4. be able to recognize the impact of culture and diversity.

  B. Family mediators should provide information to the participants about the mediator's relevant training, education and expertise.

Standard III

A family mediator shall facilitate the participants' understanding of what mediation is and assess their capacity to mediate before the participants reach an agreement to mediate.

  A.  Before family mediation begins a mediator should provide the participants with an overview of the process and its purposes, including:

      1.  informing the participants that reaching an agreement in family mediation is consensual in nature, that a mediator is an impartial facilitator, and that a mediator may not impose or force any settlement on the parties;

      2.  distinguishing family mediation from other processes designed to address family issues and disputes;

      3.  informing the participants that any agreements reached will be reviewed by the court when court approval is required;

      4.  informing the participants that they may obtain independent advice from attorneys, counsel, advocates, accountants, therapists or other professionals during the mediation process;

      5.  advising the participants, in appropriate cases, that they can seek the advice of religious figures, elders or other significant persons in their community whose opinions they value;

      5.  advising the participants, in appropriate cases, that they can seek the advice of religious figures, elders or other significant persons in their community whose opinions they value;

      6.  discussing, if applicable, the issue of separate sessions with the participants, a description of the circumstances in which the mediator may meet alone with any of the participants, or with any third party and the conditions of confidentiality concerning these separate sessions;

      7.  informing the participants that the presence or absence of other persons at a mediation, including attorneys, counselors or advocates, depends on the agreement of the participants and the mediator, unless a statute or regulation otherwise requires or the mediator believes that the presence of another person is required or may be beneficial because of a history or threat of violence or other serious coercive activity by a participant;

      8.  describing the obligations of the mediator to maintain the confidentiality of the mediation process and its results as well as any exceptions to confidentiality;

      9.  advising the participants of the circumstances under which the mediator may suspend or terminate the mediation process and that a participant has a right to suspend or terminate mediation at any time.

  B.  The participants should sign a written agreement to mediate their dispute and the terms and conditions thereof within a reasonable time after first consulting the family mediator.

C. The family mediator should be alert to the capacity and willingness of the participants to mediate before proceeding with the mediation and throughout the process. A mediator should not agree to conduct the mediation if the mediator reasonably believes one or more of the participants is unwilling or unable to participate.

D. Family mediators should not accept a dispute for mediation if they cannot satisfy the expectations of the participants concerning the timing of the process.

## Standard IV

A family mediator shall conduct the mediation process in an impartial manner. A family mediator shall disclose all actual and potential grounds of bias and conflicts of interest reasonably known to the mediator. The participants shall be free to retain the mediator by an informed, written waiver of the conflict of interest. However, if a bias or conflict of interest clearly impairs a mediator's impartiality, the mediator shall withdraw regardless of the express agreement of the participants.

A. Impartiality means freedom from favoritism or bias in word, action or appearance, and includes a commitment to assist all participants as opposed to any one individual.

B. Conflict of interest means any relationship between the mediator, any participant or the subject matter of the dispute, that compromises or appears to compromise the mediator's impartiality.

C. A family mediator should not accept a dispute for mediation if the family mediator cannot be impartial.

D. A family mediator should identify and disclose potential grounds of bias or conflict of interest upon which a mediator's impartiality might reasonably be questioned. Such disclosure should be made prior to the start of a mediation and in time to allow the participants to select an alternate mediator.

E. A family mediator should resolve all doubts in favor of disclosure. All disclosures should be made as soon as practical after the mediator becomes aware of the bias or potential conflict of interest. The duty to disclose is a continuing duty.

F. A family mediator should guard against bias or partiality based on the participants' personal characteristics, background or performance at the mediation.

G. A family mediator should avoid conflicts of interest in recommending the services of other professionals.

H. A family mediator shall not use information about participants obtained in a mediation for personal gain or advantage.

I. A family mediator should withdraw pursuant to *Standard IX* if the mediator believes the mediator's impartiality has been compromised or a conflict of interest has been identified and has not been waived by the participants.

Standard V

A family mediator shall fully disclose and explain the basis of any compensation, fees and charges to the participants.

    A.   The participants should be provided with sufficient information about fees at the outset of mediation to determine if they wish to retain the services of the mediator.

    B.   The participants' written agreement to mediate their dispute should include a description of their fee arrangement with the mediator.

    C.   A mediator should not enter into a fee agreement which is contingent upon the results of the mediation or the amount of the settlement.

    D.   A mediator should not accept a fee for referral of a matter to another mediator or to any other person.

    E.   Upon termination of mediation a mediator should return any unearned fee to the participants.

Standard VI

A family mediator shall structure the mediation process so that the participants make decisions based on sufficient information and knowledge.

    A.   The mediator should facilitate full and accurate disclosure and the acquisition and development of information during mediation so that the participants can make informed decisions. This may be accomplished by encouraging participants to consult appropriate experts.

    B.   Consistent with standards of impartiality and preserving participant self-determination, a mediator may provide the participants with information that the mediator is qualified by training or experience to provide. The mediator shall not provide therapy or legal advice.

    C.   The mediator should recommend that the participants obtain independent legal representation before concluding an agreement.

    D.   If the participants so desire, the mediator should allow attorneys, counsel or advocates for the participants to be present at the mediation sessions.

    E.   With the agreement of the participants, the mediator may document the participants' resolution of their dispute. The mediator should inform the participants that any agreement should be reviewed by an independent attorney before it is signed.

Standard VII

A family mediator shall maintain the confidentiality of all information acquired in the mediation process, unless the mediator is permitted or required to reveal the information by law or agreement of the participants.

A.  The mediator should discuss the participants' expectations of confidentiality with them prior to undertaking the mediation. The written agreement to mediate should include provisions concerning confidentiality.

B.  Prior to undertaking the mediation the mediator should inform the participants of the limitations of confidentiality such as statutory, judicially or ethically mandated reporting.

C.  The mediator shall disclose a participant's threat of suicide or violence against any person to the threatened person and the appropriate authorities if the mediator believes such threat is likely to be acted upon as permitted by law.

D.  If the mediator holds private sessions with a participant, the obligations of confidentiality concerning those sessions should be discussed and agreed upon prior to the sessions.

E.  If subpoenaed or otherwise noticed to testify or to produce documents the mediator should inform the participants immediately. The mediator should not testify or provide documents in response to a subpoena without an order of the court if the mediator reasonably believes doing so would violate an obligation of confidentiality to the participants.

## Standard VIII

A family mediator shall assist participants in determining how to promote the best interests of children.

A.  The mediator should encourage the participants to explore the range of options available for separation or post-divorce parenting arrangements and their respective costs and benefits. Referral to a specialist in child development may be appropriate for these purposes. The topics for discussion may include, among others:

1.  information about community resources and programs that can help the participants and their children cope with the consequences of family reorganization and family violence;

2.  problems that continuing conflict creates for children's development and what steps might be taken to ameliorate the effects of conflict on the children;

3.  development of a parenting plan that covers the children's physical residence and decision-making responsibilities for the children, with appropriate levels of detail as agreed to by the participants;

4.  the possible need to revise parenting plans as the developmental needs of the children evolve over time; and

5.  encouragement to the participants to develop appropriate dispute resolution mechanisms to facilitate future revisions of the parenting plan

B.  The mediator should be sensitive to the impact of culture and religion on parenting philosophy and other decisions.

C.  The mediator shall inform any court-appointed representative for the children of the mediation. If a representative for the children participates, the mediator should, at the outset, discuss the effect of that participation on the mediation process and the confidentiality of the mediation with the participants. Whether the representative of the children participates or not, the mediator shall provide the representative with the resulting agreements insofar as they relate to the children.

D.  Except in extraordinary circumstances, the children should not participate in the mediation process without the consent of both parents and the children's court-appointed representative.

E.  Prior to including the children in the mediation process, the mediator should consult with the parents and the children's court-appointed representative about whether the children should participate in the mediation process and the form of that participation.

F.  The mediator should inform all concerned about the available options for the children's participation (which may include personal participation, an interview with a mental health professional, or the mediator reporting to the parents, or a videotape statement) and discuss the costs and benefits of each with the participants.

Standard IX

A family mediator shall recognize a family situation involving child abuse or neglect and take appropriate steps to shape the mediation process accordingly.

A.  As used in these Standards, child abuse or neglect is defined by applicable state law.

B.  A mediator shall not undertake a mediation in which the family situation has been assessed to involve child abuse or neglect without appropriate and adequate training.

C.  If the mediator has reasonable grounds to believe that a child of the participants is abused or neglected within the meaning of the jurisdiction's child abuse and neglect laws, the mediator shall comply with applicable child protection laws.

    1.  The mediator should encourage the participants to explore appropriate services for the family.

    2.  The mediator should consider the appropriateness of suspending or terminating the mediation process in light of the allegations.

Standard X

A family mediator shall recognize a family situation involving domestic abuse and take appropriate steps to shape the mediation process accordingly.

A.  As used in these Standards, domestic abuse includes domestic violence as defined by applicable state law and issues of control and intimidation.

B.  A mediator shall not undertake a mediation in which the family situation has been assessed to involve domestic abuse without appropriate and adequate training.

C.  Some cases are not suitable for mediation because of safety, control or intimidation issues. A mediator should make a reasonable effort to screen for the existence of domestic abuse prior to entering into an agreement to mediate. The mediator should continue to assess for domestic abuse throughout the mediation process.

D.  If domestic abuse appears to be present the mediator shall consider taking measures to insure the safety of participants and the mediator including, among others:

1.  establishing appropriate security arrangements;

2.  holding separate sessions with the participants even without the agreement of all participants;

3.  allowing a friend, representative, advocate, counsel or attorney to attend the mediation sessions;

4.  encouraging the participants to be represented by an attorney, counsel or an advocate throughout the mediation process;

5.  referring the participants to appropriate community resources;

6.  suspending or terminating the mediation sessions, with appropriate steps to protect the safety of the participants.

E.  The mediator should facilitate the participants' formulation of parenting plans that protect the physical safety and psychological well-being of themselves and their children.

## Standard XI

A family mediator shall suspend or terminate the mediation process when the mediator reasonably believes that a participant is unable to effectively participate or for other compelling reasons.

A.  Circumstances under which a mediator should consider suspending or terminating the mediation, may include, among others:

1.  the safety of a participant or well-being of a child is threatened;

2.  a participant has or is threatening to abduct a child;

3.  a participant is unable to participate due to the influence of drugs, alcohol, or physical or mental condition;

4.  the participants are about to enter into an agreement that the mediator reasonably believes to be unconscionable;

5.  a participant is using the mediation to further illegal conduct;

6.  a participant is using the mediation process to gain an unfair advantage;

7.  if the mediator believes the mediator's impartiality has been compromised in accordance with *Standard IV.*

B.  If the mediator does suspend or terminate the mediation, the mediator should take all reasonable steps to minimize prejudice or inconvenience to the participants which may result.

## Standard XII

A family mediator shall be truthful in the advertisement and solicitation for mediation.

A.  Mediators should refrain from promises and guarantees of results. A mediator should not advertise statistical settlement data or settlement rates.

B.  Mediators should accurately represent their qualifications. In an advertisement or other communication, a mediator may make reference to meeting state, national, or private organizational qualifications only if the entity referred to has a procedure for qualifying mediators and the mediator has been duly granted the requisite status.

## Standard XIII

A family mediator shall acquire and maintain professional competence in mediation.

A.  Mediators should continuously improve their professional skills and abilities by, among other activities, participating in relevant continuing education programs and should regularly engage in self-assessment.

B.  Mediators should participate in programs of peer consultation and should help train and mentor the work of less experienced mediators.

C.  Mediators should continuously strive to understand the impact of culture and diversity on the mediator's practice.

## Appendix: Special Policy Considerations for State Regulation of Family Mediators and Court Affiliated Programs

The *Model Standards* recognize the *National Standards for Court Connected Dispute Resolution Programs* (1992). There are also state and local regulations governing such programs and family mediators. The following principles of organization and practice, however, are especially important for regulation of mediators and court-connected family mediation programs. They are worthy of separate mention.

A.  Individual states or local courts should set standards and qualifications for family mediators including procedures for evaluations and handling grievances against mediators. In developing these standards and qualifications, regulators should consult with appropriate professional groups, including professional associations of family mediators.

B.  When family mediators are appointed by a court or other institution, the appointing agency should make reasonable efforts to insure that each mediator is qualified for the appointment. If a list of family mediators qualified for court appointment exists, the requirements for being included on the list should be made public and available to all interested persons.

Confidentiality should not be construed to limit or prohibit the effective monitoring, research, evaluation or monitoring of mediation programs by responsible individuals or academic institutions provided that no identifying information about any person involved in the mediation is disclosed without their prior written consent. Under appropriate circumstances, researchers may be permitted to obtain access to statistical data and, with the permission of the participants, to individual case files, observations of live mediations, and interviews with participants.

# INDEX

[References are to pages.]

[References are to pages.]

[References are to pages.]